Noël **Coward**
Plays : Five

Relative Values, Look After Lulu!,
Waiting in the Wings, Suite in Three Keys

"He is simply a phenomenon, and one that is unlikely to occur ever again in theatre history."   Terence Rattigan

"His triumph has been to unite two things ever dissociated in the English mind: hard work and wit."   Kenneth Tynan

This volume contains the best of Coward's plays from the fifties and sixties, the last two decades of his life.

Relative Values opened in 1951 to, as Coward put it, "rave notices.   All, with the exception of the dear little Daily Mirror, enthusiastic and wonderful box office".   It ran for over a year.

The London premiere of **Look After Lulu!**, adapted from Feydeau's *Occupe-toi d'Amélie!*, took place in 1959 somewhat incongruously at the Royal Court Theatre, then associated more with "Angry Young Men" than with French farce.   However, with Vivien Leigh as Lulu, it survived bad notices and transferred to the West End.

"I wrote **Waiting in the Wings** (1960)," Coward said, "with loving care and absolute belief in its characters . . .   I consider that the play as a whole contains, beneath the froth of some of its lighter moments, the basic truth that old age needn't be nearly so dreary and sad as it is supposed to be."

In the trilogy, **Suite in Three Keys** (1966), Coward provided himself with his farewell roles and was particularly gratified at the plays' success and at his own contribution: "On the opening night I gave an excellent, un-nervous, controlled performance, thank God . . .   I am back again, like Dolly, where I belong and have always belonged."

The front cover shows a design from 1975 by Erté, reproduced by courtesy of the Grosvenor Gallery, London.   The cartoon of Noël Coward by Max Beerbohm on the back cover is from the Mander and Mitchenson Theatre Collection and is reproduced with permission.

Also by Noël Coward in the Master Playwrights series

PLAYS: ONE
Hay Fever, The Vortex, Fallen Angels, Easy Virtue

PLAYS: TWO
Private Lives, Bitter-Sweet, The Marquise, Post-Mortem

PLAYS: THREE
Design for Living, Cavalcade, Conversation Piece, To-night at 8.30 I (Hands Across the Sea, Still Life, Fumed Oak)

PLAYS: FOUR
Blithe Spirit, Present Laughter, This Happy Breed, To-night at 8.30 II (Ways and Means, The Astonished Heart, "Red Peppers").

Other Authors in the Master Playwrights series

John Arden
Brendan Behan
Edward Bond (two volumes)
Henrik Ibsen (four volumes)
Molière
Clifford Odets
Joe Orton
Harold Pinter (four volumes)
August Strindberg (two volumes)
J. M. Synge
Oscar Wilde

Further work by Noël Coward published by Methuen

POMP AND CIRCUMSTANCE (a novel)
COLLECTED SHORT STORIES

Also available

COWARD THE PLAYWRIGHT by John Lahr

NOËL COWARD

Plays: Five

Relative Values

Look After Lulu!

Waiting in the Wings

Suite in Three Keys
comprising
A Song at Twilight

Shadows of the Evening

Come into the Garden Maud

*Introduced by Raymond Mander and
Joe Mitchenson*

The Master Playwrights
METHUEN · LONDON

This collection first published in Great Britain in 1983
simultaneously in hardback and as **A Methuen Paperback** by
Methuen London Ltd, 11 New Fetter Lane, London EC4P 4EE

Relative Values was first published by Heinemann in 1958 in
Play Parade Vol. 5. It is reprinted here by arrangement with
William Heinemann Ltd.

Look After Lulu! was first published by Heinemann in 1959.

Waiting in the Wings was first published by Heinemann in 1962
in Play Parade Vol. 6.

Suite in Three Keys was first published by Heinemann in 1966.

Copyright in all the plays is by the Estate of the late Noël
Coward.

Introduction copyright © 1983 by Raymond Mander and
Joe Mitchenson

ISBN 0 413 51730 6
ISBN 0 413 51740 3

Reproduced, printed and bound in Great Britain by
Richard Clay (The Chaucer Press) Ltd,
Bungay, Suffolk

CAUTION
These plays are fully protected by copyright throughout the
world. All applications for performance etc. should be made by
professionals to Dr. Jan Van Loewen Ltd, 21 Kingly Street,
London W1R 5LB, and by *amateurs* to Samuel French Ltd,
26 Southampton Street, Strand, London WC2E 7JE.

Contents

Acknowledgements

In compiling these introductions, we have drawn on Noël Coward's own prefaces to the six volumes of *Play Parade* as well as quoting from *Present Indicative* (Heinemann 1937) and *Future Indefinite* (Heinemann 1952), the two autobiographies, for which we acknowledge our thanks. For the years not covered by these, we have drawn on Sheridan Morley's biography of Coward, *A Talent to Amuse* (Heinemann 1969) and Cole Lesley's *The Life of Noël Coward* (Jonathan Cape 1976) for which we offer further thanks.

We have had the advantage of compiling our own *Theatrical Companion to Coward* (Rockliff 1957) (now under revision) originally produced under the watchful eye of the Master himself, and from this volume we have naturally drawn information.

We also have to thank Joan Hirst, Coward's London representative, who is always on hand to answer questions, as well as "Quinney", who transferred our disparate thoughts into the printed word, and has always enjoyed casting an eagle eye over the proofs, and lastly, Colin Mabberley, Curator of our Collection, who has unflinchingly assisted us in our compilation of these introductions.

Owing to shortage of space a chronology of Coward's work for the stage and a note on the publication of his plays has had to be omitted from this volume, but it will be found in *Coward Plays: One*, *Two* and *Four* of this series.

Raymond Mander and Joe Mitchenson,
Theatre Collection
August 1982.

Introduction

Relative Values

Relative Values, "a light comedy" dedicated "For Joyce [Carey] and Cole [Lesley] in memory of Blue Harbour", was written in 1951. It followed *Ace of Clubs*, a musical play written in 1949 and produced at the Cambridge Theatre the following year.

Relative Values opened on a six week "tryout" tour at the Theatre Royal, Newcastle, on 15 October 1951 and arrived at the Savoy Theatre, London, on 28 November and stayed for 477 performances. It was directed by the author with the following cast:

CRESTWELL	Richard Leech
ALICE	Renee Hill
MRS DORA MOXTON (MOXIE)	Angela Baddeley
FELICITY, COUNTESS OF MARSHWOOD	Gladys Cooper
LADY CYNTHIA HAYLING	Dorothy Batley
THE HON. PETER INGLETON	Simon Lack
ADMIRAL SIR JOHN HAYLING	Charles Cullum
NIGEL, EARL OF MARSHWOOD	Ralph Michael
MIRANDA FRAYLE	Judy Campbell
DON LUCAS	Hugh McDermott

When the play was included in *Play Parade* Volume V Coward wrote:

Relative Values ran for over a year at the Savoy Theatre and was beautifully played by an excellent cast including Angela Baddeley, Judy Campbell, Richard Leech, Ralph Michael, Hugh McDermott and Simon Lack. Gladys Cooper as "Felicity" gave one of the most incisive, witty and altogether enchanting comedy performances that it has ever been my privilege to see. But then Gladys Cooper learned her job in her young days from four of the most brilliant actor-manager-directors who ever graced our Theatre—

Seymour Hicks, Charles Hawtrey, Dennis Eadie and Gerald du Maurier. To watch the precision with which she timed her lines (not, I hasten to add, until she had really learned them which took quite a while) was to me an exquisite pleasure. She also continued, obviously because she made no effort to do so, to look as lovely as she had ever looked, even in the old days when her picture postcards could be bought by the bushel, twopence glace and coloured but never penny plain. From the above eulogy the perceptive reader may gather that I am very fond of Gladys Cooper.

Later, in 1976, Cole Lesley was to write in his *The Life of Noël Coward*:

Rehearsals started for *Relative Values* before Noël opened at the Café de Paris with his solo performance which began on 29 October, and it became evident from the first that Gladys Cooper was going to make her biggest success in London since *The Shining Hour* nearly twenty years before. From their first skirmish during the famous Christmas party in Davos in 1922, and in between other, later skirmishes, a firm and enduring friendship had built itself up between Gladys and Noël, and this was now to be put to its severest test; Gladys could not learn her words and her part was enormously long. Especially in his comedy dialogue, not one of his carefully chosen words must be misplaced, or another word substituted, and to listen to Gladys stumbling became torture for Noël; counting rehearsals and the pre-London tour he suffered two and a half months of this torture. Gladys, with her many years of stardom and experience, seldom actually dried up, but filled in the many gaps with er, er, er, which was even more painful to his ear. We went up to the opening night in Newcastle, in agony because of her insecurity, though she herself flew brilliantly through the play with every outward sign of star-sized assurance, and so beautiful that Noël called her the Hag, or simply Hag. Theatres were packed all through the tour, but even as late as the week in Brighton, the list of Gladys's mistakes amounted during one performance to no less than twenty-eight, including when, instead of saying she was going into the study, she announced that she was going into the under-study. Good trouper that she was she rose word-perfect to the occasion of the first night in London, and she and the play got an ovation at the end. Next morning: "Well, well, what a surprise! Rave notices. All, with the exception of the dear little *Daily Mirror*, enthusiastic and wonderful box office. This should mean a smash hit—very nice too." Though never entirely forgotten, all was forgiven; Gladys remained his Darling Hag to the end, and there were no more skirmishes.

The play was revived at the Westminster Theatre on 6 September 1973 where it ran until the November with the following cast, directed by Charles Hickman:

CRESTWELL	John Stone
ALICE	Heather Bell
MRS DORA MOXTON (MOXIE)	Gwen Cherrel
FELICITY, COUNTESS OF MARSHWOOD	Margaret Lockwood
LADY CYNTHIA HAYLING	Margaret Gibson
THE HON. PETER INGLETON	Bryan Stanion
ADMIRAL SIR JOHN HAYLING	Derek Ensor
NIGEL, EARL OF MARSHWOOD	Kenneth Fortescue
MIRANDA FRAYLE	Joyce Blair
DON LUCAS	Drewe Henley

Look After Lulu!

The next play in this volume, *Look After Lulu!*, dates from 1958. It follows *Nude with Violin* (written 1954 and produced 1956) and belongs to a period in Coward's career (now a tax exile in Bermuda) when he concentrated on acting, cabaret and writing short stories.

After the London visits by the Barrault-Renaud Company and the Comédie Française in the 1950s Georges Feydeau (1862–1921) had been "discovered". Though his farces had been pilfered and adapted by English authors since the 1890s, his name had not impressed itself on the English playgoing public. His farce *Occupe-toi d'Amélie!* was first produced at the Théâtre Nouveautés, Paris, on 19 March 1908, with Armande Cassive, Marcel Simon and Suzanne Carlix in the leading parts. It was suggested by Jean-Louis

Barrault that Vivien Leigh and Laurence Olivier should ask Coward to make an adaptation; the play had not previously been translated into English.

Sheridan Morley in *A Talent to Amuse* says: "It was not a task which Coward much enjoyed; he found it difficult and frustrating to work with another playwright's plot" ... but "by early in the November of 1958 Coward had completed his adaptation of the Feydeau farce, which in view of the obvious impossibility of 'Occupy Yourself with Amelia' he had retitled *Look After Lulu!*; a mild bout of pneumonia kept him in Bermuda for the rest of that month, but as soon as he had recovered he left Spithead Lodge to start negotiations for the production of the farce on both sides of the Atlantic. Noël went first to New York, where he saw Tammy Grimes in cabaret and instantly persuaded her that she should star in the American *Lulu*, and then to London where it was arranged that Vivien Leigh would open in the English production (as she was otherwise engaged)".

The play was first produced on 18 February 1959 at the Shubert Theatre, Newhaven, Connecticut, prior to opening at the Henry Miller Theatre, New York, on 3 March. Unfortunately it was not a success and only ran 39 performances. It was directed by Cyril Ritchard with the following cast:

LULU D'ARVILLE	Tammy Grimes
BOMBA	Rory Harrity
VALERY	Craig Huebing
EMILE	Bill Berger
GABY	Barbara Loden
YVONNE	Sasha Van Schorler
PAULETTE	Grace Gaynor
PHILIPPE DE CROZE	George Baker
ADONIS	Paul Smith
GIGOT	Eric Christmas
CLAIRE	Polly Rowles
MARCEL BLANCHARD	Roddy McDowall

GENERAL KOSCHNADIEFF	Ellis Rabb
HERR VAN PUTZEBOUM	Jack Gilford
TWO BOYS FROM THE FLORIST'S	David Faulkner David Thurman
THE PRINCE OF SALESTRIA	Kurt Kasznar
ROSE	Reva Rose
OUDATTE	Earl Montgomery
CORNETTE	Kohn Alderman
THE MAYOR OF THE DISTRICT	Arthur Malet
A PHOTOGRAPHER	William Griffis
AUNT GABRIELLE	Philippa Bevans
A LITTLE GIRL	Ina Cummins
AN INSPECTOR OF POLICE	David Hurst

The English production of the play, surprisingly enough, was by The English Stage Company, notable for their *avant-garde* productions. After a preliminary week at the Theatre Royal, Newcastle, from 20 July 1959, it opened at the Royal Court Theatre on 29 July directed by Tony Richardson with the following cast:

LULU D'ARVILLE	Vivien Leigh
BOMBA	Peter Stephens
VALERY	John Gatrel
EMILE	Cecil Brock
GABY	Jeanne Watts
YVONNE	Shirley Cameron
PAULETTE	Fanny Carby
PHILIPPE DE CROZE	Robert Stephens
ADONIS	Sean Kelly
GIGOT	Peter Sallis
CLAIRE	Meriel Forbes
MARCEL BLANCHARD	Anthony Quayle
GENERAL KOSCHNADIEFF	Lawrence Davidson
HERR VAN PUTZEBOUM	George Devine
THE BOYS FROM THE FLORIST'S [*omitted at the New Theatre*]	David Ryder Arnold Yarrow
THE PRINCE OF SALESTRIA	Max Adrian

ROSE	Anne Bishop
OUDATTE	Arnold Yarrow
CORNETTE	Peter Wyatt
ROGER	Bitsa
THE MAYOR OF THE DISTRICT	Richard Goolden
A PHOTOGRAPHER	David Ryder
AUNT GABRIELLE	Barbara Hicks
A LITTLE GIRL	Elaine Miller
AN INSPECTOR OF POLICE	Michael Bates

Sheridan Morley recounts:

During the London rehearsals for *Lulu*, John Osborne is said to have wandered into the Royal Court, seen Vivien Leigh rehearsing on its stage with Anthony Quayle and Max Adrian, and assumed that in some nightmarish way he had been suddenly transported from Sloane Square to the heart of Shaftesbury Avenue. The idea had been for the Court to conquer the West End; instead it seemed that the reverse had happened.

The morning after *Lulu* opened at the Royal Court, to bad notices and a certain amount of journalistic shrieking about the betrayal of *avant-garde* values in Sloane Square, Coward flew to Athens for a fortnight's cruising around the Greek Islands aboard an Onassis family yacht. Then, tanned and rested, he returned to London to find that *Look After Lulu!* had survived its notices and that business at the Court had in fact been good enough to justify a transfer to the West End on 8 September; there *Lulu* played to adequate business at the New Theatre, just one more in a long line of Coward comedies which nobody liked except the public.

The play in all ran for 155 performances and when published in a solo edition it was dedicated "For Vivien with my love as always Noël".

Lulu was revived at the 1978 Chichester Festival Theatre season (directed by Parick Garland) and transferred to The Theatre Royal, Haymarket (with some changes in the minor roles) on 9 October with the following cast:

| LULU D'ARVILLE | Geraldine McEwan |
| BOMBA | Martin Milman |

YVONNE	Kate Percival
PAULETTE	Shelley Borkum
CHANTAL	Jance Halsey
VALERY	Rom Karol
EMILE	Michael Hughes
SIMON	John Haden
PHILIPPE DE CROZE	Gary Raymond
ADONIS	Martin Chamberlain
GIGOT	George Howe
CLAIRE	Fenella Fielding
MARCEL	Clive Francis
GENERAL KOSCHNADIEFF	Paul Hardwick
HERR VAN PUTZEBOUM	Nigel Stock
TWO FLORIST'S BOYS	{ Michael Hughes { John Haden
THE PRINCE OF SALESTRIA	Peter Bowles
ROSE	Yvette Byrne
OUDATTE	Martin Milman
ROGER	Petra
THE MAYOR OF THE DISTRICT	Robert Perceval
CORNETTE	Tom Karol
A PHOTOGRAPHER	Michael Hughes
AN INSPECTOR OF POLICE	Nigel Stock
TWO POLICEMEN	{ Michael Hughes { John Haden

This revival ran for 56 performances.

Waiting in the Wings

While waiting for the production of *Lulu* Coward began writing *Waiting in the Wings*, which he eventually finished the following year. It had its première, directed by Margaret Webster, at the Olympia Theatre, Dublin, on 8 August 1960 before arriving in London at the Duke of York's Theatre on 7 September 1960, where it ran for 188 performances with the following cast:

MAY DAVENPORT	Marie Löhr
CORA CLARKE	Una Venning

BONITA BELGRAVE	Maidie Andrews
MAUD MELROSE	Norah Blaney
DEIRDRE O'MALLEY	Maureen Delany
ESTELLE CRAVEN	Edith Day
ALMINA CLARE	Mary Clare
PERRY LASCOE	Graham Payn
MISS ARCHIE	Margot Boyd
OSGOOD MEEKER	Lewis Casson
LETTA BAINBRIDGE	Sybil Thorndike
DORA	Berry Hare
DOREEN	Jean Conroy
SARITA MYRTLE	Nora Nicholson
ZELDA FENWICK	Jessica Dunning
DOCTOR JEVONS	Eric Hillyard
ALAN BENNET	William Hutt
TOPSY BASKERVILLE	Molly Lumley (succeeded by Ethel Gabriel)

The play includes six musical numbers—"Waiting in the Wings", "Champagne", "Miss Mouse", "Over the Hill", "Come the Wild, Wild Weather", "Oh Mister Kaiser". It was first published (solo edition) in 1960 with the dedication "For Dame Sybil Thorndike with my love, admiration and gratitude".

When it was included in *Play Parade* Volume VI Coward wrote, in June 1961:

Now we come to the last play I have written to date, *Waiting in the Wings*. It opened in Dublin on 8 August 1960, where it was received with heart-warming enthusiasm by both the public and the critics. From Dublin it travelled to Liverpool and Manchester where it was greeted with equal enthusiasm. I remember in Manchester warning the company against over-optimism. "Be prepared" I said "for considerably less whole-hearted laughter and emotional response. In the first place the theatre will be much smaller than those you have been playing in and in the second place London first-night audiences are liable to arrive at the theatre in a sceptical frame of mind, particularly if the news has got round that the play they are going to see has been well received in the provinces; also the awareness that the critics are present is apt to impose a blight on the proceedings."

This little homily proved to have been unnecessary. From the moment the curtain rose on the opening performance at the Duke of York's Theatre I knew instinctively that, blight or no blight, that particular audience was warm, well-disposed and eager to find the play good. Actually it was one of the most moving first nights I have ever attended. The cast, immediately conscious that the atmosphere was favourable, played the play, if possible, better than they had ever played it before. They handled the salvos of applause, the laughter and the cheering with the grace and dignity of experienced experts, which, after all, most of them were. Marie Löhr, a young woman of seventy, who had fallen down and broken her right wrist that very afternoon, gave an assured and impeccable performance in spite of agonising pain which would have sent many a lesser actress moaning to the nearest hospital. Sybil Thorndike, to my mind one of the few really great actresses of our time, played the part I had written with such unswerving truth, restraint, lack of sentimentality and sheer beauty that I saw much of it through a haze of grateful tears. In fact each member of that remarkable company gave to my play their shining best, and for me, together with the majority of the audience, it was a great night in the Theatre. An hour after the curtain had fallen there was still a large crowd of cheering people standing in St Martin's Lane and as I stepped into my car a young man from the *Daily Express* asked me in a whining Cockney voice whether there was any truth in the rumour that I had had my face lifted. As I considered the question irrelevant to the occasion I drove away leaving him unenlightened.

The next morning when I read the reviews I was, for the first time in many years, very angry indeed. Not especially because the critics hadn't liked the play, which I was fully prepared for, but because they had neither the wit nor the generosity to pay sufficient tribute to the acting. I hasten to exonerate certain writers whose reviews in the more respectable newspapers were considered, literate and at least courteous. It was the so-called popular Press which, not unnaturally, roused my ire, for they gave to their wide circulation of readers the wholly inaccurate impression that the play had been a failure from every point of view. This, apart from its inherent personal malice, was dishonest reporting and as such should have been severely reprimanded by the editors and owners of the newspapers concerned. However, in spite of it, *Waiting in the Wings* proceeded to play to absolute capacity for three months and actually, I believe, broke the record of the Duke of York's Theatre. Just before Christmas the business, in common with most of the other shows in the West End, dropped badly. After Christmas it revived a little but not enough to carry a cast of eighteen people, and so in February the play closed in London and set forth on a tour of the provinces which I am happy to say was a triumphant success and only came to an end a few weeks ago. On the whole, including the preliminary try-out, the London run and the tour, *Waiting in the Wings* ran for nine months. If it had been a light comedy I am sure, from experience, that the bad notices in the popular Press would have had no effect. As it was a serious play on a theme which, in spite of its lighter moments, remained an intrinsically sad one, I think the original London notices may have had a delayed effect.

My own personal opinion of the play is biased by my deep affection for it. Perhaps I am still too near it to be able to recognise its "general ineptitude" and "ghastly sentimentality". Perhaps I am still too englamoured by Margaret Webster's gentle and compassionate direction, the enthusiasm and happiness of the actors concerned and the response of the audiences all over England. Perhaps I am too flattered by certain personal letters of almost overwhelming praise I have received from people of talent and integrity. Perhaps I was wrong in the first place to have written a play about old age and the imminence of death and contrived at the same time to make it entertaining.

All these "perhaps" add up to nothing. I wrote *Waiting in the Wings* with loving care and absolute belief in its character. I consider that the reconciliation between "Lotta" and "May" in Act Two Scene Three, and the meeting of Lotta and her son in Act Three Scene Two, are two of the best scenes I have ever written. I consider that the play as a whole contains, beneath the froth of some of its lighter moments, the basic truth that old age needn't be nearly so dreary and sad as it is supposed to be, provided you greet it with humour and live it with courage.

I recommend this play, more than any I have written for many years, to the reader's most earnest attention.

Despite this recommendation the play did not fulfil Coward's expectations and led eventually to a series of articles in *The Sunday Times*, aimed at the critics and expressing his growing distaste for the modern playwrights and actors of the "Scratch and mumble school" which they encouraged. With that off his chest, he began working on a musical which he had started earlier as *Later than Spring* and was now retitled *Sail Away*. It was produced in America in 1961 and London in 1962. Apart from *The Girl Who came to Supper*, an adaptation of Terence Rattigan's play *The Sleeping Prince* for which he wrote the music and lyrics only (produced in New York, 1963), he did not write again for the theatre until *Suite in Three Keys* in 1965.

Suite in Three Keys

This play, a trilogy consisting of one two-act play, *A Song at Twilight*, and two one-act plays, *Shadows of the Evening* and *Come into the Garden Maud*, was begun by Coward in 1965 as a personal vehicle for his farewell to the London stage, with Margaret Leighton and Irene Worth in support. Cole Lesley in *The Life of Noël Coward* says:

For many years Noël had cherished a dream, rather vague at first, of appearing once more on the stage in the West End. It had to be in London, nowhere else, "where I first started more than fifty years ago, to sort of round off the dinner." The dream sometimes seemed unlikely to materialise; effective star parts for men in their mid-sixties do not grow on trees, and moreover both the part and the play would have to be certain, as far as one can ever be certain, of success. The idea of Noël appearing, possibly for the last time, in a failure was unthinkable. The idea was never far from his mind for long, and more and more it grew to be the one definite ambition left for him to achieve: "I must search for or write a play to do in London as a sort of Swan Song. I would like to act once more before I fold my bedraggled wings." In the end he decided that he would have to do what he had usually done and write the vehicle for himself and, as already related, he had the idea of the comedy about Max Beerbohm and Constance Collier. To confirm what I have already dwelt upon—that *A Song at Twilight* is not autobiographical—Noël himself noted, when halfway through the writing, "My play is now more sinister, and there is Maugham in it as well as Max."

The finished plays were intended to be tried out on tour but illness struck Coward and their production which was scheduled for January 1966 had to be postponed. In the meantime Lilli Palmer had replaced Margaret Leighton, who was otherwise engaged. Eventually the first of the plays, *A Song at Twilight*, had to open "cold" at the Queen's Theatre on 14 April 1966 and the other two on 25 April, then running in repertoire for a season until the end of July (64 performances of *A Song at Twilight* and 60 of the double-bill). The plays were directed by Vivian Matalon with the following cast:

A Song at Twilight

HILDE LATYMER	Irene Worth
FELIX, *a waiter*	Seán Barrett
HUGO LATYMER	Noël Coward
CARLOTTA GRAY	Lilli Palmer

Shadows of the Evening

LINDA SAVIGNAC	Lilli Palmer
FELIX, *a waiter*	Seán Barrett
ANNE HILGAY	Irene Worth
GEORGE HILGAY	Noël Coward

Come into the Garden Maud

ANNE-MARY CONKLIN	Irene Worth
FELIX, *a waiter*	Seán Barrett
VERNER CONKLIN	Noël Coward
MAUD CARAGNANI	Lilli Palmer

Coward wrote in his diary (as quoted by Cole Lesley): "Well, the most incredible thing has happened. Not only has *A Song at Twilight* opened triumphantly but the Press notices have on the whole been extremely good. Most particularly the *Express* and *Evening Standard*! Fortunately the *Sun* struck a sour note and said, 'Coward's Return Very Tedious', which convinced me that I hadn't entirely slipped . . . the play is such a sell-out that we have had to engage extra people to cope with the ticket demand. On the opening night I gave an excellent, un-nervous, controlled performance, thank God . . . I am back again, like Dolly, where I belong and have always belonged." He added on 27 April: "After an exhausting week of two performances a day, a Sunday night and a Monday matinée, we opened *Shadows* and *Maud* on Monday night to a fantastic audience. *Shadows* I played well apparently, and the customers were attentive and controllable. *Maud* was an absolute riot from beginning to end and the ovation at the final curtain was quite, quite wonderful. I haven't experienced anything like it for many a long day and it made everything worthwhile. People came pouring on to the stage afterwards and it was altogether a heart-warming triumph."

Coward had planned to go to New York with the plays for a season but his health did not allow this and eventually, in 1974, the year following his death, *Come into the Garden Maud* and a shortened version (in two scenes) of *A Song at Twilight* was produced as *Noël Coward in Two Keys* with Anne Baxter, Jessica Tandy and Hume Cronyn.

These plays have always been considered Coward's last dramatic work but with the publication of *The Noël Coward Diaries* in 1982 it was revealed that on 16 December 1966 (his 67th birthday) he began an adaptation for the stage of *Star Quality*, a short story written and published in 1951 from a collection of six short stories. He wrote ". . . I intend to start a new play today—just as a sort of private celebration. It is to be a light comedy based on *Star Quality*, so I shall have a good deal of the dialogue already done. It should, I think, be fun to do." On 22 January he added "I have finished the second act of *Star Quality*, I am pleased with it but only up to a point. The dialogue is good but it lacks something; perhaps the something it lacks is better construction. I will press on and finish it and then leave it lie for a bit and have another look at it. My voices tell me that a certain amount of rewriting will have to be done."

The Master died in Jamaica on 26 March 1973, and the play remained unrevised. However, the world première was granted by the Trustees of the Coward estate for a Gala Benefit Performance with a distinguished cast on 21 November 1982, to commemorate the restoration of the Theatre Royal, Bath.

RAYMOND MANDER and JOE MITCHENSON

RELATIVE VALUES

CHARACTERS

CRESTWELL
ALICE
MRS. MOXTON (MOXIE)
FELICITY, COUNTESS OF MARSHWOOD
LADY HAYLING
ADMIRAL SIR JOHN HAYLING
THE HON. PETER INGLETON
THE EARL OF MARSHWOOD (NIGEL)
MIRANDA FRAYLE
DON LUCAS

The action of the play takes place in Marshwood House, East Kent.

Time: The Present.

ACT I

Scene I. Saturday afternoon. After lunch.
Scene II. A few hours later.

ACT II

Scene I. Before dinner.
Scene II. After dinner.

ACT III

The next morning.

ACT I

Scene I

Scene: Saturday. After lunch.

The most important feature of the library of Marshwood House is that it is not a library. It may have been in the past and it may be in the future, but now it is quite definitely the family living-room. There are books about of course; it is furnished comfortably and charmingly but without any particular design. The chintz covers are old and a little faded and all the furniture, which is of mixed periods, gives the impression that it has drifted into the room at one time or another, taken a liking to it, and decided to settle down.

There are double doors at the back opening into the hall. Downstage, on the audience's left, is a door leading to NIGEL'S *study. On the right, french windows open on to a flagged terrace and the garden which, like most Kentish gardens, is inwardly sure of itself but outwardly rather confused. Beyond this there are wooded hills. and the sea is not far away.*

When the curtain rises it is about two-thirty on a Saturday afternoon in July.

CRESTWELL, *the butler, a good-looking man in the middle fifties, is collecting used cocktail glasses and placing them on a tray preparatory to taking them away.* ALICE, *a young housemaid of about eighteen, is emptying ash-trays into a dustpan.*

3

ALICE: . . . and just at the very end of the film he realises that she is the one he's loved all along and they walk up a hill together hand in hand and the music gets louder and louder. . . .

CRESTWELL: Thanks, Alice. I shan't have to see her now, shall I?

ALICE: She's lovely, Mr. Crestwell. Really she is.

CRESTWELL: She'd better be.

ALICE: Don't you like her, Mr. Crestwell?

CRESTWELL: How do I know? I've never clapped eyes on her.

ALICE: But you must have seen her in something.

CRESTWELL: I've got better things to do with my spare time than to sit in the Odeon sucking sweets and gaping at a lot of nonsense.

ALICE: "Love is my Religion" is on in Deal all this week. It's one of her early ones but it's gorgeous. I went on Thursday afternoon. She's this nun, you see. . . .

CRESTWELL: Which nun?

ALICE: The one that gets captured by the Japanese.

CRESTWELL: Hurry up with those ash-trays or we shall all be captured by the Japanese.

ALICE: And they do the most terrible things to her but she won't tell where he is. . . .

CRESTWELL: Where who is?

ALICE: Don Lucas.

CRESTWELL: Get on with your work, Alice. They'll be in in a minute.

ALICE: They're in love with one another in real life, her and Don Lucas. I read about it in *Screen Romances*.

CRESTWELL: Never mind about who she's in love

with and who she isn't, it's no business of yours. And don't believe what you read in those movie magazines either—it's all a pack of lies cooked up to impress silly girls like you.

> *At this moment* MRS. MOXTON (MOXIE) *comes in. She is a pleasant looking woman of forty-six and is simply dressed as befits a superior lady's maid. Her expression, however, is grim.*

What's my Lady lost now?

MOXIE: The list for the Church Fête. She wants to show it to Lady Hayling. I put it in her bag myself this morning. (*She goes to the desk.*)

ALICE: Can Maureen come up and help with the tea to-morrow afternoon, Mr. Crestwell?

CRESTWELL: Help with the tea? What on earth for?

ALICE: I could lend her a cap and apron. No one would notice.

CRESTWELL: Two years ago, Alice, your sister Maureen was offered the job you've got now, wasn't she?

ALICE: Yes, Mr. Crestwell.

CRESTWELL: And she turned up her nose at it because she said domestic service was common. Isn't that so?

ALICE (*meekly*): Yes, Mr. Crestwell.

CRESTWELL: She is now assisting behind the bar at the 'Fisherman's Rest' in Deal, which I presume she considers more aristocratic than Marshwood House. Isn't that so, Alice?

ALICE (*uncomfortable*): I'm sure I couldn't say, Mr. Crestwell.

CRESTWELL: Why then should this fastidious girl, this runner-up for the bathing beauty competition at Ramsgate, suddenly wish to don the garb of slavery?

ALICE: Well—I—you see——

CRESTWELL (*in full flight*): Has she said to herself—
"I know that they are short-handed at Marshwood on
account of Amy having to visit her sick Granny in
Canterbury and May being in bed with shingles . . ."

MOXIE (*still rummaging at the desk*): Stop talking
nonsense, you're keeping Alice from her work.

CRESTWELL (*ignoring the interruption*): Has she said to
herself, "for the sake of Mr. Crestwell who is rapidly
going barmy, I will sacrifice my naughty pride and
spring gladly into the breach?"

ALICE: I'm sure I don't know, Mr. . . .

CRESTWELL (*thunderously*): The answer, Alice, is NO.
The answer, Alice, is that your sister, like so many of
her contemporaries, is a film-struck, good-for-nothing
little fathead! And all that she wants to help with the
tea for is to get a close-up view of Miss Miranda Frayle
and probably ask her for her autograph. And I tell you
solemnly, here and now, that if she gets it, it will be
over my dead body.

MOXIE: Run along now, Alice—you've been standing
about quite long enough.

ALICE: Yes, Mrs. Moxton.

She goes out with the tray of glasses.

MOXIE: What's the sense of talking to the girl like
that? She doesn't understand half you say.

CRESTWELL: That is a cross I have learned to bear
with fortitude, Dora. No one understands half of what
I say.

MOXIE: Then save your breath and say less.

CRESTWELL: What's the matter with you—you've
been snapping everybody's head off for the last three
days?

MOXIE (*at last finding the list*): Here it is.

CRESTWELL: What's up?

MOXIE: Nothing's up. I must take this in—Her Ladyship's waiting for it.

CRESTWELL: Ever since the news came you've been behaving like a tragedy queen. It can't matter to you all that much.

MOXIE: It does matter to me. It matters to all of us.

CRESTWELL: You can't believe those movie magazines, you know.

MOXIE: I don't read movie magazines.

CRESTWELL: Oh, yes, you do. I saw three of them in your room only last week.

MOXIE: What were you doing in my room?

CRESTWELL (*with dignity*): You asked me to fetch your work basket, and with my inherent chivalry, which all the disruptive forces of social revolution have been powerless to destroy, I nipped up three flights and got it for you.

MOXIE: I didn't ask you to go poking and prying about.

CRESTWELL (*patiently*): Your work basket, Dora, was on the table by your bed. Beside it were three magazines, *Screenland, Photoplay* and *Love Stories of the Stars*. On the cover of the latter there was a full page photograph in colour of the future Countess of Marshwood in a two-piece bathing-suit being warmly embraced by a gentleman in a one-piece bathing-suit.

MOXIE: Alice must have left them there when she was doing the room.

CRESTWELL: I accept your unconvincing explanation.

MOXIE: I suppose it's only natural that I should want to see what the new mistress of the house looked like.

CRESTWELL: This unwitting bit of espionage on my part took place last week, Dora, before any of us had the slightest idea that His Lordship intended to marry again.

MOXIE: I'm surprised at you, I am really. You've been with the family longer than I have and you don't seem to mind this—this terrible thing a bit. All you do is make jokes about it.

CRESTWELL: The trouble with you is you're too conservative.

MOXIE: Who did you vote for in the last election?

CRESTWELL: You don't have to be conservative to vote Conservative, you just plump for the lesser of two evils.

MOXIE: Why couldn't he pick someone of his own class?

CRESTWELL: Class! Oh dear, I've forgotten what the word means. Remind me to look it up in the cross-word dictionary.

MOXIE: You may have forgotten what it means but I haven't.

CRESTWELL: That, Dora, is an admission of defeat. It proves that you have wilfully deafened yourself to the clarion call of progress.

MOXIE: Clarion call of fiddlesticks.

CRESTWELL: What's happened to your early dreams and ambitions? What's happened to your divine discontent?

MOXIE: I never had any.

CRESTWELL: You'll be telling me in a minute that you are perfectly happy in the state in which it has pleased God to call you.

MOXIE: I wish you'd stop trying to be funny for one

minute. I know you're making light of the whole business on purpose, pretending it doesn't matter, but I wish you wouldn't—not to me anyhow—I really do wish you wouldn't. . . . (*She turns away*.)

CRESTWELL (*gently*): Don't take it so hard. It may not be as bad as you think.

MOXIE: You hate it as much as I do, don't you?

CRESTWELL: What if I do? There's no sense in belly-aching about it. The only thing is to look at it philo-sophically and hope for the best.

MOXIE: A common, painted hussy from Hollywood flaunting herself as the Countess of Marshwood, and you talk about hoping for the best!

CRESTWELL: Well, that's what her ladyship's trying to do. She's had Lady Hayling nagging at her all through lunch. She kept on trying to change the subject but it was no use.

MOXIE: Her ladyship's just as upset as we are, inside.

CRESTWELL: Has she said so?

MOXIE: No. But I can tell.

CRESTWELL: Have you discussed it with her?

MOXIE (*snappily*): No, I have not.

CRESTWELL: All right . . . all right . . . Miss Miranda Frayle may not be all that common, she's English born anyhow—it says so in *Photoplay*.

MOXIE: I don't care if she was born in Timbuctoo. I don't care if her blood's blue, back or yellow. I don't care if she's English, French, Russian or Chinese. I only know that when she walks into this house I shall walk out.

CRESTWELL (*drily*): You'd better start packing. They'll be here at about six.

MOXIE (*grimly*): I mean it.

CRESTWELL: It seems to me that you're taking it all a bit too seriously.

MOXIE: Maybe I am, but that's how I feel and nothing you say or anybody else says is going to change it.

CRESTWELL: Of course, a great deal depends on what she's like.

MOXIE: He oughtn't to marry her whatever she's like.

CRESTWELL: This arbitrary point of view shocks me profoundly.

MOXIE: Does it indeed?

CRESTWELL: What's happened to your *laissez faire*?

MOXIE: I expect I lost it along with my divine discontent.

> *They are interrupted by the entrance of* FELICITY, COUNTESS OF MARSHWOOD. *She is followed by* LADY HAYLING, ADMIRAL SIR JOHN HAYLING *and the* HON. PETER INGLETON.
>
> FELICITY *is a well preserved woman in the fifties. She has obviously been a beauty in her day, indeed a vestige of the maligned, foolish 'Twenties still clings to her.*
>
> LADY HAYLING, *also in the fifties, is a pleasant enough woman, but inclined to be didactic.*
>
> ADMIRAL SIR JOHN HAYLING *is about sixty. He is a typically naval man with blue eyes and a direct manner.*
>
> PETER INGLETON *might be anywhere between thirty-five and fifty. He is impeccably dressed and has a quizzical gleam in his eye.*

FELICITY: Couldn't you find it, Moxie, dear?

MOXIE (*handing her the list*): Yes, my Lady—here it is. (*She turns to go.*)

FELICITY: Don't go, for heaven't sake, I shall need your help—yours too, Crestwell. There's a full-blooded crisis on about the Church Fête. Everything's got to be changed round. . . . Where's that horrid little map of the ground, Moxie?

MOXIE (*going to the desk*): I think it's in the blotter, milady.

FELICITY: I may require you to go and murder Major Petherick, Crestwell.

CRESTWELL: Very good, my Lady.

FELICITY: He has absolutely dug his feet in about the roundabouts. I've just been talking to him on the telephone. He was quite insufferable.

MOXIE: Here's the map, my Lady.

PETER (*looking over her shoulder at the map*): What's that space there?

FELICITY: Mrs. Burrage's clock golf and the tea tent. We can't possibly move that, it would drive everybody mad.

PETER: What about there then, right at the other end? Where all those little squiggles are.

FELICITY: Those little squiggles, Peter, are graves. We can't have a roundabout grinding out 'Candy Kisses' all over the cemetery.

PETER (*pointing*): There, then.

FELICITY: Get your mind away from that corner, Peter. It's still Church property. We know the Fête is annual hell but it isn't the Day of Judgment.

CRESTWELL: The only alternative, my Lady, is to move the band.

ADMIRAL: That's out of the question. The Brigadier wouldn't hear of it. You can't hustle the Royal Marines about from pillar to post at the last minute.

PETER: I always thought that was what Marines were for.

FELICITY: Read out the list, Moxie. There might be something else that's movable.

MOXIE (*woodenly*): Tombola—Mrs. Edgecombe. Guessing the weight of the cake—Mrs. Bruce. Miss Hodmarsh's Lucky Dip——

PETER: I should never have suspected her of having one.

FELICITY: Do be quiet, Peter. Go on, Moxie.

MOXIE (*continuing*): Jumble Stall—Mrs. Pollet and Mrs. Dint. Cooling Drinks with the Stars—Miss Miranda Frayle. (*She stops.*)

FELICITY: That's not official yet because we haven't asked her, but I don't see how she can refuse, do you?

PETER: I should think it would be the least she could do.

LADY H.: I wish it was.

FELICITY: Really, Cynthia, we really can't go on about that any more—we've been at it all through lunch. . . . Moxie, you must tell Mr. Durham to paint the sign with her name in absolutely enormous letters.

MOXIE (*in a stifled voice*): Yes, my Lady.

FELICITY: What's the matter, Moxie?

MOXIE: Nothing my Lady. I've got a slight headache, that's all.

FELICITY: Have you had your lunch?

MOXIE: Yes, thank you, my Lady.

FELICITY: Then give me that tiresome list and go and lie down for a little. There's some Aspirin in my bathroom if you haven't got any.

MOXIE (*giving her back the list*): Thank you, my Lady—excuse me.

MOXIE *goes rather hurriedly out of the room.*

FELICITY: Has anything particular happened to upset Moxie, Crestwell?

CRESTWELL: I think she has been feeling a bit under the weather for the last three days, my Lady.

FELICITY: Oh dear, I do hope she's not sickening for anything. You don't happen to remember how May's shingles started, do you?

CRESTWELL: I'm afraid not, my Lady. One day she hadn't got them and the next day she had. It took us all by surprise.

FELICITY: I wonder if we ought to send for Doctor Partridge?

CRESTWELL: I think not, my Lady. My impression is that Mrs. Moxton's disorder is emotional rather than physical.

FELICITY: Emotional?

CRESTWELL: I believe that the unexpected news of His Lordship's betrothal came as a great shock to her.

ADMIRAL: It came as a great shock to all of us.

FELICITY: Has she discussed it with you, Crestwell?

CRESTWELL: Hardly at all, my Lady, until just now before you came in.

FELICITY: Without asking you to betray her confidence in any way, has she explained why she feels so very strongly about it?

CRESTWELL: As far as I could gather, my Lady, I believe it is the social aspect of the situation that is upsetting her more than anything else.

FELICITY: You mean that she considers my son to be marrying beneath him?

CRESTWELL: That is so, my Lady. I tried to reason with her, to coax her into a more tolerant frame of mind, to point out to her the changing values of this changing world, but, like Major Petherick and the roundabouts, she just dug her feet in.

FELICITY: Thank you, Crestwell.

CRESTWELL: Will that be all, my Lady?

FELICITY: Except for the roundabouts, yes. You'd better take the list and the map to Mr. Durham and see if he has any ideas.

CRESTWELL (*taking the map and list*): Very good, my Lady.

FELICITY: I have to see him after tea anyhow. But he might be able to think up something in the meantime.

CRESTWELL *goes*.

I don't know what I would do without Crestwell. Do you remember how all through the war he and Moxie and I ran this house and dealt with all those brisk W.A.A.Fs. and he never turned a hair. He was an A.R.P. Warden, too. I shall miss him horribly.

LADY H.: Why should you do without him?

FELICITY: I can't take him away from Nigel. He belongs here.

LADY H.: Are you so certain that Nigel will want you to go?

FELICITY: He won't say he wants me to go but I don't approve of resident mothers-in-law. I had quite enough of that with Joan.

PETER: I shouldn't think that this one would be very like Joan.

FELICITY: Well, she couldn't be duller at any rate. Nobody could.

LADY H.: Joan may have been dull but she was at least a lady.

FELICITY (*laughing*): Really, Cynthia!

14

LADY H.: You know perfectly well what I mean.

FELICITY: Yes, I know what you mean. Anyhow, Miranda Frayle is a good actress and she has excellent legs, which means that she will probably move well, at any rate. Joan used to walk across a ballroom as though she were trudging through deep snow.

LADY H.: But why should he want to marry this woman? He hasn't wanted to marry any of the others.

FELICITY: That's where you're wrong. He wanted to marry *all* the others. He has a tremendous sense of moral responsibility. Fortunately most of them were married already.

ADMIRAL: Judy Lavenham wasn't.

FELICITY: Poor dear Judy was in quite a different category. By the time they met she was already practically nationalised.

LADY H.: Felicity!

FELICITY: Now Joan had all the same instincts as Judy but neither the charm nor the courage to follow them. Happily dear Bogey Whittaker caught her on the hop before she had time to think, otherwise she'd be here now instead of in Kenya.

LADY H.: I cannot understand your attitude, Felicity. The fact that Nigel's first marriage was such a disaster should make you all the more anxious that his second should be a success.

FELICITY: Nigel's first marriage was not a disaster, it was a triumph. To begin with it lasted only two years, it produced a son and heir and disintegrated painlessly in the nick of time.

ADMIRAL: The nick of time?

FELICITY: Certainly. I was on the verge of strangling Joan with my bare hands when away she went. I am not a deeply religious woman but I have always regarded Bogey Whittaker as a concrete proof of the efficacy of prayer.

LADY H.: I am perfectly aware that nowadays all social barriers are being swept away and that everybody is as good as everybody else and that any suggestion of class distinction is laughed at. . . .

FELICITY: If you're aware of all that, what on earth are you making such a fuss about?

LADY H.: Because I don't believe it, any more than you do really in your heart. You know as well as I do that if Nigel is allowed to marry this synthetic, trumped up creature it will be just one more nail in all our coffins. . . .

FELICITY (*laughing*): Dearest Cynthia. You really must not let righteous indignation play such hell with your syntax.

LADY H.: It's no good trying to discuss anything seriously with you, you're quite hopeless.

FELICITY: Do take Cynthia away, John. She's getting quite hoarse from barking up the wrong trees.

LADY H.: I'm merely saying what I think.

FELICITY: Well don't, dear. It's so exhausting.

LADY H.: John agrees with me, at any rate—don't you, John?

ADMIRAL: Yes, I agree. In my opinion we ought all to put our heads together while there's still time.

PETER: Like the Andrews Sisters.

ADMIRAL: It's fairly obvious to me that Nigel must have been tricked into this in some way. After all, he's no fool.

FELICITY: But, John dear, he *is*. He's my own son and I ought to know.

PETER: I agree that Nigel has always been fairly idiotic about women. It's reasonable to suppose that there must be something nice about her for him to have fallen in love with her in the first place.

LADY H.: He was in love with Mrs. Clifford Hargrave. I should like to know what was nice about her.

FELICITY: *Mr.* Clifford Hargrave.

LADY H. (*turning away*): Really, Felicity!

FELICITY: But I mean it. He was a darling. Wasn't he, Peter?

PETER: A rather dim darling.

FELICITY: And he took it all so well, too.

ADMIRAL (*sarcastically*): Damned decent of him.

FELICITY: And he simply adored this house. We missed him dreadfully when it was all over.

LADY H.: Come along, John. It's nearly half-past three and you've got old Renshaw coming at four. See you at dinner.

ADMIRAL: You know you can rely on us to back you up, Felicity, in whatever line you choose to take.

FELICITY (*affectionately*): Yes, dear John, of course I do. But I think in this instance that masterly inactivity is the best strategy. In fact we must study the chart and take our bearings before we set our course.

PETER: Anchors aweigh.

LADY H.: Come along, John.

ADMIRAL (*ignoring* PETER. *To* FELICITY): We'll be over at about eight-thirty. Keep in good heart, my dear.

> The HAYLINGS *go out through the french windows.*
> FELICITY *sighs.*

FELICITY: I'm afraid I was beastly to poor Cynthia. But she really maddens me at moments.

PETER: Personally I think they're both cracking bores and I always have.

FELICITY: Perhaps they are, but you see they're such old friends. I've known them for so many years. Cynthia—of course, we were at school together.

PETER: I'll bet she was top of the class in Algebra and captain of the Lacrosse team.

FELICITY: She also played Bolingbroke in *Richard the Second* and her wig fell off.

PETER: She seems to have put it back.

At this moment MOXIE *comes quietly into the room. She stops in the doorway.*

FELICITY: What is it, Moxie? I haven't forgotten anything important, have I?

MOXIE: No, my Lady. I just wanted to speak to you, that's all—I'll come back later.

PETER: It's all right, Moxie dear. I'm going to the village and you can have a clear field.

MOXIE (*in rather a choked voice*): It doesn't matter, sir— I'd rather come back later.

She goes out hurriedly.

FELICITY: Oh dear.

PETER: She's obviously in a state.

FELICITY: I wish she wouldn't be, I really do. It's so catching. Why do you suppose she's taking it so dreadfully to heart?

PETER: Have you talked to her about it much?

FELICITY: No. Whenever I mention it she changes the subject. She's very deeply angry I think.

PETER: With Nigel?

FELICITY: Yes. She adores him. She always has, ever since she first came here. You know, he was only fifteen then and they used to go to matinees together and have tea afterwards at Gunters. I think she feels that he's letting down the side.

PETER: Maybe she's right.

FELICITY: There is still just a hope that she's wrong.

PETER: I think it's a pretty slim one.

FELICITY: I don't see why. After all, it isn't the first time an English peer has married an actress. In the old days they never stopped. Of course I expect there were always family rows and upsets, but it nearly always turned out all right in the long run. Look at dear Gloria Bainbridge, buried alive in Lincolnshire and absolutely indefatigable, and Lily Grantworth with all those muscular little boys. I think the aristocracy, what's left of it, owes a great deal to the theatrical profession.

PETER: Hollywood isn't quite the same as the theatrical profession. It's more flamboyant.

FELICITY: I can't see that that matters. We live in an age of publicity and we might just as well enjoy it.

PETER: You know perfectly well that you hate it. You loathe being blinded by flash bulbs whenever you go to a first night and being caught by a candid camera at the Dorchester with your mouth full of asparagus.

FELICITY: That was for charity. Anyhow, what about you? You're constantly being photographed seeing people off at railway stations and airports and you revel in it.

PETER: It's part of my job, and I don't revel in it, I detest it. You can't run a travel bureau without advertising.

FELICITY: One of the worst aspects of modern English life is that so many of one's friends have to work and they're so bad at it.

PETER: The Ingleton Rail-Sea-and-Air office is a by-word of brisk efficiency.

FELICITY: Only because of that dusty-looking girl with glasses! If she weren't there you'd never get anyone further than Folkestone.

PETER: I fail to see why you should attack me just because your son's marrying a film star and your maid's upset about it.

FELICITY: I'm upset too. I told you before, it's catching. The last three days have been hell. I've had Cynthia Hayling rasping my nerves like a buzz saw, Moxie plunged in gloom, Crestwell looking sardonic and an insufferable letter from Rose Eastry telling me to stand firm.

PETER: What's it to do with her?

FELICITY: Go and ask her. She's your aunt too.

PETER: Only in a roundabout way.

FELICITY: If I hear that word again I shall shriek.

PETER: Calm down, dear, and concentrate on the problem in hand.

FELICITY: That's exactly what I'm trying to do but everybody keeps going on and on about it so. I've made up my mind to accept Miss Miranda Frayle without prejudice, however ghastly she turns out to be.

PETER: She may not be ghastly at all. She may be absolutely enchanting. She may be simple and unaffected and fill the house all day long with her spontaneous laughter.

FELICITY: That's what I dread most.

PETER: Or she may be a little sad, a little weary and bruised by life, like she was in "Be Still Foolish Heart".

FELICITY: Was that the one where she got so dreadfully knocked about by Edward G. Robinson?

PETER: No. That was "Women Laugh at Love".

FELICITY: It's the suddenness of the whole thing that's really upsetting me more than anything else.

PETER: Is it?

FELICITY: Yes, Peter, it is and you needn't look quizzical either. That's my story and I'm sticking to it.

PETER: Very wise.

FELICITY: I have purposely refrained from analysing my emotions and rooting about among my innermost feelings because if I did I should probably discover that I am a good deal more unhappy than I think I am.

PETER: Wiser still.

FELICITY (*vehemently*): *Of course* I would rather it hadn't happened. *Of course* I would rather he had chosen someone less glittery and spectacular, someone less flagrantly unsuitable to run Marshwood and be a good stepmother to Jeremy.

PETER: Of course.

FELICITY: And of course it would have been more convenient and pleasant if he had picked someone who likes the things he likes and knows about the things he knows about.

PETER: Someone of his own class, in fact?

FELICITY: Yes—if you must have it—someone of his own class. There. Now are you satisfied?

PETER: Not satisfied exactly, but definitely reassured.

FELICITY (*crossly*): I see nothing to be reassured about. You have merely forced me to say something that I have been valiantly trying not to admit, even to myself. It's very unkind of you.

PETER: Never mind. Press on, Felicity. You're doing splendidly.

FELICITY: Don't laugh at me. It's all quite beastly,

and you know it. My instincts are at war with my reason.

PETER: Like Moxie.

FELICITY: Certainly. Moxie, too, belongs to something that's over and done with. That's what's making her miserable.

PETER: What about Crestwell?

FELICITY: How do you mean, what about Crestwell?

PETER: The same thing applies to him.

FELICITY: Crestwell is not emotional and Moxie is, he's also very adaptable and knows more about what's going on in the world than all of us put together. You should hear what he has to say about Social Revolution and the United Nations and the Decline of the West. It's fascinating.

PETER: How does he feel about Danny Kaye?

FELICITY: He reads everything too, from the *New Statesman* to the *Daily Worker*.

PETER: A fairly small range.

FELICITY: Moxie, of course, sticks to *The Times* and remains bewildered.

 The telephone rings.

Answer it, Peter, there's a dear. It's probably the Press again. They've been ringing up all day. You can evade them with more authority than I can.

PETER (*going to the telephone*): There I think you underrate yourself. (*He lifts the receiver.*) Hallo—yes, this is 2158 . . . yes—hold the line for a moment. (*To* FELICITY.) It's for you—a personal call from London.

FELICITY: Ask who it is.

PETER (*at telephone*): Who wishes to speak to her? . . . Oh—all right—hold on. (*To* FELICITY.) It's the prodigal son himself.

FELICITY: Nigel! Oh dear. (*She takes the telephone from* PETER.) Hallo . . . yes speaking . . . (*To* PETER.) The line's terrible, it sounds as though someone were snoring . . . (*At telephone.*)   Hall—hallo—Nigel?— Yes, dear, of course it is . . . What? . . . Speak louder. I can't hear a word . . . (*To* PETER.) He can't hear me either. (*At telephone.*) Where are you?—I said WHERE ARE YOU? Oh, I see—you're just leaving now —lovely, darling. How are you—both? . . . No, dear, I said How ARE You BOTH? . . . I'm doing my best, I'm screaming like a Banshee . . . BANSHEE, darling . . . B for bottle, A for Andalusia, N for Nebuchad- nezzar . . . No . . . NEBUCHADNEZZAR—N for no- body . . . It doesn't matter . . . it's not in the least important—I was only trying to explain what I was screaming like . . . (*To* PETER.) I'm going mad.

PETER: Jiggle the thing.

FELICITY: If I jiggle the thing I shall be cut off—Ah, that's better—the snoring's stopped . . . (*At telephone.*) That's better—I can hear you now—can you hear me? Good . . . Oh, what a shame . . . I expect it was because she was in a strange bed. (*To* PETER, *with her hand over the mouthpiece.*) I know I shouldn't have said that, he'll think I was being critical. (*At telephone.*) Very well, darling . . . No—nobody but Peter and the Haylings—I thought you'd like to be quiet on your first evening . . . Does she play Canasta? . . . Oh—never mind—we can all teach her—it will be lovely . . . You don't have to have a card sense for Canasta it's at least eighty per cent luck . . . all right, darling, it really doesn't matter, it was just an idea. Very well, we'll expect you between six and seven . . . Of course I am,

I'm sure she's charming . . . (*To* PETER.) I shouldn't
have said that either, it sounded patronising. (*At telephone*.) . . . No, it wasn't in the least important . . . it
sounded like Nebuchadnezzar because it was Nebuchadnezzar. I really can't explain now, it's too complicated.
All right, darling. (*She hangs up*.) That was one of
the most idiotic conversations I've ever had in my
life.

PETER: Did he sound cheerful?

FELICITY: A little irritable I thought, but that might
have been the telephone.

PETER: I expect he was nervous.

FELICITY: I wasn't beastly to him, was I? I mean I
didn't sound cross or anything?

PETER (*suddenly kissing her affectionately*): No, dear, you
were very, very good. I know it's horrid for you and I
do sympathise, really I do.

FELICITY: Well, please don't, Peter. Even a kindly
look would undermine me at the moment. It's a pity
the silly woman can't play Canasta, I was rather relying
on it. This evening's going to be hell. Be a dear and go
and find Moxie—I'd better get that over—she's probably hovering.

PETER: All right. If you fail to cheer her up, tell her
I'll drive her into Dover before tea. She dearly loves a
little outing.

FELICITY: I really don't think that will be necessary,
a nice heart-to-heart will probably do the trick.

> PETER *goes out*.
>
> *After a moment* MOXIE *enters. She is quite calm but
> her expression is set*.

It's all right, Moxie, the coast's clear.

MOXIE: Yes, my Lady.

There is a pause.

FELICITY (*kindly*): You look dreadfully grim, Moxie. What is it that's worrying you?

MOXIE: The thought of what I have to say to you, milady. That's what's worrying me.

FELICITY: Surely whatever you have to say to me can't be as awful as all that?

MOXIE: I'm afraid it is.

FELICITY (*patting the sofa by her side*): Sit down, dear, and relax a bit before you say anything at all.

MOXIE: I'd rather stand, really I would. If I sat down I might cry and make a fool of myself. (*A slight pause, and then with a great effort.*) I'm afraid I have to leave you, my Lady.

FELICITY: Leave me? Why, Moxie—what on earth? . . .

MOXIE: At once, my Lady—today. I've had some bad news.

FELICITY: Oh, my dear, I'm so awfully sorry—what is it?

MOXIE: It's my aunt, my Lady—my mother's sister— she's very seriously ill and she's all alone. . . .

FELICITY: Where?

MOXIE (*after a slight hesitation*): Southsea.

FELICITY: Why is she all alone? She must have someone to look after her?

MOXIE: Her husband looked after her, my Lady —but—but—he died suddenly two days ago. I've just had a telegram from one of the neighbours.

FELICITY: And you have to leave at once?

MOXIE: Yes, my Lady.

FELICITY: Oh, poor Moxie, how horrid for you. When do you think you'll be able to come back?

MOXIE: That's just it, my Lady. I shan't be able to come back.

FELICITY: What!

MOXIE: You see, she's all alone—and she may just sort of linger on for years.

FELICITY: Do you mean to say that you want to leave me for good—now—this minute?

MOXIE: It isn't that I want to, my Lady—do please believe that—it's that I must.

FELICITY: But this aunt of yours, what's the matter with her? What's she suffering from?

MOXIE: I don't rightly know, my Lady. The doctors don't seem to have been able to make up their minds.

FELICITY: Couldn't she go to a hospital?

MOXIE: Oh no—she can't be moved.

FELICITY: And her husband who looked after her—what did he die of so very suddenly?

MOXIE: He was run over, my Lady. By an Army lorry——

FELICITY (*inexorably*): Where?

MOXIE: Just opposite the South Parade pier.

FELICITY: How do you know all this?

MOXIE: It was in the telegram.

FELICITY: Your aunt must have very extravagant neighbours.

MOXIE (*dimly*): Yes, my Lady.

FELICITY: Moxie, how long have you been with me?

MOXIE: I came to Marshwood as housemaid twenty years ago.

FELICITY: And you became my personal maid a year later.

MOXIE: Yes.

FELICITY: And you've been my personal maid and my personal friend and part of the family ever since.

MOXIE (*obviously in distress*): Yes, my Lady.

FELICITY: So we have lived together, travelled together, laughed together and gossiped together for approximately nineteen years.

MOXIE: Yes, my Lady.

FELICITY: Can it be that during all that long time, Moxie, you have looked upon me as a drivelling idiot?

MOXIE (*turning away*): I'm sorry, my Lady—I knew it was no use—I knew you wouldn't believe it. . . .

FELICITY: I think it was the Army lorry that did it really. You're a terribly bad liar—I've noticed it on the telephone. You're upset about His Lordship's marriage. That's the trouble, isn't it?

MOXIE: Yes—yes, that's the trouble.

FELICITY: You seriously wish to leave me because of it?

MOXIE: Yes please, my Lady.

FELICITY: But why, Moxie dear? Why should it matter to you so desperately?

MOXIE: Please let me go, my Lady, and don't ask me to explain. I can't stay here—really I can't.

FELICITY: But you won't have to stay here. Not for long, at any rate. I intend to go away myself at the earliest opportunity, and you naturally will leave with me.

MOXIE: It's impossible, my Lady. I must leave at once.

FELICITY: But why?

MOXIE: I have my reasons.

FELICITY: And you won't tell me what they are?

MOXIE: I can't, my Lady. I really can't.

FELICITY: In that case there isn't anything more to be said, is there?

MOXIE (*near tears*): Oh, my Lady.

FELICITY: Obviously I can't force you to stay if you don't want to, nor can I compel you to explain if you have decided not to. I'm feeling angry at the moment, naturally enough, but unfortunately I know that the anger is only temporary. It will pass inevitably in a little while and leave me bewildered, and sad, and bitterly, bitterly disappointed. Come and say good-bye to me when you've packed.

MOXIE: Very well, my Lady. (*She goes miserably towards the door.*)

FELICITY (*rising swiftly she goes to* MOXIE *and puts her arms round her*): Oh, Moxie, Moxie—this is too utterly fantastic—I can't possibly just let it happen without doing everything in my power to prevent it—please tell me why you feel that you have to leave me, so obviously against your will—I promise you I'll try to understand whatever it is—please, Moxie. . . .

MOXIE (*breaking down*): I can't—it's too humiliating —I'm so ashamed.

FELICITY (*a thought striking her*): It isn't Nigel, is it? I mean, it isn't that he has ever . . . ?

MOXIE (*horrified*): Oh, no—no—of course it isn't . . .

FELICITY: Is it—is it perhaps that you love him— more than you can help?

MOXIE (*pulling herself together*): No, my Lady—it's nothing like that. I swear it isn't. Of course I love His Lordship. I've loved him ever since he was a boy—but not like that——

FELICITY (*soothingly*): We're all worried about this sudden engagement. But we really must all make an effort to face the situation calmly and sensibly. After all, the world has changed a great deal in our lifetime, Moxie; lots of things that mattered dreadfully when we were young, don't matter at all any more. For all we know Miranda Frayle may be simple and kind and absolutely charming, and the only really important thing is that she should make him happy, isn't it?

MOXIE: She won't.

FELICITY: We can't prove that though, can we?

MOXIE: If you searched the whole wide world with a tooth-comb you couldn't find anybody less fitted to be His Lordship's wife and the mistress of this house.

FELICITY: Why are you so sure? How do you know?

MOXIE: Because, my Lady, Miss Miranda Frayle happens to be my young sister.

CURTAIN

ACT I

SCENE II

Scene: About two hours have elapsed since the preceding Scene.
FELICITY is seated behind the tea-table. PETER is
wandering about with a cup in his hand.

FELICITY: I do wish you'd sit down, Peter! Nothing can be achieved by you charging about the room like a sort of Dodgem.

PETER: What on earth's a Dodgem?

FELICITY: One of those little motor-cars you go on in Margate and bang into everybody.

PETER: I haven't banged into anybody yet.

FELICITY: We must concentrate. This is a serious crisis.

PETER: If we concentrate until we're blue in the face we shan't get any further. There's only one possible solution and you know it. You must go abroad immediately and take Moxie with you.

FELICITY: That's not a solution at all, merely a temporary measure. And it's quite out of the question for me to go abroad immediately. My passport's in London and there are currency regulations. I used up my allowance in February, and even then I had to borrow from Henrietta.

PETER: You must borrow from her again.

FELICITY: She's in Morocco.

PETER: What's wrong with Morocco?

FELICITY: Even if I went to the Barrier Reef, I couldn't stay there indefinitely. Besides, Moxie can't stand hot climates. She breaks out in a rash.

PETER: Well, send *her* away, then—send her somewhere nice and cool.

FELICITY: I've told you once and for all that I am not going to be parted from Moxie. I couldn't live without her and I don't intend to try.

PETER: It may not be for long. We may be able to dissuade Nigel from marrying this tiresome woman, and then she could go back to Hollywood and nobody need ever know.

FELICITY: And how do you propose to go about dissuading him?

PETER: Surely when he knows that his prospective sister-in-law is his mother's maid it will shake him a bit? What was their name—their family name, I mean?

FELICITY: Birch. They had a grocer's shop in Nightingale Lane, between Brixton and Clapham. Freda, that's my future daughter-in-law, was the flighty one. Moxie's real name is Dora—she married Moxton, Edith Harrington's chauffeur. They had a child but it died, then Moxton died too, so she went back to the shop and her mother.

PETER: And Freda?

FELICITY: Oh, Freda had upped and left home long before then. Apparently she started making a beast of herself quite early. . . .

PETER: In what way?

FELICITY: Oh, the usual way. She kept on almost having babies but not quite.

PETER: Lack of concentration.

FELICITY: Then there was apparently a terrible scene and the mother had a stroke and Freda beetled off to America with a theatrical agent called Greenberg. That was the last Moxie saw of her.

PETER: Did the mother die?

FELICITY: Yes, and the shop failed, and Moxie came here as housemaid shortly afterwards.

PETER (*thoughtfully*): Twenty years is a long time.

FELICITY: Time enough to forge bonds of loyalty and affection that are impossible to break.

PETER: Perhaps Freda—Miranda—whatever her name is, wouldn't recognise her.

FELICITY: Of course she would. Moxie's hardly changed at all.

PETER: She could change, though, couldn't she?

FELICITY: How do you mean?

PETER: I have an idea.

FELICITY (*with sarcasm*): Disguise her, I suppose.

PETER: No. Promote her, that's the first thing—the disguise part can come later.

FELICITY: Peter!

PETER: No—wait a minute—it could be done, I'm sure it could.

FELICITY: What do you propose to do? Pop a tiara on her head and pretend she's the Duchess of Devonshire?

PETER: Of course not, don't be so silly—but it would be possible.

FELICITY (*exasperated*): What would be possible?

PETER: As I see it, the crux of this whole situation is that Moxie is a domestic servant, a lady's maid, in fact, a social inferior.

FELICITY: There's nothing inferior about her, social or otherwise.

PETER: All right, all right—I couldn't agree with you more—but that's beside the point.

FELICITY: What did you mean about promoting her?

PETER: Step her up—make her your companion, or your secretary.

FELICITY: But she presses my clothes and does my hair and brings me things on trays.

PETER: She doesn't do those things in public, I presume.

FELICITY: And what about Nigel? What would *he* say?

PETER: I should think if anything Nigel would be delighted. After all, she's going to be his sister.

FELICITY: Oh dear!

PETER: Did I detect in that exclamation a faint echo of old world snobbery, Felicity?

FELICITY: Of course you didn't. It's only that it's all so idiotic, so inconsistent. Moxie is Moxie. Why should it make any difference whether she's called my maid or my secretary?

PETER: Why, indeed? But it does. One must face facts. Nobody would think twice, for instance, if you took young Stephen Bristow to the opening night of the Ballet and to the Savoy Grill afterwards, would they?

FELICITY: Of course they wouldn't. He's a very charming boy.

PETER: But you wouldn't take Crestwell, would you?

FELICITY: Crestwell can't bear the Ballet. He says it's decadent.

PETER: The fact remains, you wouldn't take him. It would embarrass him and you. It would also, very slightly, embarrass your friends. Stephen Bristow is the son of a tobacconist in Folkestone. Crestwell is the son of a police constable in Sevenoaks. As far as actual class goes there is nothing to chose between them. They are both hard-working, decent Englishmen, but one happens to be a golf instructor, and the other a butler, and the social abyss yawning between them, even in these democratic days, is still unbridgeable.

FELICITY: I still don't see how the present problem can be solved by making Moxie my secretary. She can't do shorthand or type, she can't even spell very well.

PETER: Neither can you.

FELICITY: But everybody knows her as my maid. They'd all think I was dotty if I suddenly said she was my secretary.

PETER: Companion, then.

FELICITY: Where do companions eat?

PETER: Presumably with the people they're being companions to. Where is she now?

FELICITY: Upstairs in her room. I made her promise not to budge until I had had time to consider the situation from every angle.

PETER: Secretary-companion . . . she must be entirely re-dressed.

FELICITY: Oh, Peter, she'll never agree to it in a thousand years.

PETER: I don't see why.

FELICITY: She's a woman of considerable pride. She will bitterly resent the idea of stepping out of her own milieu in order to be socially acceptable to her own sister.

PETER: Let's ask her, anyhow.

FELICITY: I think before we say anything to her I should like Crestwell's opinion. Ring the bell.

PETER *rings the bell.*

PETER: We could always make a family party of it and pretend he's your long-lost cousin from South Africa.

FELICITY: Don't be so idiotic.

PETER: I bet you anything you like I can make her absolutely unrecognisable. It's only a question of make-up, really, and doing her hair.

FELICITY: Don't get too carried away now, Peter. We're not planning charades. I won't have Moxie made a fool of.

PETER: There's no question of making a fool of her. It seems to me to be a very sensible way out of a tricky situation. Why should she object to being moved a step up in the social scale?

34

FELICITY: Because it's being done for the wrong reason.

CRESTWELL *enters.*

CRESTWELL: You rang, my Lady?

FELICITY: Yes, Crestwell. Is Mrs. Moxton in her room.

CRESTWELL: Yes, my Lady. She looked depressed, so I sent her up a cup of tea.

FELICITY: How thoughtful of you, Crestwell.

CRESTWELL: I popped in to see her myself a short while ago and she perked up no end. She was just starting *The Times* crossword. I helped her a bit with it. She's quick as a knife on the clues but her spelling handicaps her terribly.

FELICITY: Oh.

PETER: You didn't happen to get 'one down', did you? It's been driving me mad. It's six letters, and I know it's a quotation from Milton.

CRESTWELL: The word is 'nursed', sir. It's *Lycidas.* "For we were nursed upon the self-same hill".

PETER: Very appropriate. Thank you, Crestwell.

FELICITY: I have been thinking for some time of making a change in the household, Crestwell.

CRESTWELL: A change, my Lady?

FELICITY: And I wanted to ask your opinion before I decide definitely. It concerns Moxie.

CRESTWELL: Yes, my Lady?

FELICITY: I wish to—to promote her—to alter her status. I was wondering how much a change would affect the other servants.

CRESTWELL: Well, there's only the cook to be considered seriously, my Lady. May is occupied with her shingles at the moment, Amy and Alice don't count, and I don't think that young Frank will be with us long, anyhow.

FELICITY: Why not?

CRESTWELL: He is not happy in his work, my Lady. Like so many of the young people of to-day he holds very definite views on social equality. He feels that all menial tasks should be done by somebody else.

PETER: And the cook?

CRESTWELL: A reasonable woman up to a point, sir. Sometimes temperamental when time or circumstances thwart her endeavours, but by no means deaf to entreaty.

FELICITY: Is she fond of Mrs. Moxton—Moxie?

CRESTWELL: Fond would be an overstatement, my Lady. She respects her, and occasionally tells her fortune with tea-leaves, but I wouldn't describe their relationship as exactly intimate.

FELICITY: What would she do if Moxie ceased to be part of the domestic staff and became my secretary?

CRESTWELL (*incredulously*): Secretary, my Lady?

FELICITY: Well—companion-secretary.

CRESTWELL: To what degree would such a metamorphosis affect the status quo, my Lady?

FELICITY: Well, I don't know really—I mean, that would all have to be gone into very carefully.

CRESTWELL: Meals, for instance?

FELICITY (*helplessly*): Oh dear—that is a problem, isn't it?

CRESTWELL: A problem, certainly, but not an insoluble one. I presume that she could eat in the dining-room when you were 'en famille' as it were?

FELICITY: Yes—I suppose so—yes, of course she could.

CRESTWELL: And on other, more formal occasions, she could have a tray upstairs. Might I suggest that we turn what used to be the Japanese room into a private sitting-room for her? Nobody ever uses it now and besides having a very agreeable view, it would consolidate her position.

FELICITY: What a wonderful idea, Crestwell! You don't think she'd be too lonely?

CRESTWELL: That is something we all have to face at one time or another, my Lady. Superior rank invariably carries with it its own burdens. I am told that newly-created Naval commanders are frequently desolate when promotion snatches them from the dusty arena of the communal wardroom.

FELICITY: I hadn't visualised Moxie as a Naval commander exactly.

CRESTWELL: Nevertheless the analogy is not too far-fetched, my Lady.

FELICITY: You haven't yet answered my original question. What do you think of the idea, Crestwell?

CRESTWELL: May I ask if you have discussed it with Mrs. Moxton herself?

PETER: Not yet. We wanted to get your reactions first.

FELICITY: You think she won't agree?

CRESTWELL: I think, taking into consideration the very special circumstances, she might.

PETER: How much do you know, Crestwell?

CRESTWELL: In common with most of the human race, sir, I know very little but imagine I know a great deal.

FELICITY: Dear Crestwell, don't be evasive, please—this is a crisis.

CRESTWELL: I suspected as much, my Lady.

FELICITY (*firmly*): Miss Miranda Frayle, His Lordship's intended bride, happens to be Mrs. Moxton's sister.

CRESTWELL: Thank you, my Lady. You may rely on my discretion.

FELICITY: You already guessed it?

CRESTWELL: By simple deduction and putting two and two together I had arrived at the conclusion that there was something a bit dodgy going on.

FELICITY: You were quite right, Crestwell. Nothing indeed could be dodgier.

CRESTWELL: A coincidence in the best tradition of English high comedy, my Lady. Consider how delightfully Mr. Somerset Maugham would handle the situation!

PETER: I can think of other writers who wouldn't exactly sneeze at the idea.

CRESTWELL: If I may say so, sir, our later playwrights would miss the more subtle nuances. They are all too brittle. Comedies of manners swiftly become obsolete when there are no longer any manners.

FELICITY: Will you help us, Crestwell?

CRESTWELL: In what way, my Lady?

FELICITY: In any way you can. You are a wise man and an exceedingly persuasive one.

CRESTWELL: Thank you, my Lady.

FELICITY: I shall never forget how you managed that dreadful W.A.A.F. who took to the bottle and kept on disappearing on her bicycle in the middle of the night.

CRESTWELL: That was more moral blackmail than persuasion, my Lady.

FELICITY: Will you go now and ask Moxie to come down?

CRESTWELL: Very good, my Lady.

He goes out with tea tray.

FELICITY: Try not to enjoy the situation too whole-heartedly, Peter.

PETER: I can't imagine why you don't marry Crestwell, Felicity. It would simplify everything.

FELICITY: It's terribly upsetting really.

PETER: It needn't be, if it's properly handled.

FELICITY: It's Moxie that I am worrying about. I've suddenly realised something—something curiously humiliating.

PETER: What?

FELICITY: I don't really know her at all.

PETER: What on earth do you mean?

FELICITY: She knows me all right, there's no doubt about that. She has studied my moods and obeyed my wishes. She knows all my problems and all my relations, in fact there are certain aspects of me that she alone knows. She has nursed me through illness, she has seen me in tears, she has seen me dressed and undressed, with my face plastered with grease or made-up to the eyes. And only once, in nineteen years, have I ever seen her in her dressing-gown and that was in the Station Hotel at Genoa when I had ptomaine poisoning from eating bad fish.

PETER: Surely true knowledge of character doesn't necessarily depend on constantly seeing people in their dressing-gowns?

FELICITY: She has done her job faithfully and well, she has given me devoted service, she has comforted me and cosseted me and received all my confidences for all those long years, and until to-day I didn't even know that she had a sister!

PETER: If she was ashamed of her, if she had cut her out of her life, it was quite natural that she shouldn't discuss her or even mention her.

FELICITY: I've told Moxie many things that I was ashamed of.

MOXIE *comes in, followed by* CRESTWELL.

MOXIE: Crestwell says that you wish to speak to me, my Lady.

FELICITY: Yes, Moxie, I do, most urgently. Will you sit down?

MOXIE: Very well, my Lady.

FELICITY: Yes, on the sofa. Crestwell, please sit down too. This is a family conference and it can't possibly be dealt with satisfactorily if everybody is standing about.

CRESTWELL: Very good, my Lady.

He and MOXIE *sit on the sofa.*

FELICITY: Peter?

PETER (*sitting*): All right. I feel as though we ought to have pencils and paper.

FELICITY: Now then, Moxie, dear. I have explained the situation confidentially to Mr. Peter. I had to discuss it with somebody, and he is an old friend whose discretion can be completely relied on.

MOXIE: I quite understand, my Lady.

FELICITY: Crestwell also. But, as a matter of fact, he had already guessed.

MOXIE (*shooting* CRESTWELL *a slightly baleful look*): Had he indeed, my Lady?

CRESTWELL: A process of natural deduction, Dora—cause and effect, you know.

40

MOXIE: I don't know any such thing. But I do know about people nosing about and not minding their own business.

FELICITY: You mustn't be cross with Crestwell, Moxie. He is eager to help us in any way he can.

MOXIE: Very kind of him, I'm sure.

FELICITY: The thought of you leaving Marshwood and me for any reason except that you were unhappy here fills me with dismay.

MOXIE: But that is the reason, my Lady. I shall be unhappy here. I couldn't very well be anything else in the circumstances.

FELICITY: I fully appreciate that, Moxie, which is why I have decided, after careful deliberation, to alter the circumstances.

MOXIE: May I ask how, my Lady?

FELICITY: I wish you from now onwards to cease being my personal maid and become my companion-secretary.

MOXIE: I am afraid I couldn't possibly do that.

FELICITY: Why not?

MOXIE: I should feel so silly, my Lady. Besides, it wouldn't be right.

CRESTWELL: Now then, Dora, don't be stubborn.

MOXIE: This is my affair, Fred, and not yours. You've interfered enough already. We will have a little talk about it later when I can speak more freely.

FELICITY: You can speak perfectly freely here, Moxie.

MOXIE: Out of consideration for Crestwell I would rather not, my Lady.

FELICITY: Why do you feel that it wouldn't be right for you to be my companion-secretary?

41

MOXIE: Well, I can't type for one thing and my writing's terrible.

CRESTWELL: The question is one of status rather than actual achievement.

FELICITY (*anxiously*): That's the whole point.

MOXIE: You mean it would embarrass my sister less to find me in a false position rather than a real one?

PETER: Touché!

MOXIE: Do you really think, my Lady, that the position of a paid companion is so very superior to that of a paid lady's maid?

FELICITY: Of course I don't, but in the eyes of the world I suppose it is.

MOXIE: How would this—this change—if it took place—really help matters?

FELICITY: Well, it would put you on a different footing in the house, Moxie. For instance, you would take your meals with us, when we were alone. . . .

MOXIE (*inexorably*): And when there were visitors?

FELICITY (*floundering*): Well—I suppose that would really depend on how many there were. We thought of making the old Japanese room into a sort of private sitting-room for you—you could occasionally have a tray up there—in peace and quiet.

MOXIE: I could even invite my sister up every now and then for a little snack, couldn't I, my Lady?

FELICITY: Don't be angry, Moxie. Please don't be angry.

MOXIE: I'm not angry, my Lady, really I'm not—and I understand what you're trying to do—but it's no good—it wouldn't work.

FELICITY: Why are you so sure it wouldn't?

MOXIE: Well, it stands to reason, doesn't it? I mean

—it's me that's the trouble—I know I couldn't carry it off. You'd much better let me go, like I said—there isn't any other way out.

PETER: But even that isn't a way out. You'll still be Lord Marshwood's sister-in-law, wherever you are.

MOXIE: Nobody need ever know.

FELICITY: I won't accept such a sacrifice from you, Moxie—nothing will induce me to. If I did, I should never forgive myself.

MOXIE: Oh, my Lady, don't take on so—you'll only start one of your headaches.

PETER: Do you absolutely refuse to consider her Ladyship's suggestion? Even as a temporary measure, until we see how the land lies?

MOXIE: It wouldn't do. It wouldn't be right.

CRESTWELL: Now look here, Dora. . . .

MOXIE (*savagely*): Unless you want to see me really lose my temper and make an exhibition of myself, you'll keep your tongue between your teeth.

FELICITY: Oh, Moxie.

MOXIE: I'm sorry, my Lady, truly sorry, but the whole business is running me ragged and that's a fact. It's more than flesh and blood can stand. I haven't slept for three nights from worrying myself sick and trying to think what could be done. I don't want to leave this house, and you, any more than you want me to go. I've belonged here for nineteen years of my life, and it's too late for me to try to start belonging anywhere else.

FELICITY: There's no question of you going away, Moxie. I want you to understand that clearly, once and for all.

43

MOXIE: I must, my Lady. This idea of play-acting and pretending to be what I'm not won't settle anything. I am what I am and I haven't got anything to be ashamed of.

CRESTWELL: We all know that, Dora, there's no sense in working yourself up.

MOXIE (*at bay*): And why shouldn't I work myself up? God knows I've got enough reason for it. It's all very fine for you, Fred Crestwell, you're safe. You've got what you call a philosophical outlook, and you never stop ramming it down all our throats until we're sick and tired of it. You're all right, you are! Nothing's going to knock you off your perch. I'm not saying you're not quite a good butler too, as butlers go, even though you are a bit sloppy with the silver!

CRESTWELL: May God forgive you for that, Dora.

MOXIE: No, I'm the one that's going to suffer over this, more than anybody, even more than you, my Lady. I know it's awkward for you and puts you in an embarrassing position, but you don't stand to lose anything by it, not really. But if this marriage takes place I shan't have anything, neither my job nor my pride in it nor the feeling that I belong anywhere. I shall be mortified until the end of my days.

FELICITY (*distressed*): Oh, Moxie!

MOXIE (*near tears*): I've always taken a pride in my work and done it to the best of my ability, and anybody who looks down on me for that can just get on with it!

CRESTWELL (*firmly*): Now see here, Dora. You just stop pitying yourself and use your loaf for a minute. Nobody's looking down on anybody. We all know you're a good worker, we all know you're upset, and

we all know why, so we needn't argue about that any
more. We also know that your martyring yourself and
going away for ever won't solve anything, but something's got to be done, for her Ladyship's sake as well as
yours, and you've got to do it. There isn't much time
and we've got to think fast.

MOXIE (*angrily*): Don't you talk to me like that!

CRESTWELL: Shut up a minute. May I make a
suggestion, my Lady?

FELICITY: Of course you may. Keep calm, Moxie,
Crestwell's right. (*To* CRESTWELL.) What is it?

CRESTWELL (*taking charge*): Well. To begin with, the
secretary-companion won't wash for one very good
reason.

PETER: What reason?

CRESTWELL: It isn't good enough.

MOXIE: Oh, Fred—how can you say such a
thing. . . .

CRESTWELL: When Dora's sister arrives in this house,
she will naturally be received as one of the family, won't
she?

FELICITY: Of course she will.

CRESTWELL: Then Dora will have to be, too.

PETER: I must say I see Crestwell's point.

FELICITY: So do I—but what I don't see is how it can
possibly be arranged.

CRESTWELL: Just a moment—begging your pardon,
my Lady.

FELICITY: Go on, Crestwell.

CRESTWELL: His Lordship's been a   y now for over
four months, hasn't he?

FELICITY: Yes.

CRESTWELL: Suppose that during that time an uncle

of Dora's—died in Australia, and left her a large sum of money, enough to give her an income for life?

FELICITY: Yes—I'm beginning to see. Go on.

CRESTWELL: Being sentimentally attached to the family as you might say, she wouldn't want to leave Marshwood, however financially independent she was, would she?

FELICITY: I don't know. Would you, Moxie?

MOXIE: Of course I wouldn't, my Lady.

CRESTWELL (*triumphantly*): Therefore she would be staying on here—at least for the time being—as a personal friend and meet her sister on equal terms rather than as one of the staff.

FELICITY: Yes, I see that, but what I don't see is how this could possibly be explained convincingly.

PETER: There isn't anyone to explain it to, apart from Nigel. You can get him alone soon after he arrives and tell him about Moxie's uncle. You can add that she's very sensitive about having been a lady's maid and that he's not to say a word.

FELICITY: What about the Haylings?

PETER: I'll deal with them. I'll pop over before dinner and tell them a little of the truth but not all of it, and swear them to secrecy.

FELICITY: Do you think you can do it, Moxie?

MOXIE: I don't like it, my Lady—it doesn't feel right somehow—I don't like it at all.

FELICITY: Neither do I. But it's worth trying, whether we like it or not.

MOXIE: Are you sure, my Lady? Quite sure?

CRESTWELL: Come on, Dora, stop shilly-shallying.

MOXIE: Shut up, Fred, I'm talking to her Ladyship. (*To* FELICITY.) What about afterwards, my Lady?

46

FELICITY: Afterwards?

MOXIE: When they are married, I mean. Shall I have to go on staying here? In the house with her?

FELICITY (*helplessly*): I don't know. We shall have to decide that when the time comes. I shall probably go away and if I do you will naturally come with me.

MOXIE: But not as a secretary-companion, or a friend of the family's, or your son's sister-in-law, only as your maid, like I've always been.

FELICITY: Very well, Moxie, that's a promise.

MOXIE: All right, then, my Lady: I'll do it, if you think I can. I'll do my best, anyway.

FELICITY: Do you think she'll recognise you?

MOXIE: I don't know—she hasn't laid eyes on me for twenty years. I've been saving a few things to say to that one, whether she recognises me or not. I can forgive her for running off and leaving me alone with Mum on my hands, but what I can't forgive her for is coming back and shoving her nose in where she doesn't belong.

PETER: Do you hate her, Moxie?

MOXIE: Of course I don't. She's not worth it. She was always an affected little piece and out for what she could get. If ever a girl needed her bottom smacking, she did.

PETER: We might arrange that after dinner.

FELICITY: Sssh, Peter. You'd better wear my Molyneux this evening. We'll discuss other clothes in the morning.

MOXIE: I'll bring your tea in half an hour early.

FELICITY: I think Mr. Peter has some ideas about your hair. You'd better listen to him, he's quite good at that sort of thing.

47

MOXIE: Very good, my Lady. (*To* PETER.) Thank you, sir.

FELICITY: I think Moxie had better have the chintz room, Crestwell. You might see that her things are moved, will you?

CRESTWELL: Very good, my Lady. I gather, to coin a phrase, that we're off?

FELICITY: We certainly are.

> *There is the sound of a car arriving, with the exuberant honking of a klaxon.*

Go along, Moxie. Good heavens, they're arriving! Fly, Moxie—quickly!

MOXIE (*giggles*): Oh, my Lady—I don't think I can . . . I really don't!

> *She goes to* FELICITY, *who takes her hand.*

FELICITY: Courage, Moxie!

MOXIE (*suddenly drawing herself up, and speaking in a changed voice*): Crestwell, tell Alice to run a bath for me, will you, please?

CRESTWELL (*obsequiously*): Very good, Mrs. Moxton.

MOXIE: And you might wipe that grin off your face while you're at it!

> *Sweeping past him and out of the room.*

CURTAIN

ACT II

Scene I

Scene: About two hours have elapsed since the preceding scene. Felicity *and* Nigel *are alone in the room. They are both dressed for dinner.* Nigel *is about thirty-five or six. He is good-looking and has charm. There is perhaps a little weakness about him, a suggestion of petulance, but one feels that, on the whole he is a pleasant fellow. At the moment however he is slightly irritable.*

Nigel: But I still don't quite understand, Mother.

Felicity: I should have thought it was simple enough.

Nigel: I'm fond of Moxie, as you know. I always have been. But I can't help feeling that this—this sudden transformation is a little drastic.

Felicity: It's her way of starting a new life, you know, like people going off to Rhodesia.

Nigel: It would be a damned sight less awkward if she had gone to Rhodesia.

Felicity: Not for me, dear. I can't bear wide open spaces. They give me whatever's the opposite of claustrophobia.

Nigel: Is it absolutely necessary for you to go wherever she goes, to be clamped to her side for the rest of your days?

Felicity: Absolutely. I'm devoted to her and she's devoted to me.

NIGEL: But surely, if she's financially independent and no longer your maid you can't expect her to fetch and carry for you and look after you.

FELICITY: Moxie would continue to look after me if she were a millionairess.

NIGEL: If you ask me I think the whole thing is absurd. You don't want to be known as an eccentric, do you?

FELICITY: I wouldn't really mind. Eccentrics have a lovely time. Look at old Maud Nethersole, she's merry as a grig from morning till night.

NIGEL: Old Maud Nethersole's not an eccentric, she's plain dotty.

FELICITY: I still don't see why you're making such a dreadful fuss. Moxie's been with us for years, she's part of the family. Why shouldn't she have meals with us and call us by our Christian names?

NIGEL: Why shouldn't she? Really, Mother!

FELICITY: Well, give me one valid reason.

NIGEL: To begin with it's unsuitable. It's also extremely embarrassing. You must see that.

FELICITY: Sylvia Fowler calls us by our Christian names, in fact she positively deafens us with them.

NIGEL: That's quite different. She's Jack Fowler's wife and we've known him all our lives.

FELICITY: She was a manicurist at Selfridges.

NIGEL: Harrods.

FELICITY: She's a perfect beast, anyhow, and she has no neck into the bargain.

NIGEL: If her head were sunk between her shoulders it still wouldn't have any bearing on what we're talking about.

FELICITY: Oh yes, it would. And it does. Why

should you be willing to accept on equal terms a loud-voiced vulgarian with no neck and turn up your nose at poor darling Moxie who has devoted the best years of her life to us?

NIGEL: I'm not turning up my nose at her, but I still think it would be uncomfortable for her and for us to have her lolling about the house all day long knocking back dry Martinis.

FELICITY: You make your ancestral home sound like Great Fosters.

NIGEL: What's Aunt Rose going to say?

FELICITY: Aunt Rose is in too much of a frizz about your marrying a film star to worry her head about Moxie.

NIGEL: How dare she be in a frizz? It's none of her damned business.

FELICITY: Neither's this.

NIGEL: Miranda's one of the most wonderful people in the world. She's given romance and happiness to millions.

FELICITY: With the apparent exception of Aunt Rose.

NIGEL: To hell with Aunt Rose.

FELICITY: Will you do as I ask? About Moxie, I mean?

NIGEL: I suppose so. But I don't approve of it and I never shall.

FELICITY: And you'll promise not to tell anyone, even Miranda?

NIGEL: How can you be so silly, Mother? Everybody's bound to know sooner or later.

FELICITY: Will you promise?

NIGEL: If you insist.

FELICITY: I do insist. It's terribly important.

NIGEL: All right, I promise.

FELICITY: After all it won't be for long. We shall be going away soon.

NIGEL: Why should you?

FELICITY: Because this is your home, darling, and I presume that you and Miranda will wish to live in it.

NIGEL: It's your home, too.

FELICITY: Only for as long as you are unattached, dear. Mothers-in-law can be horribly tedious. It wouldn't be fair to Miranda.

NIGEL: You got along with Joan all right.

FELICITY: Getting along with Joan all right was one of the most spectacular achievements of my whole life. My nervous system has never quite recovered from it.

NIGEL (*reminiscently*): Poor old Joan, she certainly was a crashing bore, wasn't she? I can't think why I ever married her.

FELICITY: I used to ponder that question myself sometimes, when she was playing the piano.

NIGEL: She thumped a bit but she wasn't all that bad.

FELICITY: We had to have it refelted after the divorce.

NIGEL: Do you like Miranda, Mother—really?

FELICITY: I only had a few words with her and then she said she wanted to go to sleep.

NIGEL: She was exhausted after the drive down. She always sleeps in the afternoon anyhow.

FELICITY: How sensible.

NIGEL (*persistently*): Do you think you are going to like her?

FELICITY: I hope so, darling. She seemed very charming. Of course she has no eyebrows.

NIGEL: Your mind seems to be running on anatomical defects this evening.

FELICITY: I didn't say it was a defect. I merely said that she hadn't got any.

NIGEL: She's awfully simple and sweet really, you know. Quite unlike what you'd think she'd be from seeing her on the screen.

FELICITY: I've only seen her as a hospital nurse, a gangster's moll, a nun, and Catherine the Great, so it's a little difficult to form any definite opinion.

NIGEL: I'm very much in love with her.

FELICITY: I'm sure you are, dear.

NIGEL: I suppose it was a great shock to you, wasn't it?

FELICITY: I think it would have been more considerate if you had prepared the ground a little beforehand.

NIGEL: It all happened so quickly.

FELICITY: What did, dear?

NIGEL: Well, meeting her and falling in love with her and asking her to marry me. It was extraordinary, really it was, like a sudden flash of light.

FELICITY: She must have been used to that, having been photographed so much, I mean.

NIGEL: It all happened at Cap d'Antibes. We found ourselves alone together on a raft——

FELICITY: Like the Kon Tiki expedition.

NIGEL: And we both knew somehow, in the first glance, that we were made for each other.

FELICITY: There can have been very little to prevent you.

NIGEL: I suppose all this laboured flippancy is merely to cover up what you really feel?

FELICITY: I don't know what I really feel yet. I haven't had time to find out.

NIGEL: You're prejudiced against her. That's fairly obvious at any rate.

FELICITY: What did you expect me to be?

NIGEL: A little more sympathetic. I know it's all very sudden and that I should have given you more warning, but you might have a little confidence in my taste and judgment.

FELICITY: Your love life since the age of eighteen, darling, has been a trifle too erratic to inspire confidence in either your taste or your judgment.

NIGEL: That's not Miranda's fault. You haven't got to know her yet. You might at least give her the benefit of the doubt.

FELICITY (*sweetly*): I do, dear. I give her the benefit of very grave doubts.

NIGEL: Well, all I can say is, it's damned unfair of you.

FELICITY (*firmly*): Don't talk nonsense, Nigel. I'm not being in the least unfair. As your mother it's perfectly natural that I should be prejudiced against the idea of Miranda Frayle becoming my daughter-in-law. I know nothing whatever about her personal habits beyond the fact that she sleeps every afternoon and can swim.

NIGEL: She's a remarkable character. She's honest and unaffected and she's never allowed her success to spoil her, she hates show-off and display, she loves the ordinary, simple things of life like living in the country and sewing and reading. She also adores children.

FELICITY: Has she ever had any?

NIGEL: No, she hasn't. But that's beside the point.

FELICITY: She's been married before, hasn't she?

NIGEL: Yes, to a man called Greenberg. He was foul to her.

FELICITY: In what way?

NIGEL: In every way. He was cruel and used to go away and leave her alone for weeks at a time.

FELICITY: That at least gave her an opportunity to catch up on her sewing and reading.

NIGEL: It's quite clear that you've hardened your heart against her so I won't say any more.

FELICITY (*after a slight pause*): I saw in the paper that Mr. Don Lucas has arrived in England.

NIGEL: What are you getting at now, Mother?

FELICITY: Mightn't that be a little awkward for Miranda?

NIGEL: Do you suppose I don't know about Don Lucas and Miranda?

FELICITY: No, dear. Their rather convulsive relationship practically comes under the heading of General Information. I merely thought that it was unfortunate that he should arrive just now. After all it is assumed by the world at large that he is the love of her life.

NIGEL: As I told you before, Mother, Miranda is completely honest. She's never attempted to conceal anything from me. I know all about her love affair with Don Lucas. It was finished and done with ages ago, three quarters of it was studio publicity anyway.

FELICITY: I'm so glad, darling.

NIGEL: It's unwise to believe what you read in the papers.

FELICITY: I know. Everyone says that, but somehow one always does.

NIGEL: Studio publicity agents are absolutely unscrupulous. Their job is to get the stars talked about at all costs. Miranda and Don Lucas were teamed together in three pictures. That was quite enough to start the whole business.

FELICITY: I remember him in the one about the Nun. He was very good.

NIGEL: He's a terrible drunk, you know.

FELICITY: How horrid for her. When do you intend to get married?

NIGEL: As soon as possible.

FELICITY: I see. Has she any family? Any relations?

NIGEL: Her mother died when she was eighteen, she was terribly cut up about it, that's one of the reasons she went to America.

FELICITY: What were the others?

NIGEL: She had to earn her living. She was a professional dancer.

FELICITY: Acrobatic or ballroom?

NIGEL: I don't know, Mother. Does it matter?

FELICITY: Of course it doesn't matter. It wouldn't matter if she'd spent her early years upside down on a trapeze. I'm merely eager to find out as much as possible about her background. Has she any brothers or sisters?

NIGEL (*reluctantly*): There was a sister, I believe. A good deal older than she was. Miranda doesn't like to talk about her much.

FELICITY: Why not?

NIGEL: Apparently she went to the bad.

FELICITY: In any specific way or just generally?

NIGEL: I'm not sure. All I know is that poor Miranda helped her as much as she could.

FELICITY: How?

NIGEL: Oh, she was constantly sending her money, but it was no good, it all went on drink.

FELICITY: Poor Miranda. She does seem to be haunted by intemperance, doesn't she? Is she still alive, the sister?

NIGEL: No, I don't think so.

FELICITY: Just as well. She might have turned up at the wedding and started throwing bottles at everybody.

NIGEL: Miranda hasn't had a particularly easy life. I expect that's why she wants to get away from it all and settle down.

FELICITY: I expect it is. The English Peerage has often proved a convenient shelter for the world weary.

NIGEL: Now you're being sarcastic.

FELICITY: I don't seem to be able to put a foot right this evening. It's very discouraging.

NIGEL: Why hasn't Crestwell brought in the cocktail things?

FELICITY: I'll ring. (*She does so.*) We're rather short-handed at the moment. May has shingles you know.

NIGEL: Good God! Are they catching?

FELICITY: I don't think so. But in any case you weren't planning to spend much of your time with her, were you?

PETER *comes in. He is wearing a dinner-jacket.*

PETER: There are two girl guides in the shrubbery. I saw them from my window.

FELICITY: What were they doing?

PETER: They weren't doing anything. They were just there.

NIGEL: If they're autograph hunters they must be sent away. Miranda is driven mad by autograph hunters.

FELICITY: Poor dear.

57

CRESTWELL *enters with a tray of cocktail implements. He is followed by* ALICE *with an ice bucket.*

There are apparently some Girl Guides in the shrubbery, Crestwell.

CRESTWELL: I know, my Lady. They've been hanging about all the afternoon. I think one of them is the little Mumby girl.

NIGEL: Have them sent away whoever they are.

FELICITY: If it's Elsie Mumby we can't possibly send her away. The whole village would be up in arms.

NIGEL: Why?

FELICITY: She pulled her little brother out of a well. She's a local heroine.

CRESTWELL: Put the ice bucket down, Alice, and go and see what they want.

ALICE: They want Miss Frayle's autograph, Mr. Crestwell. So does Miss Luton at the post office. She sent Billy down for it on his bike.

CRESTWELL: Collect their books from them, Alice, and tell them to call for them in the morning.

ALICE: Yes, Mr. Crestwell.

CRESTWELL: And don't stand about giggling with them either.

ALICE: No. Mr. Crestwell.

She goes.

FELICITY: Thank you, Crestwell. I expect we shall have quite a lot of this sort of thing to deal with.

CRESTWELL: There's the question of press reporters also, my Lady. I would like to have instructions as to what to say to them.

NIGEL: Get rid of them.

CRESTWELL: Young Willis of the *Kentish Times* has

been particularly persistent, my Lord. He's rung up seven times and called twice.

NIGEL: Tell him to go to hell.

FELICITY: Don't be silly, Nigel. We can't possibly tell old Mrs. Willis's son to go to hell. She's one of my staunchest supporters on the Cottage Hospital Committee and she made us all those wool mats for the sale of work.

CRESTWELL: If, milord, you could spare him a few moments of your time to-morrow and perhaps present him briefly to Miss Miranda Frayle it would mean a great deal to him. He's an ambitious lad and worthy of encouragement.

NIGEL: One of the reasons that I brought Miss Frayle here, Crestwell, was to protect her from newspaper men and autograph hunters and all the other pests who badger the life out of her.

FELICITY (*firmly*): You'll have to see young Willis, Nigel, and so will she. He was splendid during the election and always gives us a half-page every year for the Church Fête. (*To* CRESTWELL.) Tell young Willis to come and see me to-morrow morning.

CRESTWELL: Very good, my Lady.

He goes out.

NIGEL: Really, Mother. I do think it's very inconsiderate of you.

FELICITY: Nonsense, dear. If Miranda has decided to come and live in a small English village, she must be prepared for publicity. Will you make the cocktails or shall I?

PETER: You please, Nigel. Felicity never puts enough gin in.

NIGEL: All right. Martini for everybody?

FELICITY: Yes, please, dear.

PETER: It's quite a festive occasion after all, isn't it? What with one thing and another.

MIRANDA *comes in. Her appearance is impeccable. She is wearing a simple dinner dress, her jewellery is discreet and she is carrying a large chintz work bag.*

FELICITY: Ah, there you are, Miranda. I do hope you had a good rest.

MIRANDA (*simply*): I went to sleep in one world and woke up in another.

FELICITY: How confusing.

MIRANDA: I was tired and edgy after the drive down, and nervous too, about meeting you and Nigel's friends and wondering what you would all think of me. But when I woke up everything was different. I felt smooth and peaceful for the first time in weeks. Perhaps it was the room. What a lovely, lovely room it is. Is it haunted?

FELICITY: That rather depends on who occupies it.

PETER: When Judy Lavenham had it it used to be known as Victoria Station.

NIGEL (*from the drink table*): Shut up, Peter.

FELICITY: Come and sit down, my dear.

MIRANDS (*settling herself on the sofa*): I've brought my work. I hope nobody minds.

FELICITY: Not in the least. Why should they?

NIGEL: Martini, darling?

MIRANDA: No, thank you, dear. I'd like a soft drink if there is one.

NIGEL: Lemon juice with a little soda?

MIRANDA: Perfect. (*To* FELICITY.) I want to keep my mind absolutely clear and let every new impression sink in. You know what I mean, don't you? I want to let the atmosphere sort of take charge of me.

NIGEL: Peter—come and help.

PETER *and* NIGEL *proceed to hand round the drinks.*

FELICITY: I didn't think you'd want to meet many strangers on your first evening here, so, apart from us, there will only be Admiral and Lady Hayling dining. They are very old friends and our closest neighbours.

MIRANDA: Is there anyone else staying in the house?

FELICITY: Only Peter and—and Moxie. (*She shoots a look at* NIGEL.)

MIRANDA (*sipping her drink*): Is that a nickname?

FELICITY: Yes, I suppose it is. Her name is Mrs. Moxton. We've known her for so many years that she is practically one of the family.

MIRANDA: I do hope she'll approve of me.

NIGEL (*faintly irritated by* MIRANDA'S *humility*): Why the hell shouldn't she?

MIRANDA: Old family friends are liable to resent intruders even more than the family itself.

At this moment MOXIE *enters. She is dressed in a plain deep blue dinner-dress. Her hair is becomingly done. She wears two strings of pearls and an obviously expensive bracelet on her right wrist. She also wears large horn-rimmed glasses. She comes over to* FELICITY.

MOXIE: I hope I'm not late?

FELICITY: Of course not, Moxie, dear.

NIGEL (*with an effort*): Hallo, Moxie.

MOXIE: Welcome home, my—my goodness how well you look.

FELICITY (*hurriedly*): Miss Miranda Frayle—Mrs. Moxton.

MIRANDA (*girlishly*): How do you do? I've heard so much about you. I do really hope that we are going to be friends.

MOXIE: I feel I already know you well, Miss Frayle.

MIRANDA (*with charming impulsiveness*): Won't you call me Miranda?

MOXIE: Certainly. I should adore to.

MIRANDA (*sincerely*): Thank you for that. Thank you a great deal. I know how difficult this must be for you —for all of you. After all, you none of you know what I'm really like. You have to judge by appearances. And appearances can be deceptive, can't they?

FELICITY: Yes, fortunately. Think how uncomfortable life would be if we knew all about each other at the first glance.

MOXIE: This is a great moment. I am one of your most ardent fans.

MIRANDA (*graciously*): Thank you.

MOXIE: Be an angel, Peter, and get me a drink. I'm positively gasping.

NIGEL (*wincing, but recovering himself*): You'd better make a fresh brew, Peter. There's only iced water in the shaker. I presume you do want a Martini, Moxie?

MOXIE: Yes, please, my—my dear.

MIRANDA (*ostentatiously, putting on some glasses and rummaging in her work bag*): You've no idea how wonderful it is to be able to relax and pop on my old glasses and not worry what I look like.

NIGEL: As a matter of fact they're very becoming.

MIRANDA (*blowing him a kiss*): Thank you, sweet.

PETER (*as MIRANDA produces an embroidery frame from her bag and scrutinises it critically*): Are you a keen needle-woman, Miss Frayle?

MIRANDA: Yes. I always have been. Ever since I was a child. I used to have to do most of the sewing and mending at home. We were terribly poor, you know. I remember mother was always calling me in from playing in the street to darn stockings or put a hem on something or other. We couldn't afford a machine.

MOXIE: Playing in the street?

MIRANDA (*with a gay little laugh*): Oh yes. I was a regular little gutter child—— One of my earliest memories was making a doll's house out of an old cardboard box I'd found in the dustbin.

MOXIE: Where did you live?

MIRANDA: Oh, it was an awful slum, really—not far from the Brixton High Street.

MOXIE (*with iron control*): An awful slum?

MIRANDA (*reminiscently*): Oh yes. I can see it now—on a Saturday night with the crowds and the lights—I used to go and get mother her pint of beer at the pub and bring it home in a jug. One night there was a barrel organ and I danced to it——

MOXIE: How old were you?

MIRANDA: Oh, about five, I suppose.

MOXIE: You danced to a barrel organ outside a pub when you were five?

MIRANDA (*with a wistful smile*): Oh yes. That's how I first learnt to dance really—— (*She breaks off.*) I do hope these sordid disclosures about my childhood aren't shocking you?

NIGEL: Don't be silly, darling, of course they're not.

FELICITY: On the contrary, I find them absolutely fascinating, don't you, Moxie?

MOXIE: I certainly do.

MIRANDA: I was born in the gutter, within the sound of Bow Bells. I'm a London Cockney and I'm proud of it.

FELICITY: I'm sure you are. It must be lovely.

MIRANDA: Yesterday, without even telling Nigel, I put on some old clothes and a veil and went in a tram to Brixton—all by myself.

MOXIE: How did it look? The slum?

MIRANDA: Changed very much. Twenty years is a long time. The house was still there though. It gave me a dreadful pang to see the window of mother's room, the one she died in.

MOXIE: I expect you nursed her devotedly, didn't you?

MIRANDA (*simply*): I did the best I could, but it wasn't much.

PETER: And you were all alone? With no father or brother or sister?

MIRANDA: My father died soon after I was born. I did have one sister, she was a good deal older than me—poor old Dora.

PETER: Why—what happened to her?

MIRANDA: Oh—what always happens to people when they allow life to get the better of them.

FELICITY: In what way did life get the better of her?

MIRANDA: In every way really. You see she sort of started off on the wrong foot. I was the lucky one. I always had a conviction, deep down inside me, that somehow or other I should get on, hoist myself up out of the mire, escape from the poverty and squalor of my surroundings. I suppose I must have been born with the will to succeed. That's what's so unfair, isn't it? I mean that some people should feel like that from the very beginning and that other people shouldn't? I think that's why Dora hated me really. Because I had so much and she had so little.

PETER: Was she cruel to you?

MIRANDA: Oh no. Not exactly cruel, she just didn't understand me.

PETER: She never actually ill-treated you? She never beat you or knocked you about?

MIRANDA: Never—when she was sober.

MOXIE (*firmly*): I think I'd like another Martini, please.

PETER (*taking her glass*): I expect we all would. (*He goes to the drink table.*)

FELICITY: You haven't told us yet what happened to her. Is she still alive?

MIRANDA: No. She died some years ago. The news came to me in quite a roundabout way. I hadn't heard from her for ages. I'd been sending her pennies every now and then, you know, just to help out, and food parcels and things like that, but she never acknowledged them. I'm afraid the pennies all went on drink.

PETER: I expect the food parcels came in handy as blotting paper.

MIRANDA: Then when I heard that she had died, in horrid, sordid circumstances, it really upset me more than I could ever have believed possible. I had to go to Palm Springs, to sort of get myself straight with myself.

FELICITY: Palm Springs sound heavenly, doesn't it? Almost biblical.

MIRANDA: You see, I suddenly realised that for the first time in my life, I had failed, failed utterly. I felt guilty and ashamed, as though it was all my fault, my responsibility. Of course it wasn't really I suppose— but you know how silly one is about that kind of thing.

FELICITY: Indeed I do. Both my sisters are fairly heavy drinkers. Of course they're still alive, but I never see a telegram come into the house without saying to myself—"Caroline's gone too far at last" or "Sarah's had it!"

PETER: Here's your drink, Moxie. Felicity?

FELICITY (*taking a cocktail*): It looks very pale, dear. After all, the vermouth is there to be used, you know.

PETER (*amiably to* MIRANDA): I think it only right and proper that you should be warned about your future mother-in-law. She's famous for her meanness over inessentials.

FELICITY: I wouldn't call gin an inessential.

PETER: Of course over the major issues she'd generous to a fault. Why she'd give you the dress off her back, wouldn't she, Moxie?

MOXIE: Certainly she would, Mr.—Mr.—Mr. Bagshot was saying so only the other day.

PETER (*wickedly*): Who is Mr. Bagshot?

FELICITY (*coming to the rescue*): Mr. Bagshot is the new curate, Peter.

NIGEL: New curate? What's happened to Eustace Parker, then? Has he left?

FELICITY: Yes, dear—under a cloud.

NIGEL: You never said anything about it in your letters.

FELICITY: I couldn't, darling. There are some things you just can't put in letters.

NIGEL: But he was such a mild, inoffensive little chap. What on earth did he do?

FELICITY: We have no proof that he actually did anything. It—it was just one of those things.

NIGEL: One of what things?

PETER: One of those crazy things.

FELICITY: I'll tell you all about it later, Nigel. I really

would rather not go on about it now. Miranda, dear, surely it's time you had a proper drink? That lemonade looks so dreary.

MIRANDA: No, thank you. I hardly ever do, you know. Funnily enough it's Hollywood that taught me not to drink. And one sort of gets into the habit of disciplining oneself.

PETER: I hope, for all our sakes, for the sake of the world at large, that you haven't decided to give up acting for good.

MIRANDA: I'm afraid I have. (*She smiles at* NIGEL.) I think being married to Pete will be a whole-time job.

FELICITY: Pete?

MIRANDA (*with a laugh*): Oh dear, it slipped out. I always call him Pete, it's a sort of silly habit. He calls me Pete too, sometimes.

FELICITY: Isn't that rather muddling?

MIRANDA (*to* NIGEL): We manage to understand each other, don't we, darling?

NIGEL: It's Miranda's idea that she should give up her career. Personally I think she owes it to the public to make one picture a year at least, but she won't hear of it.

PETER: Why not?

MIRANDA: Don't you see? Don't you really see? (*Impressively*.) It's just that I love Nigel. I love him with all my heart. And I'm absolutely determined that the Countess of Marshwood shall be the longest and the greatest part I ever played.

FELICITY: I hope you won't find it too much of a strain.

NIGEL: Mother!

67

FELICITY: I know what I'm talking about. I played it for years. Nigel's dear father was my leading man. I found it a good part but technically rather exhausting.

CRESTWELL *enters.*

CRESTWELL (*announcing*): Admiral Sir John and Lady Hayling.

PETER (*in an agonised whisper to* FELICITY): My God! I forgot to warn them.

ADMIRAL *and* LADY HAYLING *come in.*

CRESTWELL *goes out.*

LADY H.: I'm sorry we're late, Felicity. Poor Eustace Parker arrived just as we were leaving and went on for hours about the Church Fête.

NIGEL: Eustace Parker?

FELICITY (*hurriedly*): Oh, I'm so glad he's back. It must all have blown over.

LADY H.: What are you talking about, Felicity?

FELICITY: Nothing, dear. I'll tell you all about it later.

ADMIRAL (*shaking hands with* NIGEL): Hallo, Nigel.

LADY H.: Welcome home, my dear. (*She kisses him.*)

FELICITY: Cynthia, John—this is Miranda. Miranda Frayle.

ADMIRAL (*gruffly*): How do you do.

LADY H. (*shaking hands with* MIRANDA): We've so often admired you—from afar.

MIRANDA (*who has risen and taken off her glasses*): Thank you.

LADY H. (*seeing* MOXIE): Moxie! You look very dressy. If you have time while we're at dinner, you might be a dear and put a few stitches in my bag, it's gaping at the side. I meant to ask Saunders to do it before I left the house but I forgot.

MOXIE (*after a slight pause*): Really, Cynthia—you'll be forgetting your head next!

LADY H. (*scandalised*): What did you say?

FELICITY (*seizing* LADY HAYLING *by the arm*): Cynthia —John too—I simply must talk to you both about the Cottage Hospital. There's the most awful crisis on about the Matron. I'm at my wit's end. She really has gone too far this time. Come into the study. I can't talk about it in front of everyone, and you're both so sane about that sort of thing—please come—— Make another cocktail, Peter, we shan't be a minute.

> FELICITY *propels the* HAYLINGS *into the study and closes the door after her.*

NIGEL: What on earth's the matter with mother this evening? She's quite hysterical.

PETER: That matron is enough to make anyone hysterical. She's a fiend incarnate.

NIGEL: If you're referring to Mrs. Gaskin, Peter, she is adored by the whole district.

PETER: This isn't Mrs. Gaskin. It's a new one.

NIGEL: Since when?

PETER (*from the drink table*): Since Mrs. Gaskin died, of course.

NIGEL: I never knew the poor old girl had died. When did it happen?

PETER: About three weeks ago, I believe.

NIGEL: What did she die of?

PETER: It's no good cross-questioning me. I wasn't here. Anyhow I feel sure that all these local incidents cannot be of the faintest interest to Miranda.

MIRANDA: But of course they are. They're part of my new life. I want to know everything. I want to learn, step by step, all about this funny, dear English world that's going to be my home. It's terribly important to me. It is, really.

NIGEL (*patting her hand affectionately*): Darling.

MIRANDA (*looking up at him devotedly*): I don't suppose it will be easy just at first, in the village, I mean, getting the people to trust me, to look upon me as a friend, but I'll win them round in the long run. Just you see!

> FELICITY *and the* HAYLINGS *come out of the study. At the same moment* CRESTWELL *enters.*

CRESTWELL (*announcing*): Dinner is served, milord.

FELICITY (*to the* HAYLINGS): Oh dear—and I snatched you away before you'd even had a cocktail.

LADY H.: We can take them in with us.

FELICITY: I think that would be the best if you really don't mind. We're starting with a soufflé.

PETER: I'll carry them for you.

FELICITY: Come along, then, everybody—Miranda—

> *She takes* MIRANDA'S *arm and goes out of the room. The others, talking cheerfully, follow. As* MOXIE *reaches the door she pauses, mutters, "Please go on—I'll come in a moment" and runs back into the room. She makes a pretence of looking for her bag. When the others have gone, she sinks down on the sofa.*

CRESTWELL: Dora.

MOXIE: I can't do it—I know I can't.

CRESTWELL: Pull yourself together.

MOXIE: I can't sit and listen to her talking about Mum like that, saying she took her jugs of beer from pubs! Mum never touched a drop in her life. She was a respectable, God-fearing woman from the day she was born until the day she died.

CRESTWELL: Come off it, Dora. She can't have been all that God-fearing the day she was born.

MOXIE: You think it's very funny, don't you?

CRESTWELL: I cannot truthfully deny that, to me, there is a certain whimsical humour in the whole curious lash-up.

MOXIE: You didn't hear her! You didn't hear the black lies she told——

CRESTWELL: There you wrong me, Dora. I contrived to acquaint myself with most of the salient points of your sister's discourse by the simple device of clamping my ear to the key-hole.

MOXIE: I'll never forgive her. Never, never, never.

CRESTWELL: Come along now. They'll be wondering what's happened to you.

MOXIE (*near tears*): Oh, Fred——

CRESTWELL: Now now—none of that. (*He grabs a half-filled Martini.*) Here—knock this back.

MOXIE: No—I'd better not—really——

CRESTWELL: Drink it. It won't hurt an old soak like you.

MOXIE *swallows it at a gulp.*

That's better. Now then. Chin up, keep a stiff upper lip, grit your teeth, put your shoulder to the wheel and—get cracking!

MOXIE: Oh, Fred.

CRESTWELL: Have you read any good books lately? (*Taking her arm.*)

CURTAIN

ACT II

Scene II

Scene: About an hour later.

    ALICE *is wandering about the room, humming to herself and piling the used cocktail glasses on to a tray.* CREST-WELL *enters.*

CRESTWELL: Get a move on now, Alice. Mrs. Crabbe will be wanting you in the kitchen.

ALICE: Yes, Mr. Crestwell.

CRESTWELL: And might I suggest, Alice, in these few brief moments of intimacy that have been vouchsafed to us, that although understandably overwhelmed by the honour of being allowed to wait at table, there is no necessity to breathe quite so heavily while doing it.

ALICE: I'm sorry, Mr. Crestwell.

CRESTWELL: When you approached the future Countess of Marshwood just now with the creamed carrots, you sounded like a goods train coming round a curve.

ALICE: I couldn't help it, really I couldn't! Seeing her tortured by the Japanese on Thursday and handing her carrots on Saturday sort of took my breath away.

CRESTWELL: If it had really done that, Alice, there would be no cause for complaint.

ALICE: Yes, Mr. Crestwell.

CRESTWELL: Nor was it entirely in accord with the higher traditions of domestic service for you to stare at Mrs. Moxton with your eyes bolting from your head and your mouth open.

ALICE: It was such a surprise, seeing her sitting at the table like that, dressed up to kill, I nearly had a fit.

CRESTWELL: If you are addicted to fits, Alice, you should have warned me in advance.

ALICE: What does it all mean, Mr. Crestwell?

CRESTWELL: What does what all mean?

ALICE: About Mrs. Moxton suddenly having meals with them instead of with us and wearing her ladyship's bracelet?

CRESTWELL: It is a social experiment based on the ancient and inaccurate assumption that, as we are all equal in the eyes of God, we should therefore be equally equal in the eyes of our fellow creatures.

ALICE: Oh!

CRESTWELL: The fact that it doesn't work out like that and never will in no way deters the idealists from pressing on valiantly towards Utopia.

ALICE: What's Utopia?

CRESTWELL: A spiritually hygienic abstraction, Alice, where everyone is hail-fellow-well met and there is no waiting at table.

ALICE: Oh, I see. Fork lunches?

There is the sound of a bell.

CRESTWELL: The front door! Who the devil can that be? Finish up now, quickly, Alice, and go back to Mrs. Crabbe.

ALICE: Yes, Mr. Crestwell.

CRESTWELL *goes hurriedly.*

ALICE, *with a sudden spurt of energy, empties the ash-trays into the waste-paper basket, collects the remaining glasses, puts them on the tray and is about to go, when the door opens and* CRESTWELL *ushers* DON LUCAS *into the room.* ALICE *stops dead in her tracks and stands staring*

at him with her mouth open. DON LUCAS *is extremely
handsome and in the late thirties. His skin is accurately
tanned, his sports clothes are impeccable within the bounds
of the best Hollywood tradition. He is also very slightly
drunk.*

CRESTWELL: I will inform his Lordship that you are
here.

DON: Hey—wait a minute—don't do that. I don't
know the Earl—it isn't him I want to see. It's Miss
Frayle I want to see—Miss Miranda Frayle.

CRESTWELL: Very good, sir. (*He turns to go.*)

DON: Before you tell her I'm here, could—— (*He
looks at* ALICE)—could I speak to you for a moment?

CRESTWELL (*to* ALICE): Take three deep breaths,
Alice, through the nose. Keep the mouth rigidly
closed and hop it.

ALICE: Yes, Mr. Crestwell.

     She goes out.

CRESTWELL: You were about to say, sir . . . ?

DON: Look here—I'm Don Lucas——

CRESTWELL: Yes, sir. I recognised you immediately.
If I may say so, sir, with pleasure not unmixed wi
dismay.

DON: I don't get you.

CRESTWELL: I gather, sir, that you wish to speak to
Miss Frayle—privately?

DON: Yeah—that's right—I do. Miss Frayle and me
—well, we're very old friends.

CRESTWELL: It is the awareness of that fact, sir, that
tinctured my spontaneous pleasure at seeing you with a
modicum of apprehension.

DON: Come again?

CRESTWELL: Sequestered as we are, sir, in our remote

Kentish vacuum, we are not entirely out of touch with the larger world beyond. We have been privileged, thanks to the silver screen and the various periodicals appertaining to it, to follow both your public and private affairs with the keenest interest. You are a very popular figure in these parts, Mr. Lucas.

DON: Thanks a lot. I could do with a Scotch if you've got one handy.

CRESTWELL: Certainly, sir. Would you like it in the form of a highball, straight, or on the rocks?

DON (*impressed*): Say! You're good. You know all the answers.

CRESTWELL: Except the one to my question, sir.

DON: Okay. You win. On the rocks.

CRESTWELL (*going to the drink table*): Very good, sir.

DON: Thanks. What's your name?

CRESTWELL (*proceeding to mix the drink*): Crestwell, sir. Frederick Crestwell.

DON: Now see here, Fred, I want your help. I'm in a bit of a jam.

CRESTWELL: What kind of jam, sir? Professional, legal, or emotional?

DON: With your fancy dialogue you could make a fortune in Hollywood as a script writer.

CRESTWELL: In my rare moments of melancholy introspection, sir, the idea has occurred to me; but I feel, on the whole, that I am happier where I am. (*He hands* DON *a glass of whisky and ice.*)

DON: Thanks. (*He takes it and has a swig.*) I want to talk to you as man to man.

CRESTWELL: Any other approach, sir, would be curious, to say the least of it.

DON: This Earl of yours. Is he really planning to

marry Miranda—Miss Frayle—or is it just a publicity stunt? I want to know what's cooking.

CRESTWELL: If you're hungry, sir, after your long drive, I am sure I could rustle up a little cold chicken and a salad.

DON (*showing signs of irritation*): Lay off the comedy a minute, will you? This means the hell of a lot to me. I heard the news on the radio three days ago and hopped a plane right away. I've got to know whether it's the real McCoy, this marriage, or whether it's just the studio publicity department pulling a fast one.

CRESTWELL: The real McCoy, I'm afraid, sir.

DON: She can't do this to me! She just can't! I've got to see her, Fred, I've got to see her alone, now, and you've got to fix it.

CRESTWELL: They're all in the middle of dinner, sir. I don't see how I could extricate her without 'shooting the works' as you might say.

DON: You needn't say it's me. Say it's a reporter from *Life Magazine*. She'd do anything for *Life Magazine*.

CRESTWELL: An unaccountable impulse shared by s many public figures.

DON: Say it's a four-page spread for the next issue with her picture on the cover. That'll fetch her. That'd fetch anybody.

CRESTWELL: I'll do my best, sir.

DON: Fred, you're a pal. Here. (*He gives him a twenty-dollar bill.*)

CRESTWELL (*looking at it*): Twenty dollars, sir! If the Government knew I had this I'd get a knighthood.

CRESTWELL *goes out.*

DON *makes a bee line for the drink table, pours himself*

*a neat Scotch, and proceeds to pace up and down the room,
obviously a prey to emotion.*

After a moment or two MIRANDA *enters. Seeing who
it is, she shuts the door hurriedly behind her.*

MIRANDA (*incredulously*): Pete!

DON (*brokenly*): Pete!

MIRANDA (*furiously*): You son-of-a-bitch!

DON (*even more brokenly*): Pete!

MIRANDA: Of all the low-down, mean tricks! I'll
never forgive you for this! Never, never, never!

DON (*going to her*): Honey—I've got to talk to you—
I've got to. I'm going out of my mind.

MIRANDA: Don't come near me. You—you snake!

DON: I've flown all across the Atlantic in a Strato-
liner without even a sleeping berth on account of they
were all full, and you call me a snake!

MIRANDA: You are too a snake. I never want to see
you again. I told you that when I left and it still goes.

DON: You don't mean that, Pete, not in your heart
you don't.

MIRANDA: I do mean it. I've cut you out of my life
like—like a withered limb.

DON: Pete!

MIRANDA: And shut up calling me Pete. That's all
over.

DON (*with a slight show of spirit*): I'm no withered
limb and you know it. (*He grips her by the shoulder.*)
Look at me!

MIRANDA (*struggling*): Let me alone!

DON (*kissing her violently*): Now then—am I a withered
limb?

MIRANDA (*breaking free from him*): How could you!
Oh, how could you!

77

DON: I'm crazy about you. I've been crazy about you for three whole years.

MIRANDA (*contemptuously*): Crazy about me! What about Beejie Lemaire, and Zenda Hicks, and that phoney Polish princess that Daryl Zanuck gave the party for?

DON: They didn't mean a thing to me, not a thing, you know they didn't! They were just ships that pass in the night.

MIRANDA: Maybe they were, but they certainly passed through your beach house in Santa Monica on their way to the open sea.

DON: So we're back at that again, are we?

MIRANDA: You bet your life we're back at that! I gave you all I had to give; my heart, my dreams, my tenderness. . . .

DON: Everything but equal billing. Remember "Be Still Foolish Heart?"

MIRANDA: You were featured under the title, which, considering it was your first big picture, was more than you had a right to expect.

DON: I got the notices, anyway.

MIRANDA: You got a rave in the *Hollywood Reporter*, and your pants torn off you in the *New Yorker*. If you call that 'getting the notices', I'll take vanilla.

DON (*incensed*): We needn't worry about that any more, though, need we? I'm bigger box office now than you ever were, even before you started slipping!

MIRANDA (*outraged*): Started slipping!

DON: Do you think I don't know why you're marrying this titled guy? Do you think the whole world doesn't know? It's because you're on the skids and have been ever since "Catherine the Great"!

MIRANDA (*livid*): On the skids, am I? It may interest you to know that M.G.M. have offered me anything I like to ask to do "The Wicked Years". They've been badgering me for weeks.

DON: They've been badgering every star in Hollywood to do that lousy script for the last eighteen months.

MIRANDA: Get out, Don! I'm sick of this! Get out!

DON: I'm not getting out of anywhere until I'm good and ready. There are a few things I'd like to say to this Earl of yours.

MIRANDA (*changing her tactics*): Don, please, go—please! For the sake of all we've meant to each other, for the sake of all the good times we've had, don't come busting in here and making a scene and spoiling everything. Please!

DON: Do you love this guy?

MIRANDA: Yes, of course I do.

DON: Really love him? As much as you loved me?

MIRANDA (*in acute distress*): Please, please go, Don—they'll be here in a minute!

DON (*inexorably*): As much as you loved me?

MIRANDA: It's different. I mean no people love other people in the same way.

DON: I'm crazy about you, Pete. I've fought against it. I've tried to forget you. Ever since we had the row, ever since that night when we said good-bye and you threw the Film Academy Award for 1949 at me, I've tried to get you out of my mind, out of my heart. . . .

MIRANDA (*moved*): Don't—please don't say any more!

DON (*going to her*): Pete!

MIRANDA: Go away, you've got to go away.

DON (*gallantly*): Okay, I'll go. I know we're all washed up. I know now that there isn't any more hope for me. I only just wanted to make sure. (*He looks at her wistfully.*) Good-bye, Pete. It was swell while it lasted.

MIRANDA (*tremulously*): Good-bye, Pete. . . .

> *Very gently, very tenderly, he takes her in his arms and kisses her. At this moment* FELICITY *comes into the room.* MIRANDA *and* DON *spring apart.*

FELICITY: I really came to rescue you, Miranda, but I see that it was unnecessary.

MIRANDA (*with commendable presence of mind*): This is one of my very old friends. We were just saying good-bye.

FELICITY: But surely he has only just arrived?

DON: I've got to get back to London.

MIRANDA (*with poise*): This is Don Lucas. Don, this is Lady Marshwood.

FELICITY (*enthusiastically*): I thought I recognised you but I simply couldn't believe my eyes. This is the most delightful surprise!

DON (*gratified*): Thank you, ma'am.

FELICITY: You're surely not intending to drive all the way to London now?

DON: I'm afraid I must . . . I . . .

FELICITY: Nonsense. I won't hear of it. That long dreary road at this time of night, in the pouring rain.

MIRANDA: It isn't raining.

FELICITY: It will be by the time he gets to Canterbury. I've never known it fail. Besides I couldn't dream of allowing Mr. Don Lucas to creep into the house and out again without letting anybody know. I should be stoned by the entire village.

MIRANDA: He's got to get to London to-night. He has an important conference the first thing in the morning.

FELICITY: Whoever heard of people having conferences on Sunday mornings? Mr. Lucas, I absolutely insist on you staying until tomorrow, at least! (*She rings the bell firmly.*)

MIRANDA: But, Lady Marshwood . . . really . . .

FELICITY (*gaily*): Dear Miranda—you really must allow me to have my own way. You're not married to Nigel yet, you know—I am still the mistress of this house and I intend to rule you all with a rod of iron until the last possible moment. (*She puts her arm affectionately and turns to* DON.) Crestwell can supply you with anything you need in the way of pyjamas and razors and toothbrushes. Please, Mr. Lucas! I shall be terribly hurt if you refuse.

MIRANDA: But . . .

DON (*looking at* MIRANDA): Thanks a lot, Lady Marshwood. I'd like to.

MIRANDA: Don!

CRESTWELL *enters.*

CRESTWELL: You rang, my Lady?

FELICITY: Oh, Crestwell—Mr. Don Lucas will be staying the night. You will see that he has everything he wants, won't you?

CRESTWELL: Certainly, my Lady. The Japanese room?

FELICITY: Yes. (*To* DON.) You haven't got any feeling about being in a Japanese room, have you? I mean, you weren't in the Pacific or anything?

DON: No, ma'am.

FELICITY: I'm so glad. It isn't all that Japanese.

anyhow—just the wallpaper and rather a washy looking painting of some carp. It has a lovely view, and when it's really clear you can see Dover Castle. Have you ever been to Dover Castle?

DON: No, ma'am. I've never been to England before.

FELICITY: I'm afraid that what with one thing and another you haven't chosen the best time to come, but we still have quite a lot to be proud of. Tell his Lordship that Mr. Lucas has arrived, will you, Crestwell, and ask them all to hurry up. We'll have coffee in here.

CRESTWELL: Very good, my Lady.

He goes out.

FELICITY: How extraordinary to think that the last time I saw you and dear Miranda together you were carrying her, practically naked, through a burning village! Wouldn't you like a drink?

DON: Thanks—thanks a lot.

FELICITY: It's all over there, do help yourself. You don't want to go back into the dining-room, do you, Miranda, and have any more of that disgusting sweet?

MIRANDA (*resigned*): No, thank you.

FELICITY: Then sit down, dear, and relax. I think we should all relax, really. It's been a tremendously exciting day, what with you and Nigel arriving and Mr. Lucas suddenly appearing out of the night and the garden over-run with Girl Guides. . . .

DON (*coming over with a fresh drink*): Girl Guides?

FELICITY: It's a very English institution. I don't know if you have them in Hollywood. It's a splendid idea really. They're trained to do practically everything from artificial respiration to making fires—with damp twigs. If the news leaks out that you're here, Mr.

Lucas, they'll probably attack the house in mass formation.

NIGEL *comes in. His expression is a trifle forbidding.*

FELICITY (*cheerfully*): Ah, there you are, Nigel—this is Mr. Don Lucas—my son, Lord Marshwood.

DON (*advancing*): Hallo there!

NIGEL (*without enthusiasm*): How do you do?

FELICITY: He's driven all the way from London to say good-bye to Miranda. They're old friends, you know.

NIGEL: Yes. I do know.

FELICITY: And believe it or not, he intended to drive all the way back again immediately! Have you ever heard anything so absurd? Fortunately I was able to persuade him to stay the night at least.

NIGEL: Stay the night!

FELICITY: Yes. Don't worry. Crestwell has everything under control. We've decided on the Japanese room because of the view.

NIGEL: Of course. A very good idea. How thoughtful of you, Mother.

LADY HAYLING, MOXIE, ADMIRAL HAYLING *and* PETER *come in.*

FELICITY (*introducing*): Cynthia—this is Mr. Don Lucas. He obviously doesn't need any introduction really, does he? Lady Hayling.

LADY H. (*shaking hands with* DON): How do you do?

FELICITY: Mrs. Moxton—Mr. Lucas—Admiral Hayling—and my nephew, Peter Ingleton.

There is a general babble of "How do you do's". LADY HAYLING sits on the sofa next to MIRANDA. MOXIE sits on a chair near FELICITY. The men stand about for the moment.

(*Conversationally*.) This is the first time Mr. Lucas has ever been to England. Imagine!

LADY H.: How extraordinary! (*To* DON.) I do hope you're enjoying it?

DON: Yes, ma'am.

ADMIRAL: I was in America once, in 1922. Norfolk, Virginia. Do you know it?

DON: No, sir.

ADMIRAL: I was commanding a light cruiser squadron in the West Indies. We had to put in at Norfolk because of boiler trouble. It was damned hot.

FELICITY: Boiler trouble sounds hot, anyhow, doesn't it?

> CRESTWELL *comes in with the coffee tray, which he places on a table.*

Thank you, Crestwell. You might put up the bridge table in the study, I think. We may want to play later.

CRESTWELL: Very good, my Lady.

> *He goes off into the library.*

FELICITY: Do you play bridge, Mr. Lucas?

DON: No, ma'am. I guess poker's more in my line.

FELICITY: My late husband adored poker. What a pity he isn't here!

> *During the ensuing dialogue,* FELICITY *pours out the coffee and* PETER *and* NIGEL *hand round the cups.*

PETER (*to* DON): Are you going to be in England long?

DON: No. I've got to get back. I've got to start on a new picture.

FELICITY: How exciting! What is it to be about— or is that a secret?

DON (*looking fixedly at* MIRANDA): No, it's no secret. It's an old story—the oldest story in the world. It's about a bum.

FELICITY: What an odd subject for a moving picture!

PETER: Felicity, 'bum' doesn't mean quite the same in America as it does in England.

DON (*unsteadily, still staring at* MIRANDA): A bum is a guy who hasn't any place to go, who hasn't got anything to live for, who just bums around wishing he was dead.

MIRANDA (*in an effort to quell him*): Don!

FELICITY: It sounds very sad. Will it have a happy ending?

DON (*brokenly*): No, ma'am—that's not the way it goes—that's not the way it goes at all—excuse me.

DON *goes hurriedly out through the french windows.*

FELICITY (*after a slight pause*): Poor Mr. Lucas! He seems upset about something. You'd better go after him, Peter, and for heaven's sake keep him away from the shrubbery, if Elsie Mumby sees him she'll give a wolf call.

PETER: All right.

He runs out after DON.

NIGEL: Did you know he was coming, Miranda?

MIRANDA: Of course I didn't.

NIGEL: I think it was very inconsiderate of you to ask him to stay, Mother.

FELICITY: It would have been far more inconsiderate to have let him go all the way back to London in the middle of the night. Not only inconsiderate but thoroughly inhospitable.

NIGEL: I was thinking of Miranda.

FELICITY: He is, too. That's what's upsetting him. We really must do all we possibly can to cheer him up. I rather wish now that we'd given him the old nursery instead of the Japanese room. It has that lovely frieze of rabbits that you liked so much when you were little.

>CRESTWELL *comes out of the library.*

CRESTWELL: The bridge table is ready, my Lady.

FELICITY: Thank you, Crestwell. You'd better leave the coffee things, we may need some more.

CRESTWELL: Very good, my Lady.

>*He goes out.*

NIGEL (*obviously suspecting some sort of plot, and also obviously very angry. He speaks icily*): You asked me before dinner, Mother, when Miranda and I were going to be married.

FELICITY: Of course I did, darling. We're all dying to know.

NIGEL: And I replied, if you remember, "As soon as possible".

FELICITY: Certainly I remember.

NIGEL: Well, I've changed my mind.

MIRANDA: Nigel!

NIGEL: It's going to be sooner than possible. It's going to be on Monday. I have the licence already. We shall drive up to London in the morning and be married in the afternoon.

FELICITY: Isn't that a little impulsive, dear?

NIGEL: I don't care how impulsive it is. That's ho it's going to be.

MOXIE (*rising to her feet*): That's not how it's going to be.

FELICITY: Moxie—please . . .

NIGEL (*to* MOXIE): I fail to see that this is any business of yours.

MOXIE (*in great distress*): I'm sorry, my Lady—I can't bear it any more, really I can't.

NIGEL: What are you talking about?

MOXIE: About you and Miss Miranda Frayle, my Lord. You're not going to marry her on Monday nor on any other day of the week. You're not going to marry her at all.

NIGEL: What's the matter with you? Have you gone out of your mind?

FELICITY: Moxie, dear—for heaven's sake don't say any more. It won't do any good.

LADY H.: Let her go on, Felicity. She might just as well now that's she's started—it will at least clear the air.

NIGEL: Clear the air?

MOXIE (*to* FELICITY): I'm sorry if you think I'm letting you down, my Lady, but I can't go through with it any longer, it doesn't feel right and it isn't right, and I shouldn't ever have started it in the first place. As he's gone this far, I would like his Lordship to know a few facts first, before he marries my sister.

MIRANDA (*in horror—jumping up*): My God! Dora!

MOXIE: That's right, dear—Dora! The one who ill-treated you when she was drunk and died in sordid circumstances!

FELICITY: Oh dear! This has really got out of control.

MIRANDA: What are you doing here? I don't understand . . . I thought you were dead!

MOXIE: You never thought any such thing—you never cared whether I was dead or alive. Well, more fool you, because here I am, alive and kicking, and if you think you're going to flounce about as mistress of this house, which has been my home for nineteen years, you've got another think coming!

MIRANDA (*with grandeur*): Please, Nigel . . . I'd like

to go to my room, if you don't mind. This is all too unpleasant.

MOXIE: Just a minute. You're going to listen to what I have to say if it's the last thing you do, and it's no use playing the fine madame any more either because the cat's out of the bag and all the airs and graces in the world won't put it back again.

MIRANDA (*furiously*): This is insufferable!

MOXIE: You're dead right it's insufferable. It all sounds very touching, you standing in a slum gazing up at the window of the room your mother died in but it may interest you to know that Mum died in St. Thomas's Hospital. And ten to one she wouldn't have died at all if you hadn't broken her heart by behaving like a tart and running off to America with that greasy little agent!

MIRANDA: How dare you speak to me like that? Don't listen to her! Don't listen to her!

MOXIE: It's all true, Freda, and you know it. And I wouldn't have said a word about it if you hadn't started showing off and making out that you were brought up in the gutter. Poverty and squalor, indeed! A London Cockney born within the sound of Bow Bells. You were born at Number Three, Station Road, Sidcup and if you can hear the sound of Bow Bells from Sidcup you must have the ears of an elk-hound!

MIRANDA (*collapsing on to the sofa*): I can't bear any more! I can't! I can't! Take me away, Nigel . . . take me away!

MOXIE: If his Lordship takes you away and marries you three times over, it won't alter the fact that I'm your sister. You'd better remember that.

FELICITY: I really think, Moxie, that you've said enough.

MOXIE: Not quite, my Lady—there's still a bit more, and my heart's heavy with it. I've got to leave this house for good, first thing in the morning. I can't be your Ladyship's maid any longer, not with the best will in the world I can't. It's all over and done with. (*Brokenly.*) Good-bye, my Lady . . .

She runs out of the room.

CURTAIN

ACT III

The next morning, at about nine-thirty.
    PETER *is lying on the sofa reading the 'Observer'.*
    CRESTWELL *enters.*

CRESTWELL: You rang, sir?

PETER: Yes, Crestwell. I'm feeling lonely. The house is like a tomb. Where is everybody?

CRESTWELL: His Lordship went out very early, sir. He said he was going for a long ride. Her Ladyship was called at the usual time, but she hasn't come down yet. Miss Frayle hasn't rung for her breakfast, neither has Mr. Lucas.

PETER: What about Moxie?

CRESTWELL: Very low-spirited, sir. She's packing.

PETER: She's really going?

CRESTWELL: Yes, to Bexhill, sir—she says she has friends there. She's catching the eleven-fifteen from Deal; being a Sunday it means three changes, but she's adamant.

PETER: Oh Lord! Poor Moxie! It does seem damned unfair.

CRESTWELL: I feel that it would be premature to abandon too hastily all hope of a happy ending, sir. Mrs. Moxton, in common with most of her sex, is inclined to allow her emotions to run away with her. Her Ladyship, on the other hand, is not.

PETER: I hope you're right, Crestwell.

CRESTWELL: If you'll forgive an archaic Shavianism, sir, I'm bloody sure I'm right!

DON LUCAS *enters, gloomily.*

PETER: Hallo! How are you?

DON: Terrible!

PETER: Hang-over?

DON: You know, pal, you could make a packet telling people's fortunes.

CRESTWELL: A horse's neck will soon put you right, sir.

DON: It'd take a giraffe's neck to make me even able to walk, let alone drive a car.

CRESTWELL: You're not thinking of leaving, sir?

DON: You bet I am! I'm getting the hell out of here as soon as I can see out of my eyes.

CRESTWELL: Leave it to me, sir, we'll have you ticking over in no time! Excuse me——

He goes out hurriedly.

PETER: Why don't you sit down?

DON: Because if I did, I'd stay down.

PETER: Last night in the garden you promised me that you'd pull yourself together and face the future with a smile.

DON: That was last night. This is to-day.

PETER: You haven't been crying again, have you?

DON: Listen, Pete . . . (*He breaks off.*) Oh, God! . . .

PETER: What's the matter?

DON: Calling you Pete . . . it kind of slipped out.

PETER: I don't mind a bit.

DON: There's only one Pete in the world for me.

PETER: I'm sure it's very charming of you to say so.

DON: You were wonderful to me last night, just

wonderful, and if you think I'll ever forget it, you're plumb crazy! We're friends, aren't we?

PETER: Of course we are.

DON: It's great to hear you say that, it is, honestly.

PETER: I'm so glad.

DON: Friendship's a rare thing, one of the rarest things in the whole God-damned world. Do you mind shaking hands on it?

PETER: Not in the least, if you feel it's really necessary.

DON (*gripping his hand firmly*): Atta boy!

FELICITY *comes in.*

FELICITY: What on earth are you doing?

PETER: Shaking hands.

FELICITY: Good morning, Mr. Lucas. You're just the one I wanted to see. Peter, be a darling and go into the garden for a minute, will you?

PETER: I'm getting rather sick of the garden.

FELICITY: The study, then—anywhere. I want to talk to Mr. Lucas privately.

PETER: Okay, pal.

He takes the 'Observer' and goes into the study.

FELICITY: Do sit down, Mr. Lucas—Don. You don't mind if I call you Don, do you? I feel somehow as if we were old friends.

DON: Thank you, ma'am.

FELICITY: And you must call me Felicity. Ma'am sounds so Royal. It makes me feel as though I were opening something.

CRESTWELL *enters, bearing a tall glass of brandy and ginger-ale and three Aspirins.*

CRESTWELL (*to* DON): Your horse's neck, sir.

DON (*taking it*): Thanks.

CRESTWELL: Swallow the three Aspirins first, sir, and then sip the drink slowly.

FELICITY (*brightly*): Quite like old times, isn't it, Crestwell? Except that the late Lord Marshwood always chewed the Aspirin.

CRESTWELL: Young Willis is here, my Lady. He's been here since eight-fifteen.

FELICITY: Tell him to wait, Crestwell. We might have a splendid scoop for him later.

CRESTWELL: Very good, my Lady.

He goes out.

DON: I guess I got a bit high last night and acted like a heel. I'm sorry.

FELICITY: Even if you had acted like the highest heel, Don, I should have understood. After all, you were under considerable emotional stress, weren't you?

DON: Yeah. I guess I was.

FELICITY: And you still are?

DON (*with vehemence*): Ma'am—Felicity—I'm going to snap out of it. I know when I'm licked.

FELICITY: Courage, Don, courage!

DON: I shouldn't have come busting down here and sticking my neck out and making a fool of myself. I see that now. It's no good being crazy about somebody if they're not crazy about you, is it? We were all washed up, Miranda and me, a long while ago only I was too dumb to believe it.

FELICITY: Are you so sure?

DON: How do you mean?

FELICITY: I am Nigel's mother, and therefore what I am going to say is doubly difficult. Can I trust you? Really trust you?

DON: Sure you can.

FELICITY: I'm also a sentimentalist and I've always believed, foolishly perhaps, that when two people really love each other nothing in the world should be allowed to break it. This proposed marriage between Miranda and my son is a mistake—a tragic, ghastly mistake, because you are the one she loves, the only one she will ever truly love. She told me so.

DON (*incredulously*): Told you so?

FELICITY (*with a gentle smile*): Not in so many words but I am a woman, Don, and I knew at once when I saw you together, from the expression in her eyes when she looked at you, the tone of her voice when she spoke to you, that her heart, her obstinate, capricious heart, belonged to you.

DON: She told me I was a snake, and she never wanted to see me again. She said I was a withered limb.

FELICITY: People never say things like that unless they're passionately in love. I'm surprised at you, Don, I am really!

DON (*rising and walking about the room*): What the hell can I do? She's going to be married. It's all set.

FELICITY: I'm disappointed in you, Don. When I think of your presence of mind and resource in that burning village, and look at you now . . .

DON: That was a movie. Real life doesn't work out like movies.

FELICITY: Not as a general rule, I admit, but I see no reason why it shouldn't, just every now and then.

DON: But what can I do?

FELICITY: Don't do anything. Just wait. Above all, keep up your courage and don't admit defeat.

> NIGEL *comes in through the french windows. He is wearing riding clothes.*

94

Good morning, darling. Did you enjoy your ride?

NIGEL: No.

FELICITY (*rising and going to the study door*): Peter——

NIGEL (*sullenly, to* DON): Good morning. I hope you slept all right.

DON (*embarrassed*): Oh yes—thanks.

PETER (*entering*): What's happening?

FELICITY: You ought to know better than to ask that, dear, nothing whatever happens on Sunday mornings. Don wants to see the church—don't you, Don? I thought you might like to show it to him. (*To* DON.) The tower's Norman, but the rest of it's a good deal later.

DON: Later?

FELICITY: You might show him old Mrs. Dunlop's house while you're at it. It isn't far.

PETER: I don't mind the church but I draw the line at old Mrs. Dunlop.

FELICITY: Oh, she's much better. She's been happy as a sandboy since her husband died. Run along, both of you.

DON: Okay, ma'am—Felicity.

PETER (*resigned*): Come on, then.

DON *and* PETER *go out*.

FELICITY: Ma'am Felicity sounds so domestically American, doesn't it? Like Grandma Moses, or Mother Goddam.

NIGEL: I want to talk to you, Mother.

FELICITY (*going to her desk*): Not just now, darling. I've got a million things to do before church. Mrs. Crabbe is waiting for the menus, and young Willis has been here since eight-fifteen.

NIGEL: Young Willis?

FELICITY: Yes, dear. If neither you nor Miranda will give him an interview, I shall have to. I do think that our first allegiance should be to the *Kentish Times*. You needn't be afraid I shall be indiscreet. I shall just fob him off with some of those stories about Miranda's early life. The fact that they're not strictly accurate won't matter in the least. They'll give him something to go on.

NIGEL: You're not to say a word to young Willis about Miranda's early life. I absolutely forbid it!

FELICITY: It can't possibly affect you, darling. The interview won't be out until the middle of the week, and you and Miranda will be away on your honeymoon. I presume you're going to have a honeymoon somewhere, aren't you?

NIGEL: It's no use trying to deceive me, Mother. It's no use trying to pretend after last night that everything's all right, because you know damn well it isn't.

FELICITY: What happened last night was embarrassing, I admit, but I can't see that it alters the situation in any way.

NIGEL: Mother!

FELICITY: You said   loudly I thought, that you had a special licence and were going to marry Miranda tomorrow afternoon. Well, that's that, isn't it? I thin' it's rather hard on the village people, of course. Everybody was so thrilled. After all, we haven't had any real excitement here since that ship foundered off the South Foreland.

NIGEL: I'm distracted, Mother. I haven't slept a wink all night. Have you seen Miranda this morning?

FELICITY: No. Have you?

NIGEL: No.

FELICITY: Then I think you should. She's probably fairly distracted too.

NIGEL: You don't like her, do you?

FELICITY: Of course I don't. I think she's a perfect ass.

NIGEL: Mother!

FELICITY: Well, what could be more asinine than inventing all that nonsense about slums and pubs and gutters, when all the time she was born perfectly respectably at Sidcup?

NIGEL: She was romanticising herself. I don't see any particular harm in that. After all, her whole life has been spent romanticising herself and very successfully too. I expect it's become a habit.

FELICITY: Well, she'll have to break herself of it. We can't have the new Lady Marshwood wandering about the countryside telling the most appalling lies to everybody.

NIGEL: She was naturally a bit nervous and ill at ease; she probably wasn't thinking what she was saying.

FELICITY: She seemed quite at ease to me, sitting there sipping away at that disgusting lemonade. Why couldn't she have a nice healthy Martini like everyone else?

NIGEL: That's unreasonable and unkind.

FELICITY: You remind me so much of your father at moments.

NIGEL: What's that got to do with it?

FELICITY: He'd never look twice at a woman unless she had an ineradicable streak of commonness. I could always trust him at house parties but never at race meetings.

NIGEL: He loved you, didn't he?

FELICITY: Good heavens, no! Not in that way. He developed a sort of rugged affection for me but he was never remotely attracted to me. He told me on our honeymoon that I had Sloane Street feet!

NIGEL: Well, perhaps he'd have been able to think of a way out of this situation. I'm damned if I can.

FELICITY: Neither can I. Isn't it maddening?

NIGEL: Of all the incredible, horrible coincidences!

FELICITY: I quite agree. But there it is, and we shall just have to rise above it, shan't we?

NIGEL: Is Moxie going?

FELICITY: Yes. To Bexhill. She's catching the eleven-fifteen from Deal.

NIGEL: Bexhill?

FELICITY: It's quite a charming place, I believe. I shall join her there in a few days when all the fuss is over. She doesn't know that of course because she's in too much of a state at the moment to see anything very clearly, poor darling.

NIGEL: You can't go and live at Bexhill!

FELICITY: I didn't say I was going to live there. I shall just stay in a hotel for a few days while I decide where I'm going to lay my old bones permanently.

NIGEL: Old bones, indeed! You haven't the slightest intention of leaving this house and you never have had.

FELICITY: There you're wrong. When you marry Miranda I shall certainly leave the house. Watching her doing that embroidery would give me a nervous collapse in a week.

NIGEL (coming out with it): How can I marry her now? In these circumstances?

FELICITY: You can't not marry somebody just because

they didn't dance to a barrel organ when they were five!

NIGEL: I think your flippancy is unforgivable, Mother, and in the worst possible taste.

FELICITY: It's no use abusing me, darling. You've made your bed and publicly announced your intention of lying on it as soon as possible. I don't see how you are to get out of it now. It's too late.

NIGEL: I didn't say I wanted to get out of it. I merely said, "How can I marry Miranda in these circumstances?" And I say it again. How can I?

FELICITY: How does Miranda feel about it?

NIGEL: I don't know. She went to bed in floods of tears last night and slammed the door.

FELICITY: Well, if I were you, dear, I should take her for a nice long walk and just hammer away until you arrive at a solution, or better still, take the car and a picnic lunch and go to St. Margaret's Bay.

> DON *and* PETER *come in through the french windows. They are both breathing heavily.*

Good heavens! Back so soon?

PETER: We couldn't get through the gates. The whole village is out!

FELICITY (*looking at* DON's *hand, which he is dabbing with a handkerchief*): Why, Don—what have you done to your hand?

PETER: It's red ink from Elsie Mumby's pen.

FELICITY: Show him where to wash, Peter.

PETER: This way. If it dries it will never come off.

> *He leads* DON *out.*

FELICITY: I had a feeling when I woke up this morning that to-day was going to be difficult and I was quite right.

99

NIGEL: Is that lachrymose oaf going to stay with us indefinitely?

FELICITY: He's not an oaf, he's perfectly charming— and if you had any sense of *noblesse oblige* you'd ask him to be your best man!

NIGEL (*bitterly*): Thank you for everything, Mother. You've been a great comfort to me.

> *He slams out of the room.*

> FELICITY *sighs, and turns to her desk* CRESTWELL *enters, bearing a tray with an immense pile of autograph books on it.*

CRESTWELL: Shall I put this lot with the others, my Lady?

FELICITY: Yes, please, Crestwell. And you'd better tell young Willis to go away. I fear we shall have no definite news until later in the day.

CRESTWELL: Yes, my Lady.

FELICITY: And, Crestwell, you might have Mr. Lucas's car brought round. We may be needing it. Did you give Miss Frayle my message?

CRESTWELL: Yes, my Lady. She should be down soon.

FELICITY: How did she look?

CRESTWELL: A bit papery, my Lady. I don't think she slept very well. She enquired about trains to London. I told her there was an eleven-fifteen fom Deal but that she'd have to change at Ashford and Maidstone.

FELICITY: I can't think why that train ever leaves at all. It doesn't seem to go anywhere that anybody wants.

> *At this moment* MIRANDA *enters. She is looking pale and is wearing black.*

CRESTWELL: Will that be all for the moment, my Lady?

FELICITY: Yes, thank you, Crestwell.

CRESTWELL *goes out into the library.*

Good morning, Miranda. I do hope you slept well?

MIRANDA: I hardly slept at all.

FELICITY: You poor dear, you must be exhausted! Would you like some coffee or Bovril or anything?

MIRANDA: No, thank you. Your butler said that you wanted to speak to me urgently.

FELICITY: How idiotic of him. It isn't in the least urgent. I only wanted to ask you a favour.

MIRANDA: A favour?

FELICITY: Yes. I want you to grant an exclusive interview to our local paper. I know you're badgered to death by such things as a rule but Willis is a special protégé and it would mean so much to him.

MIRANDA: I'm afraid I can't, Lady Marshwood. I'm going away.

FELICITY: Going away?

MIRANDA: I don't feel that I could possibly stay, not as long as my sister's in the house.

FELICITY: But she lives here. She's lived here for nineteen years.

MIRANDA: I don't care where she lives. I never want to set eyes on her again.

FELICITY: I'm afraid that's impossible. I couldn't move without her. I'm devoted to her.

MIRANDA: She insulted me and humiliated me and I shall never speak to her until the end of my days.

FELICITY: I don't suppose she'll mind that. After all, you haven't been exactly intimate for the last twenty years, have you?

MIRANDA: The situation is impossible.

FELICITY: Difficult, I grant you, but not impossible. Moxie and I won't be in the house all the time, you know. We shall go away sometimes—on little visits.

MIRANDA (*horrified*): Do you mean that you are going on living here after we're married?

FELICITY: Naturally, my dear. It happens to be my home, you know. I lived here steadily through Nigel's first marriage. Of course it didn't last very long, but that wasn't my fault. At least, I don't think it was.

MIRANDA: And Dora—Moxie—whatever you call her—she'll live here too?

FELICITY: Of course.

MIRANDA: But it's quite out of the question! It would be intolerable.

FELICITY: It would be much more intolerable for me if she went away.

MIRANDA: But you must see . . .

FELICITY: I'd be absolutely helpless without her— I'd never be in time for a single meal, my hair would be all over the place, and I should be covered in safety-pins from head to foot.

MIRANDA: Now, look here, Lady Marshwood, I think we'd better come to an understanding about this.

FELICITY: By all means. What do you suggest?

MIRANDA: I suggest that Dora should be given a nice little cottage somewhere or other, and a reasonable pension. I haven't discussed this with Nigel but I'm sure he'd agree . . .

FELICITY: I've no doubt he would, but you see, he doesn't depend on her to do his hair every morning, and I do.

MIRANDA: I admit that I haven't behaved very well

to Dora and I'm sorry for it. I'm willing to try to make it up to her in any way that I can.

FELICITY: You said just now that you never intended to speak to her again until the end of your days.

MIRANDA: I know I did and I'm sorry for that, too. I haven't slept a wink all night and my nerves are on edge.

FELICITY: Would you like some Phensic? I have some in my room. Moxie knows where it is.

MIRANDA: No, thank you.

FELICITY: We're all feeling a little jaded this morning. Nigel, of course, did the most sensible thing. He went galloping off across country. But we couldn't all do that because there aren't enough horses. As a matter of fact I believe May has a bicycle that she isn't using at the moment——

MIRANDA: You don't want me to marry Nigel, do you?

FELICITY: Not at the moment, Miranda, but I am sure I shall get used to it. I'm very adaptable. I expect we shall both have to make certain allowances just at first, but we shall doubtless jog along together all right after a while.

MIRANDA: Jog along together?

FELICITY: I know it doesn't sound very alluring put like that, but you do know what I mean, don't you?

MIRANDA: I do. I'm not quite as stupid as you think.

FELICITY: I'm so glad!

MIRANDA: I also know that you planned all that business of Dora dressing up, just to belittle me in front of Nigel, just to make me look a fool.

FELICITY: I had no idea that you yourself would contribute so generously to the final result.

MIRANDA: Then you did?

FELICITY: No, as a matter of fact, I didn't. The whole thing was improvised, foolishly I admit, to spare Moxie's feelings and your feelings, temporarily at least.

MIRANDA: Do you expect me to believe that?

FELICITY: You can believe it or not as you like, but it happens to be true. Of course I knew that the fact of you and Moxie being sisters was bound to come out eventually, but I hoped by that time that you and I would have got to know each other well enough, and like each other well, enough to discuss the situation rationally and calmly. Unhappily it didn't turn out like that.

MIRANDA: It most certainly didn't.

FELICITY: Moxie, enraged by your imaginative flights, lost her head and gave the game away and I must say I can't blame her.

MIRANDA: You may not blame her but I do.

FELICITY: The only thing you can possibly blame her for is not dying of drink.

MIRANDA (*beginning to lose her temper*): Well, I'll tell you here and now. Before I set foot in this house as Nigel's wife, she's going to be out of it for good.

FELICITY: On the contrary, she will receive you at the front door. We might even prevail upon her to drop you a curtsy. The press photographers would love it!

MIRANDA: You forget one thing. Nigel happens to be in love with me. He won't stand by and allow me to be publicly humiliated.

FELICITY: Are you so sure?

MIRANDA: What do you mean by that?

FELICITY: Nigel is my son, Miranda, and like his father before him, he has one ingrained temperamental defect. He loathes disharmony, detests scenes and runs like a stag at the first sign of a domestic crisis.

MIRANDA: Are you trying to suggest that owing to all this—this business of Dora being your maid, that he won't marry me?

FELICITY: Certainly not. Nigel is a man of his word. I am merely giving you a word of warning.

MIRANDA: I don't need any warning, thank you.

FELICITY: Really, Miranda, for a successful and world-famous woman you are quite remarkably silly.

MIRANDA: How dare you speak to me like that!

FELICITY: You forget, my dear, that I am already, virtually, your mother-in-law. And as it seems fairly obvious that we are destined to have an endless series of unpleasant scenes during the next few years, I think we might curtail this one now, don't you? (*She moves towards the door.*) We usually leave for church just before eleven.

> FELICITY *goes out.*

> MIRANDA, *left alone, wanders about for a moment, clenching and unclenching her hands.* NIGEL *enters. He has changed into a navy blue suit.*

NIGEL: Miranda! I thought you were still asleep.

MIRANDA: Still asleep! I haven't closed my eyes all night.

NIGEL: Darling—I'm so sorry.

MIRANDA: I'm going away, now, this morning. I'm catching the eleven-fifteen from Deal.

NIGEL: You can't possibly.

MIRANDA: And why not, I should like to know?

NIGEL: It's an awful train. You'll have to change twice. Ashford and Maidstone.

MIRANDA: Your mother has insulted me.

NIGEL: I'm sure she didn't mean to. You really mustn't take mother seriously. She just rattles on, you know, she doesn't mean half she says.

MIRANDA: She says she's going to live in this house—with us—is that true?

NIGEL: Of course it is. She's always lived here.

MIRANDA: Nigel!

NIGEL: Now do calm down, darling! You won't have to see much of her, except in the evenings. She has a tremendous amount to do during the day. She runs the whole place, and the village too—she's on God knows how many committees. She's practically an institution.

MIRANDA: Do you expect me to sacrifice my whole life, my career, everything, to live with an institution?

NIGEL: I never asked you to sacrifice anything. You said in Cannes that you were weary and lonely and wanted to get away from it all, and that all your fame and success was a hollow mockery. You even burst into tears when that poor young man tried to take a snapshot of you outside the Palm Beach Casino.

MIRANDA: Your mother hates me. Don't you understand? She hates me!

NIGEL: Nonsense. You're imagining things. She's probably a bit irritable this morning. After all, the scene last night was upsetting, the house is under-staffed with one maid ill and the other away, and she's got the Church Fête on Friday. She has a lot to try her.

MIRANDA: *She* has a lot to try her? What about me?

NIGEL: Now look here, Miranda . . .

MIRANDA (*near tears*): You don't love me. That's clear enough at any rate. You never came near me last night . . .

NIGEL: You slammed the door in my face.

MIRANDA: And this morning, without a word of sympathy or understanding, you went out horse-back riding.

NIGEL: We just say 'riding' in England. The horse-back is taken for granted.

MIRANDA: I'm not going to live in this house with your mother. And that's final.

NIGEL (*icily*): As my wife, Miranda, I shall expect you to live where I live and do what I ask you to do, and make every effort to be on good terms with my mother. I loathe and detest family scenes, and what is more I have no intention of putting up with them. I am quite sure that, at the first sign of a gesture from you, mother would be prepared to meet you more than halfway. And I can see no earthly reason, with good will on both sides, why you shouldn't jog along perfectly happily together.

> NIGEL *goes out with great dignity and closes the door after him.*
>
> MIRANDA *gives an inarticulate cry of rage and collapses on to the sofa in tears.*
>
> *After a moment,* DON *enters.*

DON: Pete!

MIRANDA: Go away.

DON: Don't cry. You know it always ties me up in knots to see you cry.

MIRANDA: I can't bear any more . . . I can't . . .

DON: What's happened, kid? Has that stuffed shirt said something to upset you?

MIRANDA (*controlling herself with a splendid effort*): No, Don, it's nothing. Please go away. I shall be all right in a minute . . .

DON: How can I go away and leave you—like this?

MIRANDA: You must, Don—you really must. There isn't anything you can do. (*She rises and walks away from him.*) This is my problem and I've got to grapple with it alone.

DON: If that high-hat English louse said anything to make you cry I'll poke him in the nose.

MIRANDA: No, Don, don't do that—it wouldn't do any good.

DON: Why were you crying?

MIRANDA (*gallantly*): A moment of weakness, that's all. I just felt suddenly lonely and sort of bewildered——

DON (*unhappily*): Oh, Pete! . . .

MIRANDA (*before the camera*): Life can be very cruel sometimes, Don. It can do terrible things to people, specially to over-sensitive, trusting fools like me.

DON: You're no fool, Pete. You're smart as a whip—you always have been. You're a fighter, too—that's one of the things I love best about you. You've got guts!

MIRANDA: Thanks, Don—Pete.

DON: You're not going to let this—this bunch of café society bit-players give you the run-around, are you? You—Miranda Frayle? You must be out of your mind!

MIRANDA: What's the use of talking, Pete? Maybe I am out of my mind. Maybe I have made a mess of things but I can't walk out now. I've signed the contract.

DON: You walked out of "Dreams Cannot Lie" after they'd been shooting for two weeks, contract or no contract. Where's your spirit? Why, they even suspended you for three months and you laughed in their faces! At least they can't suspend you here!

MIRANDA: They can do worse than that. They can

torture me and humiliate me. They can . . . (*She falters.*) They can break my heart.

DON (*enfolding her in his arms*): Not while I'm around they can't! I'm the guy that loves you—remember?

MIRANDA (*emotionally*): Oh, Pete! . . .

    FELICITY *enters, followed by* NIGEL *and* PETER. *They are dressed for church.*

FELICITY: Really, Miranda! This is becoming monotonous!

MIRANDA (*disengaging herself from* DON'S *embrace*): I feel that you and I have nothing further to say to each other, Lady Marshwood.

FELICITY: I'm afraid that will make our long winter evenings together rather insipid. It looks as though we shall have to have a television set after all.

NIGEL (*with dignity*): What does this mean, Miranda?

MIRANDA (*with dignity*): It means that I am going away.

NIGEL: I know you are. You said so a little while ago. I'll drive you up after lunch. You can't possibly go by train.

MIRANDA: Don is going to drive me up, before lunch. Aren't you, Don?

DON: You bet I am!

FELICITY: Well, we really can't stand about here arguing as to who drives who. We shall be late for church.

    CRESTWELL *enters.*

CRESTWELL: Mr. Don Lucas's car is at the door, my Lady.

DON (*delighted*): Okay! Come on, Pete!

NIGEL: Pete! . . . I would rather you didn't drive to London with Mr. Lucas, Miranda.

DON (*threateningly*): You can just quit ordering her about from now on, see? She's coming with me—now!

FELICITY: Please don't be belligerent, Don. It's quite unnecessary. You're not rescuing anybody from the Japanese now, you know.

DON: I'm sorry, ma'am—Felicity. But she's coming with me, right away. She's not going to stay here and be tortured and humiliated any more.

PETER (*to* FELICITY): You see, he *does* think we're the Japanese. It's a sort of occupational neurosis.

NIGEL: Shut up, Peter. (*To* MIRANDA.) You insist on leaving with Mr. Lucas?

MIRANDA: Yes, I do! I couldn't stay here. I couldn't live in this house, not with things as they are. (*She shoots a venomous look at* FELICITY.) I was a fool ever to think that I could. I'm walking out on you, Nigel. I'm sorry, but that's how it is. And you can tell my sister from me that she can go on doing your mother's hair for as long as she has any to do. Come on, Don!

MIRANDA *sweeps out.*

DON, *after an embarrassed look at* FELICITY, *follows her.*

FELICITY: Poor Miranda! She's been on edge all the morning.

NIGEL: This is all your doing, Mother. I hope you're satisfied. You engineered the whole thing. You deliberately drove her into the arms of that lout.

FELICITY: I did not. She's been in and out of his arms like a jack-in-the-box ever since he set foot in the house.

NIGEL: You've behaved abominably and I'm ashamed of you.

FELICITY: And I am most bitterly ashamed of you. You, a Peer of the Realm and a member of White's, allowing the woman you love to be whisked away from under your nose without a protest! I can hardly believe it.

NIGEL: Of all the hypocritical nonsense! You wanted to get rid of Miranda and you succeeded. You're absolutely delighted!

FELICITY: And you? Are you going to stand there and pretend that you're heart-broken? You seem to forget that I'm your mother, dear. I brought you into the world, in the middle of Ascot week, and I know you through and through. You never really loved Miranda, any more than you really loved any of the others. Of course I'm delighted. We're all delighted. And now, for heaven's sake let's go—we're terribly late, the last bell went ages ago.

MOXIE *enters, in her hat and coat.*

Ah, there you are, Moxie! I couldn't think what had happened to you!

MOXIE: I've come to say good-bye, my Lady.

FELICITY: Rubbish! Take off your hat and don't be so silly.

MOXIE: But, my Lady . . .

FELICITY: Do as I tell you, and for Heaven's sake give me some money for the collection. There's nothing more to worry about. I haven't time to go on about it now, but Crestwell will explain. . . . Come along, everybody!

MOXIE *gives* FELICITY *a coin.*

Thank you. Give Moxie a glass of sherry, she looks as if she's going to fall down. Come, Nigel, it's your first Sunday at home and you must try to look as if nothing had happened. After all, when you analyse it, nothing much has, has it?

> FELICITY *sweeps out through the french windows—* PETER *follows her.*

> NIGEL *is about to go too, but he suddenly sees* MOXIE's *expression.*

NIGEL: Cheer up, Moxie! Everything's all right, now.

> *He pats her on the shoulder affectionately, and goes out after the others.*

MOXIE (*tremulously, as he goes*): Thank you, my Lord. Thank you ever so much . . . (*She sinks down on a chair and rummages in her bag for her handkerchief.*)

CRESTWELL: Snap out of it now, Dora. You heard what he said!

MOXIE: It's all very fine for you. You haven't made a public exhibition of yourself and cried your eyes out all night long.

CRESTWELL (*going to the drink table*): Even supposing I had, I should have the sense to shut up now.

MOXIE: You haven't had the ground suddenly cut from under your feet and been shamed and humiliated by your own flesh and blood. I'll never be able to hold my head up again, and that's a fact.

CRESTWELL (*cheerfully pouring two glasses of sherry*): In that case we shall have to settle for it hanging down, shan't we? (*He hands her a glass.*) Here—away with melancholy—have a swig of this!

MOXIE (*taking the glass—dimly*): Thanks, Fred.

CRESTWELL (*fetching his own glass*): As I see the situation, Dora, you've got hold of the wrong end of the stick. You're not the one who's been shamed and humiliated. It's the other way round. Your only mistake, if I might be permitted to venture a slight criticism, is that you didn't take the golden opportunity, when you had it, to give your own flesh and blood a nice healthy slap in the chops!

MOXIE (*with a slight giggle*): Oh, Fred!

CRESTWELL (*raising his glass*): I give you a toast, Dora. I drink solemnly to you and me in our humble, but on the whole honourable calling. I drink to her Ladyship and his Lordship, groaning beneath the weight of privilege, but managing to keep their peckers up all the same. Above all I drink to the final inglorious disintegration of the most unlikely dream that ever troubled the foolish heart of man—Social Equality! (*He drinks.*)

MOXIE: No one's ever going to stop you talking, are they?

CRESTWELL: It would, I admit, be a Herculean task, but should you at any time feel disposed to have a whack at it, you have only to say the word.

MOXIE: That'll be the day and no mistake! (*She giggles again.*)

CRESTWELL: What about another nip at the Amontillado?

MOXIE: I don't mind if I do!

CURTAIN

LOOK AFTER LULU!

CHARACTERS

MARCEL BLANCHARD, a young man with expectations
    when he marries.
PHILIPPE DE CROZE, Marcel's friend and Lulu's lover.
GIGOT, a retired policeman.
THE PRINCE OF SALESTRIA
GENERAL KOSCHNADIEFF, aide-de-camp to the Prince.
HERR VAN PUTZEBOUM, Marcel's godfather.
ADONIS, a footman.
BOMBA, VALERY, EMILE, Friends of Philippe.
THE MAYOR of the District.
OUDATTE, a clerk at the Town Hall.
CORNETTE, another clerk.
AN INSPECTOR OF POLICE

LULU D'ARVILLE, a cocotte.
CLAIRE, The Duchess of Clausonnes.
YVONNE, PAULETTE, GABY, Friends of Lulu.
ROSE, a maid at Marcel's apartment.
AUNT GABRIELLE
A LITTLE GIRL

TWO BOYS, from the florist's.
A PHOTOGRAPHER

SYNOPSIS OF SCENES

ACT I   *The salon of Lulu's apartment in Paris.*
ACT II   *Marcel's bedroom.*
ACT III *Scene I. The Registrar's Office in the Town Hall.*
                Scene II. Lulu's bedroom.

ACT I

The salon of Lulu's apartment in Paris, 1908. Downstage left is a large bay window. Upstage left, facing the audience, is the main door, which gives on to the vestibule. Running across the middle of the back wall, is a glass partition through which may be seen some of the room beyond. Upstage right, at an angle, is an archway leading to the small salon. Downstage right is the door leading to Lulu's bedroom. Upstage centre, against the partition, is a grand piano with the keyboard facing left. On the piano is a box of cigars, a silver candelabrum, some matches; also on the piano, towards the right, is a gramophone and some records. In the curve of the piano stands a little kidney table on which is a tray of liqueurs and glasses. Further downstage, towards the right is a formal sofa. Downstage left is a card table. Small chairs are dotted about. There is a great deal more furniture, and a great many bibelots, pictures and potted plants. Near the door to the vestibule is an electric bell.

When the curtain rises, LULU is standing by the piano, playing the gramophone for the entertainment of her guests. The guests are smartly dressed in evening clothes. BOMBA is sitting with YVONNE on the sofa, on the arm of which PAULETTE is reclining.

> VALERY *is sitting at the card table with* EMILE
> *opposite him; they are engaged in a game of cards.*
> *The gramophone is playing a record of "Di quella*
> *pira" from "Il Trovatore" sung by Enrico Caruso.*
> *Most of the guests are listening enraptured, some with*
> *their eyes closed, some nodding their heads in time to*
> *the music and some tapping their feet.*

LULU: Isn't it gorgeous? It's hard to believe that such a sound could come out of any human throat.

BOMBA: It's hard to believe that anyone should want to listen to it when it does.

LULU: You have no ear my darling, no ear at all, but I love you in spite of it. I have a dreadful feeling I love everybody at this moment—that's what glorious music does for me.

BOMBA: Glorious music! The man's bellowing like a bull.

LULU: I've never met a bull with a range like that.

YVONNE (*giggling*): I've never met a bull at all.

LULU: There's still time if you play your cards right— just persevere.

PAULETTE: Do be quiet everybody; here's the most heaven sent voice soaring away and we do nothing but shout it down.

BOMBA: If that voice is heaven sent he'd better send it back to where it came from.

LULU: Once and for all my darling Bomba, you are not to be naughty.

BOMBA: I could sing as well as that any day of the week.

LULU: Well just don't choose to-day, there's a dear.

BOMBA: (*joining in with Caruso*): Ah-ah-ah-ah-ah! etc.

YVONNE: It's too bad. Shut *up,* Bomba.

PAULETTE: Can't somebody stop him?

LULU: Yes, I can. (*She rushes at him with a cushion, tries to smother him, but he evades her—still singing at the top of his voice. Finally he breaks away from her, strikes a tremendous attitude and joins Caruso on the last note*).

BOMBA: Ah-ah-ah-ah-ah!

PAULETTE: There now, he's ruined everything.

LULU (*to* BOMBA): You ought to be ashamed. Here am I trying my best to bring a little culture into your sordid life and all you do is make a beast of yourself.

BOMBA: I've always made a beast of myself, ever since I was a tiny boy—I glory in it. I'm a self-made beast. Ha ha!

LULU: What shall we do now?

VALERY: Put on a waltz and we can dance.

LULU: Oh no, we can't. The last time we danced old Madame Leclerc's chandelier fell down and nearly set the house on fire.

YVONNE: I remember it well; those lovely firemen and all those hoses.

LULU: *And* the bill for the chandelier.

VALERY: Put on a record of a nice brass band.

LULU: I haven't got one. (*She looks through her records*). Here's Sarah Bernhardt in the second act of 'Phedre', but it's a bit scratchy.

BOMBA: All the acts of 'Phedre' are a bit scratchy. (*He goes to the piano and lights a cigar*).

LULU: Oh, Bomba, *not* another cigar! We can't see across the room as it is.

BOMBA: Then you're very lucky—from where I am I can see Yvonne quite clearly.

YVONNE (*blowing him a kiss*): You're a beastly self-made beast—I can't think what you want with a sweet little girl like me.

BOMBA: I'll tell you later.

LULU: Once and for all Bomba, I will not have you saying that sort of thing in front of everyone—it's vulgar.

BOMBA: I'm too old to change now, and too rich. Besides, a little honest vulgarity every now and then is healthy.

PHILIPPE (*in the bedroom*): Damn, damn, damn! Hell and damnation take it!

YVONNE (*to* LULU): That, if you're interested, is the golden voice of your beloved.

PHILIPPE: Damn and blast and curse it to hell!

PAULETTE: I'm afraid he's in one of his moods.

LULU (*calling*): What's the matter, my precious angel?

PHILIPPE (*entering*): Everything's the matter. (*He is in his shirtsleeves, with his jacket over his arm. The trousers of his uniform are far, far too short.*) Will you please look at my legs?

VALERY: Must we?

LULU: I think they're very pretty legs. I never get tired of looking at them.

PHILIPPE: Well I can't go on the parade ground to-morrow like this can I? My colonel is unlikely to share your passion for looking at my legs.

LULU: You never know nowadays.

YVONNE: Why are your trousers so short, Philippe?

PHILIPPE (*patiently*): I will tell you why my trousers are so short, Yvonne. It's because I've grown since I did my military service last year. I have grown three inches in all directions.

LULU: Let me be the first to congratulate you.

PHILIPPE: Imagine if I'd had to present arms in front of the Colonel to-morrow morning looking like this——what should I have done?

LULU: Presented your legs instead I suppose. (*To* PHILIPPE) Come here, my angel, we'd better try your jacket on while we're at it. We'll do something about the trousers later.

PHILIPPE (*kissing her*): You're the light of my life, and here I am leaving you for twenty eight days. I don't think I can bear it.

LULU: You must be brave. You must also stand still—I can't let down your trousers if you wriggle.

They go up towards the piano

PHILIPPE (*as he passes* BOMBA): God what an offensive cigar!

BOMBA: Yes, isn't it? It's one of yours, my precious angel.

PHILIPPE: They seem to have a special chemical reaction when you smoke them. I can hardly see across the room.

BOMBA: I can't think why everyone keeps wanting to see across the room.

PHILIPPE: Ring the bell, Lulu, for Adonis to come and open the window. (LULU *does so*)

YVONNE: I suppose it would be vulgar if we opened it ourselves.

LULU: What's the good of having a footman if you don't use him?

YVONNE: Very delicately put.

BOMBA: I shall catch my death of cold and then you'll all be sorry.

YVONNE: What makes you think so?

121

BOMBA: You're going to wish you'd never said that. (*He advances towards her*).

YVONNE: Help! Help! He's going to attack me!

LULU: You must be used to that by now.

BOMBA *pulls* YVONNE *and* PAULETTE *on to the sofa. They struggle and squeal.*

YVONNE: Stop it! Stop it! You're spoiling my dress!

LULU (*who is letting down* PHILIPPE's *trousers by lengthening the braces*): Do be quiet all of you—all that squealing sounds so common. I do wish people would learn to behave with a little dignity when they're out in society.

BOMBA (*derisively*): Out in what?

LULU: You heard—so shut up.

PAULETTE: Valery! Emile! Please come and help us!

VALERY (*still calmly playing cards*): You're both perfectly capable of looking after yourselves.

PAULETTE: Are you my protector or are you not?

VALERY: It's never been officially decided. Anyway you're over the age of consent.

EMILE: She's been over that since 1901.

PAULETTE: There's something so lovely about true chivalry. (BOMBA *pinches her*). Ow!

LULU: This whole scene is degrading. Bomba, will you leave those girls alone! There's a time and a place for everything.

BOMBA: I know about the place, but I've never been certain about the time.

PAULETTE: Men are all alike, all they ever think about is sex.

LULU (*absently*): I know. Isn't it lovely?

ADONIS *appears in the doorway at the height of the struggle. He is very tall and good-looking, though still in his*

*teens. He is dressed in the uniform of a footman, with rows
of gold buttons.*

ADONIS: You rang, madame?

LULU: Yes, Adonis. Open the window please, as wide
as it will go. The atmosphere in here is as thick as the
Bal Tabarin at five o'clock in the morning.

ADONIS: Certainly madame. (*He opens the window.*)

LULU: And you can take away those squalid glasses
and ashtrays while you're at it. (*To* PHILIPPE). There
now, that's better. Look in the glass.

PHILIPPE (*standing on a chair and regarding himself*):
They're a bit low in the fork, aren't they?

LULU: I'm sure the Colonel won't mind.

BOMBA (*loudly*): When are we going to eat? I'm
starving.

LULU (*with immense grandeur*): We are not 'going to
eat'—we are going to partake of a buffet supper as soon
as it's bloody well ready.

YVONNE: How exciting, I've never had a buffet
supper before.

LULU: It's just the same as any other kind of supper,
except that you don't sit down.

PAULETTE: What's the point of that?

LULU: It just happens to be what all the best people
are doing nowadays.

BOMBA: Lulu ought never to have been allowed to
read that book on etiquette, it's turned her into a thun-
dering snob.

PHILIPPE (*hotly*): It hasn't done anything of the sort.
It's merely that she wishes to improve herself.

LULU: Thank you, my precious angel. But actually
it's not myself I'm so worried about, it's some of my
friends.

BOMBA: Pardon me while I shoot myself.

LULU (*grand again*): It's not a question of shooting yourself, my dear; it's merely a question of moving with the times, of reaching upwards instead of downwards which, if I may say so, you do far too often. (*With a sweeping gesture.*) A table, mes enfants!

They all go into the adjoining room, except ADONIS *who remains to tidy the drink table.* LULU *unknowingly drops her handkerchief on the way out.* ADONIS *picks up a bottle of green chartreuse, looks at it, and then pours out an enormous glassful and starts to drink it. He is facing front, gently rubbing his stomach with his free hand and occasionally rolling his eyes to heaven with pleasure.* LULU *comes back silently and, without taking her eyes off* ADONIS *for an instant, picks up her handkerchief.*

ADONIS: Sacred blue, but that is veritably delicious!

LULU: I'll give you 'Sacred blue'—guzzling down my green chartreuse. (*She gives him a resounding slap.*)

ADONIS (*jumping*): Oh! (*He quickly puts down the glass and slaps her in return.* LULU *staggers back.*)

LULU (*shocked*): Adonis! You struck me; in my own house.

ADONIS: I certainly did—and it isn't your own house, it's Philippe's.

LULU: Kindly refer to Monsieur de Croze as the Master, and put that bottle down immediately.

THE GUESTS, *hearing the altercation, return from the other room and gather in the doorway.*

PHILIPPE: What's going on?

LULU: He struck me—in my own house.

PHILIPPE: How dare you strike your mistress?

ADONIS: She's not my mistress, she's your mistress.

LULU: You're a very common boy.

ADONIS: You should know.

LULU: Take him away please—put him in prison. I can bear no more, I'm feeling quite faint.

PHILIPPE: Certainly. (*He, with the other men except* BOMBA *rush him off towards the vestibule.*)

LULU: Has anyone got any smelling salts?

PAULETTE: There are some Epsom salts in the bathroom.

BOMBA: I doubt if they would have the desired effect.

LULU: I don't know what the world's coming to, and that's a fact.

PHILIPPE (*returning with* VALERY *and* EMILE): Perhaps that will teach you to take servants out of the gutter without a reference.

LULU: He did *not* come from the gutter.

PHILIPPE: Where did he come from then?

LULU: From a very good family indeed. He was highly recommended. I would rather not discuss the matter any further, it's too unpleasant. The boy lost his temper and that's that.

PHILIPPE: He also lost his job.

LULU: Oh Philippe—No.

PHILIPPE: Wait till you see the reference *I'm* going to give him.

LULU: You're so strong dear—be merciful.

PHILIPPE: I'm kicking him out of the house *now*. (*He starts to go.*)

LULU (*restraining him*): No—no—you can't do that, he'll have nowhere to go. He'll have to sleep under one of those dreadful bridges with a newspaper over him.

PHILIPPE: You wanted to send him to prison just now.

LULU: That at least would be warmer.

YVONNE: If you're really going to kick him out of

the house, I believe I could find a nice position for him.

LULU: I'm sure you could dear.

YVONNE: I don't like to think of him walking the streets of Paris with those great big innocent eyes. Who knows what might happen to him?

LULU: I do, for one.

PHILIPPE: He could try a little hard work for a change, with those great big innocent hands.

The door to the vestibule opens and GIGOT *appears. He looks like what he is, a retired policeman.*

GIGOT: Now then, now then, what's been going on?

LULU: Papa! You've arrived in the nick of time!

GIGOT: What have you been doing to Adonis? He's sobbing his heart out.

PHILIPPE: Serve him right.

GIGOT (*to* LULU): He says you struck him—in front of everybody.

LULU: I certainly did. And he struck me—in my own house.

GIGOT: Who delivered the first blow?

LULU: I did.

GIGOT: That's a very serious admission. Stand back everybody while I collect the evidence.

LULU: Papa, you're not a policeman now, you know —Perhaps you've forgotten—you retired under a cloud in September.

GIGOT: Never mind about that, justice must be done. I represent the majesty of the law.

LULU: Fiddlesticks.

GIGOT: What was that you said?

LULU: Fiddlesticks was what I said and fiddlesticks was what I meant. You don't represent the majesty of the law darling, you represent nothing but a lot of pomposity and a very small pension.

GIGOT: Contempt of court.

LULU: Of course dear.

GIGOT: It is laid down in law that the party who delivers the first blow—to which you admit?

LULU: Certainly.

GIGOT: . . . is the guilty party. The defendant, to use his own words, says you fetched him a clip on the kisser.

LULU: Where could he have picked up such a common expression?

PHILIPPE: In the gutter where he came from.

GIGOT: He did *not* come from the gutter.

PHILIPPE: I don't care whether he came from the Palace of Versailles, he's going now.

GIGOT: Oh no, he isn't. You may pay the bills of this house my boy, but that doesn't entitle you to order people about. Now Lulu, run along like a good girl and tell Adonis you're sorry.

PHILIPPE: She shall do no such thing. (*To* LULU.) Pay no attention to the old gasbag.

LULU: Gasbag? Philippe, you are speaking of my father.

GIGOT (*ignoring him*): Do as I say, Lulu.

LULU: Anything for the sake of peace.

GIGOT: On second thoughts, it would be more appropriate for him to come to you. Now remember Lulu, no bitterness and no recriminations—one kind word or two and everything will be forgiven and forgotten. I'll ring. (*He does so.*)

PHILIPPE: This is idiotic. I'm not going to stand here and see Lulu apologising to a footman. (*He stamps out furiously.*)

LULU: There now—you've upset Philippe. On his last night at home too. Do please go back to your supper all of you. I'll deal with Adonis.

PAULETTE: You wouldn't catch me trying to get round a footman.

LULU: I wouldn't bet on it.

YVONNE: You're behaving beautifully dear—I admire you for it. I've always said there's nothing to touch Noblesse Oblige.

GIGOT: Come along, everybody. (*They all go out, talking and chattering.* LULU *is left alone; she tidies the things on the piano, desultorily.* ADONIS *appears in the doorway.*)

ADONIS: You rang, madame?

LULU: No darling—as a matter of fact father did.

ADONIS: Well, what do you want?

LULU: Are you still angry with me?

ADONIS (*looking down*): Of course I am.

LULU: Did I hurt you very much?

ADONIS: It was my feelings you hurt more than anything else.

LULU: Come over here, dear. (*He hesitates*). Please, Adonis, come and sit down. (*He goes to her.*) I didn't mean to be unkind—but you really shouldn't have drunk all that green chartreuse, it's terribly rich.

ADONIS: I couldn't help it, I was suddenly tempted.

LULU: The crème de menthe would have been much better for you—more of a digestive. You know you've got a nervous stomach.

ADONIS (*sighing*): Oh Lulu!

LULU: There, there. Put your head on my shoulder—you know I wouldn't hurt you for the world. (*She draws his head onto her shoulder.*) You know how much I love you—you know that, don't you my darling?

They kiss. PHILIPPE *appears in the doorway, holding a soup-plate. He gasps with astonishment, then beckons to the Guests. They appear, also holding soup-plates, and are equally astonished.*

ADONIS: I love you so—you're the only one in the world I really love. (*He sees* PHILIPPE, *starts, and tries to get up.*) Let me go, Lulu! Please let me go!

LULU: Don't struggle sweetheart, you're wriggling like a dear little eel—stay here and let me make a fuss of you until you feel quite, quite better again.

PHILIPPE: Well I'll be damned!

GIGOT (*coming in through the other doorway and rubbing his hands with satisfaction*): There now, that's better. That's what I like to see.

PHILIPPE (*coming forward*): Oh, so that's what you like to see, is it?

GIGOT: Of course.

PHILIPPE: Then you're a very nasty old man.

GIGOT: How dare you!

PHILIPPE: And as for your daughter, she's nothing but a. . . .

LULU: Don't say it dear—it may be true, but don't say it!

PHILIPPE: Leave this house immediately.

LULU: What on earth for?

PHILIPPE: Because I find you carrying on a disgusting affair with the footman under my very nose.

LULU: Disgusting affair!—you must be out of your mind.

GIGOT: The accusation you have just made is improper in the extreme.

LULU: I don't know what you're all making such a fuss about—it's all perfectly natural.

PHILIPPE (*wildly*): Natural! You're right—I *must* be out of my mind!

LULU: Philippe! I've suddenly realised what you are thinking—it's too humiliating, too mortifying. I can't bear it. (*She bursts into tears.*)

GIGOT: Don't upset yourself, my darling. (*He goes to her.*)

LULU (*sobbing*): I'm so ashamed, so bitterly, bitterly ashamed that the man I love should suspect me of anything so vile.

BOMBA: In fairness to Philippe, there is surely a certain basis for his suspicion.

LULU (*rising grandly to her feet*): There is *no* basis for *any*body's suspicion—Adonis happens to be my little brother.

PAULETTE (*rather sentimentally*): Her little brother!

BOMBA: He's six foot one if he's an inch.

PHILIPPE (*stunned*): Your brother!—but you never told me you had a brother!

LULU: You never asked me; the subject never came up. As a matter of fact I have a sister too.

PHILIPPE: Where is she?

LULU: In a sweet little house in Buenos Aires.

PHILIPPE (*to* LULU): If Adonis is your brother, will you kindly explain why he is your footman?

LULU: Well you see, the poor little boy was growing up and he'd never learnt a trade. In my own profession I was getting on by leaps and bounds.

BOMBA: I had no idea your progress had been so convulsive.

LULU: So I thought the best thing to do was to train him myself and take him under my wing.

GIGOT (*raptly*): The wing of an angel.

LULU: Darling Papa, we must all try not to exaggerate.

GIGOT: Family affection is a beautiful thing.

LULU: Of course, we meant to keep it a secret, but now you know, Philippe, the least you can do is to shake hands.

PHILIPPE: Me, a member of the Stock Exchange, hob-nobbing with a footman?

PAULETTE: After all, in a sort of way, he is your brother-in-law.

PHILIPPE: Oh no he isn't, not till I marry his sister.

LULU: Dearest, I never knew such a thing had ever crossed your mind.

YVONNE: Go on Philippe, do what Lulu asks you.

PHILIPPE (*reluctantly*): Oh very well. (*He shakes hands with* ADONIS.) How do you do?

ADONIS (*affably*): Mustn't grumble—how have you been keeping?

PHILIPPE: Fairly well, thanks.

LULU: Compliments fly when gentlefolk meet. Now Adonis darling, everything's all right, so you can take everybody's soup-plates and go away. (*To the Guests.*) Come along, we'll get on with our supper.

They all troop out again, PHILIPPE *and* LULU *last.* ADONIS *collects the soup-plates. Just as* PHILIPPE *and* LULU *get to the door, the bell rings and they come back into the room again.*

PHILIPPE: Whoever can be ringing my front door bell at twenty five minutes to ten?

LULU: Probably a nun with a little box. There are heaps of them in this district. (*To* ADONIS.) Go and answer the door, there's a good boy.

ADONIS: What am I to do with the soup-plates, without a rude answer?

LULU: Leave them in the hall for the moment. Go on.
He goes.

PHILIPPE: Are you expecting anybody, at this time of night?

LULU: No, I don't think so.

PHILIPPE: What do you mean, you don't think so?

LULU: Don't snap at me my precious—I can't remember everything, can I? There's so much going on.

PHILIPPE: There is indeed. A great deal too much going on.

ADONIS (*re-appearing*): There's a duchess at the door.

LULU: A duchess! She must be mad.

PHILIPPE: What does she look like?

ADONIS: I couldn't say—she's got a veil on.

LULU: Did you ask her what she wants?

ADONIS: She says she wants to talk to you—in the strictest privacy.

LULU: Good gracious. You'd better show her in, Adonis darling.

ADONIS: Righto. (*He goes.*)

PHILIPPE: Adonis darling! Either that horrid boy's a footman or he isn't—which is it to be?

LULU: Time alone will tell.

PHILIPPE: Now look here, Lulu. . . .

LULU: Don't fuss, my angel. (*Pushing him out.*) Go and join the others and leave me with Her Grace.

PHILIPPE: But why should a Duchess suddenly want to see you?

LULU: How can I possibly know until I've heard what she's got to say?

PHILIPPE: There's something fishy about it.

LULU: Never mind dear, go away and leave me to deal with it.

PHILIPPE: Oh all right.

He goes reluctantly. LULU *makes a hurried effort to tidy the room. Then* CLAIRE *silently appears in the doorway. She is beautifully gowned and heavily veiled, except that her veil, in front, only comes to the tip of her nose.*

LULU: Oh!

CLAIRE (*advancing slowly and mysteriously*): Are we alone? Are we quite, quite alone?

LULU: I'm never quite sure in this house, but I think we are.

CLAIRE: May I take it that you are Mademoiselle Lulu d'Arville?

LULU: Of course you may.

CLAIRE: Then would you please close all the doors?

LULU (*doing so*): Certainly. You don't mind if we leave the window open, do you? It's a bit stuffy.

LULU *indicates the sofa, and* CLAIRE *sits down.*

CLAIRE: I have come to you on a mission of extreme delicacy.

LULU: Just fancy.

CLAIRE: It concerns a friend of mine.

LULU: A close friend?

CLAIRE: Very close.

LULU: Living in Paris?

CLAIRE: Yes.

LULU: Dark or fair?

CLAIRE: Dark.

LULU: Animal, vegetable or mineral?

CLAIRE: I beg your pardon?

LULU: Forgive me, I got carried away.

CLAIRE: I know this friend intimately. Her tenderest thoughts are like an open book to me—haven't I seen you somewhere before?

133

LULU: I don't think so. You may have, of course—I am out and about a great deal.

CLAIRE: Curious! I feel I know that lovely face. (*She frames it with one hand.*)

LULU: Here we go.

CLAIRE: What did you say?

LULU: Nothing—I was just thinking out loud.

CLAIRE: What a gift!

LULU: Please go on, I am all attention. This friend of yours—she is in trouble?

CLAIRE: She is in despair.

LULU: Oh dear.

CLAIRE: She is a married woman.

LULU: Poor thing. I'm beginning to understand—you have come to see me about her husband?

CLAIRE: On the contrary, I have come to see you about her lover.

LULU: Hurray! At last we're on home ground.

CLAIRE: If you knew, if you only knew, how much she loves him.

LULU: Your friend?

CLAIRE: My what? Oh yes, of course, my friend. He is the first, the only lover she has ever had.

LULU: The only one—what a slowcoach!

CLAIRE: Can you imagine what it is like for a married woman to take her first lover? The agony, the rapture, the ghastly battle with her conscience?

LULU: No, I don't believe I can.

CLAIRE (*shocked*): Do you mean to say you can't remember your first lover?

LULU: Oh yes, of course I can remember *that*. I meant I couldn't remember any particular battle with my conscience. (*Nostalgically.*) He came from Copenhagen

—my friends used to call him the Great Dane.

CLAIRE: How charming! I had a Great Dane once—he used to jump onto my bed every morning.

LULU: So did mine. Ah me! So much water has passed under the bridge since then.

CLAIRE: Yes, but for my friend, for my poor friend, it hasn't. This is her only love, the only love of her life. If she should lose him, her world would come to an end. (*She buries her face in her hands.*)

LULU (*gently*): Do you love him very much?

CLAIRE: Yes I do, I do, madly, passionately, with every fibre of my being. (*She suddenly puts her hand to her mouth.*) Oh! What have you made me say?

LULU: Couldn't you trust me? Please try. You don't know me, you may never see me again—no one need ever know.

CLAIRE: You are very kind—kinder than I dared to hope you would be.

LULU: I don't understand.

CLAIRE (*violently*): Swear to me it isn't true. Swear you won't take him away from me. . . .

LULU: What on earth are you talking about?

CLAIRE (*dramatically*): You who have the world at your feet—leave me the only man I crave.

LULU: All this would be much simpler, madame, if I had the faintest idea who *is* the man you crave.

CLAIRE: Marcel of course, Marcel Blanchard. (*She kneels.*) I beg you on my bended knees not to marry him.

LULU (*laughing*): But what makes you think I'd ever marry dear old Marcel?

PHILIPPE *enters.*

PHILIPPE: Am I intruding?

CLAIRE (*rising swiftly to her feet. To* LULU): Discretion!

135

Discretion, I implore you!

PHILIPPE (*bowing politely*): Good evening, madame.

LULU: May I present my friend, Philippe de Croze.

CLAIRE (*with an effort at control*): How do you do?

LULU: There has been a misunderstanding, Philippe.

PHILIPPE: Misunderstanding?

LULU: The Duchess is labouring under the delusion that I intend to marry Marcel Blanchard.

PHILIPPE: Marry Marcel? Good God!

LULU: Please reassure her—after all he's more your friend than mine.

PHILIPPE (*to* CLAIRE): But, madame, whatever gave you such an idea in the first place?

CLAIRE: I was with him this morning, while he was dressing, I—I happened to see a letter. . . .

LULU: Which you read?

CLAIRE: Naturally. It was a letter to Marcel from a Dutchman.

LULU: Very sinister.

CLAIRE: I have been in an emotional torment ever since.

LULU: But why should a letter to Marcel from a Dutchman upset you so much?

CLAIRE: He comes from the Hook.

LULU: I suppose that could be embarrassing.

CLAIRE: He is Marcel's godfather.

LULU: I still don't quite see why. . . .

CLAIRE: In his letter he congratulated Marcel on his forthcoming marriage to Mademoiselle Lulu d'Arville.

LULU: He must be dotty.

PHILIPPE: Did you question Marcel at all?

CLAIRE: No, I couldn't confess that I'd been reading his private letters.

PHILIPPE: Anyhow, there's nothing to worry about—Marcel was at school with me, he is my oldest friend, he tells me everything.

CLAIRE: Everything?

PHILIPPE: Yes.

CLAIRE: Has he ever mentioned me?

PHILIPPE (*after a slight pause*): Never.

CLAIRE: I knew it—I knew it. He doesn't really love me—to him I'm only a toy, the plaything of an idle hour. (*She weeps.*)

LULU: Cheer up dear, that's better than nothing.

CLAIRE: No, no, I refuse to be comforted. He doesn't love me—it was too good to be true.

PHILIPPE: I lied just now madame. Marcel has talked of you constantly, but as it was in the deepest confidence, I thought. . . .

CLAIRE (*eagerly*): Prove it—tell me what he said.

PHILIPPE: He has a private name for you, hasn't he—a love name?

CLAIRE: Yes, yes, go on—say it and I'll believe you.

LULU: Go on, give her the password.

PHILIPPE: Very well, here goes—'Pussy Willow'.

CLAIRE: Ah, thank heaven, thank heaven. I wronged him in my jealous heart. He cares for me after all.

PHILIPPE: Of course he does. And what is more, if I am not mistaken, you are none other than the Duchess de Clausonnes.

CLAIRE (*clasping and unclasping her hands*): How did you guess?

LULU: Philippe's intuition is at moments almost feminine.

CLAIRE (*dramatically throwing back her veil*): All my pitiful secrets are being torn from me one by one!

LULU: Calm yourself, madame.

CLAIRE (*to* PHILIPPE): If you are Marcel's best friend, you must be none other than Philippe de Croze.

PHILIPPE: Madame is almost clairvoyante.

CLAIRE: I am slightly confused. He told me you were on the Stock Exchange—I had no idea the uniform was so attractive.

PHILIPPE: Oh this! I am leaving tonight for Rouen, to do my twenty-eight days military service.

CLAIRE (*to* LULU): My poor child, you must try to be brave. (*The bell rings.*) Who can that be?

PHILIPPE: Probably a nun with a little box—the district's black with them.

ADONIS *appears.*

LULU: Not in here Adonis, whoever it is—in the library.

ADONIS: Righto. (*He goes.*)

CLAIRE: I suppose the evening is your busiest time?

LULU: There's sometimes a certain amount of light activity in the afternoons.

ADONIS (*reappearing*): It's Monsieur Blanchard!

CLAIRE: Marcel! My God! (*She quickly lowers her veil again.*)

ADONIS: He says he won't go into the library.

CLAIRE: I am lost—what shall I do? To be discovered here, in this house, at such an hour!

LULU: Madame, please. Everything will be all right, I assure you. He loves you—make yourself known to him, I beg of you.

MARCEL *enters cheerfully.*

MARCEL: Hullo, everybody. What's all this nonsense about a library?

LULU: Someone gave me a complete set of Balzac the

other day and I had to put it somewhere.

CLAIRE (*throwing back her veil*): Marcel! My darling!
My demon lover! Don't you recognise me?

MARCEL (*surprised*): My own Pussy Willow! (*He
flings himself at her, they embrace passionately. Then, after
a moment.*) But what are you doing here, in this house,
at such an hour?

CLAIRE: I can explain everything.

PHILIPPE (*to* MARCEL): First of all, Demon Lover,
you'd better do a bit of explaining yourself.

MARCEL: What do you mean?

PHILIPPE: What's all this about you getting married
to Lulu?

MARCEL: Me marry Lulu! Whoever suggested such
a thing?

CLAIRE: I did. Oh what have I unleashed! I came
upon a letter. . . .

MARCEL: A letter of mine? And you read it? For
shame, Pussy Willow!

CLAIRE: I was seated this morning at your bureau—
my fingers were wandering about idly and they must
have opened it by mistake.

MARCEL: You doubted me!

CLAIRE: One must believe the evidence of one's own
eyes, mustn't one?

MARCEL: Not when they are blinded by wicked
suspicion.

PHILIPPE: Never mind about all that for the moment
—get on with the explaining.

MARCEL: I admit I am in trouble.

CLAIRE: What trouble? Why, oh why didn't you tell
me—I would have walked barefoot through the streets
for you.

MARCEL: Then you'd better kick off your shoes and start straight away. I'm up to my ears in debt and I haven't got one single penny I can lay my hands on, not one.

LULU: Then I'm afraid marriage is out of the question. That is my decision.

MARCEL: But I've got twelve hundred thousand francs in the Bank.

LULU: I have reconsidered my decision.

MARCEL: But I can't touch it.

LULU: I have reconsidered it again.

MARCEL: Now look here Lulu, let's get this straight, once and for all. I don't *want* to marry you.

LULU: Why ever not?

MARCEL: I only want to *pretend* to marry you.

CLAIRE: This is all hideously confusing.

MARCEL: My dear old godfather is holding the money in trust until the day I marry, or rather the day he *thinks* I marry, Lulu.

CLAIRE: The gentleman from the Hook! I see it all now.

LULU: But why did you pick on me?

MARCEL: Because he wanted me to send him a photograph of my dear little bride to be, and yours was the first one that came to hand.

LULU: Not the one in the hammock with Mr. Mortimer?

PHILIPPE: Who the devil's Mr. Mortimer?

LULU: Just an Englishman passing through Paris on his way to Baden-Baden.

CLAIRE: To take the cure, I presume?

LULU: As far as I can remember, he needed it.

MARCEL (*to* LULU): You looked so innocent in the

picture. I thought you'd melt my godfather's heart.

LULU: How did you explain Mr. Mortimer?

MARCEL: I cut him out with the nail scissors.

PHILIPPE: Well, now all that's cleared up and settled
—I hope you'll forgive me if I ask you to leave. I have
a train to catch at midnight and I want a little time to say
good-bye to Lulu.

MARCEL: But it's far from settled.

LULU: Why not? Didn't your letter ring true?

MARCEL: It rang far too true, that's the trouble. He
was so delighted that he wanted to come to Paris to see
you for himself.

PHILIPPE: He must be stopped.

MARCEL: Too late. He's in Paris already, in fact he's
on his way here now.

LULU: I shall refuse to let him in.

MARCEL: You can't do that—think of my twelve
hundred thousand francs.

LULU: Why should I, if I'm not getting any of it?

MARCEL: Ten per cent commission, if you'll go
through with it. The old boy's leaving for America
almost immediately, so we'll pretend to have the wedding after he's gone.

LULU: What's ten per cent of twelve hundred
thousand?

CLAIRE: A hundred and twenty thousand, my darling!

LULU: Done! (*She and* MARCEL *shake hands. The bell
rings.*)

MARCEL: Here he is now.

LULU: You'd better put down your veil again dear.

CLAIRE (*doing so*): I must go anyhow—back to my
ancient Duke and his joyless mansion.

ADONIS (*appearing*): General Koschnadieff!

MARCEL: But that's not my godfather!

LULU: General who?

ADONIS: Koschnadieff.

LULU: It's certainly not a Dutch name. What does he want?

ADONIS: He says he's come all the way from Salestria.

LULU: Where on earth's that?

CLAIRE: I'm not sure, but I believe it's in the extreme North of Siberia.

LULU: Good heavens, the poor man must be freezing —show him in at once. (ADONIS *goes*.)

PHILIPPE: This is too much. You know we only have a little time before I catch my train. . . .

LULU: I can't refuse to see a General who's come across the Tundra and down all those frightful Steppes especially to see me.

PHILIPPE: But Lulu. . . .

LULU: Go on, there's a dear, and take Marcel with you. I shan't be more than a few minutes. You might change your trousers while you're at it.

CLAIRE (*to* LULU): Dear Child, I don't know how to thank you enough. I must return into the shadows where I belong—I suppose you haven't a tiny back staircase down which I can glide unperceived?

LULU: Certainly. Pop along that passage and take the second door on the right.

CLAIRE (*embracing her*): Until our paths cross again. (*To* MARCEL.) Au revoir my darling—may fortune smile on your dubious endeavours.

MARCEL: Now then, Pussy Willow, no bitterness. Until tomorrow.

CLAIRE (*dramatically*): Until tomorrow!

CLAIRE *goes*. MARCEL *and* PHILIPPE *retire into the*

bedroom. LULU *flies round the room putting things to rights.*
ADONIS *ushers in* GENERAL KOSCHNADIEFF, *who is
wearing a resplendent uniform with a foreign order and a
great many medals.* ADONIS *goes.*

LULU: Monsieur—I'm afraid I haven't the pleasure.

KOSCH: General Koschnadieff, madame. (LULU *indicates that he shall sit next to her on the sofa, but he respect-
fully declines, bowing again.*) General Koschnadieff, Aide-
de-camp in Chief to Prince Nicholas of Salestria. His
Royal Highness send me all this way to see you.

LULU: Have you come very far?

KOSCH: Two thousand miles, madame. First three
days I travel across freezing wastes in my Troika.

LULU: Are you sure you wouldn't like something
warm to drink?

KOSCH: No thank you, madame.

LULU: There's nothing like a hot toddy after a cold
troika.

KOSCH: The very sight of Madame has sufficiently
heated bloodstream.

LULU: Monsieur is too flattering. But why did His
Royal Highness send you on such a dangerous journey?

KOSCH: Because he is in love, madame. When you
are madly in love you do not care about safety of other
people.

LULU: How true. But what has all this to do with
me?

KOSCH: Because you are woman he is in love with!

LULU: I can't be. I've never been to Salestria. I've
never been further north than Ostend.

KOSCH: Ah, but Prince Nicholas has been Paris—you
remember State Visit eighteen months ago?

LULU: Well?

KOSCH: There was Gala Performance at Opera House —they give opera of 'Lakme', you are in box opposite Prince. You are only lady in box full of gentlemen. . . .

LULU: My life in a nutshell.

KOSCH: Well, Prince see you, gaze at you, fall in love at first sight.

LULU: Didn't he look at 'Lakme' at all?

KOSCH: Not at all. He ask President of France your name right in middle of Bell Song.

LULU: Did the President know it?

KOSCH: Only the first few phrases.

LULU: The coloratura part *is* fairly complicated.

KOSCH: Prince's spies have been on your track for eighteen months.

LULU: Really? How romantic!

KOSCH: Yes, Prince set vast machinery of Salestrian Secret Service in motion—whole army of ruthless determined men hunt you down like animal.

LULU: They always do.

KOSCH: Finally they unearth photograph of you.

LULU: Not the one on the Eiffel Tower with Mr. Mortimer?

KOSCH: The same. It had your address on the back of it.

LULU: What a coincidence.

KOSCH: When Prince see it he say 'Jump in Troika, go Paris.' Now we must get down business. Prince will be here before you say Noschko-nichtki Kolaschnick.

LULU: What does that mean?

KOSCH: Jack Robinson.

LULU: Just fancy! One lives and learns, doesn't one?

KOSCH: Only just now Prince say 'Koschnadieff,

jump in taxi and go Mademoiselle d'Arville.'

LULU: You must be in superb physical condition. All that jumping.

KOSCH (*continuing*): He say 'Tell her I come quick spend night with her.'

LULU: I'm afraid that is quite out of the question.

KOSCH (*aghast*): You mean you refuse Prince?

LULU: Certainly I do.

KOSCH: It has never been heard of before. No one ever refuse Prince's advances since he was little tiny boy.

LULU: He must have been very forward for his age.

KOSCH: He still is.

LULU: Then it's high time he grew out of it.

KOSCH: If it is question of—how shall I say? I know, I put it this way, His Royal Highness very generous man.

LULU: That is beside the point; the point is that I am not free to accept the Prince's attentions. I already have a gentleman friend to whom I am absolutely faithful.

KOSCH: But that make it much more exciting! You deceive lover with Prince of the Blood, make passion much more frantic. This lover, where is he now?

LULU: In there—he's just changing his trousers to go to Rouen.

KOSCH: Lover go Rouen! For how long lover go Rouen?

LULU: Twenty-eight days.

KOSCH: Then everything settled—I go tell Prince.

LULU: Everything is not settled, not quite. You said just now that the Prince is a very generous man. What exactly did you mean?

KOSCH: I tell you, Prince has very nice habit—after each visit he leave ten thousand francs under clock on mantelpiece.

LULU: Ten thousand francs! That's certainly a very nice habit indeed. After all, he *is* a Prince, and in a way it's an honour, almost a Royal Command.

KOSCH: Then perhaps little madame say Yes?

LULU: Perhaps little madame say Perhaps.

MARCEL (*rushing in from the bedroom*): Lulu! It's him! He's here! I've just seen him through the window!

LULU: The Prince? Already? What ardour!

MARCEL: Prince? What are you talking about? I mean my god-father, Herr Van Putzeboum. (*The bell rings.*) There he is now.

LULU: Well, you must look after him for a minute. I have to make a great decision.

MARCEL *rushes out. During the ensuing dialogue we shall see, through the partition,* ADONIS *conducting* VAN PUTZEBOUM. *The latter and* MARCEL *meet and embrace.* ADONIS *retires.*

KOSCH: I go now, jump into my fiacre, but I come back within the hour.

LULU: Au revoir General.

KOSCH: Au revoir mademoiselle. Kalnick eelo ninchavick patchnog.

LULU: I'm sure you say that to every girl you meet!

KOSCHNADIEFF *leaves.* MARCEL *comes in, preceding* VAN PUTZEBOUM.

MARCEL: Godfather dear, may I present. . . .

VAN P.: Ach no, pliss not be tellink me, let me be guessink. Das ist—der leetle one—Mademoiselle d'Arville, thine leetle brite to be? (*He goes to* LULU, *kisses her hand.*)

LULU: We have all heard *so* much about you.

VAN P.: You will be forgivink mein lankwich pliss—

I was beink born in Stuttgart, but now I am commink from der Hook.

LULU: Perhaps you'd like something to drink? There's nothing like dry sherry after a damp Hook.

VAN P. (*to* MARCEL): But thine fiancee is charmink, wairy charmink, like ein leetle snowdrop.

LULU: What a sweet thing to say—thank you, godfather dear.

VAN P.: Already she calls me gottfader! You hear dat?

MARCEL: Well Lulu, aren't you going to kiss your new godfather? You're almost one of the family now, you know?

VAN P.: Der leetle snowdrop is givink me ein kiss? (LULU *hesitates.*) Ach, she is showink her modesty. I am understandink, she is beink fiancee for der first time, she is not knowink der men before. (LULU *offers her cheek.*) Her cheek is like ein rose petal. Iss goot, kissink ein womans who is always being chaste.

LULU: Who told him?

VAN P.: Und now, leetle one, iss time I gif you mein weddink present.

LULU: A present for me? What is it, godfather dear?

VAN P.: Iss not moch. Iss only beink ein diamont necklace. (*He takes a scarlet case out of his inside pocket.*)

LULU: A diamond necklace! But I have done nothing to deserve it.

VAN P.: Ja, ja, you are doink moch. You are making mein gottson wairy, wairy happy. (*He presents her with the case.*)

LULU (*opening the case*): Oh do look, Marcel! Isn't it beautiful! (*To* VAN PUTZEBOUM.) Thank you a thousand times, godfather dear. Are they being diamonds of the first water?

VAN P.: All iss of der wairy first water. Und der grosse diamont, hangink from der end, iss beink ein solitaire.

LULU: Poor thing. (*She puts on the necklace.*)

VAN P.: Diamonts iss not really right for innocent young madchen—but leetle snowdrop become married woman wairy soon now.

MARCEL: Ja, and on der wairy same day, I become wairy rich man.

VAN P. Iss better really I give pouquet of peautiful flowers for innocent young madchen.

LULU (*quickly*): Oh no, godfather dear, not flowers— I always think diamonds last longer, don't you?

VAN P.: Haf you not been receivink der grosse pouquet I send you from der florist round der corner?

LULU: Are you giving me flowers as well? I shall become thoroughly spoiled. No, I haven't received them yet, godfather dear.

VAN P.: Ach, dat florist, dere has been ein grosse mix-up. Perhaps you will be letting me use der telephone; you haf telephone, nein?

LULU: Certainly I have a telephone—I find it most useful. I keep it in the bedroom.

VAN P. Ach, dat florist round der corner! I say to him 'You are knowink Mademoiselle d'Arville?' He say 'Ja, I am knowink Mademoiselle d'Arville, she is livink mit Philippe de Croze' I say 'Nein, nein, I am talking of Mademoiselle Lulu d'Arville, der fiancee of mein gottson.'

PHILIPPE (*coming in from the bedroom*): There we are, I've changed my trousers. That looks better, doesn't it?

VAN P.: You will kindly present der chentleman?

MARCEL (*losing his head*): What? Oh yes, certainly. This is Monsieur . . . Monsieur. . . .

LULU: Chopart.

PHILIPPE: Who?

LULU (*firmly*): Chopart. Paul—Paul Chopart, my cousin from Fontainebleau.

VAN P.: Ach, so you woss commink from Fontainebleau?

PHILIPPE: Well, I wasn't actually. Actually I was *going* to Rouen.

VAN P.: Der cousin of mademoiselle! You haf all mein compliments. I am Jacob Putzeboum, from der Hook. (*They shake hands.*)

PHILIPPE: How do you do?

MARCEL (*nervously*): Come along, godfather dear. This way for the telephone. (*He takes* VAN PUTZEBOUM *towards the bedroom door.*)

VAN P.: I will be giving der florist what for! (*He goes into the bedroom.*)

PHILIPPE: What florist is he talking about?

LULU: The one who's sending me the basket of flowers.

PHILIPPE: What basket of flowers? It's the first I've heard about it.

LULU: Oh really! What is the matter with you tonight? Don't you understand? That was why I had to say you were my cousin—Paul Chopart from Fontainebleau.

PHILIPPE: No, I don't understand. I don't understand anything any more.

MARCEL: Never mind, it'll soon be over. You'll be off to Rouen, the old boy off to America, I shall be a rich man, and you can have your name back.

PHILIPPE: Thank you.

VAN P. (*appearing at the bedroom door*): Mademoiselle, help me pliss. I get through to florist, but iss wairy bad connection. So sawry. (*He disappears.*)

LULU (*going towards the bedroom*): (*As she passes* PHILIPPE.) Oh, I nearly forgot. You haven't seen my new diamond necklace, have you?

PHILIPPE: Oh yes, I have. I was nearly blinded by it as a matter of fact. Where did you get *that*, I should like to know?

LULU (*cooingly*): My precious angel! (*She gives him a kiss.*) It was a present from my new godfather. To his little snowdrop! (*She gives a saucy little backward kick and disappears into the bedroom.*)

PHILIPPE: That exit was too skittish. She's up to something.

MARCEL (*soothingly*): Merely high spirits.

PHILIPPE: I don't like any of this; and it's all your fault. Is that old bore really your godfather?

MARCEL: Of course he is. And when he's gone to America Lulu will have ten per cent of twelve hundred thousand francs *and* a diamond necklace. What's wrong with that?

PHILIPPE: I tell you I don't like it.

MARCEL: For God's sake be reasonable. We're old friends, after all—you can trust me.

PHILIPPE (*ranging about the room*): I wish I didn't have to go away.

MARCEL: Cheer up, twenty-eight days isn't very long. It'll go in a flash and when you come back I shall be a rich man and we can celebrate.

PHILIPPE: Can I really trust you Marcel?

MARCEL: Of course you can.

PHILIPPE: If I agree to all this intrigue about you and Lulu and your godfather, will you make me a promise in return?

MARCEL: Certainly—anything you like.

PHILIPPE: I'm worried about Lulu. I really am very fond of her, you know.

MARCEL: Of course.

PHILIPPE: And I don't like leaving her alone and unprotected.

MARCEL: Very understandable.

PHILIPPE: Please don't imagine for a moment that I don't trust her absolutely.

MARCEL: Perish the thought.

PHILIPPE: But she is indubitably on the flighty side.

MARCEL: Indubitably.

PHILIPPE: Therefore all I ask of you is this—when I am gone will you, as my greatest friend, look after her?

MARCEL: Is *that* all? Why of course I will—with the greatest pleasure.

PHILIPPE: Pay her little friendly attentions. Take her to the Zoo.

MARCEL: Certainly, if she hasn't already been. I'd make any sacrifice for you, you know that.

PHILIPPE: I don't think she's ever done the Louvre really thoroughly, and there's always Napoleon's Tomb.

MARCEL: Alas yes.

PHILIPPE: I can rely on you?

MARCEL: To the tomb.

PHILIPPE: Dear old friend! Look after Lulu!

They shake hands warmly, then separate. LULU *and* VAN PUTZEBOUM *come out of the bedroom.*

VAN P.: Telephone iss no goot connection—it make growling and snarling but no voice come. I think best maybe I go round corner for seeing florist myself. Would you be commink mit me, Marcel?

MARCEL: Of course, godfather dear.

VAN P. (*to* LULU): Back in a twinklink we will be commink.

LULU: You are too kind to me—everybody's too kind to me. It's really wearing me out.

VAN P.: Auf weidersehen, mein liebchen.

LULU: By all means.

MARCEL *and* VAN PUTZEBOUM *go*.

PHILIPPE: Damn Marcel, damn his godfather, damn everything.

LULU (*going to him*): Don't be angry, my precious angel.

PHILIPPE: We haven't had one minute together all the evening.

LULU: Well we've got one now, so let's make the most of it. (*She kisses him fondly*.)

PHILIPPE: Do you realise that for the next twenty-eight days I shall be living like a monk?

LULU: I've never been quite sure how monks *do* live —apart from having their heads shaved and making those delicious liqueurs.

PHILIPPE: I love you, Lulu.

LULU: I love you too—and now Fate is tearing us asunder. Life can be terribly cruel, can't it?

PHILIPPE: If only we were on a desert island, away from it all.

LULU (*dreamily*): Like the Swiss Family Robinson.

PHILIPPE: I could build you a house with my bare hands of palm and wattle.

LULU (*kissing him*): What's wattle?

PHILIPPE: A sort of flowering shrub. And I could

come home to you every evening at sunset with a lot of fish.

LULU: How beautiful.

PHILIPPE: And we could lie together in each other's arms under a Frangipani.

LULU: What's that?

PHILIPPE: Another flowering shrub. And millions of tropical stars would come out one by one.

LULU: Wouldn't that take rather a long time?

PHILIPPE: Time wouldn't exist. (*The bell rings.*)

LULU: Well it does now, dear, and we're wasting it.

She takes him by the hand and leads him into the bedroom.

GIGOT *enters from the anteroom in time to see them disappear.* ADONIS *comes in.*

ADONIS: This way boys, this way.

GIGOT: Which boys? What's happening?

ADONIS: They're from the florist's shop round the corner.

Enter TWO FLORIST'S BOYS *in messengers' uniform. They are carrying, one on each side of it, an immense basket of flowers which they eventually put down near the card table. They are followed by* MARCEL *and* VAN PUTZEBOUM.

GIGOT (*very bewildered*): What's going on?

VAN P.: Where woss mein leetle snowdrop? Who is dis chentleman beink?

MARCEL: He is being your little snowdrop's father.

VAN P.: But diss iss wunderbar! (*He shakes* GIGOT'S *hand like a pump handle.*) You are a most lucky man!

The doorbell rings.

ADONIS: There's that damned doorbell again! (*He goes.*)

All the Guests troop in.

YVONNE: Where's Lulu? She hasn't eaten a thing!

GIGOT: She's in the bedroom, making an important telephone call.

VAN P.: Ach, dat telephone—we must hope dat she iss makink der goot connection.

PAULETTE (*seeing the flowers*): Oh, what gorgeous blooms!

YVONNE: Where did they come from?

VAN P.: Dey are for mein leetle gott-daughter to be.

BOMBA: Which little god-daughter?

VALERY: What does he mean?

MARCEL: This is my godfather everybody. Herr Van Putzeboum, from the Hook.

ADONIS (*announcing grandly*): His Royal Highness Prince Nicholas of Salestria!

GIGOT: Royal Highness? Prince? In this house! Where have you put him?

ADONIS: I haven't put him anywhere—he's coming up the stairs.

YVONNE: Fancy! Royalty—at this time of night!

GIGOT: Quickly, we must keep our heads. This is a great moment. A Royal prince and we're not ready for him. (*To the* FLORIST'S BOYS.) Come here, boy, you stand there. And you stand there, boy. (*To* MARCEL.) You stand there. (*To* VAN PUTZEBOUM.) And you stand there. (*Thus forming a guard of honour by the doorway. Then, rushing to the piano.*) We must light the candles! Where are the matches. Adonis, boy, don't just stand there, light the candles!

ADONIS: Whatever for?

GIGOT: Because we're receiving royalty, fathead. (ADONIS *lights the candles.*) Are the flowers in position? Are you all in position? My God, we should have a band! (*He rushes to the gramophone and puts on the record of the Marseillaise.*) Now I think we're ready. (*He looks round to make sure.*) Adonis! You may show in His Royal Highness.

ADONIS *goes.* GIGOT *goes to the doorway, facing out, holding the candelabrum. The Marseillaise begins, then, after a slight pause,* GIGOT *begins to back into the room with great dignity, preceding* THE PRINCE, *who is followed by* KOSCHNADIEFF, *with* ADONIS *bringing up the rear. The guard of honour bows as* THE PRINCE *walks slowly by,* YVONNE *and* PAULETTE *curtsey.* BOMBA *and* VALERY *bow.*

PRINCE: So kind, so kind—but I did not expect a party.

GIGOT (*bowing low*): We are honoured indeed, Your Highness.

PRINCE: Who is this gentleman, Koschnadieff? Who are all these people? Kindly explain.

GIGOT: I am the father of Mademoiselle Lulu d'Arville, Your Highness.

PRINCE: Are you indeed. And why are you holding a candlestick? Were you about to go to bed?

GIGOT: No, Your Highness, no—the candles are in your honour.

PRINCE: So kind, so kind—we are most grateful. The flowers also?

GIGOT (*embarrassed*): Well, Your Highness, as a matter of fact. . . .

PRINCE: Most thoughtful. Where *is* your delightful daughter?

GIGOT: She is in her bedroom, Your Highness.

PRINCE: Already? How flattering. We are most touched.

GIGOT: She is making an important telephone call.

I will go and bring her at once. (*He backs towards the bedroom door, opens the door, which is immediately slammed in his face.* THE PRINCE *meanwhile chats nonchalantly to* KOSCHNADIEFF. GIGOT *tries the handle, then taps on the door.*

LULU'S VOICE: For goodness sake, go away and leave us in peace!

PHILIPPE (*appearing in the doorway in a bath towel*): There is absolutely no admittance—no admittance whatsoever! (*He quickly retires and shuts the door.*)

GIGOT: My God, what shall I do? (*He pulls himself together and goes back to* THE PRINCE.) I am afraid there has been a slight hitch. I shall have to beg Your Highness to wait for a moment in the anteroom. I'm so sorry for the delay.

PRINCE: The night is young. There is no hurry. There is no hurry at all.

GIGOT: Then perhaps Your Highness will step this way.

The Marseillaise swells to a crescendo, GIGOT *picks up the candelabrum again then, bowing, he leads the way. The others fall in behind the* PRINCE *and the whole imposing procession marches slowly out again.*

CURTAIN

ACT II

Murcel's bedroom. Downstage left is a large window in a recess, deep enough to hold a banquette (or window seat) and not interfere with the curtains when they are drawn. The curtains should have tie-backs, not necessarily in use, long enough and pretty enough for LULU *to use as sash for her dress when needed. Further up on the left is a large bed at an angle so that the bottom of the bed and the left hand side of it are visible to the audience. On the left side of the bed is a chair and on the right a night table.*

Centre back is the main door; this door, though facing the audience, is round a corner from, and further upstage than the bed, so that an occupant of the bed could not see it.

To the right of the door is a console table. Further down right is the fireplace with a looking glass above the mantel, and downstage right is the door to the bathroom.

Towards the right of centre stage is a writing table, placed at an angle. There is a chair at the desk and in front of the desk is a sofa. This group of objects must be out of the way of a straight line drawn from the bed to the bathroom door.

Above the night table is a small reading light, controlled from the bed by a hanging switch. Also a hanging push for an electric bell. Also a switch for the centre ceiling light. On the night table should be a tumbler or vase

*holding water. On the table-desk are writing materials, a
candlestick and an evening dress rolled up.*

*On the console table are Lulu's hat and a grotesque
mask.*

> *The window curtains are still drawn and the room
> is almost dark, lit only by the light burning above the
> bed.* MARCEL *is fast asleep, breathing somewhat
> heavily. He turns once or twice. A pause. There is
> a knock at the door, then the door opens and* ROSE,
> *the maid, brings in his coffee on a tray. She is pretty
> and smartly dressed in maid's uniform, but is apple-
> cheeked and from the country. She goes and puts the
> tray down and then goes to the bedside.*

ROSE: Monsieur Marcel! (*Silence. Then louder.*) Monsieur Marcel! (*Silence. She shouts.*) Monsieur Marcel!
(*There is a slight sound of life.*) It's half past twelve. (*Another sound.*) It's nearly lunch time—it's twelve-thirty-
five.

MARCEL (*dreamily*): I don't care if it's twenty-five
minutes to one.

ROSE (*returning to the charge*): I have brought you your
coffee sir.

MARCEL (*jumping up, furious*): What did you say you'd
done?

ROSE: I only said I'd brought your coffee sir.

MARCEL: How dare you bring me my coffee at this
ungodly hour?

ROSE: I'm sorry if I'm late sir, I'm sure.

MARCEL: Late! Do you realise that dawn is only just
breaking over the city?

ROSE: Is it sir?

MARCEL: What did you say your name was?

ROSE: Rose, sir.

MARCEL: How long have you been with me, Rose?

ROSE: Since ten o'clock yesterday morning.

MARCEL: Then you should have got used to my ways by now. You'll have to pull up your socks, Rose.

ROSE: Very good, sir. (*She gives him the tray.*)

MARCEL: You'd also better pull the curtains.

ROSE: Certainly, sir.

MARCEL: Has the dawn actually broken yet?

ROSE (*draws the curtains, sunlight streams into the room*): Oh yes, it's been fairly light ever since five o'clock.

MARCEL: Five o'clock in the morning! How could you possibly know?

ROSE: In my Auntie's house I always got up at five. There were a hundred and twenty pullets to feed, two cows to be milked and Bidi Bom Bom to be curry-combed.

MARCEL: Who the devil was Bidi Bom Bom?

ROSE: A horse, of course.

MARCEL: You will find life with me less agricultural.

ROSE: I'm sure I shall sir.

MARCEL: You'll have to change your rhythm.

ROSE: I'll do my best, sir. (*She goes.*)

MARCEL *rolls about luxuriously in the bed. Finally one of his feet touch an object at the bottom of the bed. He gives a loud cry, then jumps to a kneeling position.*

MARCEL: Good God! Whatever's that? (*He lifts the bedclothes a little and peers down.*) Oh, it's you Roger—you bad boy! What are you doing in the bed—you know perfectly well that's not allowed. (*Wheedling.*) Come along then, there's a good dog—how often has father told you. (*Sternly.*) *Roger!* Come out of there at once sir—otherwise no walky-walky.

He leans over and rings the bell which can be heard in the distance. There is an upheaval under the bedclothes and he throws them back a little. Eventually LULU *emerges. She stretches her arms, then rubs her eyes.*

LULU: Good morning.

MARCEL: Good God! What are you doing here?

LULU: I have no idea—don't *you* know?

MARCEL: How did you get here?

LULU: Don't you know that either? Because I'm sure I don't—I don't even know *when* I got here.

MARCEL: You must go away at once. Supposing someone were to come in and see you! (*There is a knock at the door.*) There you are, what did I tell you?

MARCEL *quickly puts a pillow over* LULU'S *head and leans an elbow on it nonchalantly.* ROSE *comes in.*

ROSE: Did you want me, sir?

MARCEL: Yes, I did, Rose. I wanted you to take Roger away and tie him up in the garden.

ROSE: But I just left Roger in the kitchen, sir—he's having his boudoir biscuits.

MARCEL: Then there's no need for us to worry, is there Rose?

ROSE: Are you feeling quite well sir?

MARCEL: Of course I am. Why?

ROSE: I merely wondered, sir.

She goes. MARCEL *removes the pillow and shakes* LULU.

MARCEL: Lulu, please, please wake up.

LULU: Oh Marcel, how can you be so cruel—when I'm feeling so sleepy?

MARCEL: We are in a critical situation.

LULU: Marcel, before we go any further I want you to tell me one thing truthfully. What are you doing in my bed, you naughty boy?

MARCEL: But I'm not in your bed—you're in mine.

LULU: Am I? So I am! (*Looking round.*) What a lovely room—I had no idea you had such charming taste. I love that little chest of drawers—is it Louis Quinze?

MARCEL: No, Seize.

LULU: I knew it must be one of those Louis.

MARCEL: How long have you been here?

LULU: How do I know? I've been fast asleep.

MARCEL: This is terrible.

LULU: You don't mean . . . you don't suppose . . . that we actually spent the night together?

MARCEL: We cannot rule out that possibility.

LULU: Oh Marcel! How disgraceful! I *wonder* if we did?

MARCEL: I suppose there's nobody we could ask?

LULU: I can't remember. My head feels fuzzy. Oh dear!

MARCEL: We ought to be ashamed of ourselves.

LULU: Only if we're sure there's something to be ashamed of.

MARCEL: What is Philippe going to say when he finds out that I've betrayed his confidence?

LULU: Don't tell him. What the eye doesn't see the heart doesn't grieve over.

MARCEL: How can you, Lulu? That's a very immoral attitude to take.

LULU: But very sensible. What's the use of stirring up trouble?

MARCEL: When I think of the night he went away, and how he said so trustingly 'Look after Lulu for me. Watch over her. Take her to the Zoo.'

LULU (*dreamily*): Did he really say that?

MARCEL: Yes. He also mentioned the Louvre and Napoleon's Tomb.

LULU: He must love me to distraction.

MARCEL (*getting out of bed and striding about the room. He is wearing a nightshirt*): How could we have got ourselves into such a frightful situation?

LULU: I haven't the faintest idea.

MARCEL (*clasping his head*): If only I could remember. What did we do exactly?

LULU (*she gets out of bed and then goes and sits on the end of it.* MARCEL *joins her*): I know that first of all we had two or three bottles of champagne with Bomba and the girls. Then we all went up to Montmartre to the fair. . . .

MARCEL: And bought funny masks to frighten everybody. . . .

LULU: And a box of fireworks.

MARCEL: What did we do with the fireworks?

LULU: We all went to the Dead Rat and I let them off in the ladies' cloakroom. Then after the police had gone, we went to the Mad Virgin and had some more champagne and then to the Three Snails and had some more champagne and then we went to old Madame Popodopolus and had ouzo and crème de menthe.

MARCEL: Ouzo! My head's going round!

LULU: I'm not surprised.

MARCEL: How did we get back here?

LULU: Because I fell down in the Place Pigalle and you said you had some ammonia.

MARCEL: And did I?

LULU: No—but you had some more champagne instead.

MARCEL: Why did we have it in the bedroom?

LULU: Because it was where you thought the ammonia was, but it wasn't.

MARCEL: Well, now that we've got everything explained I feel better.

LULU: I don't. I feel awful. (*She gets into bed again.*)

MARCEL: None of that. You must find your clothes and go into the dressing room and put them on.

LULU: Don't bully me. I want to go to sleep for ever and ever and ever.

MARCEL: Where did you put your dress?

LULU: I don't know—it sort of left me.

MARCEL (*He puts on the mask, and claps Lulu's hat on the top of it. LULU laughs*):
Ah, here it is. I've found it.

LULU: Where?

MARCEL: On the table.

LULU: What a funny place for it to be.

MARCEL: You'd better put it on.

LULU: I shall do no such thing. I never wear evening dress before breakfast.

MARCEL (*he takes off the hat, then picks up her dress, out of the folds of which falls a small, longish box*): What's this?

LULU: What's what? I wish you'd stop asking me questions—my head's splitting.

MARCEL: This box.

LULU: It's the remains of the fireworks from last night. (*She jumps out of bed.*) Shall we have a tiny display? Just to celebrate?

MARCEL: I've done enough celebrating to last me for years. (*He goes into the bathroom.*)

ROSE *suddenly comes in. She is holding some letters and a ball of string.*

LULU (*she snatches up her dress and holds it in front of her*): Oh!

ROSE: Did you wish to see Monsieur Blanchard, madame?

LULU (*with assurance*): Yes, please. I just happened to be passing. Is he at home?

ROSE: I'm not quite sure, madame. He was, a moment ago.

LULU: Have you been with him long?

ROSE: Since yesterday, madame.

LULU: I'm sure you'll be very happy here. (*She looks round.*) Such exquisite taste—look at that dear little Louis Seize chest of drawers, for example.

ROSE: Louis Quinze, madame.

LULU: You are interested in very old furniture?

ROSE: Oh yes, madame.

LULU: You should see my apartment—it's crammed with it.

MARCEL *comes back, without the mask, sees* ROSE, *gives a start, then runs to* LULU, *grabs her dress which he holds in front of him to hide them both.* LULU *and he are back to back.*

MARCEL: Well Rose, what is it now?

ROSE: There's a lady to see you.

MARCEL: A lady? Who is she?

ROSE: She gave no name sir.

MARCEL: How very mysterious. What did she look like?

ROSE: Charming, sir, and very well dressed. She said she'd call again, just on the chance.

MARCEL: Very good, Rose—you're doing beautifully.

ROSE: I aim to please sir.

MARCEL: What's all that?

ROSE: The letters sir—the concierge just brought them up. And the ball of string you asked me to get last night.

MARCEL: A ball of string! Why did I ask you to get a ball of string?

ROSE: A house is not a home, sir, without string.

MARCEL: How right you are. I think you'd better go now—as you see, I am very busy.

ROSE: Oh yes, sir, I can see that clearly. (*She goes.*)

MARCEL: That girl's an absolute treasure—so imperturbable.

LULU: Did she come to you with good references?

MARCEL: Excellent.

LULU: She'll probably go away with a few more.

MARCEL: Do hurry up Lulu, and put on your dress. You really must leave the house as soon as possible.

LULU: I can't.

MARCEL: Why not?

LULU: I can't be seen in the street in evening dress at this time of day, can I?

MARCEL: Go on the Metro.

LULU: What would people think?

MARCEL: Merely that you were on your way to see Tristan and Isolde.

LULU: You and your grand friends—I don't even *know* Tristan and Isolde.

MARCEL: It's just as well—they're a bit loud.

LULU: I shall write a note to father and ask him to pop round with a coat and skirt. (*She goes to the writing table and starts to write.*)

MARCEL: All right, only hurry up.

165

LULU: That maid of yours can take it.

MARCEL (*reading his mail*): I've had a letter from my Aunt Gabrielle.

LULU: What does she say?

MARCEL: She's lost her poor old Schnauzer.

LULU (*absently*): She's probably better off without it.

MARCEL (*looking over her shoulder*): What have you said?

LULU (*reading*): I've said 'My Dear Little Father, I am at Marcel Blanchard's, 3 Avenue Matignan. Please bring me a coat and skirt. A thousand kisses. Lulu.' Will that do?

MARCEL: Very concise. It says exactly what you mean to say and no more.

LULU: Now for the address. Inspector Gigot, 120 rue de Rivoli.

MARCEL: My God, this is awful!

LULU: What is?

MARCEL: A letter from my godfather.

LULU: He's certainly a keen letter writer.

MARCEL: It starts 'Mein liebe Patenkind' . . . he was born in Stuttgart, you know.

LULU: Yes I know—but now he is commink from der Hook.

MARCEL (*reading*): 'I am making you a big surprise. I am beink in Paris since this morning most early and am meaning to come and see you this afternoon.'

LULU: Well, that's pretty concise too.

MARCEL: That's not all, there's a postcript. (*He reads.*) 'Tonight I will be giving the little dinner for you and your fiancée and her father.'

LULU: You'll have to refuse. I can't possibly come.

MARCEL: Why not?

LULU: Because I already have a most important dinner engagement.

MARCEL: Who with?

LULU (*wildly*): Dear old Madame Dupont. Her leg's in a plaster cast so I can't possibly let her down.

MARCEL: You'll have to, this is terribly important to all of us. You must back me up—after all the old boy did give you a diamond necklace.

LULU: Oh all right, but it's very tiresome. It means I shall have to write another letter. (*She starts to write.*)

MARCEL (*after a pause*): Why is her leg in a plaster cast?

LULU: Why is who's leg in what?

MARCEL: Dear old Madame Dupont's of course.

LULU: I don't know. It always has been—ever since she was a tiny tot.

MARCEL: You're lying, Lulu.

LULU: How can I concentrate when you keep asking silly questions?

MARCEL: Who are you really supposed to be dining with?

LULU: With His Royal Highness The Prince of Salestria, so there.

MARCEL (*shocked*): Oh Lulu! And I promised Philippe to protect you from that kind of thing.

LULU: Nonsense. You only promised to take me to the Zoo. Ring the bell, there's a dear.

MARCEL (*doing so*): There's no doubt about it—women were deceivers ever.

LULU: Don't stand there moralising in your night shirt. Here's the letter. Be careful, the ink isn't dry. You'd better blow on it.

MARCEL (*he does so*): Now the envelope.

167

LULU: Blow on that too.

He blows on it and, without looking, picks up the letter to Gigot, puts it in the envelope and seals it. LULU *does the same with the remaining letter and envelope. There is a knock at the door.* ROSE *comes in.*

ROSE: You rang sir?

MARCEL: Yes, Rose. I want you to take this letter to the rue de Rivoli and this one to the Hotel Continental just round the corner.

ROSE: Can I take Roger sir? He hasn't had his walky-walky yet and the kitchen's beginning to look rather untidy.

MARCEL: By all means.

ROSE (*smilingly, to* LULU): I see you called again after all, madame.

LULU: Yes Rose. I just happened to be in the neighbourhood.

ROSE *goes off.*

MARCEL: That girl's getting brighter every minute.

LULU: Yes. I'd like to throttle her. (*She gets into bed.*) I really must lie down again while I'm waiting for Daddy —I'm exhausted.

A bell rings. She jumps up again.

MARCEL: Who can that be?

LULU: Probably Tristan and Isolde.

ROSE'S VOICE: Were you looking for the Master, madame?

CLAIRES VOICE: Yes, I am, but please dont announce me, I want to surprise him.

LULU: It's the Duchess!

MARCEL: She surprised me all right.

LULU: What shall we do—this is dreadful. She mustn't find me here!

MARCEL: You must hide.

LULU: Where?

MARCEL: Under the bed. (LULU *starts to get under the bed.* MARCEL *gives her a push from behind with his foot.*) Go on—right under!

MARCEL *rushes to the window and draws the curtains. The room is now in darkness. He regains the bed with one leap and lies flat. The door opens a little, letting in a shaft of light from the passage outside.* CLAIRE'S *head appears.*

CLAIRE: Coo-hoo! May I come in?

MARCEL: It depends who it is.

CLAIRE: But don't you know who it is? Can't you tell by the beating of your heart?

MARCEL: Don't tell me it's my own little Pussy Willow!

CLAIRE: It is! It is! (*She rushes to the bedside and gropes about for* MARCEL, *feels his face.*) Oh, now I've poked my finger in your lovely blue eye!

MARCEL: Don't worry. Actually it was my lovely blue mouth.

CLAIRE: My darling!

MARCEL: My darling!

LULU (*Under the bed*): My foot!

CLAIRE: What was that?

LULU: It's gone to sleep.

MARCEL: What was what?

CLAIRE: I heard something.

MARCEL: Perhaps it was a mouse.

CLAIRE (*screaming*): A mouse!

MARCEL: Yes, they sometimes creep in from the fields.

CLAIRE: What fields?

MARCEL: The Champs Elysées.

CLAIRE: If there's a mouse in the house I shall scream the place down.

MARCEL: There, there. Keep calm my darling—fancy a great big Pussy Willow being afraid of a tiny mouse.

CLAIRE: I *am* afraid of tiny mice and it's no good pretending I'm not. Switch on the light, I beg of you.

MARCEL: It's by you—over the table.

CLAIRE *feels about for the switch, and knocks over the ball of string which rolls under the bed.* (*The ball of string doesn't actually fall,* CLAIRE *can slip it behind the bolster and let it drop to the floor, so that* LULU *can get it when needed.*)

CLAIRE: Now what have I knocked over? It's gone under the bed. (*She gets down on her knees and starts to get under the bed.*)

MARCEL: Leave it, leave it—it's only a ball of string.

CLAIRE: Why do you have a ball of string by your bed, my angel?

MARCEL: For tying up my Christmas presents.

CLAIRE: But it's only the tenth of June!

MARCEL (*he pulls her up*): I always do my Christmas shopping early because of the crowds.

LULU: Now my other foot's dropped off.

CLAIRE: There's that same noise.

MARCEL: It's probably the same mouse.

CLAIRE: I can't bear it.

MARCEL: I expect the poor little thing's panic stricken.

CLAIRE: So am I. I shall have to get into bed. (*She quickly takes off her coat and starts to undo her dress.*)

MARCEL: Oh no, you mustn't do that!—I'll get out

instead. (*He starts to get out but she pushes him back by the legs.*)

CLAIRE: Don't you want your little Pussy Willow to come into bed with you?

MARCEL: Yes, of course I do—it would be lovely, only. . . .

CLAIRE: Only what?

MARCEL: There's no need. I'll put on the light, then you won't feel frightened any more.

He presses the switch, which lights the ceiling light, not the little light over the bed.

CLAIRE: All the same I'd rather get into bed.

LULU: There's nothing like the direct approach.

CLAIRE: Oh, now it sounds louder, it must be a rat.

MARCEL: They sometimes creep in from the catacombs. (*She flies to the bed and gets into it.*) No, no, you mustn't do that! (*He jumps out the other side.*) Let's both go into the dressing room.

LULU: Hurray!

CLAIRE: Marcel, you've got to do something about that horrid rat. Why don't you send for Roger to come and chase it away?

MARCEL: Because he's gone to the rue de Rivoli with a letter.

CLAIRE: What a clever dog he is.

LULU *has been tugging at the counterpane on* MARCEL'S *side of the bed to attract his attention—she eventually gets hold of his wrist and gives it a tug, so that he falls from his kneeling position, with his legs in the air.*

CLAIRE: Now what's the matter?

MARCEL: Nothing—nothing. I'm just doing my exercises. (*He pedals with his legs.*) You ought to try it.

If you'd do this fifty times a day you'd soon have legs like tree trunks.

LULU: She's got those already.

It can now be seen that LULU *has found the ball of string and is tying it to the counterpane.*

MARCEL (*to* CLAIRE): What are you doing?

CLAIRE: I'm going to turn on this little light and turn out the others. (*She does so.*) Then I'm coming to bed. I'm so tired—I had such a bad night last night.

LULU: So did we.

CLAIRE: I had the most horrible nightmares. I kept waking up shaking like a leaf.

LULU: Jelly.

CLAIRE: What did you say?

MARCEL: I didn't say anything.

CLAIRE: Yes, you did—you said 'Jelly'.

MARCEL: Why should I say 'Jelly'.

CLAIRE: There's something odd about you this morning. You seem distrait.

MARCEL: Nonsense, I'm perfectly calm.

LULU: Cool as a cucumber.

MARCEL: What did you say?

CLAIRE: I didn't say anything.

MARCEL: I distinctly heard you say something about a cucumber.

CLAIRE: Oh my darling, that's pure hysteria. Perhaps I'm still dreaming. Perhaps this is still part of the nightmare. Perhaps I'm not here at all. Pinch me, my angel.

MARCEL: If you insist. (*He pinches her.*)

CLAIRE (*a little scream*): Oh!

CLAIRE: I've had a dreadful sense of impending doom ever since three-thirty this morning.

MARCEL: Why three-thirty?

CLAIRE: It was then that I saw the apparition.

MARCEL: Apparition?

CLAIRE: It was a tall figure in a long white robe, waving it's arms.

MARCEL: Perhaps it was the Duke, putting on his nightshirt.

LULU: Or taking it off.

CLAIRE: And for the whole rest of the night I was tormented by strange noises and movements. All the objects in my bedroom seemed to take on a sinister life of their own. (LULU *pulls the counterpane by little jerks until it falls off the end of the bed.*) Oh! The counterpane's gone!

MARCEL: Never mind—leave it.

CLAIRE (*lets out a great cry as she sees the counterpane, under which is* LULU, *moving like a caterpillar across the floor towards the bathroom*): Ah—ah—ah! (*She gives one leap over* MARCEL'S *body, out of bed, and goes over towards the window.*) Marcel, look! The bedspread! It's gone to the bathroom all by itself!

MARCEL (*jumps to his knees and looks over the end of the bed*): Has it really? Good Lord! I didn't see a thing.

CLAIRE: Didn't you? Oh, didn't you my darling?— then my nightmare has returned.

At this moment, by the light from the opened bathroom door, we see the counterpane coming back, by little jumps, all by itself, to the bottom of the bed.

CLAIRE (*she screams again*): Ah—ah—ah! (*She jumps onto the bed and off again the other side, runs round in agitated little movements, and in the end gets up on the table.* MARCEL *jumps out of bed the other side and runs about, but finally summons up enough courage to go towards the bedspread which gives one or two last twitches and heaves and then settles down, inanimate.*) Don't go anywhere near it, my darling— who knows what it might do. Oh, my darling you're so brave!

MARCEL (*he advances towards the counterpane, then retreats, several times, gives it one or two dabs with his toe, and then jumps on it triumphantly*): Got it! (*He picks it up.*)

CLAIRE (*hurriedly getting off the table*): My hero! You're the bravest man in the world! (*She flies to his arms.*)

MARCEL: Please don't exaggerate, it was nothing— it would take more than that to frighten me. (*The counterpane is snatched from his hold and goes back to the foot of the bed. This time they both scream and MARCEL practically collapses. CLAIRE has to support his limp weight for a time.*)

CLAIRE: Help—help! Someone! Anyone! Help! I must put on my hat. (*She lets MARCEL fall to the floor and hurriedly goes and gets her hat and puts it on.*)

MARCEL: Claire, please don't scream like that—you gave me quite a fright.

CLAIRE *rushes agitatedly towards the bathroom but at this moment* LULU *comes out. She has put on the mask, also a white bathrobe with the hood over her head. In each hand she is holding a lighted sparkler which she waves about. She makes herself small, like a gnome, and advances towards* CLAIRE *with little hops and jumps.* CLAIRE *gives a long piercing scream which she maintains until, after* LULU *has chased her round the room once or twice, she runs out of the room for good.* LULU *plunges the sparklers in the glass of water and takes off the mask and robe.*

LULU: Well, that's got rid of her.

MARCEL: Oh Lulu, how could you? (*He draws the curtains, letting in the daylight again.*)

LULU: Were you really frightened, my little hero?

MARCEL: Of course not. I knew it was you all the time, but how did you manage to make it come back by itself?

LULU: By tying the string round the bedpost and pulling it, silly. Now we can relax. (*She jumps onto the bed.*)

MARCEL (*seeing her and going towards the bed*): Oh no, you don't. I've had quite enough people in my bed for one day. (*The bell rings. He jumps.*) What's that?

LULU: You really mustn't be so nervous Marcel. It's probably only Daddy bringing my coat and skirt.

VAN P's. VOICE: Nein, nein—I will go up and make the surprise.

MARCEL: My God, my godfather!

LULU: Never a dull moment. . . .

MARCEL: He mustn't see you. You must get back under the bed.

LULU: Certainly not. I'm sick of playing Mousey-mousey.

There is a knock at the door, MARCEL *looks wildly round, but can think of nothing better to do than jump into bed and pull the sheets over their heads.* VAN PUTZEBOUM *comes in and tiptoes to the bed. Once there, with one movement, he whips the sheet off* LULU *and* MARCEL.

MARCEL: You can't come in. Oh it's you, godfather dear—how are you?

VAN P.: Mademoiselle d'Arville! Fancy I am finding you here like diss.

LULU: It is a small world, isn't it?

VAN P.: Iss it not beink a leetle unconventional that you are already in der bed together?

LULU: Perhaps—but you see, I happened to be strolling down the Avenue Matignan and it's . . . it's such a lovely day. And I felt like going for a walk in the country.

VAN P.: Lyink in bed with mein gottson iss not beink exactly a walk in der country.

LULU: Of course it isn't, but you see. . . .

VAN P.: I am seeink what I am believink.

LULU: You must let me explain, godfather dear—it's all quite simple.

VAN P.: And you are thinking that I am quite simple also?

LULU: No, godfather, it's not that at all. When I got to the corner of the street I suddenly thought of Roger.

VAN P.: Who is beink Roger?

LULU: Roger is Marcel's little dog. And he never gets enough exercise, so I called to ask Marcel if I could take him for a walk, but I was five minutes too late— Roger had just gone to the rue de Rivoli with a letter, and the letter was to ask my father to bring me a coat and skirt.

VAN P.: I am tryink to understand, but it iss beink complicated.

LULU: So while I was waiting for the coat and skirt . . . I . . . I . . . just popped into bed for a minute or two. I mean I couldn't just stand about without a coat and skirt on, could I?

VAN P.: This I am understandink. But for a moment I wass worried—seeink you in der bed together make me think perhaps you are already married, but I am wairy plissed you are not.

MARCEL: It is now we who are not understanding, godfather dear.

VAN P.: Ach, this iss der big surprise—I am not going to America after all. I am waiting here in Paris until after wedding. I want to see mein gottson happy. I want to be here to hand him his fortune on his wedding day.

MARCEL (*horrified*): How very kind!

LULU (*horrified*): What a wonderful surprise!

VAN P.: We will have peautiful weddink, nein?

LULU: Oh, Ja.

VAN P.: Mit ein grosse weddink cake. But I am keepink you from doink odder tings, so I will go now and have my hairs cut for tonight, but back I will be commink in half an hour. When your fader is commink with der coat and skirt you will tell him about tonight?

LULU (*hopelessly*): Of course. But you won't say a word to him, will you, about . . . about what you've seen?

VAN P.: Do not fear. I am not spoilsport. I am man of der world and my lips I am sealink. Auf wiedersehen! (*He blows them kisses and goes.* MARCEL *shuts the door and leans against it, his eyes closed.*)

LULU: Well—how are you going to get out of *that,* I should like to know?

MARCEL: I've no idea, my brain has gone quite numb all of a sudden. Can't you think of something?—you were so inventive with that ball of string just now.

LULU: Oh, he's ruined everything, the silly old fool.

The door is pushed open, nearly knocking MARCEL *over.* VAN PUTZEBOUM *comes back*

VAN P.: Your fader! Quick! Your fader, op der stairs he iss commink!

LULU: Well, what of it?

VAN P.: But fader mosst not see leetle snowdrop in bed before der weddink, iss wairy unlucky!

LULU: So it is, I quite forgot. Never mind, I'll just nip into the bathroom. (*She does so.*)

VAN P. (*to* MARCEL. *Fanning himself:*) Iss wairy narrow escape, nein?

Enter GIGOT

GIGOT: Good afternoon. How is everyone? I thought I should find my daughter here—where is she?

MARCEL: She's gone to see Madame Dupont—her leg's in a plaster cast you know.

VAN P.: You are thinkink to find your daughter in betroom of fiancé?—I am beink ashamed of you.

GIGOT: It doesn't really matter. It's Marcel I want to see.

MARCEL: Well, godfather dear, we mustn't keep you if you're going to get your hair cut.

VAN P.: Auf wiedersehen, Monsieur Gigot—at dinner again we shall be meetink.

GIGOT: Dinner?—it's the first I've heard of it.

VAN P.: Iss all arranged, Marcel will explain. I will now be leavink. (*He goes.*)

GIGOT: I can never understand what that old man's talking about. Why hasn't he gone to America?

MARCEL: I'll tell you why he hasn't gone to America. It's because he wants to see me married to Lulu before his very eyes.

GIGOT: Now listen, Marcel—this joke's gone far enough. You'll be getting my daughter seriously compromised if you're not careful. She hasn't been home all night as it is.

MARCEL: How extraordinary! Where *could* she have been?

LULU *puts her head out of the bathroom door.*

LULU: Good afternoon, father.

GIGOT: So you *are* here, after all.

LULU: Of course I am—where did you think I was?

GIGOT: Marcel just said. . . .

LULU: Marcel's not himself today—he's been raving ever since he woke up. Have you got it?

GIGOT: Have I got what?

LULU: My coat and skirt of course. Didn't you get my letter?

GIGOT: Letter?

LULU: Really darling, you are too tiresome. Here I am with nothing but my evening dress.

GIGOT (*looking at her nightshirt*): So I see.

LULU: If you didn't get my letter why are you here anyhow?

GIGOT: I came to warn you.

LULU: What about?

GIGOT: About Philippe. He's back. He's finished his twenty-eight days.

LULU: He can't have. He only went away last Sunday.

GIGOT: The whole regiment's been sent home—with mumps.

LULU: Mumps—how dreadful! Mumps can be terribly embarrassing for men of military age—don't you remember poor Uncle Claude?

GIGOT: I certainly do.

LULU (*to* MARCEL): He had to cancel his golden wedding.

GIGOT: Never mind about Uncle Claude for the moment—we've got to think what to say to Philippe. I told him you'd gone for a little stroll before breakfast.

LULU: Did he believe you?

GIGOT: He looked suspicious. You'd better come home immediately.

LULU: How can I? I haven't a thing to wear.

THE PRINCE'S VOICE: I wish to see the owner of this establishment.

MARCEL: Who the devil's that? (*He opens the door a little and quickly shuts it again.*) It's the Prince of Salestria!

GIGOT (*excitedly*): His Royal Highness! We're *never* ready for him. Where are the candles?

MARCEL: There aren't any.

GIGOT: What *will* he think?

LULU: If he sees me like this I *know* what he'll think.
She jumps onto the window seat and gets behind a curtain.
MARCEL *flattens himself against a wall.*

PRINCE (*at the threshold*): Ah, Monsieur Gigot. How surprising.

GIGOT (*bowing*): Good afternoon, Your Royal Highness.

PRINCE: I hardly expected to find you in a place of this kind. Where is your delightful daughter?

GIGOT: She went out for a little stroll before breakfast.

PRINCE: It must have been more than a little stroll as it's now after lunch.

GIGOT: Lulu, the Prince is asking for you.

LULU: Tell him I'm getting dressed.

PRINCE: A charming thought, but unnecessary.

LULU (*there are movements behind the curtain, and the band that holds back the curtain disappears. It is long and wide at the ends; when LULU emerges she has tied it round her waist, thus forming a sash and making (more or less) a dress out of the nightshirt. She curtseys*): Your Royal Highness!

PRINCE (*kissing her hand*): Allow me to compliment you on your gown.

LULU: It's just a little something I ran up myself.

PRINCE: How agile.

LULU: May I ask Your Royal Highness to what we owe this unexpected honour?

PRINCE: Unexpected? I came immediately I received your letter.

LULU: Letter . . . Oh Marcel! (*She looks at him wildly.*)

PRINCE (*producing letter*): 'My dear Little Father' (*He smiles.*) I found that touching, really most touching. All my subjects call me Little Father, even the serfs—some of them of course with every reason.

LULU: How picturesque.

PRINCE: I had a little difficulty about the coat and skirt, but General Koschnadieff is bringing a large selection.

LULU: I'm sorry to give Your Royal Highness so much trouble. Actually I only wanted one.

PRINCE: Nonsense my dear—one would be meagre. You should never be meagre in thought or deed.

LULU: Your Royal Highness is most generous.

PRINCE (*consulting the letter again*): Now then—where do I find the proprietor of this establishment? What's his name—Monsieur Blanchard? (*He puts the letter back in his pocket.*)

LULU (*indicating* MARCEL): Allow me to present— Monsieur Blanchard. (MARCEL *bows from his unobtrusive place against the wall.*)

PRINCE: How do you do? My aide-de-camp will be here in a moment and will complete the little transaction.

MARCEL: Will he sir? Thanks very much sir. (*Spreads his hands and raises his shoulders in bewilderment to* LULU, *who shakes her head and puts a finger to her lips.*)

PRINCE: Now that that's settled, perhaps we can begin to enjoy ourselves.

LULU: By all means, sir. Are you fond of fireworks?
—we still have some left over.

PRINCE: I'm afraid I do not care for fireworks. They
always remind me of the night my father was assassin-
ated.

LULU: Oh sir—how dreadful.

PRINCE: It was a gala night in the Winter Palace. We
had just been to see 'Tristan and Isolde.'

LULU (*to* MARCEL): They *do* get about, don't they?

ROSE *opens the door.*

ROSE: There's a man outside, in uniform. Shall I
show him in?

MARCEL: Why not? It's apparently Visitors' Day.

ROSE: Step this way, please.

Enter KOSCHNADIEFF, *carrying a very large box.* ROSE
goes.

KOSCH. (*gives the Salestrian salute, then bows*): Altessia!
I bring coats and skirts. If they no good more on way.
Galeries Lafayette most excited.

LULU: I don't wonder—I'm excited too. I must try
them on at once. Have I Your Royal Highness's permission?

PRINCE: Certainly. Although it seems waste of
time.

LULU: Come along, father—bring the box. (*She goes
to the bathroom,* GIGOT *gives her the box then he goes off
through the main door.*)

PRINCE: That will be all for the moment, Koschnadieff. Karlousk nichtzia ipansk knood.

KOSCHNADIEFF *goes.*

MARCEL: What does that mean?

PRINCE: I was merely instructing my aide-de-camp
to keep watch on the stairs. He usually does on these

occasions. There are anarchists everywhere—one cannot be too careful.

MARCEL: Have I your Royal Highness's permission to put some clothes on also?

PRINCE: Certainly if you wish—I have no idea what the form is in this kind of place.

MARCEL: This kind of place?

PRINCE: You know what I mean.

MARCEL: I'm afraid I don't quite sir, but in any case I hope you like it.

PRINCE: I've seen better.

MARCEL (*disappointed*): Oh sir.

PRINCE (*looking round*): Not enough mirrors.

MARCEL: That's a very attractive little desk, don't you think?

PRINCE (*giving it a glance*): Louis Quatorze, and fake at that. Now then, what is the price of the room exactly?

MARCEL: It costs me eighteen hundred francs, sir.

PRINCE: A day?

MARCEL: Oh no sir—eighteen hundred francs a year.

PRINCE: I shall be unlikely to want it for a year.

MARCEL (*puzzled*): I am honoured that Your Royal Highness should think of wanting it at all.

PRINCE: One must go somewhere. And after all, this is a very agreeable neighbourhood.

MARCEL: It's particularly charming in Spring—the chestnut blossoms you know—like candles.

PRINCE: I cannot imagine why everyone assumes that I like candles.

MARCEL: Personally I don't care for them one way or another.

PRINCE: Now then, to our muttons.

MARCEL: To our what, sir?

PRINCE: Muttons—it's a French expression. We can't stand about here for ever.

MARCEL: Perhaps Your Royal Highness would like to sit down?

PRINCE: Never mind about that. We might as well get this little matter settled. How much does the apartment cost by the day?

MARCEL: That's rather a tricky question to answer, sir. It's never cropped up before.

PRINCE: Hasn't it? You surprise me—but then I don't fully understand the customs of your country.

MARCEL: I don't think I fully understand what you mean, sir.

PRINCE: It's perfectly simple. I want to know the price of this room per day.

MARCEL: Oh Lord! That's a teaser—arithmetic's never been my long suit. Let me see now . . . eighteen hundred francs per year. . . .

PRINCE: Please take your time. I am in no hurry, no hurry at all.

During the ensuing dialogue, the PRINCE *wanders nonchalantly about the room, looking at the pictures, out of the window, etc.*

MARCEL: Right. (*Thinking.*) Now suppose we call it one hundred francs a month. . . .

PRINCE (*absently examining a picture*): By all means.

MARCEL: One hundred francs a month multiplied by by twelve makes . . . makes . . . don't tell me—please don't tell me, it's on the tip of my tongue . . . (*he thinks hard for a while then, triumphantly*) twelve hundred!

PRINCE: Bravo!

MARCEL: Now twelves into eighteen goes once, any fool knows that, which leaves eight.

PRINCE: Six.

MARCEL: Oh no sir, I don't think so, really I don't—
I was always brought up to believe it left eight.

PRINCE (*firmly*): And *I* was brought up to believe
that it left six—I had an English governess called Miss
Beresford.

MARCEL: Then there's obviously nothing more to be
said. Six it is.

PRINCE: Good.

MARCEL: Now twelve times six hundred makes.
. . .

PRINCE: Twelve hundred dozen.

MARCEL (*pitifully*): Oh sir—do please allow me to do
it my own way.

PRINCE: Very well, go on.

MARCEL: Let us suppose that six hundred is half of
twelve hundred. . . .

PRINCE: A revolutionary idea.

MARCEL: And that twelve hundred represents what
we called one hundred francs per month. . . .

PRINCE: When?

MARCEL: Just now—don't you remember?

PRINCE: Vaguely.

MARCEL: Now six hundred would be exactly half of
that, and half of the one hundred would be fifty, so I
shall put that on one side and carry the hundred. . . .

PRINCE: Where?

MARCEL (*ignoring him*): Therefore, with the fifty I put
on one side, it makes the answer . . . (*with a sigh of relief*)
one hundred and fifty!

PRINCE: One hundred and fifty francs a day?

MARCEL: Oh no, sir—per month. I've been dividing
by twelve—don't you remember?

PRINCE: Vaguely. But how much does that make it by the day?

MARCEL: Do you really want me to go on with this sir? We might be here all night.

PRINCE: We *must* get this business cut and dried.

MARCEL: If only Miss Beresford were here!

PRINCE: I'm afraid that's out of the question. She died years ago in Vladivostock—we laid her to rest in the English cemetery.

MARCEL: How considerate.

PRINCE: We fired a volley over her grave and killed several seagulls—Vladivostock is on the coast you know.

MARCEL: I always thought it was inland.

PRINCE: You must have been thinking of Nishni-Novgorod.

MARCEL: Of course—how idiotic of me. Where were we?

PRINCE: One hundred and fifty francs per month.

MARCEL: That's right.

PRINCE: It doesn't sound right to me.

MARCEL: Wait a minute, sir. (*With the point of his toe he traces division signs and figures on the carpet. Sometimes he has to rub them out and start again.*) Let's divide a hundred and fifty by thirty. Now—fifteen goes into thirty twice, that's falling off a log, so I think I'd better put that little two over there and carry the thirty. (*Horrified.*) Oh God, what's that seven doing? Hold on a moment—the five is right I know. Now then—seven . . . nine . . . nought . . . nought . . . nought. . . .

THE PRINCE *walks over the sum.*

Oh, sir, look what you've done. You've made it come to seventy-nine thousand!

PRINCE: I *beg* your pardon. I *am* so sorry.

MARCEL: Now I don't know where I was. (*Suddenly a great light breaks over his face.*) Oh, sir, it's suddenly come to me! Of *course*. One should always cross off all the noughts before one starts, shouldn't one? (*He crosses off the noughts.*) So it's all quite simple really—child's play. Three into fifteen goes five—Five francs a day!

PRINCE: Is that all? Well, we mustn't expect the Ritz for five francs a day, must we? I'll tell the General.

MARCEL: Tell the General what, sir?

PRINCE: That it's five francs a day.

MARCEL: Do you think he'd be interested sir?

PRINCE: Of course. He always looks after those sort of things for me, it's part of his job. (*He calls.*) Koschnadieff!

KOSCH (*entering*): Swoya Altessia na bouk papelsoya mimi? (Has Your Highness any further need of me?)

PRINCE: Nack. Woulia malousk twarla stchikopne quanti prencha to the proprietor? (No. Would you give twenty francs etc.)

KOSCH: Oh, stchi, momolak. (Oh yes, certainly.) (*He gets out his purse and offers* MARCEL *twenty francs.*) Quanti prencha!

MARCEL: I don't understand, sir.

PRINCE: Great heavens above, man, what do you think we've been doing for the last half hour? There are your five francs for the room, please take it and keep the change.

KOSCH (*to* MARCEL): Titipoff polna coromal scrown.

MARCEL (*reluctantly taking it*): Well, if you *ab*solutely insist. It's frightfully good of you sir.

KOSCH: Sta Swoya Altessia lo madîbom, me pipilski me tadipouk. (*If Your Highness has no further need of me, I will go.*)

PRINCE: Nack, Koschnadieff. Bonadia. (*No, good day.*)

MARCEL: Allow me, General. (*He goes with* KOSCHNA-DIEFF.)

KOSCH (*bowing at, the door*): Marmalouk! (*Au revoir.*)

They go. THE PRINCE *sits on the side of the bed. After a slight pause, there is a knock at the door.*

PRINCE: Come! (*Enter* ROSE, *carrying a pair of sheets over her arm.*)

ROSE: I've come to make the bed, sir.

PRINCE: How very thoughtful of the management.

ROSE: It's all in the day's work, sir.

PRINCE: I wonder they can afford it for only five francs.

ROSE: I don't know what it costs, I'm sure. I only started yesterday.

During the ensuing dialogue THE PRINCE *helps* ROSE *to make the bed.*

PRINCE: Ah, so you're new to the game are you? Do you come from the country?

ROSE: Yes, sir—I was brought up on a farm. (*Busily making bed.*)

PRINCE: Then life can hold few surprises for you.

ROSE: I wouldn't exactly say that, sir.

PRINCE: Are you happy here?

ROSE: Quite, sir—so far, that is. Of course Roger makes extra work.

PRINCE: Roger?

ROSE: He's very intelligent, but he keeps begging me to throw things for him.

PRINCE (*philosophically*): Well, it takes all sorts to make a world.

ROSE: Also he's a fiend for bedroom slippers. I've had to smack him three times this morning.

PRINCE: I suppose you must expect that sort of thing if you come to work in a place like this.

ROSE: And you should just see what he can do with a ball of string.

PRINCE: There's no doubt about it—the French have very peculiar ways.

ROSE: I must go now, and give him his biscuits.

She goes. THE PRINCE *sits on the bed.* LULU *comes from the dressing room, serene in her new ensemble.*

LULU (*pirouetting and showing off her new clothes*): Does Your Royal Highness approve?

PRINCE (*opening his arms*): At last, at last! We are alone at last! Come to me immediately, my pretty creature.

LULU (*hanging back*): Oh, sir.

PRINCE: I have been waiting so long for this wonderful moment. All across the wastes of Siberia, the mountains, the forests, the deserts, I've thought of nothing else.

LULU (*sitting firmly on his knee*): Your Royal Highness quite overwhelms me.

PRINCE (*twining his arms round her*): What is that intoxicating perfume that sends the blood coursing madly through my veins?

LULU: Jockey Club.

PRINCE (*trying to kiss her*): Adorable coquette! Why, oh why did you put on such a thick coat and skirt and such a very large hat?

LULU: My darling! (*They embrace.*)

> MARCEL *and* GIGOT *come flying in.* LULU *and* THE
> PRINCE *jump up.*

GIGOT: Quick! Quick! Everybody out!

LULU: Why? What's happened?

MARCEL: It's Van Putzeboum!

PRINCE: An anarchist!

LULU: Oh quickly sir! He mustn't see you!

PRINCE: No, of course not—he may have a bomb.
Thank you so much.

> *They all go scurrying off in a body, crowd into the bathroom
> and shut the door.* ROSE *appears in the doorway.*

ROSE: I'm sure it's quite all right for *you* to come in,
sir.

> *Enter* VAN PUTZEBOUM.

VAN P.: But where woss everybody going?

ROSE: I really don't know. You couldn't breathe in
here just now. One minute they're here and the next
minute they're not. (*The doorbell rings.*) There's the bell
again—I don't know whether my legs can stand it.

> ROSE *goes.* VAN PUTZEBOUM *goes over to the window
> and looks out. The bathroom door opens and* LULU's *and all
> the other heads peep out, see* VAN PUTZEBOUM, *and quickly
> shut it again.* VAN PUTZEBOUM *idly picks up the mask,
> tries it on and looks at himself in the glass. Enter* PHILIPPE.

PHILIPPE: Now then, Marcel, enough of that nonsense.

> VAN PUTZEBOUM *quickly takes off the mask.*

VAN P.: Ah, Monsieur Chopart! You woss commink
from Fontainebleau?

PHILIPPE: Well no, I wasn't actually. Actually I was
coming from Rouen.

VAN P.: Der brave soldier—I remember now. Why
woss you back so soon?

PHILIPPE: Because we all had mumps.

VAN P.: Mumps iss beink wairy bad for soldiers. You are commink here to see you future cousin-to-be?

PHILIPPE: My what?

VAN P.: When my gottson marries your cousin, he will be your cousin, nein?

PHILIPPE: Oh yes, I see. I see. And you sir, I understood you were in America?

VAN P.: I not go America after all. I stay here in Paris to see der weddink. I tell mein gottson dis mornink.

PHILIPPE: *Did* you—and what did he say to that?

VAN P.: Woss wairy touched—wairy touched and plissed, so woss der leetle snowdrop.

PHILIPPE: Oh, so they were, were they?

VAN P.: Ja. Der weddink is all beink arranged for one week on Wednesday commink. And iss not beink one moment too soon, if I am asked.

PHILIPPE: What do you mean by that, sir?

VAN P.: Diss wairy mornink I see dem—Ah, I am forgettink, I have made der promise not to be tellink.

PHILIPPE: Oh that's all right, sir—I'm Marcel's closest friend, he tells me everything anyway.

VAN P.: Das ist true, and also you are cousin of der snowdrop—wairy well, but iss secret, ja?

PHILIPPE: Oh yes, of course sir, I promise.

VAN P.: Well, dis wairy mornink, I find dem togedder in dis wairy bet!

PHILIPPE: You *what*?

VAN P.: Ja, in dis wairy bet. Dey woss lookink wairy sweet togedder, like der Babes in der Woot.

PHILIPPE: Oh the traitor! When I think . . . ! (*He becomes demented and stamps about, holding his clenched fists to his temples.*) Oh! Oh! Oh! (*With each 'Oh!' he bangs his fist on the bed.*) When I think . . . ! .

VAN P.: What you tink?

PHILIPPE: When I think how I said to him 'Look after Lulu. She will be quite safe in your care!'

VAN P.: So sawry, so sawry. I am not knowink you are carink so much for your cousin. But you will not be tellink what I am tellink you?

PHILIPPE: Tell them? Of course I am going to tell them. I'm going to do more than tell them—I'm going to teach them a sharp lesson. How dare they—oh, how dare they, with me far away in Rouen, serving my country!

VAN P. (*following* PHILIPPE *about and pleading*): But you prawmise me. Pliss kip prawmise. Iss better keep prawmise, say noddings, prawmise me you say noddings —*pliss.*

PHILIPPE: (*after a pause, suddenly straightening himself*) Very well, Herr Van Putzeboum. I will keep my promise —I won't say a word to anyone.

VAN P.: Goot—that iss beink most sensible.

PHILIPPE: But I intend to teach them a lesson all the same. Where the devil are they? Where is everybody? MARCEL!

Enter MARCEL *from the bathroom.*

MARCEL: Philippe! What a splendid surprise! When did you get back?

PHILIPPE: Early this morning.

MARCEL: You should have sent us a telegram—we'd have met you at the station.

PHILIPPE: We?

MARCEL: Of course. All of us.

Enter LULU *from the bathroom, followed by* GIGOT.

LULU (*flying to* PHILIPPE): My precious angel!

PHILIPPE (*between clenched teeth*): My precious angel!

LULU: My hero! Safe home from the wars! I've missed you every minute of the day and night.

PHILIPPE: I hope you haven't been too desperately lonely.

LULU (*bravely*): I've tried to be brave, to carry on my life as usual—but my heart was in Rouen.

PHILIPPE: You didn't find that inconvenient?

LULU: There's a chill note in your voice, my darling. Is anything wrong?

PHILIPPE: What could be wrong? Thank you Marcel, for keeping your promise to me with such devotion.

LULU: Marcel has been wonderful. I don't know where I'd have been without him.

PHILIPPE: It's where you've been with him that counts.

LULU: Marcel! I do believe my precious angel is a weeny bit jealous.

PHILIPPE: Jealous—what nonsense! I know who I can trust and who I can't. I'm just racking my brains to think of a way of repaying you, Marcel.

MARCEL: There's nothing to repay. It's been a great, great pleasure.

VAN P.: Now everybody is beink happy I will go and have my hairs cut.

MARCEL (*speeding him*): Very well godfather dear— we'll see you later.

VAN P.: Auf wiedersehen, mein leetle snowdrop. (*He goes.*)

MARCEL (*shuts the door and leans against it with relief.*) I wish he'd get his throat cut while he's at it.

VAN PUTZEBOUM *opens the door again and knocks*

MARCEL *over*

VAN P.: Iss der barber beink wairy far away?

MARCEL (*urging him out again*): No, no—there's one just round the corner—turn to the right and you can't miss it.

VAN PUTZEBOUM *goes again*.

PHILIPPE: What's he doing in Paris anyhow? I thought he was going to America.

MARCEL: Oh, Philippe! If you knew, if you only knew!

LULU: Poor Marcel's in dreadful trouble again.

PHILIPPE: He seems to attract misfortune, doesn't he?

MARCEL: The old fool has decided not to leave Paris until he has seen the actual wedding.

PHILIPPE: The actual wedding?

MARCEL: What the hell are we to do?

PHILIPPE: It's perfectly simple.

MARCEL: What do you mean?

PHILIPPE: If he wants a wedding, he shall have one.

MARCEL: How can he? A., you don't want me to marry Lulu and B. I don't want to either.

GIGOT: One can't always do what one wants. I had to marry her mother.

PHILIPPE: Of course I don't want you to marry my Lulu—so good (*he kisses her*) so true (*kiss*), so faithful! (*kiss.*)

LULU: Precious angel!

PHILIPPE (*firmly*): Listen. You've got to deceive old Putzeboum and you've also got to convince him—right?

MARCEL: Right. But how?

PHILIPPE: Leave it all to me—I've had an idea—Toto Bardac!

LULU: Who's Toto Bardac?

PHILIPPE: He's the shining light of the Stock Exchange Dramatic Society. You've heard of that, I suppose?

LULU: Of course. They're always doing 'Les Cloches de Corneville.'

PHILIPPE: He's the best mimic in the world and a great friend of mine.

MARCEL: I don't understand.

PHILIPPE: I shall ask him to make up like the Mayor and marry you in the Town Hall. We'll invite everybody—it'll be the wedding of the year.

MARCEL: Do you think we dare?

PHILIPPE: Why not? All Toto will have to do is to keep a straight face and read out the Marriage Act from Civil Law—don't you see?

LULU: Of course—it's the only solution. You're a genius!

MARCEL (wringing PHILIPPE's hand): A friend in need is a friend indeed.

KOSCHNADIEFF (bursting in): Where's His Royal Highness?

PHILIPPE: What Royal Highness?

LULU: He popped into the bathroom for a moment.

KOSCH: The Ambassador has had an urgent despatch from Salestria. There's trouble brewing among the peasants.

MARCEL: Does that mean revolution?

KOSCH: I'm afraid so. Those serfs are always revolting.

CLAIRE (rushing in agitated): Marcel! Marcel!

MARCEL: Why have you returned, Pussy Willow?

CLAIRE: My voices told me my darling was in trouble.

MARCEL: Your voices were dead right.

CLAIRE: I had a terrible presentiment on the Left Bank.

PHILIPPE: Calm yourself madame—all is well. Marcel and Lulu are going to be married in the Town Hall next Wednesday.

CLAIRE (*with a loud cry*): I knew it! My life is over! *She faints.*

LULU: Salts! Vinegar! Cut her laces!

MARCEL: Some water, Rose—quickly!

ROSE: Certainly sir. (*She rushes into the bathroom.*)

MARCEL (*bending over* CLAIRE): Wake up, wake up, Pussy Willow! Things are not as black as they seem.

CLAIRE (*weakly, opening her eyes*): Where am I?

MARCEL: Safe in the arms of your demon lover.

ROSE *comes out of the bathroom with a glass of water, followed by* THE PRINCE *wrapped in a bath towel.*

PRINCE (*crossly*): What on earth is happening?

LULU: A great deal Your Royal Highness, but it's all perfectly simple. Marcel and I are going to pretend to be married at the Town Hall next Wednesday by Toto Bardac who sometimes appears in 'Les Cloches de Corneville' for the Stock Exchange Dramatic Society, because if we don't Herr Van Putzeboum won't go back to the Hook and won't give Marcel his twelve hundred thousand francs of which I am to receive ten per cent, Philippe de Croze's regiment has got mumps and so he has returned unexpectedly, and the Duchess of Clausonnes has just fainted because she had a presentiment on the Left Bank, in addition to which there's a small revolution in Salestria.

PRINCE: This is becoming farcical!

QUICK CURTAIN

ACT III: Scene I

A room at the Town Hall, of which we only see a large angle.
Upstage left, across the corner of the angle, are the main
doors from the corridor outside, with two wide steps leading
into the room.

On the right, on a raised platform, is the Mayor's table,
covered in a baize cloth, red or green according to the decor.
This faces across stage, opposite to the main doors. Up-
stage of it, but not on the platform, are a small table and
chair, and another small table and chair are on the down-
stage side of the platform.

On the wall above the Mayor's table is a bust of the
Republic with flags. Facing the Mayor's table are two
chairs with arms, for the bride and bridegroom, with two
more ordinary chairs on either side of them. At the end
of this row, upstage, are two more chairs placed at a right
angle with the row, i.e., facing the audience, and next to
the upstage clerk's table.

Behind this first row of chairs is another row of five
chairs and behind these are two long wooden benches without
backs. These four rows of seats should be set somewhat
fan-wise, with the wide end of the fan towards the audience,
so that the occupants will be as visible as possible.

Near the downstage table and chair is a little backless
bench just big enough to hold two, parallel with the foot-
lights.

*On the Mayor's table is an inkstand, a copy of the Civil
Code and assorted documents. On each of the smaller
tables is a register.*

*Upstage right, near the clerk's table is a small door
leading to the Mayor's Parlour.*

*When the curtain rises, a few guests are scattered
about. ROSE is seated at the upstage end of the first
bench, so that ROGER, who is with her, is invisible.
OUDATTE, the clerk, is fussing about with the arrangements. GABY comes in and strolls down the aisle (or
what would be an aisle if there were seats on the
audience side of it) and sits down in the front row.*

OUDATTE: Everybody back on the benches please—
the chairs are reserved for the bridal party.

GABY: Sorry I'm sure. (*She gets up and goes to a seat on
a bench. To* OUDATTE.) What time does the balloon
go up?

OUDATTE: Three o'clock on the dot.

ROSE: Roger! Stop scratching!

GABY: What a dear little dog.

ROSE: He belongs to the bridegroom. (*Fondly.*) He's
come to see his great big master get married, hasn't he
then!

EMILE *and* VALERY *enter and stroll down the aisle to the
front row.*

EMILE: I sent a cruet. There's no lid to the pepper
pot but at least it's antique.

VALERY: Where did you find it?

EMILE: In one of those trays on the Quais.

VALERY: I sent them an Empire sauce boat.

EMILE: Genuine?

VALERY: You can't expect genuine antiques at a false wedding.

EMILE: Sssh! Somebody might hear.

OUDATTE: Everybody back on the benches please—the chairs are reserved for the bridal party.

EMILE *and* VALERY *get up, then get seated on one of the benches.*

GABY: Are they really going through with it?

EMILE: Of course.

GABY: How did they get the Mayor to agree?

EMILE: It isn't the Mayor at all. It's Toto Bardac.

GABY: No! It's the best joke I've ever heard.

CORNETTE, *the other clerk, comes hurrying in.*

CORNETTE: Oudatte! Oudatte!

OUDATTE: Cornette—where the devil have you been? The Mayor's been looking for you for the last half hour.

CORNETTE: I had to go for my treatment.

OUDATTE: Hasn't it cleared up yet?

CORNETTE: They've stopped it spreading, but it still itches.

ROSE (*loudly*): Stop *scratching*, Roger.

THE MAYOR *puts his head round his door and thunders.*

MAYOR: Cornette! Where have you been? You're late again. (*He disappears.*)

CORNETTE: Sorry Your Worship. Coming, Your Worship. (*Hurries off.*)

GABY: I don't care what you say, that looks like the Mayor to me.

VALERY: Of course—that's the whole point. Toto's a master of make-up.

YVONNE *and* PAULETTE *come in and stroll down to the front.*

YVONNE: I thought we'd never get here. Hello Gaby!

Hello, Emile!

PAULETTE: How are you feeling after last night?

EMILE: Ghastly.

YVONNE: Nothing's happened yet, has it?

VALERY: No, there's still a few moments to go.

OUDATTE: Everybody back on the benches please—the chairs are reserved for the bridal party.

YVONNE *and* PAULETTE *get up and go through the same performance.*

YVONNE: If I'd known we were going to be made to sit on a hard bench I'd have brought a cushion.

GABY (*looking at her back as she passes*): Are you sure you haven't dear? (*General Laughter.*)

A PHOTOGRAPHER, *a pale and nervous young man, comes. in, carrying a large camera on a folded tripod, and a folded black sheet. He tries to get by* YVONNE *and* PAULETTE *who have not yet sat down.*

PHOTOGRAPHER: I beg your pardon—thank you so much. I'm the official photographer.

YVONNE: Is it wise to have an official photographer when the whole thing's a fake?

EMILE: Not so loud, Yvonne—somebody might hear.

THE MAYOR (*popping his head out of his door*): Oudatte! Oudatte! (*He disappears.*)

OUDATTE: There's His Worship, I must go.

PHOTOGRAPHER: Excuse me, excuse me—it's one minute to three. I must get into a position where I can do my job without being jolted.

OUDATTE: That's your problem. (*He goes into the Mayor's Parlour.*)

YVONNE: It's been my problem for years. (*More laughter.*)

ROSE: Be *quiet*, Roger!

PAULETTE: Fancy bringing a dog to a wedding in the first place. I never heard of such a thing.

ROSE: When my uncle was married a whole pack of beagles followed him up the aisle.

YVONNE: Was he a Master of Hounds?

ROSE: No, a pork butcher.

At this moment, outside in the corridor, a band strikes up the March from 'The Prophet.' Everyone is electrified and there is a general scuffling back into the proper seats. OUDATTE comes rushing out of the Mayor's Parlour. ROGER starts to bark.

OUDATTE: The carriages have arrived! Everyone back in their seats please! (*To* ROSE.) You must keep that dog quiet or else he'll have to go.

ROSE: It's only the music—it always over-stimulates him. Quiet Roger—be a good boy.

THE PHOTOGRAPHER *sets up his camera right in the middle of the main doorway and envelopes himself in a long black sheet.*

YVONNE: I can't see a thing—he's right in front of me.

PAULETTE: Tell him to move over a bit—he's blocking the view.

There is a general babble of conversation which dies down when LULU *appears at the top of the steps, leaning on her father's arm. She is dressed as a bride in a veil and orange blossom.* GIGOT *is in evening dress, holding a bowler hat in his free hand. They enter very slowly, followed by* MARCEL *with his* AUNT GABRIELLE *on his arm—she is very tall and very thin and dressed in black from top to toe. Then comes* ADONIS *in a dinner jacket, a little too small and tight for him; holding by the hand a* LITTLE GIRL *dressed as a bridesmaid and carrying a large bouquet. They are followed by the four witnesses,* PHILIPPE, VAN PUTZEBOUM, GENERAL

KOSCHNADIEFF *and* BOMBA.

OUDATTE *leads the procession till* LULU *and* GIGOT *achieve the right hand side of the stage.*

GABY (*calling as* LULU *goes by*): You look lovely dear.

LULU (*graciously*): Thank you. Thank you.

All the ensuing dialogues take place while OUDATTE *is showing them to their places.*

MARCEL: Cheer up Aunt Gabrielle.

AUNT GABRIELLE: I can't help it—it's all so moving. It seems only yesterday that you were a tiny boy romping at bedtime with your little cousins.

MARCEL: I still do when they come to Paris.

AUNT GABRIELLE *shakes open a large black-bordered handkerchief, covers her face with it and sobs quietly.*

ADONIS (*to* LITTLE GIRL): Stop sniffling.

LITTLE GIRL: I can't help it—it's the flowers.

ADONIS: You can blow your nose, can't you?

LITTLE GIRL: No I can't, so there. (*She puts her tongue out at him.*)

ADONIS: You've got a handkerchief, haven't you?

LITTLE GIRL: Of course I have.

ADONIS: Well use it.

LITTLE GIRL: I can't, it's folded.

ADONIS: You're a dirty little pig.

LITTLE GIRL: And you're a great fat beast.

ADONIS: Sit down and shut up. (*They sit down on the little bench near* OUDATTE'S *table, with their backs to the audience.*)

VAN PUTZEBOUM: Iss wairy peautiful, der French weddinks.

PHILIPPE: The most moving part of the ceremony is yet to come. (*He and* VAN PUTZEBOUM *go to their places.*)

KOSCH (*to* BOMBA): And so His Royal Highness say to me 'Jump into cab—go Town Hall, represent me as witness.'

BOMBA: Couldn't he come himself?

KOSCH: No, he was just jumping into bath.

OUDATTE: Will the witnesses kindly step this way? The bride's witnesses here, and the bridegroom's here, please. (*All the witnesses sit.*) Now I think we are ready. I will go and inform His Worship. (*He goes into the Mayor's Parlour.*)

MARCEL (*in a stage whisper*): Is Toto all right?

PHILIPPE: Of course.

MARCEL: How is his make-up?

PHILIPPE: Fantastic. You won't believe your eyes.

MARCEL (*to* LULU): Toto's all right—his make-up's wonderful.

LULU (*to* GIGOT): Toto's all right—his make-up's wonderful.

GIGOT (*to* AUNT GABRIELLE): Toto's made up and ready, so everything's all right.

AUNT GABRIELLE: How very nice. But then all the arrangements have been beautifully done—it's lovely, quite quite lovely. (*She cries again.*)

VAN P. (*loudly*): Iss the Mayor's name being Toto?

PHILIPPE: No, no—certainly not. I'll explain later.

OUDATTE *comes out of the Mayor's Parlour, goes up onto the platform and starts fussing with papers.*

ADONIS: What's the matter? (*The* LITTLE GIRL *whispers in his ear.*) You can't now—the wedding's just beginning.

LITTLE GIRL: I must.

ADONIS: You should have gone before you left your mother's.

LITTLE GIRL (*whimpering*): I did. But I want to go again.

LULU: What is it Adonis darling? (ADONIS *goes and whispers to her.*) Well I suppose you'd better take her.

ADONIS: I don't know where it is.

LULU: Ask somebody.

ADONIS (*beckoning to* OUDATTE): Excuse me sir.

OUDATTE (*irritably*): What is it? (ADONIS *whispers to him.*) For the little lady? Certainly—come this way.

GIGOT: Go on Adonis, go with her.

LITTLE GIRL (*screaming*): I don't want him to come with me—he called me a pig.

ADONIS (*grabbing her*): Pig or no pig—come on. (*He drags her off screaming.*)

AUNT GABRIELLE: The poor little thing's over-excited.

ROGER *barks.*

MARCEL (*standing up and turning round*): Roger, stop that noise at once, sir.

ROSE: He's over-excited too.

MARCEL (*he sits down again. Looking at his watch*): I wish old Toto would hurry up—it's ten past three already.

LULU: And I've got to meet the Prince at four.

MARCEL: Do you mean to say you're not coming to the reception? What will everyone think?

LULU: I can't help what they think. He's leaving first thing in the morning for Salestria, poor darling—and I did promise.

MARCEL: What on earth shall I say to Philippe?

LULU: Tell him I've gone to Napoleon's Tomb.

OUDATTE (*mounting the dais*): His Worship the Mayor!

(*He comes down and goes to his table downstage.*)

Enter THE MAYOR, *a very stern gentleman in a frock coat with a sash and his chain of office. He has a large lump on the left side of his forehead. He mounts the dais and stands behind his table. He has been followed by* CORNETTE *who goes to his own table on the upstage side of the dais. Everyone stands up. This achieved,* THE MAYOR *makes a sign for them all to sit down again. They do so.*

MARCEL (*to* PHILIPPE): Is that really Toto?

PHILIPPE: Of course it is.

MARCEL: It's unbelievable—I've never seen anything like it. Look, Lulu—isn't he marvellous?

LULU: I shall get the giggles—I know I shall.

MARCEL: For heaven's sake don't. You might break him up.

PHILIPPE: Don't worry. Toto never breaks up, whatever happens.

MAYOR: No more talking please!

OUDATTE: Quiet, everybody!

MAYOR: Will the bridegroom please stand up? (MARCEL *stands.*) What is your name in full?

MARCEL: Marcel Joseph Blanchard. (*He sits down.*)

MAYOR: And mademoiselle?

LULU (*standing*): Louise Clementine Gigot. (*She sits down.*)

MAYOR: Thank you, mademoiselle.

GIGOT (*to* AUNT GABRIELLE): She was called Clementine after her mother, you know.

AUNT GABRIELLE: How sweet. Where is her mother?

GIGOT: We're not quite sure. She travels a great deal.

AUNT GABRIELLE: Do you ever hear from her?

GIGOT: Occasionally. We had a postcard from Thursday Island last Tuesday.

MAYOR: We will begin with the reading of the Marriage Act. Monsieur Cornette!

THE MAYOR *sits down, turning upstage towards Cornette's table. He rests his elbow on his table, his head on his hand, so that the lump on his forehead is visible.* CORNETTE *reads the Marriage Act right through, starting loudly, then diminishing to a murmur during what follows. The other characters must speak in stage whispers.*)

CORNETTE: This being the 24th of June in the year 1908, etc. (*The Marriage Act is given in full at the end of the scene.*)

LULU (*sotto voce*): Marcel—have you noticed his bump?

MARCEL: Of course. (*He giggles.*) Isn't he wonderful?

LULU: How did he do it?

MARCEL: I don't know.

LULU: Philippe, how did Toto make that bump?

PHILIPPE: Rubber and putty, I think. I told you he was a master of make-up.

LULU: It doesn't seem possible, does it? Father, look at Toto's bump.

GIGOT: Fantastic—what's it made of? (*He leans forward to get a better view.*)

LULU: Rubber and putty.

MAYOR (*suddenly*): Quiet during the reading of the Marriage Act! (GIGOT *jumps back.* THE MAYOR *resumes his original position.*)

GIGOT (*to* AUNT GABRIELLE): That bump's made of rubber and putty.

AUNT G.: Just fancy. My dear father had one just like it, only *not* on his forehead. (*She has to get out her handkerchief again.*)

GIGOT *turns round and passes the news on to the row behind.* 'They say that bump is made of rubber and putty,' 'It isn't possible!' 'What did you say?' 'Rubber and putty?' *The words* 'Rubber and putty' *are passed from one to the other, the people in the back rows leaning forward, and and some half-standing up until the news reaches them. At the end of it all,* KOSCHNADIEFF *is left standing.*

MAYOR: Well sir?

KOSCH: I heard her once, in 'Rigoletto'.

MAYOR: Heard who? What are you talking about?

KOSCH: Adeline Patti.

MAYOR: Please sit down sir. This is no time for casual reminiscence.

KOSCHNADIEFF *sits down.*

AUNT G. (*in a piercing whisper*): I heard her in 'The Daughter Of The Regiment.'

MARCEL (*not having quite heard*): They all had mumps.

AUNT G.: Who did?

LULU: Philippe's regiment.

THE MAYOR *makes a gesture of despair to* OUDATTE, *who returns it.*

CORNETTE (*finishing the Marriage Act*): . . . having publicly pronounced in the name of the law that Marcel Blanchard and Louise Gigot shall be united in marriage.

KOSCH: Bravo!

ALL: Sssh!

MAYOR: Will you please stand up? (LULU, MARCEL *and* GIGOT *all stand up. To* GIGOT.) Please sit down. (*They all sit down again.*) No, no, no—I am talking to you sir. Kindly remain seated. (LULU *and* MARCEL *stand up again.*) Hippolyte Napoleon Gigot, do you consent to the marriage of your daughter Louise Clementine with Marcel Joseph Blanchard?

GIGOT: With the greatest pleasure.

MAYOR: There is no need to express your pleasure sir.

GIGOT: But it's true—she's my own little daughter.

MAYOR: Answer Yes or No.

GIGOT: Absolutely.

MAYOR (*raising his eyes to heaven*): Is it Yes or No?

GIGOT: Of course it's yes—that's why we're all here, isn't it? (*He looks round triumphantly.*)

MAYOR: I will not have such levity at a time like this. I insist on absolute silence during the reading of Articles 212 to 226 of the Civil Code. Article 212. . . .

ADONIS *and the* LITTLE GIRL *have come in the main doors. There is a general Ah! of satisfaction at their return. As they get to their little bench* KOSCHNADIEFF *calls sotto voce* 'Bravo!'

MAYOR: Article 212. . . .

LULU (*leaning forward, to* ADONIS): Is everything all right?

ADONIS: I couldn't get her out. She's been shut up in there for twenty minutes, eating nougat.

Everyone whispers 'What a dear little girl', "Isn't she sweet' *etc.*

MAYOR: Will you please be quiet! Article 212:— They shall give to one another mutual assistance, help and fidelity. Article 213. The man shall protect his wife and the woman shall obey her husband. Article 214. The woman shall be a comfort to her husband in sickness and in health, and shall live in peace with him wheresoever he shall live; the man shall provide the woman with those things necessary to life in accordance with his state and according to his faculties. Article 226. . . .

OUDATTE (*at the beginning of Article* 212, *above, he goes*

208

to the LITTLE GIRL *with a large metal plate*): Would you be good enough, little lady? (LITTLE GIRL *takes it, holds out her hand to* ADONIS, *who goes with her reluctantly.* OUDATTE *conducts them to the top of the first row, and the* LITTLE GIRL *starts to take up the collection. This goes on all through the reading of the Articles.*)

VAN P.: Wass ist beink for?

OUDATTE: It's for the poor of the parish, sir. (*He whispers to everyone as they go by* 'It's for the poor and destitute', 'Thank you, it's for the poor of the parish' *etc.*)

   Just as THE MAYOR *gets to the words* 'Article 226', *the* LITTLE GIRL *trips, falls down, and drops the plate and money with a clatter.* ROGER *barks. Everyone at the back gets up to crane.*

MAYOR: What is all this noise?

ADONIS: The bridesmaid fell down with the plate sir.

MAYOR: Then pick her up again.

LITTLE GIRL (*screaming*): I've cut my knee.

ADONIS (*hauling her up*): If you don't keep quiet I'll cut your throat. (*He hits her and drags her back to their bench, still screaming.* OUDATTE *and the people nearest pick up the money.*)

   CLAIRE *suddenly materialises in the doorway.*

CLAIRE: I trust I'm not too late for the ceremony?

PHOTOGRAPHER: I'm afraid you missed the best part of it.

CLAIRE: How tragic. I am the Duchess of Clausonnes.

PHOTOGRAPHER (*impressed*): Please stand still for a moment.

CLAIRE: No photographs I implore you—the light is too harsh and the moment too sacred.

LULU (*seeing her and waving*): Coo-whoo!

CLAIRE (*waving back tragically*): Coo-whoo!

MAYOR: Do you take for your lawful wedded wife Louise. . . .

LULU (*nudging* MARCEL): It's the Duchess!

MARCEL (*started*): Claire?

MAYOR: *No*—Louise, Louise Clementine Gigot.

MARCEL: I do.

CLAIRE: Although I know it all to be a masquerade it still cuts me to the heart.

MAYOR: Quiet please! (*To* LULU). Louise Clementine Gigot!

LULU: It was sweet of her to come, wasn't it? I mean—considering everything.

MAYOR (*firmly*): Mademoiselle! Am I to have your attention or not?

LULU: I'm most awfully sorry.

MAYOR: Do you take Marcel Joseph Blanchard for your lawful wedded husband.

LULU (*giggling*): Of course—don't be so silly.

MAYOR (*crossly*): I *beg* your pardon!

LULU (*laughing*): I think you're marvellous, really I do.

MAYOR: That is quite beside the point. Do you or do you not take Marcel Joseph Blanchard for your lawful wedded husband?

LULU: I do.

MAYOR: Then in the name of the law, I pronounce you man and wife!

KOSCH: Bravo!

ALL (*carried away by* KOSCHNADIEFF): Bravo! Bravo! (*They applaud,* ROGER *barks,* AUNT GABRIELLE *sobs.*)

MAYOR (*banging on the table*): Once and for all, this is not a place of entertainment.

MARCEL (*to* PHILIPPE): It's the next best thing though.

Isn't he superb?

OUDATTE: Now would you step this way to sign the registers please? (*He leads* MARCEL *and the witnesses up to* CORNETTE'S *table, then* LULU *and* GIGOT *to his own table downstage.* THE MAYOR *also comes down.*)

MAYOR: Would you please sign the register there, (*pointing.*) Mademoiselle Gigot? (*After she has signed.*) Thank you, *Madame Blanchard.*

LULU *goes back to her chair.* MARCEL *comes down to the* MAYOR.

MAYOR: Well sir, I'm afraid I am unable to compliment you on the behaviour of your friends.

MARCEL: Oh well, I wouldn't have been surprised if they hadn't laughed more than they did—you were so awfully good you know.

MAYOR: Good? What do you mean?

VAN PUTZEBOUM *comes towards them.*

MARCEL: Sssh! Don't say a word in front of my godfather, will you—everything depends on it.

MAYOR: I have no wish to speak to your godfather sir. (*He goes up onto the platform.*)

MARCEL (*to* VAN PUTZEBOUM): Everything went splendidly, didn't it?

OUDATTE: Will everyone take their places please, for the Mayor's address! (*Everyone hurries back.*)

MAYOR: Thank you, Oudatte. Monsieur and Madame Blanchard! Although I haven't found among you and your friends the sort of conduct which I believe I have a right to expect during a ceremony of this solemnity. . .

LULU: Isn't he killing?

Murmurings among the assembly. MARCEL *gives* PHILIPPE *a broad wink.*

MAYOR: . . . I nevertheless must conform to usage.

In sparing you the tedium of a long speech. . . .

KOSCH: Bravo!

MAYOR: I will content myself with wishing you both long life, happiness and prosperity.

ALL (*applauding*): Bravo! Bravo!

MARCEL: Thank you very much. (*Confidentially, going to him.*) I only said that about my godfather just now because he's the only one who—well, you know. . . .

MAYOR: No sir, I do not know.

LULU (*also going towards him*): I think you have been magnificent, sir, right up to the last. And as for that bump, (*She gives it a little tweek.*) it's a masterpiece.

MAYOR: I can only conclude, madame, that you are either intoxicated or have taken leave of your senses. (*He goes to the Mayor's Parlour, followed by* CORNETTE.)

LULU: Isn't he divine? He's kept it up right to the end.

OUDATTE: Ladies and Gentlemen, the ceremony is now over. Will you please come this way, past the bride and bridegroom.

LULU *and* MARCEL *stand by the first chair of the first row, and the others all pass by to give them their congratulations.* AUNT GABRIELLE *and* GIGOT *first, and they then stand on the right of* LULU *and* MARCEL. *The rest shake hands with, or kiss, the bride and bridegroom, murmuring* 'All my congratulations', 'It was a beautiful wedding', 'You look lovely' *etc.* GIGOT *says* 'We'll see you at the reception. It's upstairs at Filet's, just across the road.' ROSE *is the last to pass by, leading or carrying* ROGER.

ROSE: Give paw to your Master, then.

MARCEL: Who's been a good dog?

ROSE: Now he shall have his walky-walky.

All the GUESTS *go, leaving* LULU, MARCEL, CLAIRE,
VAN PUTZEBOUM. PHILIPPE *and* KOSCHNADIEFF *are
chatting by the door.* OUDATTE *is writing at his table.*

VAN P.: It was beink a peautiful weddink. I hurry
now to bring you der deet of trost.

MARCEL: Thank you a thousand times, godfather
dear.

VAN P.: It will be at der reception I am seeink you.
Auf wiedersehen! (*He goes.*)

MARCEL (*to* CLAIRE): My Pussy Willow! It's all over
and I am a rich man at last! (*They embrace.*)

CLAIRE: My beloved! I will be waiting for you,
veiled, in the corridor. (*She goes.*)

OUDATTE (*coming forward*): Here you are, sir. Here is
your marriage certificate, all signed and sealed.

MARCEL: My *what*? Oh yes, of course. Thanks very
much. (*He gives* OUDATTE *a tip.*)

OUDATTE: Thank you sir—my best respects to you
both. (*He bows and goes into the Mayor's Parlour.*)

LULU: We really ought to have it framed. Darling
Philippe hasn't left out a single detail.

KOSCHNADIEFF *approaches, tapping his watch and
making significant signs to* LULU *that they should be off.*
PHILIPPE *remains near the door.*

LULU: Good heavens, I was forgetting—the poor
Prince, I mustn't keep him waiting. It's nearly four
o'clock.

MARCEL: But you must come to the reception for a
minute. You can't have a wedding reception without
the bride.

LULU: Oh yes you can—the joke's over now. Don't
tell Philippe where I've gone. I'll see you later. Come,
General!

She and KOSCHNADIEFF *go to the steps of the main doors.*

PHILIPPE: Where are you off to in such a hurry?

LULU: The Louvre. (*They go.*)

MARCEL (*wringing* PHILIPPE's *hand*): I'll never be able to thank you for all you've done. The whole thing was brilliantly organised.

PHILIPPE: I must say I thought it was pretty convincing myself.

MARCEL: Convincing! It was absolutely superb, right down to the smallest detail. As for Toto Bardac— he was magnificent.

PHILIPPE (*smiling*): Yes he was, wasn't he?

MARCEL: He ought to go on the stage professionally.

PHILIPPE (*still smiling*): Yes he should, shouldn't he?

MARCEL: How did you manage to get the real Mayor out of the way?

PHILIPPE: I didn't.

MARCEL: What do you mean?

PHILIPPE: That *was* the real Mayor.

MARCEL: The real Mayor! What are you talking about?

PHILIPPE (*enjoying himself*): You signed a real register, that is a real marriage certificate you are holding in your hand. You really are married to Lulu.

MARCEL: Philippe! What are you saying? Why are you smiling like that?

PHILIPPE: I'm smiling because you fell so neatly into my trap, Marcel.

MARCEL (*frantically*): Trap! I don't understand.

PHILIPPE: You don't suppose I didn't know about your carryings on with Lulu while I was away, do you?

MARCEL: I didn't. We're innocent, both of us, I swear we are.

PHILIPPE: It doesn't matter now whether you're innocent or not. You're married. For better or for worse, till death do you part.

MARCEL: Philippe!

PHILIPPE (*at the door*): Look after Lulu for me. I *know* she'll be safe with you.

He goes. THE MAYOR *comes out of his parlour, putting on his gloves. He is minus his sash and chain.* MARCEL *rushes to him.*

MARCEL: Tell me it isn't true! Oh, Monsieur Bardac —tell me it isn't true!

MAYOR: God bless my soul! What's the matter now? —you've been behaving like a maniac all the afternoon.

MARCEL: I beg you to tell me the truth—you really are Toto Bardac, aren't you?

MAYOR: Toto Bardac? Who the devil is Toto Bardac?

MARCEL: Oh my God!

MAYOR (*with impressive dignity*): My name is Paul-Emile Etienne Seidman and I am the Mayor of this District, elected according to the laws of the Fourth Republic.

MARCEL: You can't be—this is a ghastly nightmare! Swear to me I'm only dreaming—swear to me. . . .

He falls in a fainting condition and THE MAYOR *catches him on one arm.* CLAIRE *puts her head round the door.*

CLAIR: Coo-whoo!

MAYOR: Coo-*who*?

CLAIRE: What has happened? (*flying to him.*) What have you done to my demon lover?

MAYOR: He seemed to be worried as to whether or not he was legally married, and when I assured him he was, he fainted.

CLAIRE (*dramatically*): Legally married!

MAYOR: Of course. That's what he came here for, wasn't it?

CLAIRE: Am I to take it that you've never appeared in 'Les Cloches de Corneville?'

MAYOR: Madame! I fear I. . . .

CLAIRE: Are you or are you not Toto Bardac, the shining light of the Stock Exchange Dramatic Society?

MAYOR (*furiously*): No I am *not*! I am the Mayor of this District, elected according to the laws of the Fourth Republic!

CLAIRE (*flinging out her arms*): Dear Heaven! I have been duped! I stretched out my arms too wide and now I am knee deep in broken dreams.

SHE *faints, and* THE MAYOR *catches her on his other arm.*

CURTAIN

THE MARRIAGE ACT IN FULL

This being the 24th of June in the year 1908, at three
o'clock in the afternoon, before us, the Mayor of this
District, and before these witnesses assembled in the
Town Hall of this District, for the purpose of uniting in
marriage, on the one hand Marcel Joseph Blanchard,
bachelor, aged twenty-eight years, Avenue Matignan,
eldest legitimate son of Joseph Blanchard, banker, and
of Caroline-Emilienne Toupet his wife, both deceased;
and on the other hand Louise Clementine Gigot, aged
twenty-six years, 120 rue de Rivoli, daughter of Hippolyte Napoleon Gigot, former officer of police, of the
same address, and of Clementine Laloyau of Thursday
Island. The father is here present as consenting party.
After having received, before the Mayor and witnesses
here present, the contracting parties, each in turn, and
they having declared their intention of taking, the one
the other, for man and wife, we publicly pronounce in
the name of the law that Marcel Blanchard and Louise
Gigot shall be united in marriage.

ACT III: Scene II

Lulu's bedroom. Downstage left is the main door, which leads to the salon. Downstage right, at an angle, is the bed, against the foot of which is a small settee. Upstage from the bed, on the right, is the window. Upstage centre is the door to the bathroom and on the left of the door, at an angle, is the fireplace, with a looking glass above it. On the right of the door is a sofa. Lying on the settee at the foot of the bed is Lulu's négligée.

    The Prince, *in his underclothes, is pacing up and down the room. His clothes are lying on the small sofa by the window. The bed is a little disordered, as though someone had been lying on it. After a little while* Koschnadieff *hurries in, his hat in his hand.*

Prince: Koschnadieff! You are abominably late—what has detained you?

Kosch: Altessia! It was the wedding—I could not get away sooner.

Prince: Was the ceremony a splendid one?

Kosch: Magnificent in some respects, curious in others.

Prince: Did everything go according to plan?

Kosch: Yes, I think so, but difficult make head nor

tail. French weddings most complicated. Very confusing.

PRINCE: I presume that Mademoiselle Lulu returned with you?

KOSCH: Yes, Altessia—she is waiting. I came to know if you were ready to receive her, but I can see that you are.

PRINCE: I have been ready to receive her for an hour. I have been pacing back and forth like a caged animal. My passion for this woman, Koschnadieff, is driving me to distraction. For the love of god bring her to me—I can wait no longer.

KOSCH (*going to the doorway*): Mademoiselle! (*To* PRINCE.) Here comes the bride.

LULU *enters and curtseys to* THE PRINCE.

LULU: Your Royal Highness! Oh!

PRINCE: What is it, my dear?

LULU: I didn't expect you to be quite so informally dressed.

PRINCE: I thought I would make myself at home while I was waiting. Actually I lay down and tried to sleep for a little, but it was no good—the pounding of my heart was too deafening. But now at long last my turbulent dreams are to be realised. Koschnadieff, you may retire.

KOSCH (*bowing*): Altessia! Marmalouk! Kultak nagonsk neeka baglat. (*He goes.*)

LULU: What does that mean?

PRINCE: It is famous proverb of my country. It means match to gunpowder make big bang.

LULU: How romantic!

PRINCE (*advancing amorously*): At last! At last we are alone!

LULU (*retreating*): But Sir, it's four o'clock in the afternoon.

PRINCE: Time is only relative—in my country it is seventeen minutes past eleven.

LULU: I understood you merely wished to say Goodbye.

PRINCE: Adorable coquette! Why, oh why do you persist in torturing me?

LULU: Oh sir!

PRINCE: Tomorrow I make the long journey home. I may never see you again.

LULU: Then the least I can do is take off my veil.

PRINCE: Take off your dress too, my plump little pigeon.

LULU (*at the looking glass, taking off her veil*): My hair's a sight—I look like a bison.

PRINCE: Let me have the exquisite delight of unhooking your dress.

LULU: Exquisite delight or not, I'm afraid you'll have to—I can't possibly unhook it myself.

PRINCE (*starting to do so*): Did the wedding go well?

LULU (*with a mouthful of hairpins*): Oh yes—Toto Bardac was marvellous. He had a bump on his head made of rubber and putty.

PRINCE: I once heard her in 'The Barber of Seville'. 'Una Voce Poco Fa.'

LULU: What did you say?

PRINCE: I said 'Una Voce Poco Fa.'

LULU: Why?

PRINCE: It's her big aria. In my opinion nobody can come near her.

LULU: Poor thing. She ought to have it seen to. Be careful—you're pinching me.

PRINCE: I'm sorry, my hands are trembling.

LULU: I was trembling all through the cermony, trying not to laugh.

PRINCE: Herr Van Putzeboum suspected nothing?

LULU: Nothing.

PRINCE: What a good job. I adore the practical jokes —we play a great many in my family. The wet sponge in the bed is the best of all, don't you think?

LULU: What a happy childhood you must have had. (*She lets her dress fall to the ground, steps out of it.* THE PRINCE *takes it and lays it carefully on the sofa.*)

PRINCE (*turning round*): Ah, what a vision! What exquisite beauty! (*He advances towards her.*) At last! At last!

He is about to enfold her in his arms when there is a ring at the bell

LULU (*jumping*): Oh dear!

PRINCE: Who can that be?

LULU: I don't know. It might be two Salvation Army lasses with a little box. They often call about tea-time.

PRINCE: I thought everyone had gone to the reception?

LULU: So they have. But the cook has left her eldest daughter to answer the door—she's only nine but very capable.

PRINCE: My beloved! (*He returns to the embrace. There is a knock at the door.*) Damn!

LULU (*calling*): Whoever you are, go away—I'm in conference.

MARCEL *opens the door and staggers in.*

MARCEL: Lulu! Oh, Lulu!

LULU: You have no right to be here, Marcel.

PRINCE (*with great charm*): We cannot be inhospitable.

After all, he *is* the bridegroom. (*He wrings* MARCEL'S *hand.*) You must be a very happy man.

MARCEL: I'm the most miserable man in the world.

LULU: What on earth's the matter?

MARCEL (*sinking into a chair and burying his head in his hands*): We have been betrayed! All is lost!

LULU: What are you talking about? For heaven's sake explain.

MARCEL: The Mayor was *not* Toto Bardac.

PRINCE: How disappointing. He was so funny in 'The Little Michus.' I saw it four times.

LULU: If he was not Toto Bardac, who was he?

MARCEL: Paul-Emile Seidman.

PRINCE: Great heavens—is he at large again?

MARCEL: He is the Mayor of this District, elected according to the laws of the Fourth Republic.

LULU: Marcel, what are you saying?

MARCEL: I am saying that our wedding was perfectly legal, and that we are man and wife. Philippe organised the whole thing.

LULU: But why? Why should he?

MARCEL: Out of revenge.

LULU: Revenge? What on earth for?

MARCEL: He found out we'd spent the night together.

LULU: You mean I really am Madame Marcel Blanchard?

MARCEL: Of course. (*He beats his forehead*). It's appalling!

LULU: I don't think it's very polite of you to make such a dreadful fuss.

MARCEL: I have no desire to be married to you, Lulu. I told you that before.

LULU: I can't see why you should be so against the

idea. I'm sound in wind and limb and fairly popular.

PRINCE: I think, if I may say so sir, that your attitude *is* a trifle discourteous.

MARCEL: But I am not *in love* with Lulu.

LULU: I don't see why you shouldn't try to be—anyone would think I was the Hunchback of Notre Dame.

MARCEL: You know perfectly well I'm in love with my Pussy Willow.

PRINCE (*To* LULU): I fear I am confused. What is his Pussy Willow?

LULU: It isn't a what, it's a who.

PRINCE: I am still more confused.

LULU: It's actually the Duchess of Clausonnes. She's married to one of the oldest Dukes in France which makes her a bit restive.

PRINCE: Naturally.

LULU: She's besotted about Marcel and happened to read a letter from his godfather congratulating him on being engaged to me which of course he wasn't.

PRINCE: Pray continue. I am all attention.

LULU: Then of course Philippe came back unexpectedly from Rouen and everything would have been all right if Marcel had taken me to the Zoo instead of Montmartre and if I hadn't fallen down in the Place Pigalle and gone home with him to find the ammonia which he hadn't got.

PRINCE: I quite understand.

LULU: So, now I am really Marcel's wife and a respectable married woman, it's high time I put some clothes on.

PRINCE: Not yet! Not yet! Our rendezvous hasn't even begun.

LULU: But sir, you must see the situation has changed.

I have a husband—I cannot bring myself to betray him so *very* soon after the wedding. Don't you agree, Marcel?

MARCEL: Damn the wedding. Damn everything.

LULU: That's not the way to speak dear. I'm surprised at you. (*She puts on her négligée.*)

PRINCE (*pleading*): But tomorrow I return to Salestria! I may never see you again. How can you live on in my memory if I have nothing to remember?

LULU: I'll give you a photograph. I have quite a nice one taken with Mr. Mortimer at the Gare du Nord.

PRINCE: Do you mean that the cup of ecstasy is to be dashed from my lips?

LULU: Do not despair, Sir. I'm sure that one of these days you'll meet Miss Right.

PRINCE: I've already met her. She and Miss Beresford were inseparable.

LULU: Please understand and forgive, Sir. This must be goodbye. I now have my husband to think of.

PRINCE (*with dignity*): Very well, madame, as you wish. I would never dream of insisting. (*He goes towards his clothes.*) I will leave you, Monsieur Blanchard, to your new found happiness.

MARCEL (*jumping up*): Oh no you won't. I'm not going to let things stay like this.

LULU: You *are* being disagreeable dear. I can't think what's come over you.

MARCEL: I shall get a divorce immediately.

LULU: But we've only just got married!

MARCEL: I can't help that—the marriage is null and void. I was tricked into it. I was not a consenting party.

LULU: Oh yes you were. You said 'Yes', didn't you?

MARCEL: Yes, but I didn't mean it any more than you did.

LULU: Yes is Yes all the world over.

PRINCE: In my country it is Schti.

MARCEL (*wildly*): To hell with you and your country.

LULU: Marcel!

PRINCE: Do you realise at whom you are shouting?

MARCEL: I do and I don't care. I'm going to get a divorce if it's the last thing I do, and what's more I've got a damned good idea how to do it. (*He goes to the window and flings it open.*)

LULU: Stop him, Sir—he's going to throw himself out of the window!

MARCEL: I'm not going to do any such thing.

LULU: What *are* you going to do then?

MARCEL: This! (*He throws all the Prince's clothes out of the window, then runs quickly to the door and out.* LULU *runs after him and rattles the handle but finds the door is locked.*)

LULU: The beast! He's locked us in.

PRINCE: This is intolerable.

LULU (*she goes to the window and looks out*): There he is, going down the steps. Marcel! Marcel!

PRINCE: Tell him to pick my clothes up and bring them back immediately.

LULU: Marcel! Marcel! Bring His Royal Highness's clothes back immediately.

PRINCE: The fellow's obviously unhinged.

LULU: Oh dear—he's just hung your trousers on the railings. Now he's running across the road, Look, look! He's gone straight into the Police Station.

PRINCE (*going to the window*): The Police Station!

LULU: I know what he's up to. He's gone to bring a witness back here to collect evidence.

PRINCE: Evidence of what?

LULU: You know—of our being found in thingamajig.

PRINCE: What, my love bird, is thingamajig?

LULU: It's a legal term for whatever it is that people are caught in when they're doing what we're doing, only of course we haven't done it.

PRINCE: I quite understand.

LULU: It sounds sort of Italian—like the name of an opera.

PRINCE: Well, that rules out 'The Bartered Bride.'

LULU (*clasping her head in her hands*): I wish I could remember it.

PRINCE: 'Cavalleria Rusticana.'

LULU: You're getting warmer.

PRINCE: 'Norma.'

LULU: No.

PRINCE: 'Cosi Fan Tutti.'

LULU: That's it—at least I think it is. Anyhow, it's what Marcel wants to catch us in.

PRINCE: To be caught in 'Cosi Fan Tutti' in my position would be extremely embarrassing. Is there no other way out?

LULU: Only the bathroom, but the window's very small and it's three floors up.

PRINCE: What are we to do then?

LULU: I suppose we could knot some sheets together and lower you to the ground—we can't just sit here doing nothing.

There are sounds of footsteps and voices.

PRINCE: Look out! Someone's coming!

LULU (*dramatically*): My husband! The bathroom, quick!

THE PRINCE *rushes to the bathroom and shuts the door. There is the sound of a key in the lock of the main door. The door opens and* MARCEL *comes in.*

MARCEL: This way Inspector—please come in.

LULU (*to* MARCEL): Snake in the grass!

INSPECTOR (*in the doorway*): You men there, guard all the exits. (*He comes into the room.*)

LULU: Good afternoon, Inspector.

INSPECTOR: Good afternoon, madame.

LULU: I've seen you so often from my balcony. How charming to meet you at last.

INSPECTOR: Madame is most flattering.

LULU: How *do* you manage to keep your police station so spick and span? Those window boxes are a pleasure to the eye.

INSPECTOR: One of my younger officers is devoted to flowers. He has a green thumb.

LULU: Not the one with the red face?

INSPECTOR: Madame is most observant.

MARCEL: Never mind about Madame being observant; that's your job. I brought you here to take careful notes of all the various points of evidence. In the first place, look at the bed—how would you describe it?

INSPECTOR: I should describe it as rumpled, sir.

MARCEL: And how would you describe my wife's appearance?

INSPECTOR (*gallantly*): Ravishing sir.

LULU: Thank you, Inspector.

MARCEL: Never mind about that. How would you say she was dressed?

INSPECTOR: Well that is usually called 'Deshabille' sir. I'm afraid it always sounds rather bad in court—Judges are apt to come down on 'Deshabille' like a ton of bricks.

MARCEL: And this! Her wedding dress that she discarded so wantonly only a little while ago.

INSPECTOR: Is this true madame?

MARCEL: Dare you deny it?

LULU: Of course not. Don't be so silly.

MARCEL: And where is your paramour now?

LULU (*with a nod over her shoulder*): In the bathroom.

INSPECTOR: This is most regrettable. (*He puts his hat on, goes to the bathroom door, tries the handle unsuccessfully and then knocks sharply.*) We know you're in there, so you might as well come out at once.

THE PRINCE *comes out with a face towel over his head.*

MARCEL: Take a good look at him Inspector. How would you say he was dressed?

INSPECTOR: He is wearing what is described as a minimum of clothing sir.

MARCEL: Exactly.

INSPECTOR: There is no doubt about it, you have a very strong case.

PRINCE (*with dignity*): If I am in a state of undress, it is because this gentleman threw my clothes out of the window.

INSPECTOR: Which proves that you couldn't have had them on in the first place.

MARCEL: Bravo, Inspector.

INSPECTOR: What is your name and address?

PRINCE: I am travelling incognito. I have nothing more to say.

MARCEL: Incognito my eye! (*He whips off the towel.*) This is His Royal Highness Prince Nicholas of Salestria.

INSPECTOR (*taking off his hat and bowing*): Oh no, sir! I beg your pardon, sir! I'm very sorry sir.

MARCEL: What are you talking about?

INSPECTOR: We don't like to get mixed up with Royalty sir, especially when they're travelling incognito.

Incognito comes roughly under the heading of Diplomatic Immunity.

MARCEL: I can't help that. To all intents and purposes you have caught this man and my wife in . . . in . . . (*He pauses.*) In what you call it.

LULU: 'Cavalleria Rusticana.'

PRINCE: 'Cosi Fan Tutti.'

INSPECTOR: Flagrante delicto!

LULU: I told you it sounded Italian.

INSPECTOR (*to* THE PRINCE): I am sorry to have inconvenienced you sir. As far as the Police are concerned, the case is closed.

PRINCE: Thank you Inspector. You're a very sensible man.

MARCEL: But what about me? As a husband I have been grievously wronged.

INSPECTOR: You have an extremely poor case and I've a good mind to take you in charge.

MARCEL: What for? What have I done?

INSPECTOR: You have made a false declaration and brought me here under false pretences. (*To* LULU.) I regret my intrusion, madame. Perhaps as a slight gesture of contrition you would accept a few lobelias.

LULU: I should be charmed.

PRINCE: You have been most understanding, Inspector. You have my gratitude and my Embassy will see to it that you are more tangibly rewarded.

INSPECTOR: Your Royal Highness is too gracious. (*In the doorway.*) All right men—everyone back over the road. (*He bows and goes.*)

MARCEL: Well I'll be damned!

PRINCE: You have, if I may say so made an ass of yourself.

LULU: Don't be too hard on him sir—he's had a difficult day.

PRINCE: If it were not for my affection for your wife, I would have you horse-whipped.

LULU: Do please try to keep calm Sir.

PRINCE: I am perfectly calm, but rather chilly. (*To* MARCEL.) Go and get me some clothes immediately.

MARCEL: Where from?

LULU: There's a very good shop in the rue de la Paix —Featherstone, Winthrop and Crouch. They have an English cutter.

MARCEL: They'd be shut by now.

LULU: Weatherby, Benson, Marlborough and Slope might still be open.

PRINCE: I shall have no time for fittings—I'm leaving tomorrow. Lend me some of yours.

MARCEL: I can't. I haven't any here.

PRINCE: Give me the ones you've got on.

MARCEL: They wouldn't fit you, Sir.

PRINCE: Take them off at once and don't argue.

MARCEL: Sssh! Someone's coming up the stairs.

LULU: It's probably only Madame Leclerc in the flat below. She always gets back from her cello lesson about this time.

PHILIPPE (*outside*): Can I come in?

LULU: It's Philippe—the traitor. He's come to gloat over us.

MARCEL: I'll teach him to gloat. (*He shouts.*) Come in!

PHILIPPE (*entering*): I just dropped in to see how the honeymoon was going. (*He sees* THE PRINCE.) Oh, Your Royal Highness, what an unexpected pleasure. How well you're looking.

PRINCE (*icily*): Thank you.

PHILIPPE: How sensible of you to discard your uniform on such a hot afternoon.

PRINCE: You are impertinent sir.

MARCEL (*ominously*): Close the door, Philippe.

PHILIPPE (*doing so*): By all means.

MARCEL: Now then. (*To* THE PRINCE.) You said just now that you were in need of a pair of trousers, Sir?

PRINCE: Indeed I did.

MARCEL: And a coat?

PRINCE: Certainly.

MARCEL: Good. Off with them, Philippe.

PHILIPPE: What are you talking about?

MARCEL: Your trousers. Take them off at once.

PHILIPPE: I'll see you damned first.

MARCEL (*he takes out a small revolver*): Take off your trousers or I'll shoot you like a dog.

PHILIPPE: Are you out of your mind?

MARCEL: I'm perfectly sane and, as you know, an excellent shot. I can shoot the core out of an apple at two hundred yards.

PRINCE (*humming a few bars nonchalantly*): Tiddy bom, tiddy bom, tiddy bom bom bom.

LULU: What are you humming, Sir?

PRINCE: The overture to 'William Tell.' It just dropped into my mind.

MARCEL: Go on, Philippe. I mean what I say. I shan't shoot to kill, merely to maim.

PHILIPPE: I don't believe you.

MARCEL: We'll see about that. (*He fires into the floor. There is the sound of a tremendous crash below.*)

LULU: Oh dear. There goes Madame Leclerc's chandelier again.

MARCEL (*advancing slowly towards* PHILIPPE): They

must be off by the time I count three.

PHILIPPE (*backing*): Don't be so idiotic.

MARCEL (*inflexibly*): One. Two. (*A pause.* PHILIPPE *hurriedly takes off his trousers and coat.* MARCEL *throws the clothes one by one to* THE PRINCE *who catches them and quickly puts them on.*)

PHILIPPE: This situation is ridiculous.

LULU: You'd never believe it if you saw it on the stage, would you?

MARCEL (*to* THE PRINCE): Do you need his under-clothes, Sir?

PRINCE: God forbid.

PHILIPPE: How can you stand there Lulu, and see me so humiliated?

LULU: Quite easily.

PHILIPPE: After all we've been to each other!

LULU: You should have thought of that before you arranged that wedding.

MARCEL: Now, Your Royal Highness—are you quite ready?

PRINCE: Ready for what?

MARCEL: To leave, Sir. I really think it would be advisable for you to return to your Embassy as soon as possible. Your presence here would interfere with my plans—you understand?

PRINCE: I am beginning to understand. You are a very clever fellow and most resourceful. (*To* LULU.) I fear, madame, that this must be goodbye.

LULU: Oh Sir!

PRINCE: It has been a most romantic episode but a trifle too erratic—I feel rather tired. After all, I shall have my memories, though not perhaps quite of the kind I had hoped for. I beg of you not to forget the photograph with Mr. Mortimer.

LULU: Your Royal Highness is most magnanimous. Au revoir, but not adieu.

PRINCE: The word for that in my country is 'Groubenska boul.' The peasants of course employ the more familiar phrase 'Yamoleck.'

LULU (*curtseying*): Yamoleck, Your Royal Highness and, from the bottom of my heart, Groubenska boul!

THE PRINCE *kisses her and goes out, humming absently the Overture from 'William Tell.'*

MARCEL: Well, so far so good.

LULU (*pensively*): I wish he'd been able to stay a little longer—I was growing quite fond of him.

PHILIPPE: I've had enough of this. (*He goes towards the door.*)

MARCEL (*barring the way*): If you move out of this room I'll shoot.

PHILIPPE: Put that silly revolver away and don't be such a damned fool.

MARCEL: Look after Philippe for a few moments Lulu—I have to pop across to the Police Station.

PHILIPPE: Police Station? What on earth for?

MARCEL: To fetch an eye-witness. Do you know what you are, Philippe, my dear old friend? You're my wife's lover!

LULU: Of course he is dear, everybody knows that.

MARCEL: And you're going to be discovered in her bedroom on the very day of our wedding. In your underclothes.

LULU: Oh, Marcel! I see the whole thing. You *are* clever!

There is a knock at the door.

MARCEL: Come in!

Enter THE INSPECTOR *carrying a window-box of lobelias.*

LULU: How very fortunate. We were just about to send for you.

INSPECTOR: These are for your balcony Madame, with the compliments of the whole Station.

LULU (*graciously accepting the box*): How kind.

INSPECTOR: All they need is a little care and a lot of water.

LULU: I'll do my best.

INSPECTOR: Is His Royal Highness still here?

LULU: He left a moment ago. You've only just missed him.

INSPECTOR: What a pity. His clothes have just been handed in by an elderly lady with a cello.

MARCEL: Never mind. I'll see that they're sent on.

INSPECTOR (*to* PHILIPPE): Good evening, sir.

PHILIPPE: Good evening.

INSPECTOR: You're feeling the heat, no doubt? It's been an oppressive day.

LULU: It certainly has.

MARCEL: Inspector, would you be good enough to take down some notes as evidence? I've just surprised my wife with her lover.

INSPECTOR: What again? And so soon?

LULU: Yes. I'm afraid I'm giving you an *awful* lot of trouble.

INSPECTOR: It's all in the day's work, Madame.

PHILIPPE: Marcel, for heaven's sake. . . .

MARCEL: Shut up.

INSPECTOR: I suppose the evidence will be roughly the same as before sir? Bed rumpled, etcetera?

MARCEL: Yes, exactly the same.

234

INSPECTOR (*as he scribbles on a pad*): Bed rumpled, underclothes, deshabille. . . .

PHILIPPE: Hold on a minute. This whole situation has been unscrupulously fabricated. . . .

LULU: So was the wedding Philippe dear. And you must admit it serves you right.

INSPECTOR (*to* MARCEL. *Closing his notebook*): Well, that's more than enough evidence. In my opinion you have what they call a water-tight case sir.

MARCEL: Thank you, Inspector.

INSPECTOR: I'll go back to the Station and formally lodge it in the Police files. Goodbye Madame.

LULU: Thank you again for the lobelias.

MARCEL: I'll see you out. (THE INSPECTOR *bows and they both go.*)

PHILIPPE: This is an absolute outrage.

LULU: Outrage or not, you're going to be a co-respondent.

PHILIPPE: I'm damned if I will.

LULU: You really are behaving very rudely. Don't you love me any more?

PHILIPPE: That's beside the point.

LULU: Oh my precious, jealous angel—are you quite quite sure? (*She goes to him.*)

PHILIPPE: Now then Lulu—none of that.

LULU (*twining her arms round him*): How could you ever believe I was unfaithful to you?

PHILIPPE: Because Van Putzeboum found you and Marcel in bed together.

LULU: If only you'd let me explain.

PHILIPPE: I'm waiting.

LULU: Well, it was quite simple really, and none of it would have happened if Marcel hadn't sent my photo-

graph to his godfather and we hadn't bought the fireworks and been thrown out of the Dead Rat and you
hadn't asked Marcel to take me to the Zoo which you
know perfectly well bores me stiff and I hadn't fallen
down in the Place Pigalle and your regiment hadn't had
mumps and you hadn't come back and made a jealous
pig of yourself because you love me more than anyone
in the world and it's no use pretending that you don't. . . .

PHILIPPE: Say no more my darling. I quite understand. How could I ever have doubted you for a moment?

LULU: You wouldn't have if only it hadn't been for
Marcel insisting on pretending to be engaged to me on
account of the twelve hundred thousand francs out of
which he promised me ten per cent and if you hadn't. . . .

PHILIPPE: Stop! Stop! You're driving me mad!

MARCEL (*popping his head round the door*): Philippe—I
nearly forgot.

PHILIPPE: Forgot what?

MARCEL: To ask you to do me a favour.

PHILIPPE: What is it?

MARCEL (*blowing them kisses*): "Look After Lulu!"
(*He bangs the door.*)

LULU: My precious angel!

They are in each other's arms.

CURTAIN

WAITING IN THE WINGS

A play in 3 Acts

CHARACTERS

MAY DAVENPORT	Marie Lohr
CORA CLARKE	Una Venning
BONITA BELGRAVE	Maidie Andrews
MAUDIE MELROSE	Norah Blaney
DEIRDRE O'MALLEY	Maureen Delaney
ALMINA CLARE	Mary Clare
ESTELLE CRAVEN	Edith Day
PERRY LASCOE	Graham Payn
MISS ARCHIE	Margot Boyd
OSGOOD MEEKER	Lewis Casson
LOTTA BAINBRIDGE	Sybil Thorndike
DORA	Betty Hare
DOREEN	Jean Conroy
SARITA MYRTLE	Nora Nicholson
ZELDA FENWICK	Jessica Dunning
DOCTOR JEVONS	Eric Hillyard
ALAN BENNET	William Hutt
TOPSY BASKERVILLE	Molly Lumley

The action of the play takes place in "The Wings," a Charity home for retired actresses.
The Time is the Present.

ACT I

Scene I. A Sunday afternoon in June.
Scene II. Three a.m. on a Monday morning.
　　　　　A month later.

ACT II

Scene I. A Sunday afternoon in September.
Scene II. Several hours later.
Scene III. A week later.

ACT III

Scene I. The evening of Christmas Day.
Scene II. A Sunday afternoon in June.

PRELIMINARY NOTE

'The Wings' is a small charity home for retired actresses. It differs from other organisations of its kind in that it provides only for those who have been stars or leading ladies and who, through age, lack of providence, misfortune, etc., have been reduced to poverty.

Some of these have been granted a pension of four pounds a week by the King George's Pension Fund; others have small, pitifully small, incomes of their own.

No actress under the age of sixty is eligible for admittance to the Home.

'The Wings' is subscribed to by public funds and was founded in 1925 by Sir Hilary Brooks, a leading actor-manager and producer of his day.

The organisation is controlled from London by a committee of leading actors and actresses who attend meetings once a month and make decisions on policy, investments, etc.

SET DESCRIPTION

'The Wings' is comfortable without being luxurious. It is situated in the Thames Valley not far from Bourne End and has a pleasant garden with a view of the river in the distance. The furniture is mixed. There are some fairly good 'pieces' here and there which have been donated at various times. There is, inevitably, a set of framed play-bills of earlier days and dominating the main living-room or 'lounge' is a very large but not very good oil painting of Ellen Terry. There is also an impressive bronze bust of the late Sir Hilary Brooks.

The lounge in which the action of the play takes place was originally three rooms: hall, dining-room and drawing-room. But these were amalgamated into one when the house was bought and it is now large, airy and cheerful.

Upstage, on the audience's left, there is a staircase leading to a small landing and the upper rooms of the house. Below the staircase are three french windows opening on to a flagged terrace which overlooks the garden and the distant Thames.

Downstage, below the windows, is a door leading to the library, which is now known as the television room.

In the crook of the stairs is an antiquated but still playable Bechstein Grand. To the right of this, double doors lead into the hall, the dining-room and the front door. There is a large fireplace on the right with above it a green baize door leading to the servants' quarters and below it a door leading to Miss Archibald's office. There are comfortable chairs and sofas upholstered in faded chintz.

ACT I

SCENE I

When the curtain rises it is just after lunch on a sunny Sunday afternoon in June. Bonita Belgrave *and* Cora Clarke *are playing cards at a card table near the fireplace in which a small log fire is burning because, although it is a summer day, it is an English summer day and therefore unpredictable.* Bonita, *in her late sixties, has reddish blonde hair and is wearing a well cut, but none too new beige jersey dress, two strings of pearls with earrings to match and a lucky-charm bracelet. She is a gay, bright woman with a strongly developed theatrical sense of humour. She appeared with considerable success in revues and musical comedies during the* 1914–18 *War and in the 'twenties and 'thirties forsook the musical for the legitimate stage. She was never a great star but was popular in supporting parts, worked hard for* ENSA *during the Second World War and was forced, owing to advancing years and lack of offers, to retire in* 1950. Cora, *who is a year or two older, is very brightly made-up with the rouge on her cheeks placed high. She wears a pink cotton afternoon dress and has a grey cardigan jacket slung over her shoulders. From beneath her coloured turban peep a few very black curls. She has several bead necklaces and a gold chain with a locket.*

Maudie Melrose, *a diminutive soubrette of seventy, is*

*curled up in an armchair reading the 'Sunday Times'. She
has rather sparse red hair, a neat blue print dress, enormous
horn-rimmed glasses and a vast bag into which she plunges
occasionally for her cigarettes and matches. In the years
before the first war when she made her début she appeared
with success in several musical comedies. Vivacity was her
strong suit. She was always an excellent musician and, in
her youth, had a piercing soprano voice of startling
volume. She appeared sporadically in the period between
wars but her life, on the whole, has been a long and fairly
fruitless struggle.*

MAY DAVENPORT, *aged about seventy-five, is seated bolt
upright by the fire working slowly and majestically on an
embroidery frame. A cup of coffee is beside her on a small
table, from which she occasionally takes a majestic sip. She
was an authentic star in her day and specialised in Shakespeare and the more ponderous Restoration comedies. Her
movements are slow and immensely dignified and she wears a
black velvet dress which in earlier years might have been
described as a tea-gown. Her hair is coal-black but she has
allowed it graciously to go a little grey at the sides. Her
discreetly made-up face is still structurally beautiful and
she wears a narrow black velvet ribbon round her neck.*

Outside on the terrace ALMINA CLARE, *eighty-five, and*
ESTELLE CRAVEN, *seventy-four, can be seen through the
open french windows. They are muffled up against the June
weather and sitting on deck-chairs.* ESTELLE, *white-
haired and permanently wistful, is knitting.* ALMINA,
*immensely fat, has dropped off to sleep over the 'Sunday
Express'. They have both been on the stage all their lives
and have played leading parts from time to time but genuine
stardom has eluded them.*

BONITA (*to* CORA): Well, that's that. You owe me two and six.

CORA: You owe me a shilling from last Sunday.

BONITA: In that case you only owe me one and six.

CORA: We'd better hold it over until next time we play.

BONITA: I thought you'd say that.

CORA (*sharply*): Why – may I ask?

BONITA (*sweetly*): Because you always do, dear.

MAUDIE (*looking up from the 'Sunday Times'*): I see they're hoping to get Buck Randy for the Midnight Matinée this year.

MAY: Who in heaven's name is Buck Randy?

MAUDIE: Really, May – you *must* have heard of Buck Randy. He's the rage of America.

MAY: I haven't been to America since 1913. What does he do?

MAUDIE: He sings, stripped to the waist, to a zither.

MAY: Why should he be stripped to the waist?

BONITA: Because he's supposed to have the most beautiful male body in the world, dear. He was Mr America of 1955 and 1956.

MAY: Why a zither?

MAUDIE: He accompanies himself on it. Last year one of his records sold over two million. He has to have police protection wherever he goes.

MAY: I'm not surprised.

MAUDIE (*back at the 'Sunday Times'*): They say that Carolita Pagadicci is going to appear too. She's flying over from Rome especially.

MAY: Is that the one with the vast bust who came last year and just stood about?

CORA: I'm sure it's very kind of all of them to take so much trouble for a bunch of old has-beens like us.

BONITA: Speak for yourself, dear.

CORA: I know they get a lot of publicity out of it but even so I shouldn't think from their point of view it was worth all the effort.

MAY: It is always possible, my dear Cora, that just one or two of them might do it from sheer kindness of heart.

CORA: I said it was kind of them to take the trouble and Bonita flew at me.

BONITA: I didn't fly at you for that. It was because you said we were a bunch of old has-beens.

CORA: We wouldn't be here if we weren't.

MAY: In essence you are quite right, my dear Cora, and I am sure that there are many who would salute your rather devastating honesty. On the other hand there is a wide gulf between honesty and crudeness. Please remember before you say things like that again that it is painful to some of us to be so vulgarly reminded that we are dependent on the charity of our younger colleagues.

CORA: Oh dear! I'm sure I'm sorry I spoke.

MAY: So are we all, Cora. So are we all.

At this moment DEIRDRE O'MALLEY *stamps in from the television room. She is a spry, white-haired old woman of eighty-two attired in dusty black.*

DEIRDRE (*in a strong brogue*): I'm telling you all here and now that I would like to take the windpipe of the man who invented television in me ould rheumatic hands and strangle the bloody life out of him.

BONITA: Has it gone wrong again?

DEIRDRE: It has indeed and for no reason in the world other than pure devilment. I was sitting there quiet as the grave listening to Father Dugan giving his Sunday afternoon talk when suddenly the damned contraption gets up to its blasphemous tricks and before me very eyes

I see the blessed Father begin to wobble about like a dancing dervish with one side of his saintly face pulled out of shape as though it was made of india-rubber.

BONITA (*getting up*): Miss Archie will fix it, dear. I'll go and ask her.

DEIRDRE: I'm grateful for the thought but spare yourself the trouble. By the time Miss Archie's fiddled with the damn thing the blessed Father will have finished his talk and be having his tea. I'm going up to have me forty winks. (*She starts to go upstairs.*) It's a dark world we're living in when a bit of soulless machinery can suddenly turn a holy man into a figure of fun. (*She disappears into the upper regions.*)

BONITA (*laughing and sitting on the sofa near to* MAY): That old girl's wonderful, she really is. You must have seen her in the old days, May; was she really good?

MAY (*after a moment's thought*): Good, but unreliable. She's never played a scene the same way twice.

At this moment ALMINA CLARE *and* ESTELLE CRAVEN *come in from the terrace.* ALMINA *waddles over to the sofa and subsides on it with a sigh.* ESTELLE *goes across to the fireplace and warms her hands.*

ESTELLE: I'm perished to the bone and it's no good pretending I'm not.

ALMINA (*quaveringly*): Do you think we shall ever get it?

BONITA: Get what, dear?

ALMINA: The solarium lounge.

MAUDIE: The letter went off to the committee over two weeks ago.

BONITA: It probably came up at Friday's meeting.

ALMINA: Even if they say yes I shall be dead and gone before they get round to building it. My heart's been pounding again, I hardly slept a wink last night.

MAY: You know perfectly well, Almina, that that's only indigestion. Doctor Jevons told you so. You eat far too much far too quickly.

ESTELLE: That east wind comes straight across the valley and cuts you in two.

CORA: The committee could well afford it if they chose. Perry told me so himself.

MAY: As official secretary to the Fund he had no right to. That young man talks far too much.

BONITA: Now then, May, you know perfectly well you dote on him, we all do. You gossip away with him for hours whenever you get the chance.

MAY: What nonsense you talk, my dear Bonita.

MAUDIE: I suppose he'll be down as usual this afternoon.

CORA: Of course he will, it's Sunday. Also he'll be sure to come today in order to welcome——

BONITA (*warningly*): Cora!

CORA (*with a hurried glance at* MAY): Well, you know what I mean.

MAY (*after a slightly awkward silence*): In order to welcome who?

MAUDIE (*embarrassed*): We've got a new addition to our cosy little family arriving this afternoon.

MAY: Why wasn't I told? Who is it?

BONITA: Oh dear, the cat's out of the bag now with a vengeance. I suppose we'd better say.

MAY: What are you all talking about? Why all this mystery?

BONITA: It's Lotta Bainbridge.

MAY (*stiffening*): Lotta Bainbridge.

BONITA: Yes.

MAY (*ominously*): Lotta Bainbridge – coming here?

BONITA (*hurriedly*): We all thought – knowing that you and she are not exactly the best of friends – that it would be better not to say anything about it.

MAY: How long have you known?

MAUDIE: Perry told us last Sunday.

MAY (*accusingly*): You mean you were all prepared to let me meet her face to face without even warning me.

BONITA: Old Dora, her dresser, who's been with her for years, is leaving her to get married, and the maisonnette she had just off the Fulham Road is being pulled down to make way for office buildings——

MAY (*rising*): I am not in the least interested in where she lives and what is being pulled down. I only know that I find your combined conspiracy of silence difficult to forgive. (*She moves towards the stairs.*)

MAUDIE (*jumping up from her chair and putting her hand on her arm*): It was only that we didn't want to upset you.

MAY: Do you seriously imagine that it would have upset me less to find her here in this house without being prepared?

BONITA: Don't be angry with us, May. After all, it was a long, long time ago, wasn't it? The quarrel, I mean——

MAY (*beginning to go upstairs*): There was no quarrel, my dear Bonita. You have been misinformed.

BONITA (*weakly*): Well, whatever it was then——

MAY: I have not spoken to Lotta Bainbridge for thirty years and I have no intention of doing so now.

MAUDIE: Oh May, dear – don't be like that – it's all over and done with.

MAY (*grandly*): One of you had better explain the situation to her when she arrives. Don't be afraid she won't understand. She'll understand perfectly.

MAY *goes off to her room. There is an embarrassed silence for a moment or two.*

BONITA: Well, that's that, isn't it?

MAUDIE: I suppose we ought to have told her, really.

BONITA: They'll probably settle down together in time; they can't go on not speaking for ever, but the next few weeks are going to be hell.

MAUDIE: Who was it that said that there was something beautiful about growing old?

BONITA: Whoever it was, I have news for him.

ESTELLE: Since I've been here I somehow can't remember not being old.

BONITA: Perhaps that's something to do with having played character parts for so long.

ESTELLE: I was an ingénue for years. I was very very pretty and my eyes were enormous. They're quite small now.

MAUDIE: What started it – the feud between her and May?

BONITA: Come off it, Maudie. You weren't toddling home from school with your pencil box in 1918.

MAUDIE (*equably*): As a matter of fact that's exactly what I was doing, eight times a week. I was in *Miss Mouse* at the Adelphi and I had a number in the last act called 'Don't play the fool with a school-girl!' It used to stop the show.

CORA: As far as I can remember it was the notices that stopped the show.

At this moment there is the noise of a motor-bicycle coming to a noisy halt.

CORA: Here's Perry. He's earlier than usual.

BONITA (*immediately opening her bag and touching up her face*): Bless his heart.

MAUDIE: Don't trouble to do that, dear – it's locking the stable door.

BONITA: All right, all right, I know – it's just habit.

ALMINA: He'll tell us whether we're going to get the solarium or not.

CORA: Oh no, he won't. He'll just say that the committee has it under consideration.

BONITA: In any case we shall know by his tone whether there's any hope.

CORA: I don't know why you're all working yourselves up about that damned solarium. It'll be waste of money even if we do get it. Just so much more glass for the rain to beat against.

BONITA: That's right, dear. Keep us all in hysterics.

PERRY LASCOE *comes in briskly from the hall. He is a nice-looking young man somewhere between thirty-eight and forty. He is wearing a sports coat, grey flannel trousers and a highly-coloured pullover. Some years ago he had a certain success as a musical comedy juvenile but realising, wisely, that although he could sing and dance adequately he had little hope of becoming a star, h* renounced the shadow for the substance and took on the job of being secretary to 'The Wings' Fund. Most of the inmates adore him because he jokes with them and jollies them along and is fundamentally kind.*

PERRY: My dears, I'm in trouble.

MAUDIE: What sort of trouble?

PERRY: I knocked over a milk cart in Maidenhead. Fortunately they were mostly empties. The milkman was livid. Where's old May?

BONITA: Upstairs.

PERRY: Good.

BONITA: Not so good. She knows.

PERRY: Oh Lord! Who told her?

MAUDIE: We all did, we had to.

PERRY: Well, maybe it's all for the best.

BONITA: It isn't. She's hopping mad.

PERRY: Oh, poor Lotta. She's got enough to put up with without this.

CORA: When's she arriving?

PERRY: Any time now. Billy Musgrove lent her his car and Dora's bringing her, with all her bits and pieces.

MAUDIE: Have you seen her?

PERRY: Yes, last week. I went along to her flat and had tea with her and made all the final arrangements.

BONITA: How did she look?

PERRY: Sort of miserable, but she tried not to show it. I don't think she minds about the flat so much, it's Dora leaving her that's really got her down. Where's the Colonel?

CORA: In her office, deciding whether we're going to have shepherd's pie or macaroni cheese for supper, I expect.

ALMINA: We had macaroni cheese last night and it nearly killed me.

At this moment SYLVIA ARCHIBALD *comes out of her office.* MISS ARCHIE *is the resident superintendent of 'The Wings'. She is a woman of about fifty; her gruff and rather masculine manner conceals a vulnerable heart and an amiable disposition. She is fairly popular with the inmates although at moments she is a trifle overbearing. Her build is on the bulky side, which doesn't prevent her from wearing corduroy trousers and rather tight woollen sweaters. She worked diligently for ENSA during World War II and retired at the end of it with the rank of Colonel. This, incidentally, is her greatest pride.*

MISS ARCHIE: There are you, Perry. I thought I heard the old bike.

PERRY: Hallo, ducks! The old bike's older than ever since the last half hour. She grazed her knees against a milk cart.

MISS ARCHIE (*whistling*): Good Lord! Ten days confined to barracks for you, my lad.

PERRY: I love to hear you talk like that, Archie. It reminds me of my uncle Edgar.

MISS ARCHIE: Never mind about your uncle Edgar now, Perry. What time is Lotta Bainbridge arriving?

PERRY: At any moment, I should think. She's coming down in Billy Musgrove's car.

MISS ARCHIE: Nobody ever tells me anything. Has Osgood been yet?

BONITA: No. He's late.

PERRY: How *is* poor old Martha?

MISS ARCHIE: She was a bit under the weather on Friday and yesterday, but she always perks up on Sundays.

CORA: Do you suppose we've all got to live to be as old as that?

MAUDIE: I hope to God we don't.

ESTELLE: Old Osgood himself must be seventy if he's a day.

MAUDIE: Were they ever lovers, do you think? – I mean in the old days.

PERRY (*laughing*): Good heavens, no! He's twenty-five years younger than she is, to start with. No, no, it's just star-worship, a sort of an obsession. He used to wait outside stage-doors for her when she was in her heyday and he was only a young boy. Rain or shine, there he'd be with his bunch of violets.

MAUDIE: He still brings her violets.

PERRY: I know. It really is rather sweet, isn't it?

CORA: I was in the last play she ever did. We all loathed her.

There is the sound of the front-door bell.

MISS ARCHIE: There he is now, I expect. I'll answer it, Doreen's gone to the village. (*She goes out into the hall.*)

PERRY: Is Doreen working out all right?

CORA: She has adenoids and no time sense but she's better than that awful Gladys.

PERRY: I rather liked Gladys, she was like a bad character performance in Act Three.

MISS ARCHIE *comes in from the hall with* OSGOOD MEEKER, *an elderly bald-headed man, nattily dressed and rather dim. He carries a bunch of violets.*

OSGOOD (*with a courtly manner*): Good afternoon, ladies.

BONITA: Hallo, Osgood. How are you?

OSGOOD: Fine, thank you, my dear, a little twinge every now and then, you know, but apart from that, fit as a fiddle.

MISS ARCHIE: I'll take you up.

OSGOOD: No, please don't trouble, Miss Archie. I know the way. She is expecting me, isn't she?

MISS ARCHIE: Yes, Mr Meeker. She's always expecting you.

OSGOOD: Has she been – er – happier this last week?

MISS ARCHIE: Oh, yes. She was a little low on Friday and yesterday, but nothing to worry about.

OSGOOD: I'll go on up then. (*He starts up the stairs.*)

MISS ARCHIE: I'll have a cup of tea for you when you come down.

OSGOOD: Thank you, my dear, thank you. That will be delightful. (*He disappears from view.*)

MAUDIE: Do you think she recognises him?

MISS ARCHIE: Oh, yes. He's never caught her on one of her bad days. She gets quite gay with him sometimes, and tells him risky stories about the past, her memory's fantastic, at least for things that happened a long while ago.

PERRY: That's quite usual, isn't it? I mean, when people get old they can recall, say, Queen Victoria's Jubilee, and not be able to remember what happened last week.

CORA: Nothing did.

ESTELLE: One thing I can remember, and that is that we wrote a round robin to the committee two weeks ago about having a solarium lounge so that we could enjoy the sun without being frozen to death. Did they read it?

PERRY: Yes. It came up at Friday's meeting.

BONITA: What did they say?

PERRY: They said they'd consider it.

CORA: There now – what did I tell you?

ESTELLE: Is there any hope, do you think?

PERRY: Of course there is. We must always look on the bright side.

CORA: None of that bedside manner stuff, Perry. You don't think they're going to let us have it, do you?

PERRY: I tell you they said they'd consider it – I really don't know.

BONITA: You could tell from the way they discussed it which way the wind was blowing, couldn't you?

CORA: Didn't anyone even suggest sending for an estimate?

PERRY (*unhappily*): I gave them an estimate – with the letter.

CORA: How do you mean?

PERRY: Hodges and Creal did it for me. Miss Archie and I measured the whole terrace last Sunday evening, after you'd gone to bed.

BONITA: I thought I heard someone scuffling about under my window. I thought it was burglars.

CORA: No burglar'd be fool enough to prowl round this house.

MISS ARCHIE: How much was the estimate? How much did Hodges and Creal say it would cost?

PERRY: Two thousand five hundred.

BONITA: God Almighty! What are they planning to build it of, uranium?

MISS ARCHIE: It's the frontage, I expect. It's a very wide frontage, and glass costs an awful lot.

BONITA: Were any of the committee in favour of it?

PERRY (*flatly*): One or two, but not the majority.

CORA: Do you mean to say the Fund couldn't afford it – even after poor Maurice's legacy?

PERRY: That's already been invested.

CORA: What did Pam Harlow say?

PERRY: She was in favour of it, but Boodie Nethersole wasn't.

CORA: Oh, she wasn't, wasn't she?

MISS ARCHIE (*warningly*): I say, Perry old chap, you know you're not supposed to discuss the committee.

BONITA (*irritably*): Oh go and form fours for a minute, dear, this is important to all of us.

CORA: Boodie Nethersole indeed! I'd like to strangle her.

BONITA: So would I if I could find her neck.

MISS ARCHIE: I say – steady.

CORA: She has no right to be on the committee anyhow, she can't act her way out of a paper bag and never could.

PERRY: She's had four whacking successes in the last five years.

BONITA: What did she say exactly?

PERRY: I really can't say any more. She was just a bit more bossy about it than the others.

BONITA: You mean she swung them round, against the idea?

PERRY: Yes – I suppose so.

ESTELLE: Perhaps it was too much to ask. The house is very comfortable on the whole, but it would have been nice to be able to enjoy the sun when it comes out without having to face that awful east wind.

PERRY: I promise I'll bring it up again at the next meeting, when there aren't quite so many of them there. Actually last Friday was a bit of a teaser, anyhow, a whole lot of things seemed to come together at the same time, there was the Atco mower, the broken railings at the end of the garden, to say nothing of the new boiler, which cost a small fortune.

BONITA: I can't believe that glassing that terrace in would cost two thousand five hundred pounds.

PERRY: That's what Hodges and Creal say.

BONITA: Well, Hodges and Creal must be barmy.

ALMINA: I knew nothing would come of it – I always said so, right from the very beginning.

ESTELLE: I feel it's all my fault really for having suggested it in the first place. Now you're all disappointed and I'm to blame. (*She is near tears.*)

BONITA: Cheer up, dear – it doesn't matter all that much.

ESTELLE: I was so looking forward to it – we all were – it would have been so lovely—— (*She weeps and searches in her work bag for her handkerchief.*)

PERRY (*putting his arms round her*): Don't cry, my old duck egg – I'll swing it somehow, you see if I don't. I'll get another estimate from another firm, one that isn't quite so posh as Hodges and Creal, and we'll knock a bit off here and a bit off there, and I'll get the committee to agree, if it's the last thing I do.

BONITA: That Boodie Nethersole! I'll have a few words to say to her the next time she comes bouncing down here in her bloody Bentley.

MISS ARCHIE: You'll only get Perry into trouble if you do.

PERRY: She didn't mean to be unkind, she just got worked up.

MAUDIE: Showing off, that's all she was doing.

CORA: Oh, for heaven's sake let's change the subject. As Bonita said, it doesn't matter all that much anyhow. A little while ago we'd none of us even heard of a solarium, we've all got one foot in the grave anyway.

BONITA: Excuse me while I slip into my shroud.

At this moment there is the sound of the front-door bell.

PERRY: That'll be Lotta, I expect.

MISS ARCHIE: Be a good chap, Perry, and yell for Ted to take up the bags – he's in the kitchen. I'll go to the door.

PERRY: Aye aye, sir. (*He goes off through the green baize door.*)

MISS ARCHIE (*briskly*): I hate welcoming new arrivals, they always look sort of lost. (*She goes off into the hall.*)

CORA: It's nothing to what they look after they've been here for a few months.

BONITA: Why do you say that, Cora? You know you don't really mean it.

CORA: Perhaps I was trying to be funny.

MAUDIE: There's nothing very funny about arriving here for the first time. I know I cried myself to sleep for a whole week.

ESTELLE: But you're happy here now though, aren't you? On the whole, I mean?

CORA: Are you?

ESTELLE: Don't, please, don't – I can't bear it. (*She gets up, grabs her work bag and hurries upstairs. The others look after her in silence.*)

BONITA: There now.

MISS ARCHIE *returns followed by* LOTTA BAINBRIDGE *and her maid,* DORA. LOTTA *is a well preserved woman in her early seventies. Her hair, which was once blonde, is now ash-coloured. She wears a small hat and a dust coat over a plain but well-cut dress. She is well made-up and calmly cheerful.* DORA, *in her forties, is fat and morose. She has obviously been crying.*

LOTTA (*with a smile*): Well, this is all very exciting – rather like going to a new school – except of course that at a new school one doesn't meet old friends. Cora! – I haven't seen you for years. (*She kisses her.*) Miss Melrose – (*She shakes hands with* MAUDIE, *who has risen to greet her.*) We're not exactly old friends but I have admired you so often – I remember you years ago singing a most enchant-ing song dressed as a school-girl – I've forgotten the name of the play——

MAUDIE: It was *Miss Mouse* at the Adelphi.

LOTTA: *Miss Mouse* – of course it was; dear old Harry Henderson was the comedian, wasn't he? He played in a play with me you know, just before he died – at the Garrick I think it was——

BONITA: *June Weather*.

LOTTA: How clever of you to remember – it was quite

a success but terribly sentimental. You're Bonita Belgrave, aren't you? – I'd recognise you anywhere. I knew you were here because we have a great friend in common, Lucas Bradshaw.

BONITA: Luke Bradshaw! I didn't know he was still alive. How is the old soak?

LOTTA: Still soaking, I'm afraid, but only every now and then. He comes to see me sometimes in his more lucid moments and we reminisce about the good old days.

CORA: A lot of that goes on here.

LOTTA: Between ourselves, you know, I'm really getting a bit tired of the good old days – but I suppose it is fun, once in a while, to wander back for a little.

MISS ARCHIE: You know Almina Clare.

LOTTA: Of course I do. Almina! (*She kisses her.*) You really are very naughty to have put on so much weight. You used to be as thin as a rail.

ALMINA: I like eating and there's no reason to diet any more.

LOTTA: No, I suppose there isn't really. I've done it for so many years that it's become a habit – I know that I shall automatically refuse bread and potatoes until the day I die.

PERRY *comes back from the kitchen.*

PERRY: Welcome to St Trinian's, Miss Bainbridge.

LOTTA: Why, Mr Lascoe. (*Shakes hands.*) I'd no idea you would be here to greet me – how very nice. (*Looking at Sir Hilary's bust.*) I remember that bust of Hilary. He was sitting for it when we were playing in *Brief Candles*. It took nearly three months, he nearly went mad. You know how impatient he always was, never still for a minute. (*She leads* DORA *forward by the hand.*) This is my beloved Dora. She's going to be married in a month's

time. We don't talk about being separated much because
we burst into tears. Why don't you go upstairs, Dora,
and do just a little unpacking for me, as a sort of final
gesture? Would you be very kind and show her where my
room is, Miss Archibald?

MISS ARCHIE: Certainly. Follow me, Dora.

DORA *shoots a tearful look at* LOTTA *and obediently
shuffles off upstairs in the wake of* MISS ARCHIE.

LOTTA (*slipping off her coat and sinking on to the sofa*): Oh
dear! I really felt quite nervous when I came in, like a
first night. But I feel better now. Old Martha Carrington's here, isn't she?

PERRY: Yes, but she never leaves her room.

LOTTA: She must be at least a hundred.

PERRY: Not quite, but she's coming along nicely.

CORA: May Davenport's here, too.

LOTTA: Yes. Yes, I know she is. I wonder who painted
that picture of dear Ellen Terry. It really isn't very good,
is it? But even flat painting can't quite subdue her
radiance, can it?

BONITA (*suddenly going up to* LOTTA *and kissing her*): It's
awfully nice to have you here, Miss Bainbridge – we're
all tremendously thrilled.

LOTTA (*nearly undone for a moment*): Thank you, dear –
thank you very much.

PERRY (*to cover a little silence*): You'll love Miss Archie
when you get to know her.

LOTTA: I'm sure I shall.

PERRY: She slips into uniform at the drop of a hat.
She retired from ENSA at the end of the war with the
rank of full Colonel. But underneath that gruff exterior
there beats a heart of pure gold.

LOTTA: I suppose I really should go upstairs and help

Dora and see my room but I don't feel I want to just yet, I shall be seeing quite enough of it in the years to come.

MAUDIE: It's one of the best ones, it looks out over the kitchen garden.

LOTTA (*wryly*): How lovely.

BONITA: Don't dread it, please don't dread any of it, it's not nearly so bad as you think – really it isn't.

LOTTA: I've tried not to think very much during the last few weeks, it seemed more sensible. I'm very fortunate to have this place to come to, I suppose we all are, really.

CORA: That's a matter of opinion.

BONITA: Oh, shut up, Cora.

LOTTA: I remember driving down here with Hilary years ago a few months after he had opened it. It was a lovely summer day – we had tea in the garden. Little did I think then that one day I should be coming here to live.

BONITA: It's quite a pleasant life, really. We have television and sometimes we go to the movies in Maidenhead and have tea at the Picture House café – the bus stop is only five minutes walk.

LOTTA (*absently*): I must catch up on my movies – I've been shamefully neglectful lately.

BONITA: Why don't you sit here quietly for a little and relax and sort of get accustomed to the atmosphere? It's about time for our afternoon snooze anyhow. Are you coming up, Cora?

CORA (*reluctantly*): Yes – I suppose so. (*She rises.*)

LOTTA (*with an effort*): You all know that May Davenport and I have not been on speaking terms for many many years, don't you?

CORA: Yes – yes, we do.

BONITA: Don't worry – it'll all work out in the long run.

LOTTA: The situation is not without humour. It is certainly ironic that Fate should arrange so neatly for May and me to end our days under the same roof. Personally I can't help seeing the funny side of it, but I doubt that May does.

BONITA: She doesn't, not at the moment, but she probably will in time.

LOTTA: Sense of humour was never one of her outstanding characteristics.

MAUDIE: She sometimes says awfully funny things.

LOTTA: She always did, but generally unintentionally. All I want to explain to you is that I am fully armed with olive branches. I couldn't bear to think that my coming here was in any way an embarrassment to you. I shall do my best, but please don't blame me too much if I fail. May is fairly implacable.

CORA: I suppose it would be too much to ask what caused the feud in the first place?

LOTTA: Yes, Cora, it would. In any case it would be redundant because I am well aware that you know the whole story.

BONITA: If ever I've heard a cue for exit, Cora, that's it. Come on up.

ALMINA (*heaving herself up from the sofa with an effort*): Oh, dear.

PERRY (*helping her*): Come on, love – you can make it, if you don't weaken.

MAUDIE (*putting her glasses into her bag and folding her newspaper*): See you later, Miss Bainbridge.

LOTTA: Au revoir, Miss Mouse.

MAUDIE (*laughing*): Oh, it wasn't me that was 'Miss Mouse' – I was only the soubrette. It was poor Dolly Drexell, actually it was the last thing she did before she went off her rocker – you remember her, don't you?

LOTTA: Vaguely.

MAUDIE: China-blue eyes and no middle register.

MAUDIE *goes upstairs followed more slowly by* ALMINA. CORA *and* BONITA *go after them.*

BONITA: We mustn't forget to ask Miss Archie to fix the television before tonight. There's a new quizz game.

CORA: I hate quiz games.

BONITA: You never actually *played* 'Rebecca of Sunnybrook Farm', dear, did you?

They disappear upstairs.

PERRY: Would you really like to be left alone for a bit?

LOTTA: No. I'm quite happy. Dora will be down in a minute anyhow, then, if you don't mind, I should like you to leave us – it will be a rather painful good-bye scene, I'm afraid. She's been working up for it all day.

PERRY (*offering his cigarette case*): Cigarette?

LOTTA (*taking one*): Thank you.

PERRY: Is Billy's car taking her back to London? (*He lights her cigarette.*)

LOTTA: Yes. It was dear of him to lend it to me. She'll go back to the flat and do all the final tidying-up. Poor old Dora. I shall miss her dreadfully.

PERRY: Have you seen him – the husband to be?

LOTTA: Yes, once, she brought him to tea. He seemed nice enough – massive, but with a very small head.

PERRY: Does he really love her?

LOTTA: I couldn't really tell. He stared at her fixedly all the time, if that is anything to go by. It's wonderful for her, really, after all she's not exactly in the first flush of youth. I'm afraid it's a bit late for her to have children of her own, but she'll be able to look after those two step-daughters. I expect she'll miss me a lot at first, but she'll soon get over it.

PERRY: Everybody gets over everything in time.

LOTTA (*with a smile*): I do so hope you're right.

PERRY: You'll soon get to like it here. I'm sure you will.

LOTTA: I'm sure I shall, too.

PERRY: If there's anything that really upsets you, that you really hate, do let me know privately and, if necessary, I can tactfully bring it up before the committee.

LOTTA: Thank you, you're very kind. I don't suppose there will be.

PERRY: Well, just remember – if you need me I'll be down like a flash.

LOTTA: You gave up the theatre very young, didn't you?

PERRY: Yes, six years ago, when I was thirty-three.

LOTTA: Why?

PERRY: I started out believing that I was going to be a star and then I suddenly realised that I wasn't.

LOTTA: I see. (*After a pause.*) Do you regret it?

PERRY: No, not really. Every now and then I get a pang or two when I see some young man prancing about the stage – I say to myself 'I could have done that better' but really, deep down, I'm not altogether sure that I could have.

LOTTA: And you like this job? You like having to cope with all these old shadows?

PERRY: It's a fixed salary to start with, so Mum's taken care of, and I love the – the old shadows. The committee gets me down a bit sometimes, but you can't have everything.

MISS ARCHIE *comes briskly down the stairs.*

MISS ARCHIE: Dora's nearly finished Miss Bainbridge. She'll be down in a minute. Unless you'd care to go up?

LOTTA: No. I'd rather wait here I think.

MISS ARCHIE: Buzz off for a minute, Perry, there's a good chap. I'd like to have a little chat with Miss Bainbridge.

PERRY: Where shall I buzz to?

MISS ARCHIE: Go and have a look at the Telly.

PERRY: I can't, it's bust.

MISS ARCHIE: I bet that's old Deirdre, she's always losing her temper and kicking it. I'll deal with it later.

PERRY: I'll brave the east wind in the garden.

MISS ARCHIE: Good.

PERRY: Good-bye for the moment, Miss Bainbridge.

LOTTA: Thank you – thank you for being so considerate and kind.

PERRY *goes out through the french windows and disappears into the garden.*

MISS ARCHIE: Good value, that lad. We get on like a house on fire.

LOTTA: I'm glad. I'm sure it's awfully important that you should.

MISS ARCHIE: You're dead right it is. Before he came they had a woman secretary, nearly drove me round the bend I can tell you, always in a frizz about something and absolutely terrified of the committee. I used to say to her over and over again, 'Listen, old girl – a commitee's something you've got to stand up to, and, what's more, they're grateful to you for it in the long run. They don't know what they're talking about half the time anyhow.' You know what actors and actresses are like on a committee? Always getting over-enthusiastic over inessentials and going off at tangents.

LOTTA: Oh, yes indeed. I served on this committee myself for three years in the 'thirties.

MISS ARCHIE: Oh Lord! I certainly put my neck out that time, didn't I?

LOTTA: Not at all. I agree with you on the whole. I remember at the time being horribly aware of my own inadequacy. I was often away on tour and obliged to miss several meetings in a row, then I'd come back and be asked to give my opinion on problems I knew nothing about. I wish now that I had taken a little more trouble. I'm sure we all tried to visualise it all from the point of view of the inmates themselves, but I'm not sure that we succeeded.

MISS ARCHIE: It's running pretty smoothly now, thank the Lord. Perry's liaison officer between the committee and me – we have our ups and downs occasionally, of course, but most of the time we manage to keep on an even keel. Now then, in regard to rules and regulations——

LOTTA (*ruefully*): Oh dear!

MISS ARCHIE: Don't be alarmed, there aren't many restrictions.

LOTTA (*ironically*): Are we allowed out alone?

MISS ARCHIE: Good Lord, yes. You can go anywhere you like.

LOTTA: Not quite, I'm afraid.

MISS ARCHIE: One rule we're very firm about is No Pets.

LOTTA: Yes, I know. Perry Lascoe explained that to me last week. I had my little dog put to sleep the day before yesterday. I bought him at the Army and Navy stores nine years ago when he was a tiny puppy. He was very devoted to me and I don't think he would have been happy with anyone else.

MISS ARCHIE: I say, I'm most awfully sorry, that's damned hard luck.

LOTTA: Please don't sympathise with me about it. It's the only thing, among my present rather dismal circumstances, that is liable to break me down.

MISS ARCHIE: I quite understand.

DORA *appears at the top of the stairs and comes slowly down.*

LOTTA: Here comes Dora. I wonder if you'd be very kind and leave us alone for a few minutes, she has to get back to London. You can brief me about the rest of the rules and regulations later on. I'm afraid there'll be lots of time.

MISS ARCHIE: Of course. Well, cheerio for the moment. I'll be in my office if you want anything. (*She nods cheerfully to* DORA *and goes out.*)

LOTTA: How's the room, Dora?

DORA: Quite nice, dear. It's a bit chintzy but there's a pretty view and it is quiet.

LOTTA: Where is it?

DORA: Second door to the right along the passage. Do you want to come up now?

LOTTA: No. I'll save it until after you've gone.

DORA (*breaking down*): I can't go away and leave you here, dear – I thought I could but I can't.

LOTTA: Don't talk nonsense, Dora. Of course you can, you must, there's nothing else to be done, anyhow. You know that as well as I do.

DORA (*sobbing*): I can't bear it – after all these years – I just can't bear it.

LOTTA (*putting her arm round her*): Pull yourself together, my dear, for my sake as well as for your own.

DORA: I'll tell Frank he'd better go off and marry

someone else, I swear to God I will. You and me will find a flat somewhere and go along as we always have – I can't go off and leave you in a sort of workhouse.

LOTTA (*smiling*): It isn't a workhouse, Dora. It's a very smart home for retired actresses. And in a few days, when the first strangeness has worn off, I'm quite sure I shall be far happier here and far less lonely than I should be in a flat. You have many more years than I have to live and enjoy. For heaven's sake see to it that you enjoy them. You have Frank and the two girls to look after, and you couldn't have stayed with me much longer anyhow because I couldn't afford it. And if I died I should have had nothing to leave you and you'd be alone. I couldn't bear the thought of that. We've talked about this over and over again. Please, please, dear Dora, don't cry any more. It isn't nearly so sad as it looks. You've promised, remember, to come down and see me next Sunday fortnight.

DORA (*with an effort*): Yes – yes, I know.

LOTTA: I shall look forward to it, and I shall write to you first thing to-morrow, and let you know how my first meeting with May went off.

DORA: Horrible old cat!

LOTTA: Now, now, now – she may have mellowed with the years.

DORA: I'll give her 'mellow' if I get within spitting distance of her.

LOTTA (*suddenly kissing her*): Dora – darling old Dora. I want you now this very minute to go out of the house, get into the car and drive away. Don't let's either of us say another word. I'm beginning to feel a little tremulous myself. Please. Please – dearest old friend – away with you. (*She gives her a little push.* DORA, *crying again, goes.*)

DORA (*at the door*): I've put the snapshot of Poochie on the mantelpiece, the one with the ball in his mouth.

LOTTA (*with a break in her voice*): Thank you, Dora – thank you.

DORA *goes out.* LOTTA, *left alone, bites her lip in a determined effort to control her tears, then she purposefully gathers up her coat and handbag and walks slowly and firmly up the stairs.*

CURTAIN

ACT I

Scene II

A month has elapsed since Act I, Scene I.

> *The time is about three a.m. on a Monday morning. The lights are on, the curtains are drawn and there is a fire in the grate.*

> *When the curtain rises* Doreen *comes in from the service door carrying a tray on which there are some plates of sandwiches.* Doreen *is a rather untidy girl of about twenty-three.*

> Miss Archie *comes out of her office. She is wearing a khaki-coloured man's dressing-gown, and rather old fur-lined bedroom slippers.*

Miss Archie: They ought to be here soon. Is the soup on?

Doreen: Yes, Miss Archibald.

Miss Archie: You'd better have a kettle going, too; some of them will probably want tea.

Doreen: Yes, Miss Archibald.

Miss Archie: Sorry to keep you up, Doreen. You can have an extra hour in the morning. They'll all be kipping late after to-night. (*She goes to the windows and drawing aside the curtain peers into the darkness.*) Still raining. Damn it!

That means that the roads will be greasy and Baxter will have to drive slowly.

DOREEN: The show's to-morrow night, isn't it, Miss Archibald?

MISS ARCHIE: Yes. (*She glances at her wrist-watch.*) To-night, really. It's three o'clock in the morning.

DOREEN: Is it true that Buck Randy's in it?

MISS ARCHIE: Yes. I think so.

DOREEN (*ecstatically*): Oooo – smashing!

MISS ARCHIE: You've never seen him, have you?

DOREEN: He was on in *In London To-night* last week. The man made him take off his shirt and sing a song – it was lovely. Will it be on the Telly? – the show, I mean?

MISS ARCHIE: Only an hour of it.

DOREEN: Can I pop in and have a look? I promise I'll turn it off afterwards.

MISS ARCHIE: You'll be asleep. It doesn't start until twelve. That's why it's called a Midnight Matinée.

DOREEN: I'll wake up, I'll set my alarm clock. Please let me, Miss Archibald.

MISS ARCHIE: All right. I expect some of the ladies will stay up for some of it if they're not too tired after tonight. They don't sleep much anyhow.

At this moment SARITA MYRTLE, *clad in a nightgown and dressing-gown, appears at the top of the stairs. She is a wispy old lady in the late seventies.*

SARITA: Everyone has forgotten me, the house is empty and I'm left alone.

MISS ARCHIE: Miss Myrtle, you're very naughty. You ought to be in bed, you know you ought.

SARITA: Please let me come down to the fire, my room is so cold.

Miss Archie: You know that's not true, dear, it's right next to the linen closet.

Sarita (*descending the stairs*): Out, damnéd spot! Out I say! One two: why then, 'tis time to do't.

Miss Archie (*firmly*): You must *not* quote Macbeth in this house, Miss Myrtle. You know how it upsets everybody.

Sarita (*with a slight giggle*): There isn't anybody to upset – all the rooms on the landing are 'empty, vast and wandering air' – perhaps it is the end of the world—— (*She catches sight of the spread card table.*) Good Heavens! Sandwiches! Whoever thought of sandwiches on the day of judgment?

Miss Archie: It isn't the day of judgment, old dear, it's three o'clock on Monday morning and you must go back to bed.

Sarita: But why the sandwiches?

Miss Archie (*patiently*): They're for the others when they come back from the Palladium. You went with them last year, don't you remember?

Sarita: Why didn't I go this year?

Miss Archie: Because Doctor Jevons said it would be bad for you. He said your heart wasn't up to it.

Sarita: There isn't anything wrong with my heart. It's my head that betrays me. It's so noisy. The island is full of noises. My head is an island. An island is a piece of land entirely surrounded by water. Please may I have a glass of water?

Miss Archie: Run into the kitchen and get her one, there's a good girl.

Doreen (*awe-stricken*): Ooo dear! (*She runs out.*)

Miss Archie (*to* Doreen): Go back to bed now and I'll bring the water up to you.

SARITA: Who is that girl who runs about?

MISS ARCHIE: You know Doreen. She brings you your breakfast every morning.

SARITA: Doreen is a very common name, don't you think?

MISS ARCHIE: Well, that's not her fault.

SARITA: All names ending in 'een' are common, Doreen, Maureen, Noreen——

MISS ARCHIE (*humouring her*): Eileen and Kathleen are all right, aren't they?

SARITA: Eileen and Kathleen who?

DOREEN (*returning with a glass of water*): Here you are, Miss Myrtle.

SARITA: What is this for?

MISS ARCHIE: You asked for a glass of water.

SARITA (*graciously accepting it*): Thank you, my dear child – thank you very much. I hope you enjoyed the performance.

DOREEN (*startled – to* MISS ARCHIE): What does she mean?

MISS ARCHIE: Never mind – just say 'yes', it saves time.

DOREEN: Yes, Miss Myrtle.

SARITA: I am afraid it was a rather dull matinée audience. It was the boat race, I expect; their minds were divided.

MISS ARCHIE: Take her back to bed, Doreen.

SARITA (*sitting down on the sofa and taking a sandwich*): I don't care for ham sandwiches as a rule, but to-night I'm hungry as a hunter.

There is the sound of a motor-horn outside.

MISS ARCHIE: Here they are. Run and open the door, Doreen. (*To* SARITA.) You really must go back to bed,

Miss Myrtle. I don't know what Doctor Jevons would say if he saw you wandering about the house in the middle of the night in your dressing-gown.

SARITA (*suddenly bursting into tears*): Please don't send me back to bed – it's so lonely and cold upstairs with all those empty rooms – please let me stay here – please, please, please——

MISS ARCHIE (*distracted*): There, there, old dear, there's nothing to cry about. (*She puts her arm round her rather clumsily.*) You can stay here for a bit if you really want to, but do try not to get over-excited.

SARITA (*cheering up*): I don't know who you are, but you smell like horses.

At this moment, BONITA, CORA, ALMINA, DEIRDRE *and* ESTELLE *come in. They are followed in a moment or two by* MAUDIE, MAY *and* LOTTA.

ESTELLE: It's raining cats and dogs. I thought we'd never get here.

BONITA: Good God, what's Sarita doing? Oughtn't she to be in bed?

MISS ARCHIE (*helplessly*): She woke up and came down a few minutes ago and I can't get her back.

BONITA (*kissing* SARITA): Hallo, dear – I haven't seen you for a long time.

SARITA (*munching her sandwich*): I've been away on tour.

DOREEN *comes back.*

MISS ARCHIE: You can bring in the soup now, Doreen.

DOREEN (*she goes off*): Yes, Miss Archibald.

CORA (*sinking into an armchair*): I'm absolutely exhausted. I thought that ass with the zither would never stop.

ALMINA: He was certainly very handsome.

CORA: His handsomeness palled on me after the first three quarters of an hour.

MAUDIE: Personally I'm going straight up to bed, I'll take a couple of sandwiches with me – I don't want any soup, it might wake me up. (*She goes amid a general murmur of good-nights.*)

MISS ARCHIE: How was the rehearsal?

LOTTA: Very good, but I fear much too long. I suppose they have to have all those microphones. They spoil it for me rather.

CORA: None of them nowadays can project their voice beyond a whisper.

LOTTA: I thought Marjorie Atherton's dance with all the men was very charming.

CORA: Very, considering that she can't put one foot in front of the other.

ESTELLE: The thing that worried me most was poor Sylvia doing that prologue. I can't believe that her dress was meant to look like that, and she didn't know the words very well, did she?

LOTTA: Sylvia's always been bad on words. I should have thought those two seasons at Stratford would have cured her, but they haven't.

CORA: She'd have been better advised to go to Tring.

LOTTA (*laughing*): Cora. You really are disgraceful.

DOREEN *comes back with a tray on which there are several bowls of soup. She puts it down rather awkwardly on the card table.* CORA *moves the plate of sandwiches out of the way.*

SARITA: There's that girl who brings me my breakfast. What's she doing here?

ALMINA (*in a false, rather cooing voice*): That's Doreen, dear – you know Doreen, don't you?

SARITA (*graciously*): Of course I do. We shared digs in

Wolverhampton years and years ago. The landlady was an absolute horror and one night she locked us out and we hammered and hammered on the door and I had to crawl in through the scullery window. (*To* DOREEN.) Don't you remember?

DOREEN (*startled*): Well, Miss Myrtle, I——

BONITA: Of course she remembers, who would forget a thing like that?

MISS ARCHIE: You can hop off to bed now, Doreen.

DOREEN: Thank you, Miss Archie.

LOTTA: Thank you for waiting up for us, Doreen. I'm afraid you must be very tired.

DOREEN: It's a pleasure I'm sure, miss.

SARITA: Don't forget to turn the gas out on the landing, we promised Mrs Worsley we would and we don't want any more scenes.

DOREEN: Okay, Miss Myrtle. (*She goes into the servants' quarters.*)

SARITA: Head like a sieve, that girl, no concentration, she dried up dead in the first act last night, just stood there with her mouth opening and shutting silently, like a carp. Poor Ronnie was frantic.

MISS ARCHIE (*taking her gently by the arm*): Bedtime now, old dear.

SARITA (*rising without protest*): I know – I know – can't afford to lose our beauty sleep – train call to-morrow at nine-thirty – oh dear! (MISS ARCHIE *leads her upstairs.*) I must remember to give a little present to that girl who keeps on running about. What *is* her name?

MISS ARCHIE: Doreen, dear.

SARITA: Poor child, fancy being saddled with a name like that. It sounds like an eye lotion. (*She and* MISS ARCHIE *disappear.*)

BONITA: Well, here's to The Midnight Matinée from which all our blessings flow. (*She raises her bowl of soup.*)

LOTTA: And all those very kind people who worked so hard for it.

CORA: Some of them worked a damned sight too hard, particularly that American woman dressed as a cowgirl. I thought she'd burst a blood vessel.

ALMINA: The audience adored her.

CORA: That audience would adore anything.

BONITA: Well, I for one am grateful to them. If they didn't enjoy themselves they wouldn't come again, and if they didn't come again we should be up the creek, so here's to them! (*She raises her bowl of soup.*)

LOTTA: Hear, hear.

ESTELLE: Do you think she'll ever get any better, poor old Sarita, or just go on and on getting madder and madder?

BONITA: She'll probably stay about the same. She's quite happy most of the time, at least that's what Doctor Jevons says.

LOTTA: It's a form of escape, isn't it?

BONITA: Yes, I suppose so.

LOTTA: Miss Archie's wonderful with her.

BONITA: Miss Archie's a pretty good sort, taken all round.

CORA: If only she didn't make us feel we ought to present arms all the time.

LOTTA *comes over to* MAY *with a bowl of soup.*

LOTTA: Here's some soup, May. (*The others all watch while* MAY *turns her head away in silence*.) I said here's some soup, May. Would you like it or not? (MAY *still ignores her.*) Are you never going to break down?

DEIRDRE: Holy Mother of God, May Davenport, it's shame you should be feeling, walking through the last years of your life with your head so high and your heart full of hatred.

MAY: Please don't talk to me like that, and mind your own business.

LOTTA: It is Deirdre's business, May. It's the business of all of us in this house to live together as amicably as possible without causing each other any embarrassment.

DEIRDRE: If you'll take my advice you'll pay no attention to her. She's warming her cold heart at the fire of her own hatred. Take that away and she'll freeze to death, you mark my words.

LOTTA (*with a smile*): I'll mark them, Deirdre. But I fear at the present moment they are not being very helpful.

DEIRDRE (*rising*): Well, for me the sweet waters of oblivion. I'll say a couple of Hail Marys before I drop off, just in case the Blessed Saviour should see fit to gather me to his bosom in the middle of the night.

LOTTA: I somehow don't feel that he will. Good-night, Deirdre.

DEIRDRE *disappears upstairs.*

LOTTA (*firmly*): May, I want to talk to you.

MAY *rises and without looking at her goes towards the stairs.* LOTTA *intercepts her.*

MAY (*icily*): Please let me pass.

LOTTA: I have no intention of letting you pass, nor have I any intention of allowing you to carry on this idiocy any longer. We have now been in this house together for a month without addressing a word to each other and the situation is intolerable. You are going to listen to what I have to say, so you had better make up your mind to it.

MAY: I am not. (*She makes another movement towards the stairs.*)

LOTTA (*gripping her firmly by the shoulder*): Stay where you are.

MAY: Leave go of me immediately. You must be out of your mind!

LOTTA: Listen to me. I implore you to listen to me. Not for my sake. I don't care if you never speak to me again, but for the sake of all the other people in this house, this age-old feud must be resolved here and now. It poisons the air we breathe and we have no right, either of us, to infect others with our personal spleen. If we were living our ordinary lives it would be different, we could go on avoiding each other as we have done for thirty years, but here we can't. Here, we are forced to see each other morning, noon and night until we die. We had better face one harsh fact, May. We have fallen on evil days and there is no sense in making them more evil than they need be. We haven't many years left and very, very little to look forward to. Let's for God's sake forget the past and welcome our limited future with as much grace as possible.

MAY: Eloquently put, Lotta. I would be the last to deny your sentimental appeal to an audience. It was all you ever had. Please remove your hands from my shoulders and allow me to go to bed.

LOTTA (*doing so and turning away*): Very well.

MAY *goes upstairs in dead silence.* LOTTA *goes over to the mantelpiece and leans her head on her hands.*

BONITA: Once a ham always a ham!

LOTTA (*hopelessly and near tears*): I did my best. I shan't try any more. It's waste of time and there's so little left. (*She bites her lip and forces a smile.*) Thank God!

CURTAIN

ACT II

SCENE I

It is a Sunday afternoon in September. When the curtain rises the stage is empty. There is the sound of the front-door bell. DOREEN comes out of the green baize door and goes into the hall. She ushers in PERRY and ZELDA FENWICK.

ZELDA is in her middle thirties. She is nice-looking, trim and wears well-cut trousers and a sports shirt.

PERRY: Where is everyone, Doreen?

DOREEN: Upstairs, I think, all except Miss Clarke and Miss Davenport; they've gone for a walk.

PERRY: Is Miss Archie in her office? You might tell her we're here.

DOREEN: Okay, sir. (*She goes to MISS ARCHIE's door and knocks. MISS ARCHIE's voice shouts 'Come in' gruffly and she goes in.*)

ZELDA (*looking round*): Quite a nice room. (*Seeing Sir Hilary's bust.*) Who's that?

PERRY: Sir Hilary Brooks. He founded the place.

ZELDA: My mother was crazy about him when she was young, used to wait in pit queues for hours and hours. I have a feeling he was rather an old ham. (*She looks at the picture of Ellen Terry.*) My grandmother was crazy about her.

PERRY: A keen theatre-going family.

ZELDA: Good Lord yes, they never stopped. I was dragged screaming to matinées from the age of four onwards.

PERRY: Didn't you enjoy them?

ZELDA: Not the jolly pantomimes and children's plays, and that was all I got until I was well into my teens. I can't think of *Peter Pan* to this day without a shudder.

PERRY: I love *Peter Pan*.

ZELDA: That's because you've got a mother-fixation. All sensitive lads with mother-fixations worship *Peter Pan*.

PERRY: I expect I have a crocodile fixation too.

DOREEN *comes out of* MISS ARCHIE'S *room*.

DOREEN: Miss Archibald says she won't be a minute.

PERRY: Thanks, Doreen.

DOREEN *goes out*.

ZELDA: Who is the oldest inmate here?

PERRY: Martha Carrington. She's pushing ninety-five.

ZELDA: Good Lord!

PERRY: And what's more, she still has a beau, Osgood Meeker. He's just a kiddie of seventy. He comes to visit her every Sunday, rain or shine. He's probably up with her now. He always brings her violets.

ZELDA (*whipping out a notebook and scribbling in it*): Good. That's the sort of stuff I want.

PERRY (*apprehensively*): You will be careful, won't you? – I mean – don't mention names more than you can help.

ZELDA: Don't worry, I'll be discretion itself. It's just possible, though, that one or two of them might recognise me.

PERRY: I doubt it, your photograph never appears in your column.

ZELDA: My name does.

PERRY: I'll introduce you as Miss - Miss Starkey.

ZELDA: Why Starkey, for Heaven's sake?

PERRY: *Peter Pan* again, it's an obsession with me.

ZELDA: Where are they going to put the what-you-may-call-it if they get it?

PERRY: Solarium. (*He points to the terrace.*) There. We want to glass the whole terrace in and do away with the french windows. It would mean an awful lot to them to be able to enjoy the sun without the wind. As it is, they can hardly ever use the terrace unless the weather's absolutely perfect.

ZELDA (*going to the french windows and opening one*): Yes. I see what you mean. The damned house was built in the wrong place to start with.

MISS ARCHIE *comes out of her office.*

MISS ARCHIE: Hallo, Perry - I didn't hear the old bike.

PERRY: No. I came down with a friend. Miss Starkey - Miss Archibald.

MISS ARCHIE (*wringing* ZELDA's *hand*): How do you do?

PERRY: She drives like a fiend. I think she has a Stirling Moss fixation.

MISS ARCHIE (*laughing heartily*): Good show!

ZELDA: I've got an old Jag convertible, quite a nice little job.

MISS ARCHIE: Whew! I should just say so indeed. What can you do in her?

ZELDA: Up to a hundred and twenty on the open road.

MISS ARCHIE: Wizard!

PERRY: Perhaps I'd better leave you girls to your feminine secrets while I go and put on a pipe or something.

MISS ARCHIE (*ignoring him*): I had an M.G. just after the war but I ran it into a lorry.

PERRY: Butter fingers.

ZELDA: Were you Waafs, Wrens or Ats?

MISS ARCHIE: Ensa.

ZELDA: Lord! That must have been a bit tricky, having to deal with all those actors.

MISS ARCHIE (*slightly defensive on behalf of her old regiment*): It was damned interesting. My job of course was mainly administrative, but I managed to get about a good bit, Cairo, Bombay, Burma—— Better than staying at home and pen-pushing in some Ministry.

ZELDA: I was a Wren. Malta for two years.

MISS ARCHIE: Good for you!

PERRY: And now to rescue Wendy!

MAY *and* CORA *come in from the hall. They are both dressed for walking.*

CORA: Hallo, Perry!

PERRY: May I introduce an old friend of mine – Miss Starkey – Miss Cora Clarke.

CORA (*shaking hands*): How do you do?

PERRY: And Miss May Davenport.

MAY (*bowing*): How do you do?

ZELDA: My father was one of your greatest admirers, Miss Davenport.

MAY: I fear you must be confusing your father with your grandfather, my dear.

PERRY (*hurriedly*): Have you had a nice walk?

MAY: Very pleasant. We managed to hobble to the tow-path and back. Cora insists that such arduous expeditions are good for us, but I am not entirely convinced. (*She looks at* ZELDA's *trousers.*) Have you been riding?

ZELDA: Riding? Oh no, we've just driven down from London.

MAY (*smiling remotely*): How foolish of me.

PERRY: Miss Starkey was most anxious to come and see 'The Wings' and everything, so I brought her down to tea.

CORA: How nice. (*To* ZELDA.) If you'll forgive us for the moment, we'll go upstairs and take off our things. Are you coming up, May?

MAY: Yes. *A bientôt*, Miss Starkey.

They go slowly upstairs.

MISS ARCHIE (*to* ZELDA): Cigarette? (*She produces a packet of Players.*)

ZELDA (*taking one*): Thanks.

PERRY: Is Osgood here today?

MISS ARCHIE: Of course. He never misses a Sunday.

ZELDA (*looking to see that* MAY *is out of earshot*): Lotta Bainbridge is here, isn't she?

MISS ARCHIE: Yes. She came in June.

ZELDA (*thoughtfully*): Lotta Bainbridge and May Davenport. Wasn't there a famous quarrel or something? I seem to remember hearing about it.

MISS ARCHIE: Yes, there was.

ZELDA: What was it about?

MISS ARCHIE (*guardedly*): I don't know – it was ages ago anyhow.

ZELDA: Have they kissed and made friends?

MISS ARCHIE (*uncomfortable*): Well, no – not exactly. Actually it's a bit tricky.

ZELDA: There's a good story in that, isn't there?

MISS ARCHIE (*puzzled*): Story – how do you mean?

ZELDA: 'Old foes still feuding in the twilight of their lives!'

MISS ARCHIE: Sounds like newspaper stuff.

PERRY (*nervously*): Yes – it does rather – doesn't it?

At this moment OSGOOD MEEKER *appears at the top of the stairs.*

OSGOOD: Ah, there you are, Miss Archie. I didn't see you when I arrived. I went straight up as usual – I hope you don't mind.

MISS ARCHIE: Of course not.

OSGOOD: She's in splendid form to-day, positively blooming.

PERRY: This is Miss Starkey – Mr. Meeker.

OSGOOD (*shaking hands*): How do you do?

ZELDA: I understand that you visit Miss Carrington every Sunday?

OSGOOD: Oh yes – yes, ever since she first arrived here, years ago. It has become quite a little ritual, hasn't it, Miss Archie?

MISS ARCHIE: Rather.

OSGOOD: I think – I hope that it gives her pleasure, it seems to.

MISS ARCHIE: Of course it does, Mr. Meeker. She looks forward to it all through the week.

ZELDA: How long is it since she retired?

OSGOOD: Oh, many, many years, forty or more. I last saw her in the 'thirties in *The Late Mrs Robart* at the St. James's. She was getting on in years even then, but she was as witty and stylish as ever. She had a special way of moving about the stage that was all her own, effortless, and with such infinite grace. I saw her for the first time in 1906 in *The Lavender Girl.*

ZELDA: *The Lavender Girl.* That's certainly going back a bit.

OSGOOD: I was only eighteen at the time and I quite

lost my heart. Those were her great years, of course, her musical comedy years, there was nobody like her and there never will be again. All London was at her feet.

ZELDA: I remember my parents talking about her. She hadn't much of a voice, had she?

OSGOOD: She hadn't much of anything really, except magic, but she had a great deal of that.

ZELDA: And now she's dying upstairs?

OSGOOD: Oh no, Miss – Miss Starkey, living upstairs. I don't think she will ever die, not quite.

ZELDA: Bully for you, Mr. Meeker.

OSGOOD: I'm afraid I don't quite understand.

MISS ARCHIE (*saving the situation*): Would you like to have your tea in my office as usual, Mr. Meeker, or will you wait and have it with all of us in the dining-room?

OSGOOD: Neither today, thank you, Miss Archie. I have an appointment in London. I can just catch the four-forty if I hurry.

MISS ARCHIE: You're quite sure? It's no trouble.

OSGOOD: Quite sure. Thank you all the same. You're always so kind. Good-bye, Mr. Lascoe.

PERRY: Good-bye – until next Sunday.

OSGOOD: Oh yes – yes – next Sunday. Good-bye, Miss Starkey. (*He bows politely.*) Your parents were quite right, she hadn't much of a voice, but it didn't matter – I really do assure you it didn't matter in the least. (*He goes.*)

ZELDA: There's certainly gold in these yar hills. (*To* MISS ARCHIE.) Would it be all right if I took a few shots of the house from the garden? The light's still good.

MISS ARCHIE (*more and more puzzled*): Shots?

ZELDA: Snapshots. For my memory book. My camera's in the car.

PERRY: I'll get it.

ZELDA: No – don't you trouble. I'd like to wander round on my own for a bit anyhow. I shan't be long. (*She goes out into the hall and disappears.*)

MISS ARCHIE: What's going on?

PERRY: How do you mean?

MISS ARCHIE: Who is she, Perry?

PERRY: I told you. Miss Starkey. She's an old friend of mine.

MISS ARCHIE: You're up to something.

PERRY: Don't be silly. What could I be up to?

MISS ARCHIE: She's Press, isn't she?

PERRY (*after a pause*): Yes – she's Zelda Fenwick.

MISS ARCHIE: Zelda Fenwick! The one that writes all that hogwash in the *Clarion*?

PERRY (*unhappily*): Yes.

MISS ARCHIE: Good God! have you gone out of your mind? You know Press interviews are dead against the rules.

PERRY: She has a lot of influence.

MISS ARCHIE: Do any of the committee know she's here?

PERRY: Of course not. It was my idea.

MISS ARCHIE: Look here, my lad, you're going to get yourself into serious trouble.

PERRY: I don't care. I want the old girls to get that solarium. The committee has dug its feet in, I've done everything I can to persuade them but they're as stubborn as mules. The Fund could afford it perfectly well. I've got another estimate, from Weatherby's, only eighteen hundred.

MISS ARCHIE: What's all this got to do with Zelda Fenwick?

PERRY: I said that if she'd promise to make an appeal

for us on T.V. I'd arrange for her to have an exclusive story on 'The Wings'.

MISS ARCHIE: You'll get the sack! You'll get us both the sack! Why the hell didn't you consult me first?

PERRY: You needn't know anything about it. I'll take the rap.

MISS ARCHIE: I can't agree to it. You'll have to get her out, and quick, pack up the whole idea.

PERRY: There's no need to get into such a frizz. She's promised to let me see whatever she writes before it goes in.

MISS ARCHIE: I've heard that one before. I don't like it, Perry – I don't like it one little bit. It's going dead against regulations.

PERRY: The old girls have built up this solarium in their minds as the one thing in the world they really want. I don't see why they should be deprived of it just because one dizzy fathead like Boodie Nethersole has enough personality to sway the committee. We could easily have used some of Maurice Kane's legacy for it, but she jumped on that too and talked a lot of hot air about needless expenditure——

MISS ARCHIE: Who were in favour of it?

PERRY: Laura, Dame Maggie, old Cecil Murdoch and of course dear old Jane, but she's always in favour of everything. A few of the others were wavering but they allowed themselves to be overruled.

MISS ARCHIE (*rising and striding about*): Damn it – I don't know what to think.

PERRY: It isn't needless expenditure anyway. It will make a very real difference to their health and their comfort.

MISS ARCHIE: All right, I'll play ball. We shall probably find ourselves up the old creek but they can't fire us both.

PERRY: They can but they won't. They'd have to find replacements, and the few of them that really take an interest and do the work, like Laura and Dame Maggie, know damn well that that's easier said than done.

MISS ARCHIE: Look out, someone's coming. Let's go into the office.

PERRY: Right.

They go hurriedly into the office. SARITA *appears at the top of the stairs and comes cautiously down. She is, as usual, in a nightgown, bedroom slippers and a quilted blue dressing-gown. She goes over to the fireplace and sits in* MAY'S *chair with a little giggle.* ZELDA *comes in from the terrace.*

ZELDA (*seeing* SARITA): Oh!

SARITA (*grandly*): How do you do? I'm afraid my sister is at a rehearsal but she is sure to be back soon. Won't you sit down?

ZELDA: Thank you. (*She sits on the sofa.*)

SARITA (*reaching for a matchbox and striking a match*): Isn't that pretty?

ZELDA (*slightly bewildered*): Yes. Very pretty.

SARITA: When we were very young we used to have boxes of coloured matches on Guy Fawkes day and the tips of them were different from ordinary matches, longer and fatter, like little black sausages. When you struck them they were like red and green stars.

ZELDA: You must forgive my ignorance but I don't know your name. Mine is Zelda F—— Starkey.

SARITA: Miserable Starkey!

ZELDA (*ignoring this*): What's yours?

SARITA: I am Sarita Myrtle. I expect that surprises you, doesn't it?

ZELDA (*at sea*): Oh yes – oh yes, of course.

SARITA: I've always looked so much younger than my age, it's an advantage in a way of course, but one can't go on playing ingénues for ever, can one?

ZELDA: How long have you been here?

SARITA: Oh, quite a while.

ZELDA: It's a very nice house, isn't it?

SARITA: Capacity.

ZELDA (*pressing on*): Are you happy on the whole?

SARITA: Oh yes, except on matinée days, I hate those tea-trays, so distracting.

ZELDA: Are they kind to you?

SARITA: Oh yes. Sometimes they're a little dull in the first act, but they generally warm up.

ZELDA: Is your room comfortable?

SARITA: It's cold. *She* says it isn't because it's next to the linen closet, but she doesn't always speak the truth, I'm afraid.

ZELDA: Is 'she' Miss Archibald?

SARITA: Yes, I think so. It's difficult to be quite sure, people's faces change so, it's very confusing. (*She strikes another match.*) There!

DEIRDRE *and* ESTELLE *come out of the television room.*

DEIRDRE (*hurrying across to* SARITA): Holy Mother of God, what the hell are you doing with those matches, Sarita Myrtle? Is it burning us all to cinders that you're after? (*She firmly takes the box from her.*) Go back to your bed this very minute.

SARITA (*sociably*): How do you do?

DEIRDRE: Never you mind how I do. Come on now, away with you before Miss Archie catches you and claps you in irons. Take her other arm, Estelle.

SARITA: For Heaven's sake lower your voice, Rupert,

the children will hear. (*She moves away*.)

ESTELLE (*approaching her*): Come, dear——

SARITA (*backing*): Henceforward, Mr Cartwright, we must regard one another as strangers. I can say no more – farewell. (*She goes swiftly up the stairs and disappears*.)

DEIRDRE: You'd better go after her, Estelle, and see that she's safe in her bed. You have more of a way with her than I have.

ESTELLE (*resigned*): Very well. I hope this isn't the beginning of one of her bad spells. (*To* ZELDA.) Excuse me. (*She goes upstairs after* SARITA.)

DEIRDRE: The poor ould thing's a bit weak in the head.

ZELDA: I gathered that.

DEIRDRE: My name is Deirdre O'Malley. Are you a friend of Miss Archie's?

ZELDA: No. As a matter of fact I came down with Perry Lascoe. I'm just a stray visitor. I've heard so much about 'The Wings' and I wanted to see it for myself. My name is Starkey.

DEIRDRE: It's a pleasure to meet you, I'm sure. A new face is always a bit of a treat – we get tired of looking at our own ould ones year in year out.

ZELDA: Have you been here long?

DEIRDRE: Nearly twenty years. I've seen a lot of them come and go but the Blessed Lord has seen fit to let me linger on.

ZELDA: Are you happy here?

DEIRDRE: We're as happy as you could expect a bunch of old women to be when the tide of life has turned away from them and left them high and dry watching the dark shadows growing longer and longer and waiting for the grave.

ZELDA: Is the food good?

DEIRDRE: That's a practical question and deserves a practical answer. No, it isn't.

ZELDA: What's wrong with it?

DEIRDRE: You're not one of the committee, are you?

ZELDA: No.

DEIRDRE: Good. I'd have a few home truths to tell you if you were.

ZELDA: Don't you approve of the committee?

DEIRDRE: Approve of them! (*She gives a short laugh.*) They don't give us a chance to approve of them. We don't clap eyes on them from one year's end to the other. Just one or two of them have the grace to come down here once in a blue moon. They wander about, asking questions without listening to the answers, then they're given tea and we all sit about, watching them trying to remember what our names are. Then they drive away in all their finery and we're left feeling like a lot of animals in the Zoo. I'm sometimes surprised that they don't prod us with their umbrellas and throw us buns!

ZELDA: Aren't you being a little bitter, Miss O'Malley?

DEIRDRE: Bitter, is it? You'd be bitter if the last years of your life were controlled by a lot of gabbing flipperty-gibbets who don't really give a hoot in hell whether you're alive or dead.

At this moment BONITA *and* MAUDIE *come down the stairs.*

MAUDIE (*as they come down*): . . . she wouldn't stay off, of course and give the understudy a chance, not her, and the result was that the whole company got mumps and the show had to close.

BONITA: I had mumps once in Inverness. I nearly

went mad! (*She arrives at the bottom of the stairs and sees* ZELDA.) Oh – how do you do?

DEIRDRE: This is a friend of Perry's, Miss – Miss—— (*She looks inquiringly at* ZELDA.)

ZELDA: Starkey.

BONITA: I'm Bonita Belgrave and this is Maud Melrose. (*She shakes hands with* ZELDA.)

MAUDIE (*doing the same*): How do you do—— Where *is* Perry?

ZELDA: I don't know. He seems to have disappeared.

ALMINA *and* ESTELLE *come down the stairs, followed by* MAY *and* CORA.

ALMINA: If I got a notice like that I'd never lift my head up again.

ESTELLE: The *Sunday Times* was quite good.

ALMINA: Yes, but I couldn't understand half of it, too many French words and that Edwigger what's-her-name being dragged in all the time.

ESTELLE: Not Edwigger, dear. Edveege. Edveege Fooyare.

By this time they have arrived at the bottom of the stairs. PERRY *and* MISS ARCHIE *come out of the office and the conversation overlaps and becomes general.* PERRY *introduces* ZELDA *to* ALMINA *and* ESTELLE.

BONITA: Why Perry – I thought you had deserted us!

PERRY: No. Miss Archie and I have been having a little gossip.

BONITA (*to* ZELDA): Is that your car outside?

ZELDA: Yes.

BONITA: It's a beauty, isn't it? I saw it from the lavatory window.

MAY: Really, my dear Bonita. There is no need to be

over-explicit. (*She sits in her chair and produces from her work-bag her embroidery frame and coloured wools.*)

BONITA: Well, I couldn't have seen it from my own window because it faces in the opposite direction.

DEIRDRE (*mournfully*): When I think of the changes in the world during the span of my own miserable lifetime, me head reels, and that's no lie.

CORA: Your life span hasn't been in the least miserable, Deirdre. You've enjoyed every minute of it and still do.

DEIRDRE: And what is there to enjoy I should like to know? Loitering about here in me dotage getting feebler and wearier with every blessed breath I take?

CORA: Pay no attention to Deirdre, Miss Starkey. She loves talking like that.

MAY: She also takes considerable pleasure in embarrassing the rest of us.

DEIRDRE: Maybe it's the unacceptable ring of truth behind me words that embarrasses you, May Davenport.

MAY: I wish you would either address me as 'May' or 'Miss Davenport', Deirdre. May Davenport sounds like a roll call.

DEIRDRE: You can save your almighty arrogance until you get to the final roll call, Miss May Davenport.

MISS ARCHIE (*firmly*): Now then, Deirdre. That's no way to talk when there are strangers present.

DEIRDRE: Nothing I do is right, nothing I say is right. If I fell into the dark waters of the river this very night, I doubt if anyone would lift a finger to help me.

MAY (*sepulchrally*): The Irish can never resist cheap sentimentality.

BONITA: Oh, May, don't make things worse, for heaven's sake.

LOTTA *comes down the stairs.*

LOTTA: What on earth's happening?

BONITA: Nothing much. Deirdre's getting a bit out of hand, that's all.

DEIRDRE (*attempting to rise but held firmly back by* CORA): Out of hand, is it——

CORA: Yes, it is. Be quiet.

PERRY: Lotta I don't think you've met Miss Starkey.

ZELDA (*advancing*):   Hallo – how are you?

LOTTA (*shaking hands and staring at her*): Miss Starkey?

ZELDA: Yes. I came down with Perry. We're old friends.

LOTTA: Is Starkey your private name?

ZELDA: Private name? – I——

LOTTA: You're really Zelda Fenwick, aren't you – the one who writes the 'People are News' column in the *Sunday Clarion*?

ZELDA (*after a slight pause*): Yes. Yes I am.

MISS ARCHIE: Oh Lord – that's torn it!

MAY (*rising*): Is this true, Perry?

PERRY (*guiltily*): Yes. Perfectly true.

LOTTA (*to* ZELDA): I saw you on television a few weeks ago. (*She turns to* PERRY.) I think, Perry, that it would have been more polite and considerate if you had introduced Miss Fenwick by her proper name.

PERRY (*miserably*): I'll explain it later. I'll explain it all later.

LOTTA: I'm sure that no explanation is in the least necessary. It's merely a little confusing, that's all.

MAY: I beg to differ. A great deal of explanation is necessary. (*To* ZELDA.) May I ask, Miss Fenwick, if you are here in a professional capacity?

ZELDA (*with spirit*): I am always in a professional

capacity, Miss Davenport. That is an essential part of my job.

MAY: Is the committee aware of your visit to us?

ZELDA: No. And, if I may say so, I rather resent your tone. I am not answerable to you for my actions or to your committee.

PERRY: Just a minute – please let me explain.

MAY (*in rich tones*): Be quiet, Perry.

LOTTA (*with considerable authority*): It seems to me that the situation is being rather over-dramatised. (MAY *starts to interrupt but* LOTTA *silences her.*) No, May. I'm afraid I must insist on speaking. I would like Miss Fenwick clearly to understand that we are delighted to welcome her here. We have, as a rule, very few visitors. I am sure, however, that Miss Fenwick herself will be the first to realise that it will place us all in a most humiliating position if she mentions either 'The Wings' itself or any of its occupants in her newspaper. In the first place it would be a breach of the rules of this—— (*she smiles*) – this rather 'specialised' charity, and in the second place I am sure that, even in her professional capacity, she would not wish either to betray our confidence or abuse our hospitality. I am right, aren't I, Miss Fenwick?

ZELDA (*awkwardly*): Well – er – as a matter of fact——

LOTTA: You will promise, won't you, even if you had it in mind to write a story about us, *not* to write it? Our own professional careers are long ago over and done with, some of our names may still be remembered by a few people but those get fewer and fewer as the years go by. We are quite content that it should be so. We are happy enough here, living out our days in this most agreeable backwater. The last thing we want any more is publicity. It would shed too harsh a light on us, show up all our lines and wrinkles, betray to the world how old and tired we are. That would be an unkind thing to do. We are still actresses in our hearts, we still have our little vanities and prides. We'd like to be remembered as we were, not as we are. You will give us your promise, won't you?

ZELDA: I appreciate what you say, Miss Bainbridge. But I'm afraid I must be honest with you. My editor has been trying to get a story on this place for years. I know you will understand that it isn't only in the Theatre that the job must come first. I cannot promise not to write about 'The Wings' but I can promise to do all I can to help. I had already arranged with Perry that if he let me come here I would make a personal appeal on Television for your solarium.

CORA: Solarium – Good God! Are we to sell our souls to get that damned solarium!

LOTTA: Oh, Cora – please——

MAY: I'm ashamed of you, Perry. Mortally, mortally ashamed.

MISS ARCHIE: Here, steady on. It's no good flying off the handle at Perry. He only did it for the best.

ESTELLE (*wailing*): It's all my fault – I was the one who suggested it in the first place.

DEIRDRE (*rising dramatically*): Shame on you, Miss Whatever-your-name-is! Shame on you for worming your way in here like a wolf in sheep's clothing and talking to us as sweet as honey while all the time you were gouging out the secrets of our hearts for your shoddy catchpenny newspaper. Shame on you I say! And may the Holy Mother of God forgive you for making a mock of a houseful of poor defenceless old women who are only asking to be left in peace and quiet. The devil's curse on you for being a double-faced, scheming hypocrite! Write what you like and be damned to you! I've said my say. (*She sits down again.*)

LOTTA: You certainly have, Deirdre. And I for one would like to throttle you.

ZELDA: I can't stand any more of this. Are you coming, Perry?

PERRY (*wretchedly*): No. I'm staying here.

ZELDA (*curtly*): Good-bye, everybody. I'm sorry to have caused such a hullabaloo. (*She marches out.*)

MAY (*in stentorian tones*): The whole thing is an outrage – an outrage!

CORA: For Heaven's sake calm down, May.

MAY: The committee must be warned immediately, pressure must be brought to bear.

CORA: Personally I think a great deal of fuss is being made about nothing. What does it really matter whether she writes about us or not?

MAY: We shall be publicly degraded.

CORA: Nonsense! She'll probably write a lot of sentimental rubbish which will embarrass us for a little until we forget it and everyone else does too. Let's go into tea and talk about something else.

PERRY: I really am sorry. I did it for the best, honestly I did.

LOTTA: I'm sure you did, Perry, but, if you will forgive my saying so, it was an error in taste.

She sweeps out, the others follow, all talking at once. ESTELLE *is weeping and being comforted by* ALMINA. MISS ARCHIE *is last, and turns at the door.*

MISS ARCHIE: Come on, old chap.

PERRY: I don't want any tea.

MISS ARCHIE: Cheer up! It'll all blow over.

PERRY: An error in taste. I suppose it was really – but I didn't see it like that.

MISS ARCHIE: I don't feel like tea either. Let's pop into my office and have a slug of something a bit stronger. I've got a bottle of Gordon's in case of emergencies.

PERRY: Thanks, pal.

MISS ARCHIE: We're in this together. We might as well celebrate.

They move towards the office. MISS ARCHIE *puts her arm comfortingly round* PERRY'S *shoulder.*

The stage is empty for a moment.

SARITA *appears at the top of the stairs and comes quietly down. She makes a bee line for the matches, strikes one and watches it burn delightedly – then, hearing someone coming, she drops down in front of the sofa.* DOREEN *comes in from the service door with the tea tray and goes off into the dining-room with it.* SARITA *gets up, gives a little giggle, collects another box of matches as well as the one she has already, and goes quietly upstairs again.*

CURTAIN

ACT II

SCENE II

The same night, actually the early hours of the morning. The
stage is dark but there is still a faint glow from the remains
of the fire. There is silence for a few moments, which is
broken by a scream from upstairs. BONITA *comes swiftly*
down the stairs in a dressing-gown and bangs frantically on
MISS ARCHIE'S *door.*

BONITA: Miss Archie! Miss Archie – come quickly –
Sarita's room is on fire!

She opens the door and disappears inside.

There is a sound of further screaming and hubbub upstairs
and smoke is seen coming from the archway leading to the
bedrooms. The noise increases. MISS ARCHIE, *clad in swan-*
stripe pyjamas, comes flying out of her room and rushes
upstairs. BONITA *follows her more slowly. At the top of the*
stairs MISS ARCHIE *almost collides with* MAY, *who is*
wearing a crimson dressing-gown and has a sort of turban
round her head. Her manner, as usual, is majestic. MISS
ARCHIE *pushes by her and disappears.*

MAY (*descending*): Has anyone telephoned the Fire
Brigade?

BONITA (*meeting her at the foot of the stairs*): No – not
yet.

MAY: Then I suggest we do so immediately. (*Briskly.*) Come and help me find the number. I've left my glasses upstairs.

BONITA (*agitatedly*): So have I.

MAY: In that case we will dial 999. 9 comes one before the 0. We can't miss it.

MAY *methodically switches on the lights and they go into* MISS ARCHIE'S *room. Meanwhile more smoke billows out from the upstairs archway.* ALMINA, ESTELLE *and* MAUDIE *appear in their night things, choking, and come down the stairs, followed by* DEIRDRE *in a towering rage.*

DEIRDRE (*also choking*): The damned old fool! I knew this would happen – burnt to bloody crisps in our beds we should have been if I hadn't smelt the smoke.

MISS ARCHIE *reappears briefly, yanks a fire-extinguisher off the wall and goes back into the smoke. There is a confused murmur of voices.* ALMINA *and* ESTELLE *having reached the bottom of the stairs collapse on to the sofa.* MAUDIE *pulls back the curtains and opens the window.* MISS ARCHIE'S *voice is heard –*

MISS ARCHIE (*upstairs*): Bang the nozzle against the wall – there!

There is a loud swishing noise and a scream.

ESTELLE (*wailing*): Poor Sarita – oh, poor Sarita!

DEIRDRE: Poor Sarita, my eye! She ought to be locked up in a padded cell.

LOTTA *and* CORA *appear at the top of the stairs one on each side of* SARITA, *who is wrapped in a blanket. They bring her downstairs.* MISS ARCHIE *appears.*

MISS ARCHIE: It's all right – everything's under control. It was only the curtains that caught and I've got them out. (*She disappears again.*)

BONITA *rushes out of* MISS ARCHIE'S *room.*

BONITA: Has anyone got any glasses ? We can't see the damned dial. We've tried 999 but nothing happened.

MAUDIE: It doesn't matter. It was only the curtains and Miss Archie's put them out.

BONITA *goes back into* MISS ARCHIE'S *room to tell* MAY. LOTTA *and* CORA *deposit* SARITA *in an armchair*.

SARITA *(cheerfully)*: It looked so pretty – so very pretty.

DEIRDRE *(snorting)*: Pretty indeed! It's small thanks to you, Sarita Myrtle, that we're not all charred corpses at this very minute.

CORA: For God's sake, shut that window somebody! Having escaped death by burning it would be idiotic to die of pneumonia.

MAUDIE *(plaintively)*: I only opened it to let the smoke out. We were suffocating. *(She closes the window.)*

MAY *comes out of* MISS ARCHIE'S *room, followed by* BONITA. *She sits in her accustomed chair*. BONITA *puts some coal on the fire*.

SARITA *(picking at her blanket)*: Why am I wearing this strange garment ? Is it to be an oriental production ?

MAY: How did she get hold of the matches ?

BONITA: She must have pinched them when nobody was looking and hidden them somewhere. You know Miss Archie always searches her room thoroughly every night.

DEIRDRE: It's as much as our lives are worth to have her in the house a minute longer.

MAY: Calm down, Deirdre.

DEIRDRE: I'll calm down when I feel like it and not before and you can put that in your high and mighty pipe and smoke it, May Davenport.

BONITA: I'm going to wake Doreen. Miss Archie can't cope with everything by herself. *(She goes out through the service door.)*

MAUDIE: Do you think we ought to telephone to Doctor Jevons?

CORA: What for?

MAUDIE: For Sarita, of course. He might give her a sedative or something.

DEIRDRE: You might tell him to bring a strait-jacket while he's at it.

LOTTA: Do be quiet, Deirdre. It's unkind to say things like that. (*She pauses.*) Oh dear – I wonder how poor old Martha is – I'd better go and see.

MAUDIE: I'll go, Lotta – stay where you are. I've got to get some cigarettes anyhow. I'm shaking like a leaf.

MAUDIE *goes upstairs and disappears through the archway. The smoke has by now subsided.* BONITA *comes back through the service door, followed by* DOREEN, *who is attired in a pink Japanese kimono. Her hair is in kirby grips.*

BONITA (*giving her a slight push*): Run along up and help Miss Archie.

DOREEN: Okay, Miss Belgrave. (*As she goes.*) Ooh! What a terrible smell of burning.

DEIRDRE: What do you expect with the whole house blazing to the skies? The girl's a half-wit.

LOTTA: The house isn't blazing to the skies, Deirdre.

DEIRDRE: It might well be if I hadn't noticed that smoke curling under me door like a grey serpent.

BONITA: I know what I could do with and that's a nip of whisky. I've got some in my room. How about you, Cora?

CORA: Thanks.

BONITA: Any other offers? Lotta – May?

MAY: No thank you, my dear Bonita.

LOTTA: I should love a little. You're very kind.

BONITA (*going upstairs*): I'll fetch the bottle. (*She disappears.*)

LOTTA: Stay by Sarita, Cora, while I go and find some glasses. (LOTTA *goes off through the service door.*)

SARITA: What are we all waiting here for in the middle of the night? Is someone going to read a play to us?

DEIRDRE: I'd throttle anybody who tried.

MAUDIE *reappears carrying her bag.*

MAUDIE (*coming downstairs*): Martha's all right. She's fast asleep, but poor Miss Archie's wet through. Cigarette, anybody?

CORA: Thanks. I'd love one.

MAUDIE *hands round a packet of Players.* CORA *and* ESTELLE *take one.* MAY *refuses with an austere smile.* LOTTA *returns with a tray of glasses and a jug of water.*

MAUDIE: Old Martha's fast asleep, Lotta. She didn't hear a thing.

MAUDIE *strikes a match and lights* CORA'S *and* ESTELLE'S *cigarettes; being superstitious, she then blows the match out and lights another for herself.*

SARITA (*clapping her hands authoritatively*): Light all the candles, François, post-haste, Madame la Marquise will be weary after her journey in the diligence.

DEIRDRE: For the love of God, don't let her get her hands on those matches.

BONITA *appears with a bottle of whisky.*

BONITA (*coming down*): Here's the booze, girls!

MAY (*disapprovingly*): Really, Bonita!

BONITA (*while she pours out little nips for everyone*): Miss Archie's having a wonderful time upstairs. Charging about in her swan-stripes and shouting orders like a sergeant-major. She and Doreen are moving Sarita's things into the room at the end of the passage.

ALMINA: Oh dear – that's the one next to mine. I shan't sleep a wink, I know I shan't, my heart's pounding as it is.

MAUDIE: Take some bismuth, dear, and a couple of Phensic.

MISS ARCHIE appears at the top of the stairs and comes down. Her pyjamas are sopping wet but she is calmly victorious. DOREEN follows her.

MISS ARCHIE: That was a close shave and no mistake. Thank God the jolly old extinguisher worked all right.

CORA: It seems to have worked almost too well. You're soaking.

MISS ARCHIE: That was when the damn thing just went off. I was holding it the wrong way round.

BONITA (*handing her a glass of whisky*): Have a drop of this, *Mon Colonel* and slip into something loose before you catch your death.

MISS ARCHIE: Thanks. I could do with a snifter.

LOTTA: I think your presence of mind was absolutely splendid, Miss Archie. We're all very grateful to you.

MAY (*sepulchrally*): Hear, hear.

Everyone looks surprised that MAY should even acknowledge anything said by LOTTA.

LOTTA (*with a smile*): I'm glad you agree with me, May.

She looks MAY full in the eye. MAY meets her gaze and turns her head away.

MAUDIE (*breaking the silence*): We were wondering if we ought to telephone to Doctor Jevons?

MISS ARCHIE: Time enough for that in the morning. (*She lowers her voice and nods towards SARITA.*) I've got a pill that'll put her out like a light.

CORA: An unfortunate simile.

MISS ARCHIE: Would anyone like a cup of char? It wouldn't take a minute to boil the kettle.

ESTELLE: No thanks, not on top of the whisky.

LOTTA: Not for me, thank you.

There are general murmurs of dissent.

MISS ARCHIE: In that case you'd better get back to bed, Doreen.

DOREEN: Okay, Miss Archibald. (*She goes off through the service door.*)

CORA: I think it's time we all went back to bed.

MISS ARCHIE: I'll just slip out of these and pop on a dressing-gown, then we'll take Sarita up. I shan't be two shakes. (MISS ARCHIE *goes into her room.*)

ESTELLE: Come on up, Almina. There's no sense in just sitting about. (*She rises.*)

ALMINA: I suppose it's the shock but I'm feeling all trembly.

ESTELLE: Well, the shock's over now, so there's nothing to feel trembly about any more. Come along.

ALMINA (*heaving herself up*): Shock's a very dangerous thing. A friend of mine once saw a man run over by a bus in Newcastle and three days later she fell down dead.

ESTELLE: Come on, dear. It's no use being morbid.

ESTELLE *takes* ALMINA'S *arm and they go slowly upstairs together.*

SARITA: I fell in love with Herbert in Newcastle.

BONITA: Herbert who?

SARITA: My Herbert, of course. We used to go to Whitley Bay on non-matinée days and hold hands and look at the sea.

MAUDIE: I think I'll go up too. Deirdre?

DEIRDRE: All right. (*She gets up and shoots a malevolent glance at* SARITA.) A fine moment to be jabbering about holding hands in Whitley Bay when you've just committed arson.

MAUDIE *and* DEIRDRE *go upstairs.*

MISS ARCHIE *comes* out of her room wearing her flannel dressing-gown and slippers. She goes to SARITA.

MISS ARCHIE: Come along, old dear. Time for Bedfordshire.

SARITA: My brother Armand and I were all in all to each other, he the little father, I the tiny mother.

BONITA: Good Lord! The Scarlet Pimpernel.

MISS ARCHIE: Give me a hand, Bonita.

They both help SARITA *out of the chair. She breaks away from them and moves swiftly to the stairs.*

SARITA: I am sorry if I have done anything wrong but please do not touch me. I cannot bear people to touch me. (*She goes upstairs followed hurriedly by* BONITA *and* MISS ARCHIE.)

BONITA: I hope you've got that pill handy. She's twanging like a fiddle-string.

MISS ARCHIE: Quickly – head her off from going to her own room. I don't want her to see it as it is.

They reach the top of the stairs at the same time as SARITA.

SARITA (*turning*): The sea was rather muddy and there was always a wind but there was a freshness in the air and we were in love.

MISS ARCHIE: Come along, old dear.

The three of them disappear.

CORA (*in a muffled voice*): Oh God! It's intolerable – intolerable. (*She sinks into a chair and buries her face in her hands.*)

LOTTA (*going to her and putting her arm round her shoulders*): Of course it is, but it's no use allowing yourself to be upset by it. There's nothing to be done.

CORA: I suppose she'll have to be sent away – eventually.

LOTTA: Yes. I suppose she will.

CORA: What happens when the mind goes like that? Does it make it better or worse? – living, I mean.

LOTTA: Who knows? More bearable perhaps. I don't think Sarita's unhappy.

CORA (*pulling herself together and getting up*): I expect she's to be envied really. At least she doesn't realise what a bore it is, all this sitting about and waiting. Are you coming up, May?

MAY: No. I'm going to stay by the fire for a little.

LOTTA (*cheerfully*): So am I.

MAY *looks at* LOTTA *sharply and then looks away again.* CORA *stares at them both for a moment, then, without another word, she goes upstairs and disappears. There is a long silence.* MAY *takes up her work bag, which is by her chair, and takes out her embroidery frame. She shoots* LOTTA *another swift look and, fumbling in her bag again, produces her wool, needle and spectacle case. She gives a little grunt of satisfaction.* LOTTA *sits quietly staring in front of her. The silence continues.*

MAY (*at last*): They were here all the time. (LOTTA *without replying looks at her inquiringly.* MAY *meets her eyes and forces a wintry little smile.*) My glasses. They were here all the time in my work bag.

LOTTA (*gently*):

'And frosts were slain and flowers begotten
     And in green underwood and cover
     Blossom by blossom the Spring begins'.

MAY: The fire's nearly out.

LOTTA: There's enough heat left, really. It's not very cold.

MAY: Were you happy with him?

LOTTA: Yes. I was happy with him until the day he died.

MAY: That's something gained at any rate, isn't it?

LOTTA (*lightly*): He was a monster sometimes, of course. Those black Irish rages.

MAY: Yes. I remember them well. (*She looks at* LOTTA *curiously and says, without emotion.*) Why did you take him from me?

LOTTA: I didn't. He came to me of his own free will. You must have known that. He wasn't the sort of character that anyone could take from anyone else.

MAY (*dispassionately*): You were prettier than I was.

LOTTA: You know perfectly well that that had nothing to do with it. The spark is struck or it isn't. It's seldom the fault of any one person.

MAY: Any one person can achieve a lot by determination.

LOTTA: Would you like a scrap of accurate but rather unpleasant information?

MAY: What do you mean?

LOTTA: I can tell you now. I couldn't before. You never gave me the chance anyhow.

MAY: What are you talking about?

LOTTA: There was somebody else.

MAY: Somebody else?

LOTTA: Yes. Between the time he left you and came to me.

MAY: I don't believe it.

LOTTA: It's quite true. Her name was Lavinia, Lavinia Parsons.

MAY (*incredulously*): Not that dreadful girl who played Ophelia with poor old Ernest?

LOTTA: That's the one.

MAY: Are you telling me this in order to exonerate yourself?

LOTTA (*with a touch of asperity*): No, May. I'm not apologising to you, you know, not asking for your forgiveness. I see no reason to exonerate myself. Charles fell in love with me and I fell in love with him and we were married. I have no regrets.

MAY (*drily*): You are very fortunate. I have, a great many.

LOTTA: Well, don't. It's a waste of time.

MAY: What became of your first husband, Webster Whatever-his-name-was?

LOTTA (*evenly*): His name was Webster Bennet. After our divorce in 1924 he went to Canada and died there a few years later.

MAY: You had a son, didn't you?

LOTTA: Yes. I had a son.

MAY: Is he alive?

LOTTA: Yes. He went to Canada with his father. He is there still. He has had two wives, the first one apparently was a disaster, the second one seems satisfactory. They have three children.

MAY: Does he write to you often?

LOTTA: I haven't heard from him for seventeen years.

MAY (*gruffly*): I'm sorry, Lotta, very sorry.

LOTTA: Thank you, that's kind of you. I was unhappy about it for a long time but I'm not any more. He was always his father's boy more than mine. I don't think he ever cared for me much, except of course when he was little.

MAY: Why did you come here? Was it absolutely necessary?

LOTTA (*looking down*): Yes, absolutely. I have a minute income of two hundred pounds a year and nothing saved;

the last two plays I did were failures and – and there was nothing else to be done, also I found I couldn't learn lines any more – that broke my nerve.

MAY: That's what really finished me, too. I was always a slow study at the best of times, the strain became intolerable and humiliating, more humiliating even than this.

LOTTA: I refuse to consider this humiliating. I think we've earned this honestly, really I do.

MAY: Perhaps we have, Lotta, perhaps we have.

LOTTA: Bonita's left her bottle of whisky. Would you like a sip?

MAY: A very small one.

LOTTA (*going to the table and pouring out two drinks*): All right.

MAY (*ruminatively*): Lavinia Parsons. He must have been mad!

LOTTA (*handing her her drink*): She was prettier than you and prettier than me and a great deal younger than both of us.

MAY (*thoughtfully*): I must buy a bottle of whisky tomorrow in Maidenhead. What is really the best sort?

LOTTA: Oh, I don't know. There's Haig and Black and White – they're all much of a muchness unless one happens to be a connoisseur, and we're neither of us that.

MAY (*rising and holding up her glass*): Well, Lotta – we meet again.

LOTTA: Yes, May dear, we meet again. (*She also holds up her glass.*) Happy days!

MAY: Happy days!

    They both drink and then stand quite still for a moment looking at each other. In their eyes there is a glint of tears.

CURTAIN

ACT II

SCENE III

A week has elapsed. It is just after lunch on Sunday. MAY is sitting in her usual chair doing her embroidery. BONITA and MAUDIE are on the sofa reading 'The Sunday Clarion'. CORA is playing 'Patience' at the card table. LOTTA is sitting in an armchair also reading the 'Clarion'. DEIRDRE and ALMINA are playing draughts at a table down left. ESTELLE is seated below the fireplace knitting.

DEIRDRE (*triumphantly*): I huff you – there – away you go – one – two – three!

ALMINA: Oh dear. I never saw it.

LOTTA: You really must listen to this, May, it really is too ghastly. (*She laughs.*)

MAY: I have already told you I do not wish to hear a word of it.

LOTTA (*reading*): 'Old foes still feuding in the twilight of their lives!' It's in large black letters, May. The first time we've ever been co-starred!

MAY: I can see nothing to laugh at.

LOTTA: Why not? It's not worth taking seriously.

MAY: For all of us to be publicly humiliated in the Press may appeal to your sense of humour, Lotta; it does not to mine.

LOTTA: It's vulgar and inaccurate and full of treacly sentimentality, I admit, but somehow it isn't as bad as I feared.

MAY: I cannot imagine how it could have been much worse.

LOTTA: It might have been a good deal more vindictive. I wouldn't have been surprised, after Deirdre's little outburst.

DEIRDRE: I said what I had in my heart to say to the fawning deceitful creature and I don't regret a word of it.

LOTTA: Then you should, Deirdre. You were much too violent and, above all, tactless.

DEIRDRE: I'll hold to my opinion and you hold to yours and we'll agree to differ. (*To* ALMINA.) Huff you again! Is it dropping off into a doze you are, Almina?

ALMINA: I wasn't concentrating. I was listening to what the others were saying.

DEIRDRE: Well, stick to one thing at a time or you'll find yourself trapped in a corner like a hunted animal and shrieking for mercy.

CORA: Deirdre can make even a game of draughts sound like a Lyceum melodrama.

DEIRDRE: And what's wrong with that I should like to know. The Lyceum melodrama at least gave you your money's worth. An honest bit of blood and thunder's a lot more healthy and entertaining than all this modern creeping about in the pitch dark and complaining.

MAY: For once I am in complete agreement with Deirdre.

DEIRDRE: The skies will fall I shouldn't wonder.

ALMINA: I huff you!

DEIRDRE: You were in no position to huff me a minute

ago, Almina. It's moving the pieces you've been after when me back was turned.

BONITA (*poring over the newspaper*): She's even dragged poor old Osgood in! It's lower down in the column after the bit about us all sitting in the garden at dusk listening to the rooks cawing and wistfully remembering our former triumphs.

CORA: Sitting in the garden at dusk indeed! We should be eaten alive.

BONITA (*reading*): 'Faithful unto death'. 'A love that never died!'

MAY (*jabbing her needle viciously into her embroidery*): Disgusting!

LOTTA: She seemed quite a well educated young woman, it's curious that she should write so abominably.

MAY: No other sort of writing would be accepted by that horrible rag. 'The infection of vulgarity that will subdue the world': I read that in a library book the other day and it is true of this whole dreadful age. I'm thankful that I am old and near the end of my time. All the standards are lowered, all the values have changed. There is no elegance, dignity or reticence left. 'Milton, thou should'st be living at this hour – England hath need of thee'.

CORA (*laconically*): Curtain!

LOTTA: I'm afraid that if Milton really were living at this hour there wouldn't be much he could do about it. (*She goes on reading for a moment.*) Oh, really! Listen to this—— (*She reads.*) 'I wonder if we ordinary people realise how much we owe to these old faithful servants of the public, wearily playing out the last act of their lives, all passion spent, all glamour gone, unwanted and forgotten. Just waiting – waiting in "The Wings"!'

BONITA: Pass me a basin or a bucket, somebody.

MAY (*reprovingly*): Bonita, please——!

MAUDIE (*getting up and going to the piano*): That would make a wonderful number—— (*She plays a few chords and sings*):

> 'Waiting in the Wings – Waiting in the Wings –
> 'Older than God, On we plod,
> Waiting in the Wings'——

BONITA (*joining in*): 'Hopping about the garden like a lot of Douglas Byngs'.

MAUDIE (*with a bravura finish*): 'Waiting – Waiting – Waiting in the Wings!'

They all applaud and laugh. OSGOOD MEEKER *comes in timidly from the hall. He is carrying his usual bunch of violets.*

OSGOOD: Good afternoon. I hope I'm not interrupting anything?

LOTTA: Of course you're not, we're just feeling rather skittish.

OSGOOD: The front door was on the latch so I didn't bother to ring the bell.

BONITA: Quite right. You're one of the family anyhow.

OSGOOD: How kind of you to say that, how very kind. I suppose it will be all right if I go straight up?

MAUDIE: I'm sure it will – I'll call Miss Archie if you like.

OSGOOD (*going to the stairs*): No – no – please don't trouble. I know the way. (*He goes up the stairs, stops and turns.*) There's such a nice article about all of you in the *Sunday Clarion*. I read it in the train coming down – it almost brought tears to my eyes, so sensitively written, most touching – most touching! (*He disappears.*)

314

LOTTA: There you are, you see! An honest reaction from an ordinary member of the public.

BONITA: I give up.

CORA: It only goes to prove that we are all far too touchy.

MAY: The poor man must be out of his mind.

There is the sound of a motor-bicycle.

CORA: Here's Perry.

LOTTA: Poor boy. I feel so sorry for him.

MAY: Personally, I find it hard to forgive him for un-leashing all this vulgarity on our heads.

DEIRDRE: Then it's shame you should be feeling, May Davenport.

CORA: Oh, for heaven's sake don't let's start all that again!

DEIRDRE: The poor lad was misguided, I grant you, but it was all planned to help us in the long run.

ESTELLE: So you think he's come to say good-bye? That this is the last time we shall see him?

LOTTA (*briskly*): No. They'll have to give him a month or so at least, if only to give them time to replace him.

PERRY *comes in. His usual cheerfulness is not apparent.*

PERRY: Hallo, everybody.

MAUDIE: Oh, Perry! (*She goes impulsively and kisses him.*)

PERRY: I see that one of you has forgiven me at least.

LOTTA: Nonsense! We've all forgiven you ages ago, except May, and she's only holding out so that you can make an extra fuss of her.

MAY: Really, Lotta! How can you say such things?

PERRY: I suppose you've all read it?

CORA: We certainly have.

315

PERRY: It's no use me saying I'm sorry any more, is it? – I mean – I did write and try to explain——

LOTTA: It was a very nice letter, Perry. Miss Archie read it out to us.

CORA: But that was before the special meeting. What happened?

PERRY: Exactly what I expected would happen.

BONITA: Oh, Perry.

PERRY: It was hell.

ESTELLE (*wretchedly*): Oh, poor Perry! It was all my fault for ever thinking of the horrid old solarium in the first place. I shall never forgive myself – never——

BONITA: Now then, Estelle – none of that.

MAUDIE: What happened exactly, Perry? Tell us.

PERRY: Oh, they all flew at me and Boodie Nethersole said a lot about me exceeding my duties and assuming responsibilities that I had no right to assume, etc., etc.

BONITA: Silly bitch!

MAY: Bonita – please!

LOTTA: Go on, Perry.

PERRY: Dame Maggie had already telephoned to the editor of the *Clarion* to have Zelda's piece stopped but he flatly refused. Then after a lot more talk they told me that I should have to go but that I could stay on until they found someone to replace me. Then they all went away with long faces like mutes at a funeral and that was that. I was sacked.

LOTTA: Oh, Perry, I really am most distressed. We all are.

PERRY (*with the suspicion of a twinkle in his eye*): Even May?

MAY (*busy with her embroidery*): I'm sure I hope it will be a lesson to you in the future.

316

LOTTA: Really, May! I think you are being unnecessarily disagreeable.

DEIRDRE: And what would you expect from granite but a heart of stone?

LOTTA (*crossly*): Do be quiet, Deirdre!

DEIDRE (*flaring up*): And why should I be quiet? The poor lad loses his job. And on top of that he's talked to by May Davenport as though he were a juvenile delinquent hauled up before the bar of justice for rape and bloody murder!

PERRY (*going to her*): Just one minute, Deirdre, please – I haven't quite finished my story.

LOTTA (*quickly – sensing a change in his tone*): Go on then, Perry. Finish it.

PERRY (*enjoying himself*): There was another meeting called yesterday. A much smaller one. Dame Maggie was in the chair and Boodie, thank God, was playing her matinée.

LOTTA: I hope I've guessed what happened – go on.

PERRY: The resolution of Thursday's meeting, by some oversight, had not been minuted. And so, after rather a kind little lecture, I was reinstated.

MAUDIE: Hurray!

LOTTA: How perfectly splendid!

PERRY: And would you all like to know why I was reinstated? Why there was such a sudden change in the weather?

MAY (*in authoritative tones*): Perry, I absolutely forbid you to say another word.

PERRY: Just allow me five. (*He goes to her.*) Thank you, dear, dear May. (*He kisses her warmly on both cheeks and goes hurriedly into* MISS ARCHIE's *office.*)

BONITA (*after a stunned silence*): Well, I'll be damned!

DEIRDRE: What in the name of the Blessed Saints did he do that for?

LOTTA: You've been very sly, May. I'm surprised at you. Did you write to Maggie?

MAY: I'd prefer not to discuss it.

BONITA: You must tell us, you really must-please, May.

MAY: I telephoned to Dame Maggie from Miss Archie's office on Thursday evening while you were all at supper. I explained that the whole thing had been a foolish mistake on Perry's part and that he was too important to all of us to be summarily dismissed for such a trivial misdemeanour. I added that we were all prepared to write strong letters of protest to the committee.

DEIRDRE: Well, blow me down and bury me bones if that's not the biggest surprise I've ever had in me life. Hats off to you, May Davenport!

MAY: Once and for all, will you *stop* calling me May Davenport!

There is the sound of the front door bell.

MAUDIE: Who's that, I wonder?

CORA: Doctor Jevons, I expect.

LOTTA (*stricken*): Of course, yes. I'd quite forgotten. How horrid!

DOREEN *comes out of the service door and goes into the hall.*

BONITA: I'd forgotten too for the moment, what with the *Clarion* article and Perry arriving and everything. Poor old love—— (*She sighs.*) I suppose it's all for the best, really.

DOREEN *ushers in* DOCTOR JEVONS *and then goes off again.* DOCTOR JEVONS *is a pleasant-looking young man in the thirties.*

DR JEVONS: Good afternoon, ladies.

MAY: Good afternoon, Doctor Jevons.

DR JEVONS: Is Miss Archie in her office?

LOTTA: No, she's upstairs. It's not an ambulance, is it?

DR JEVONS: No, no – nothing like that. Just my old Hillman. I'm driving her myself.

LOTTA: Now nice of you! I'm so glad.

DR JEVONS: I'll go on up. (*He crosses to the stairs.*) May I suggest something – without appearing to be unduly officious?

MAY: Of course, Doctor. What is it?

DR JEVONS: I think it would be advisable if no 'good-byes' were said or implied. Just behave ordinarily, as though nothing had happened.

CORA: Very well, Doctor. We quite understand.

LOTTA: It is absolutely necessary for her to go – to go away, isn't it?

DR JEVONS: In my opinion. yes, but I do assure you there is nothing to worry about. She will be well and most kindly taken care of, and never made to feel that she is in any way – er – out of line.

LOTTA: Thank you. I'm so glad.

DOCTOR JEVONS *goes upstairs. There is a long silence.*

BONITA: I wonder how he can be so certain, that there's nothing to worry about, I mean?

LOTTA: There is no absolute certainty, I suppose. But he is a good doctor and a sensible, kindly man. I'd be inclined to trust his word.

CORA: In any case there really isn't any alternative.

MAUDIE: No, I suppose not, but it does seem awful somehow.

MAY (*firmly*): Of course there's no alternative. She obviously must go somewhere where she can be under proper supervision, somewhere where she isn't dangerous to anyone else.

BONITA: The poor old duck didn't mean to be dangerous.

MAY: I am not suggesting that she did, Bonita. But the fact remains, she was.

PERRY *comes out of the office.*

PERRY: Was that the doctor?

ESTELLE: Yes. He's gone up.

PERRY: I've just been having a look at Miss Archie's official report. She told me all about it on the telephone, of course, but it looks more startling somehow, in black and white. Did she realise what she had done?

DEIRDRE: Of course she did. She was as pleased as Punch – jumping up and down and clapping her hands like a two-year-old.

CORA: You're exaggerating, Deirdre, as usual.

PERRY: Does she know that she is being sent to – being sent away?

CORA: Miss Archie explained to her tactfully this morning that she was going to stay with some new friends, but she didn't seem to take it in.

PERRY: Oh, poor old girl. I do hope she won't mind.

LOTTA: That's what haunts me, the idea of her waking up in strange surroundings and being suddenly lonely and afraid.

MAUDIE: Oh, don't – I can't bear it.

MAY: There's no point in being sentimental about it, my dear Lotta. She must be properly cared for.

CORA: She *has* been getting progressively dottier during these past years.

DEIRDRE: An aunt of mine went off her head when I was a wee girl, I remember it well. There was no shilly-shallying about in those days. They came for her in the middle of Sunday dinner and hauled her off to the asylum like a sack of potatoes.

LOTTA: Oh Deirdre, really——

PERRY: I think they're coming down now.

ESTELLE (*emotionally*): Oh dear – I don't think I can bear it. I shall only cry and make a fool of myself.

ALMINA: Let's go into the television room – help me up.

CORA: Stay where you are. The doctor said we were to behave as though nothing had happened.

LOTTA: We'd better talk, I think.

BONITA (*miserably*): I can't think of anything to say.

LOTTA: Play the piano, Maudie. Play anything that comes into your head.

MAUDIE: Oh no – I couldn't.

LOTTA: Please – just to cover up the silence – quickly.

MAUD (*going to the piano*): All right.

She starts to play a light Chopin waltz. MISS ARCHIE, DOCTOR JEVONS *and* SARITA *appear at the top of the stairs.*

SARITA *is in a grey coat and skirt and wears a small hat.* MISS ARCHIE *is carrying her suitcase.*

DOCTOR JEVONS *holds his hand lightly under* SARITA'S *elbow as they come down.*

CORA *deals herself a new hand of 'Patience' with intense concentration.* MAY *embroiders implacably.* BONITA *produces a cigarette and is about to light it when she thinks better of it and puts it back in her case.*

The others remain more or less immobile watching covertly. SARITA *stops dead at the foot of the stairs.*

SARITA: What a charming hotel! It has quite an atmosphere of home, hasn't it?

MISS ARCHIE: That's right, dear. Come along.

SARITA (*listening a moment to* MAUD'S *playing and nodding her head in time to the music*): I remember that tune – it's Chopin, isn't it?

MAUDIE (*still playing – rather tremulously*): Yes, dear. It's Chopin.

SARITA: I made an exit to it in *Lady Mary's Secret* many many years ago. (*She smiles at* DOCTOR JEVONS.) Long before your day, young man. It was a lovely long exit and I wore a white evening dress and just as I got to the door I turned slowly and threw a red rose to my leading man. It was only a property rose, of course, and he didn't always catch it, but it always brought the house down.

She goes slowly towards the hall, DOCTOR JEVONS *slips his arm through hers. She turns again at the door and addresses the room.*

Au revoir, my dears. I won't say good-bye because it is so unlucky. It has been such a really lovely engagement. Good luck to you all.

She goes out with DOCTOR JEVONS. MISS ARCHIE *follows with the suitcase. In the silence* MAUDIE'S *playing falters and she bends her head over the keys.*

CURTAIN

ACT III

SCENE I

It is about nine-thirty on the evening of Christmas Day. The room shows signs of jestivity. There are some paper decorations here and there and, above the fireplace, a decorated Christmas tree. When the curtain rises DOREEN *is collecting an armful of discarded paper wrappings. She goes through the service door with them and returns for more.*

MISS ARCHIE, resplendent in uniform, but wearing a rather coquettish paper cap, comes in from the hall. There is a buzz of conversation and laughter heard from the dining-room.

MISS ARCHIE: You can leave all that mess until tomorrow, Doreen. Go and get the coffee and then cut along home to your family – you've had quite a day.

DOREEN: Okay, Miss Archie – thanks.

MISS ARCHIE: There are a couple of boxes of crackers left over, you can take them to your little brother.

DOREEN: Thanks ever so.

MISS ARCHIE: I hope he is getting along all right?

DOREEN: Oh yes. The doctor says his left leg will never be quite the same, and he'll always have a bit of a limp, but he doesn't seem to mind.

Miss Archie: Good for him! (*There is the sound of the front-door bell.*) Now who the devil can that be at this time of night? Run and see, there's a good girl, I'll take these.

She relieves Doreen *of an armful of papers and goes off with them through the service door.* Doreen *goes into the hall, and, a moment later, ushers in* Zelda Fenwick. Zelda, *dressed for the evening, is wearing black corduroy trousers, a black velvet jacket, a white shirt and a red scarf. She is carrying a large and obviously heavy package – which she deposits on the piano.*

Doreen: I'll tell Miss Archie you're here.

Zelda: Thank you.

Doreen *goes.* Zelda *listens for a moment to the noise from the dining-room and lights a cigarette.* Miss Archie *returns.*

Miss Archie (*nonplussed*): Oh!

Zelda: Good evening.

Miss Archie (*awkwardly*): I didn't realise who it was, I mean, Doreen didn't say——

Zelda: Happy Christmas!

Miss Archie (*with an anxious glance towards the dining-room*): The same to you.

Zelda: I've been at a party in Maidenhead and I'm on my way back to London. I thought I'd call in for a moment, with a peace offering.

Miss Archie: Peace offering?

Zelda: That's it on the piano. It's a case of champagne.

Miss Archie: Champagne – good Lord! I really don't think that——

Zelda: I gather that I am still in the dog house?

Miss Archie: Well, Miss Fenwick – I wouldn't

exactly say that – but of course they were a bit upset at the time, and it's no use saying they weren't.

ZELDA: Please don't be embarrassed. I'm only staying for a moment. You needn't even say I've been here if you don't want to. You can pretend the champagne was just left at the door. I hasten to add that I am not here in a professional capacity, for once. It's just that I had rather a guilty conscience.

MISS ARCHIE: I see.

ZELDA: Not about what I wrote, please don't misunderstand me, that was part of my job, but because I didn't keep my word.

MISS ARCHIE: I don't quite know what you mean.

ZELDA: I promised Perry I'd make an appeal on my T.V. programme.

MISS ARCHIE: Oh that – yes – I remember.

ZELDA: But the T.V. people were against it, and so was my editor, so – so I gave in.

MISS ARCHIE: Please don't worry any more about it. It's all over and forgotten. Can I offer you a drink?

ZELDA: No, thanks, I must go, I've got a friend outside in the car. My boss asked me to give you this – for 'The Wings'. (*She takes an envelope out of her pocket and gives it to* MISS ARCHIE.)

MISS ARCHIE: Your boss?

ZELDA: His Lordship. He's a barking old tyrant but he is in mortal dread of hell's fire and so he occasionally likes to make a gesture. It may be a form of spiritual insurance or it may even be genuine kindness, with him it's difficult to tell. At any rate – this is it.

MISS ARCHIE (*opening the envelope and taking out a cheque*): Good God! Two thousand pounds!

ZELDA: It's for the solarium.

MISS ARCHIE: I can't believe it.

ZELDA: There are no strings attached. It's a private donation for a specific purpose, so see that the committee don't use it for anything else. I'll be getting along now. Give my love to the inmates, even that old Irish battle-axe.

MISS ARCHIE: Please stay a minute.

ZELDA: No, I think I'd better go.

MISS ARCHIE: At least give them a chance to say thank you.

ZELDA: I don't want them to say thank you: they have to say thank you every day of their lives, they must be sick to death of it. I'm off.

MISS ARCHIE: Perhaps you'll let me say it then – on their behalf.

ZELDA (*with a smile*): All right – fire away.

MISS ARCHIE (*obviously moved, but trying to control it*): Thank you. (*She wrings* ZELDA's *hand.*)

ZELDA: Be careful – I need my hand to drive the car.

MISS ARCHIE (*huskily*): Sorry.

ZELDA: You know, curiously enough, that paper cap is rather becoming. (*She smiles.*) Good-night, Colonel.

MISS ARCHIE *stands quite still for a moment staring at the cheque in her hand. She puts it carefully back in its envelope and places the envelope on the mantelpiece. She then produces a handkerchief from her sleeve and blows her nose violently.* DOREEN *staggers in through the service door with a large coffee tray.*

DOREEN: Do they want it in the dining-room, or in here?

MISS ARCHIE: In here – put it on the table.

DOREEN: Okay, Miss Archie. Will that be all? (*She puts the tray on the table.*)

MISS ARCHIE: Yes, Doreen, that'll be all.

DOREEN: Ta ever so for the brooch – it's smashing!

MISS ARCHIE: I'm glad you like it.

DOREEN: Well – bye-bye for now.

MISS ARCHIE: Bye-bye for now.

DOREEN goes out. MISS ARCHIE goes over to a tray of drinks on a side table, pours herself out a stiff brandy and swallows it in one gulp.

Led by LOTTA, MAY and OSGOOD MEEKER, the others come in from the dining-room laughing and talking. OSGOOD and PERRY are wearing dinner-jackets. They are all, more or less, in evening dress and most of them still have on paper caps.

MAY makes a bee line for her special chair and settles down with her embroidery frame. The others dispose of themselves in due course.

LOTTA: The turkey was delicious, Miss Archie, in fact the whole dinner was perfect.

ALMINA: It will take me at least three days to get over it.

LOTTA: We really ought to say thank you to Mrs Blake, is she still here?

MISS ARCHIE: No, she's gone home.

LOTTA: We must remember in the morning.

BONITA and ESTELLE go to the table and begin to pour out the coffee.

BONITA: Coffee, everybody?

ALMINA: Not for me, I shouldn't sleep a wink.

PERRY (*seeing the package on the piano*): Hallo – what's this?

MISS ARCHIE: It's a case of champagne.

BONITA: A *case* of champagne! Somebody must have gone mad.

MAY: Where on earth did it come from?

MISS ARCHIE: I expect you'll be angry when I tell you.

MAY: Why?

MISS ARCHIE: Zelda Fenwick brought it – a few minutes ago – she was on her way up to London and she just dropped in – to wish you all a happy Christmas.

ESTELLE: Zelda Fenwick – good heavens!

MISS ARCHIE: She said it was a peace offering.

CORA: Are we to be photographed drinking it?

MISS ARCHIE: No. There were no ulterior motives. She meant it kindly – I assure you she did.

PERRY: I think it was very decent of her.

DEIRDRE: Send it back – we don't want to be beholden to her.

LOTTA: I think that would be ungracious.

DEIRDRE: Champagne indeed – for a lot of defeated, miserable old crones.

MAY: We know the Irish have a peculiar gift for highly-coloured phraseology, Deirdre, but, like everything else, they overdo it.

LOTTA: We are *not* defeated, miserable old crones, Deirdre. We are well cared for, very comfortable, and we have just enjoyed a most excellent Christmas dinner. I think it was extremely generous of Miss Fenwick to bring us a case of champagne and I propose that we open a bottle immediately and drink her health.

BONITA: Hear, hear!

MISS ARCHIE: Miss Fenwick brought something else too. (*She goes to the mantelpiece and shows them the envelope.*) It's this.

MAUDIE: What is it?

MISS ARCHIE: A present to 'The Wings' from her boss, Lord Charkley. It's a cheque for two thousand pounds, for the solarium.

There is a stunned silence.

PERRY (*breaking it*): Well, I'll be damned!

CORA (*incredulously*): Two thousand pounds!

ESTELLE: It can't be true – it can't be true——

PERRY *runs to the mantelpiece, tears the cheque out of the envelope and stares at it.*

PERRY (*awe-stricken*): It *is* true – two thousand bloody pounds!

MAY (*routine disapproval*): Really, Perry——

CORA: Where's the catch in it? There must be a catch somewhere.

MISS ARCHIE: She said that there were no strings attached, that it was a private donation and that I was to inform the committee that it was for the solarium and nothing else.

PERRY (*devoutly*): Boodie Nethersole, thou should'st be with us at this hour!

BONITA: To hell with Boodie Nethersole – to hell with the committee! – This is the most wonderful thing that ever happened.

MAY: I don't think you should say 'To hell with the committee', Bonita, even in fun. They do their best and they *did* send all of us those pretty little powder compacts.

LOTTA (*laughing*): Oh, May!

MISS ARCHIE: Come on, Perry my lad – bring that case of booze into the kitchen and let's bash it open.

PERRY: Right. (*He takes the package and goes off through the service door.*)

MISS ARCHIE (*following him*): I'm afraid we'll have to use tumblers – there aren't any champagne glasses. (*She disappears.*)

CORA: Whoever heard of a home for defeated old crones without champagne glasses!

Everyone laughs except ESTELLE – *who bursts into tears.*

ESTELLE: Oh, I am glad – so very very glad——

CORA: Cheer up, dear – there really isn't anything to cry about.

ESTELLE: I can't help it – I always cry when something nice happens.

DEIRDRE: The world's too full of sorrow and suffering for you to waste your foolish tears on a scrap of happiness, Estelle. Save 'em until you need 'em, and you will, one of these fine days, mark my words.

MAY (*with a note of irritation*): I sometimes wonder, Deirdre, if you ever believe *anything* you say!

DEIRDRE (*belligerently*): And what might you be meaning by that?

MAY: I would like to know what inspires your continual harping on misery and age and the imminence of death. Are you so afraid of it? Are you whistling in the dark?

DEIRDRE: I've never been afraid of anyone or anything, May Davenport, since the day I was born.

MAY: In that case it would be kinder to spare the feelings of those who are less courageous.

DEIRDRE: The Blessed Lord will gather me to his bosom when my time comes and that'll be that.

MAY: Presumably the Blessed Lord will gather us all to his bosom when our time comes. I see no reason to suppose that you have an exclusive monopoly. In the meantime I suggest that you allow us to endure our remaining years as cheerfully as possible.

BONITA: Hurray!

DEIRDRE: That's right – take sides against me, all of you – just because I'm old and weary and a foreigner among you.

CORA: You've got more vitality than all of us put together, so be quiet and stop overacting.

DEIRDRE: So I'm overacting now, am I?

MAY (*majestically*): Yes, Deirdre, you are, and you always did.

BONITA: Never mind about all that now. Let's stop arguing, after all it is Christmas——

There is the sound of a champagne cork popping in the kitchen.

I don't think I've heard that sound since they turned Daly's into a cinema.

MISS ARCHIE returns carrying a tray of glasses, followed by PERRY *with two bottles of champagne.*

ALMINA: This will be the death of me, I know it will, on top of all that brandy sauce.

CORA: I hope it's a good year.

PERRY (*looking at a bottle*): Bollinger 1938.

CORA (*gloomily*): Never mind.

MISS ARCHIE passes round the glasses and PERRY *follows her, filling them as he goes.*

MAUDIE: Only a drop for me – really.

OSGOOD: Do you think it would be all right if I took a little sip up to Martha? I think it would please her.

MISS ARCHIE: Of course – damned good idea – Perry——

PERRY pours champagne into two glasses and MISS ARCHIE *hands them to* OSGOOD.

OSGOOD: Thank you. (*He begins to go upstairs.*) She won't be asleep, will she?

MISS ARCHIE: She may be dozing but she never really settles down for the night before eleven.

OSGOOD: If she is, I'll wake her gently. A little unexpected treat never hurt anyone. (*He disappears upstairs.*)

BONITA: You know that man breaks my heart, he really does. Fancy anyone loving anyone as much as that, over all those years.

MAY (*splendidly*):

'Love's not Time's fool though rosy lips and cheeks
  Within his bending sickle's compass come,
  Love alters not with his brief hours and weeks
  But bears it out even to the edge of doom.'

DEIRDRE: And who's harping on death now, I should like to know?

MAY (*briskly*): William Shakespeare.

DEIRDRE (*with a snort*): I might have known it.

MAY: An unlikely contingency.

PERRY: I propose we drink a toast to Zelda Fenwick and Lord Charkley. Will those in favour raise their glasses?

CORA: I suppose it's the least we can do, really.

They all raise their glasses and murmur 'Zelda Fenwick and Lord Charkley'. MAUDIE *goes to the piano and bangs out* 'For they are jolly good fellows'. *Everybody joins in and they finish with a flourish and applaud and laugh.* MAUDIE *continues to play softly through the ensuing dialogue.*

PERRY (*with the bottle – to* BONITA): Have another whack – there's lots more in the kitchen.

BONITA: Certainly. I shall have a hangover in the morning but who cares? (*He pours her some.*)

PERRY: May?

MAY: Only a very little. (*He goes round refilling glasses.*)

ALMINA: Oh no, I daren't, really, I daren't.

PERRY: Come on – a little of what you fancy does you good.

ALMINA: I don't know *what* Doctor Jevons would say.

BONITA (*meditatively*): There's always something glamorous about champagne, isn't there? I wonder why.

DEIRDRE: Because it's a devil's brew and very expensive.

BONITA: When did you first taste it, May, can you remember?

MAY: Certainly I can. It was at my brother's wedding in Wimbledon in 1898. I was a bridesmaid and it gave me hiccups.

ALMINA: When I was at the Gaiety with Millie James she used to have a magnum in her dressing-room every night. That was in 1904.

MAY: Poor Millie. The results were only too apparent in 1905.

PERRY: When was your first go at it, Bonita?

BONITA: Before a dress rehearsal of *Aladdin* in Manchester when I was sixteen. The assistant stage manager brought some to the digs and we all got soused.

ESTELLE: What were you playing?

BONITA: The Spirit of the Lamp and I fell into the orchestra pit, lamp and all.

MAUDIE (*breaking into song – at the piano*):
    'Champagne – Champagne – Champagne
      So sublime, so divine, so profane
      It fizzes and bubbles
      And banishes troubles
      Champagne – Champagne – Champagne!'

BONITA: That's a common little lyric if ever I heard one.

MAUDIE: It's the waltz from *Miss Mouse* – Poor Dolly Drexell sang it at the end of the second act, she had a big head-dress of ostrich feathers and they kept on getting into her mouth.

LOTTA: Play the other one, Maudie – the one I like——

MAUDIE: Oh dear – I can't remember much of it – wait a minute—— (*She pauses for a second and then plays a few chords and begins to sing.*) 'Won't you come and live in my house – Miss Mouse?' – Now you all have to repeat 'Miss Mouse' – let's start again. 'Won't you come and live in my house – Miss Mouse?'

ALL (*singing*): 'Miss Mouse'.

MAUDIE: 'It's as neat as any apple pie house – Miss Mouse'.

ALL (*singing*): 'Miss Mouse'.

MAUDIE (*singing*):
> 'I will give you honey from the bees
> Bread and milk and lovely bits of cheese
> Please please please please please please please
> Come and live in my house——' All together

ALL (*singing*):
> 'Come and live in my house'.

MAUDIE (*singing*):
> 'Come and live in my house – Miss Mouse!'
> *Everyone laughs and applauds.*

– Now once more – all together.

She repeats the refrain and they all join in with a will.

LOTTA (*laughing*): That really is the most idiotic song I ever heard.

MAUDIE: Come on, Bonita – 'Over the hill I'll find you'.

BONITA: Good God, no – it's too long ago – I couldn't.

MAUDIE: We'll sing it with you – come on. (*She plays some introductory chords.*)

BONITA (*starting to sing, in a husky, uncertain voice*):
> 'Over the hill I'll find you

            There by the murmuring stream'.
(*Speaking.*) Help me somebody——
    MAUDIE (*prompting*):
        'And the birds in the woods——
    BONITA (*continuing*):
        'And the birds in the woods behind you
        Will echo our secret dream.
        There in the twilight waiting
        Gentle, serene and still
        All the cares of the day
        Will have vanished away
        When I find you – over the hill'.
        Everybody applauds.
    DEIRDRE: Sentimental poppycock.
    MAY: The words are a little sugary but it's a very
pretty tune.
    MAUDIE: What was that number you did in *Two's a
Crowd*, Perry?
    PERRY: Oh no, Maudie, I couldn't – I couldn't, really
– I'd dry up dead.
    BONITA: Come on, dear, don't be coy, you're among
friends. Play it, Maudie.
    MAUDIE: E flat?
    PERRY: No – that's too high – a tone down.
    MAUDIE: D flat then – come on—— (*She plays some
introductory chords.*)
    PERRY (*starting to sing hesitantly, he falters and stops*):
Damn!
    MAUDIE: Start again.
        He starts again and sings 'Come the Wild, Wild Weather'.
    He sings it gently and very sweetly. When he finishes MAY
    gets up and kisses him.
    PERRY (*singing*): Time may hold in store for us.

Glory or defeat
Maybe never more for us
Life will seem so sweet
Time will change so many things
Tides will ebb and flow
But wherever fate may lead us
Always we shall know

Come the wild, wild weather
Come the wind, come the rain
Come the little white flakes of snow
Come the joy, come the pain
We shall still be together
When our life's journey ends
For wherever we chance to go
We shall always be friends
We may find while we're travelling
      through the years
Moments of joy and love and happiness
Reason for grief, reason for tears
Come the wild, wild weather
If we've lost or we've won
We'll remember these words we say
Till our story is done.

MAY: That was charming, dear boy – really charming.

LOTTA: I'd have given anything in the world to have been able to sing when I was young but I never could – not a note.

DEIRDRE: Play something larky for the love of heaven – you'll have us all crying our eyes out in a minute.

MAY: An Irish jig perhaps?

DEIRDRE: And what's wrong with that I should like to know?

MAUDIE: Come on then, Deirdre——

She starts to play a jig. DEIRDRE *rises to her feet and begins to dance it. Everyone claps their hands in time to the music. She becomes more and more abandoned. Suddenly she stops and gives a little cry.* MAUDIE *stops playing.*

LOTTA: Deirdre – what's the matter?

DEIRDRE (*in a faint voice, clutching her heart*): Mother of God, it's happening – it's happening to me – it's happening – to me——

She gives a small gasp and falls back on to the sofa. There is a stunned silence. PERRY *and* MISS ARCHIE *run to her.*

LOTTA: Brandy – quickly——

She goes swiftly to the side table and pours some brandy into a glass. PERRY *and* MISS ARCHIE *lift* DEIRDRE *into a more comfortable position, but her head falls back.*

MAY: You'd better telephone for Doctor Jevons, Perry.

PERRY: Right. (*He runs off into* MISS ARCHIE'S *office.*)

LOTTA *comes over with the brandy and tries to force a little between* DEIRDRE'S *lips. After a moment or two she desists and wipes* DEIRDRE'S *mouth gently with her handkerchief.*

LOTTA (*feeling for* DEIRDRE'S *pulse*): I don't think there's much that Doctor Jevons could do.

CORA: You don't mean – you don't mean——?

LOTTA: I'm not sure, but I think so.

Everyone stands in silence looking at DEIRDRE. ESTELLE *bursts into tears.* MAY *takes* DEIRDRE'S *hands and folds them on her breast, then she straightens herself.*

MAY: The luck of the Irish!

CURTAIN

337

ACT III

Scene II

The time is after lunch on a sunny afternoon in June. Beyond the french windows the solarium can be seen in all its glory.

    ALMINA, ESTELLE, BONITA, CORA *and* MAUDIE *are sitting in it enjoying the afternoon sun.* MAY *is in her usual chair by the fire working away at her 'petit point'.*

    LOTTA *is seated on the sofa reading a book. After a moment or two she closes it firmly and puts it on the table.*

LOTTA: Well, I plodded through it.

MAY: Poor Marion, it's a tissue of lies from beginning to end.

LOTTA: I enjoyed the first chapters about her childhood. She says that one of her earliest memories was the crunch of carriage wheels on the drive when Mummy and Daddy came home from the Opera.

MAY: She was born over a tobacconist's shop in the Wilton Road.

LOTTA: Do you think we should write our memoirs, May?

MAY: I most certainly do not.

LOTTA: At least they'd be more interesting than Marion Brodie's. Think of all that we could remember!

MAY: Think of all that we can't forget.

LOTTA: Now then, May – none of that.

CORA *comes in from the solarium.*

CORA (*as she goes*): I can't bear sitting under that ghastly glass another minute – it's like a Turkish bath. (*She disappears into the television room.*)

MAY: Cora was always a grumbler. Even when she was doing quite well. Nothing ever satisfied her.

LOTTA: I only saw her once when she was with Hilary at the Adelphi in the 'twenties. She wore several ropes of pearls and an astrakhan hat.

MAY: She always had delusions of grandeur.

LOTTA: I suspect that she hates being here more than any of us.

MAY (*with a note of bitterness*): I wouldn't be too sure of that.

LOTTA (*curiously*): Do you still hate it – so very much?

MAY (*putting down her embroidery frame*): Still hate it? Yes, Lotta, I do. I hate it with all my heart and soul. I have tried to be resigned, and even pretended to myself that I was succeeding, but it wasn't true, it's never been true for a moment. I am formally grateful for being housed and fed, but I resent every minute of every day, and every meal that is provided for me chokes me with humiliation. I was always over-proud, which was one of the reasons that I was never very popular in the theatre, but worse, far worse, than my pride was my stupid improvidence. For that I am paying a bitter price and the bitterest part of it is that I know I have only myself to blame for my contemptible destiny. (*She takes up her work again.*) And now, if you don't mind, I should like to change the subject.

LOTTA (*with a smile*): I see you haven't entirely lost your arrogance, May. You still like to dictate terms.

MAY: What do you mean?

LOTTA: *I* might not want to change the subject. I too might wish to bare my soul a little and discuss the carelessness and the follies and the idiocies that have brought me low.

MAY (*searchingly*): Do you?

LOTTA: No, dear, I don't. I am resigned, you see, and fairly content.

MAY: I suppose it's a question of temperament.

LOTTA: Are you implying that you possess more of that dubious asset than I do?

MAY: I'm not implying anything.

LOTTA (*thoughtfully*): Perhaps it is because I always played gentler parts than you. I was always a dreadfully sweet actress. I made my début as Cordelia.

MAY: One of the most pompous and disagreeable girls Shakespeare ever wrote.

LOTTA (*laughing*): Very well, dear – you win!

There is a ring of the front-door bell.

MAY: I wonder who that can be.

LOTTA: Probably Osgood.

MAY: He generally comes straight in. The front door's not locked.

LOTTA: Per aps it's some of the committee.

MAY: I hope to heaven it isn't. They're always so overpoweringly cheerful.

DOREEN *comes in from the hall.*

DOREEN: It's a gentleman to see you, Miss Bainbridge.

LOTTA (*surprised*): To see me?

DOREEN: Yes. He said it was important.

LOTTA: Did he give any name?

DOREEN: Yes. Mr. Alan Bennet.

LOTTA (*putting her hand to her throat for a moment and*

closing her eyes): Oh! (*With an effort.*) Ask him to come in, Doreen.

DOREEN: Okay, Miss. (*She goes out.*)

MAY (*concerned*): Lotta – it isn't – it can't be——?

LOTTA: I'm afraid it is.

MAY(*gathering up her work*): I'd better leave you.

LOTTA: No, no – please don't – not for a moment.

DOREEN *ushers in* ALAN BENNET *and goes off through the service door.* ALAN *is in the late forties. He is neatly dressed but there is an indefinable quality of failure about him.*

His manner is nervous.

ALAN: Hallo, Mother.

LOTTA (*rising*): Alan – what an extraordinary surprise – I mean – I had no idea you were in England.

ALAN: I flew in from Toronto yesterday.

They stare at each other uncertainly for a moment, then LOTTA *moves forward and kisses him.*

LOTTA (*turning*): May – this is my son – Miss May Davenport.

MAY: How do you do? (*She rises.*)

ALAN (*nervously shaking her hand*): I've certainly heard your name before, Miss Davenport.

MAY: How very kind of you to say so! I'll leave you now, Lotta.

LOTTA: No, please don't. Alan and I can easily talk in the garden or somewhere.

MAY: Nonsense, I'll join Cora in the television room. I don't really care for television but I'm persevering. Good-bye for the moment, Mr. Bennet.

ALAN: I hope we meet again.

MAY (*going to the television room*): Perhaps you will be staying to tea, in which case we are bound to. (*She goes.*)

Lotta (*after a slight pause*): Sit down, Alan, and have a cigarette.

Alan: I'm afraid I don't smoke.

Lotta: How wise. I never stop.

*She takes a cigarette from a box, lights it and sits on the sofa. *Alan* sits uneasily in* May's *chair.*

Alan: Well – well – well!

Lotta (*with a faint smile*): Well – well – well – indeed!

Alan: You look splendid, Mother, you really do – I'd have known you anywhere.

Lotta: I doubt that, thirty-three years is a long time.

Alan (*guiltily*): Yes – yes, it is – isn't it.

Lotta (*with an effort*): How is Cynthia?

Alan: She's fine.

Lotta: I'm so glad.

Alan: She's put on a bit of weight, you know, but I suppose that's only to be expected.

Lotta: Yes – I suppose it is.

Alan: She sent you her love.

Lotta: Thank you – thank you very much.

Alan: She was quite envious of me coming back home, she's never been out of Canada in her life, you know.

Lotta: No – I didn't know.

Alan: She was born in Winnipeg and then her whole family moved to Montreal in 1928.

Lotta: Is it large?

Alan: Winnipeg?

Lotta: No, her family.

Alan: Yes – she has three sisters and a brother in Ecuador.

Lotta: I'm never quite sure where Ecuador is.

ALAN: It's in South America, between Colombia and Peru.

LOTTA: Oh. (*After another pause.*) How are the children?

ALAN: Fine. I've brought some snapshots to show you. (*He produces a wallet from his pocket and from it some small photographs.*) I'm afraid they're not very good but they give you an idea.

LOTTA: I'll put on my glasses. (*She fishes in her bag, finds her glasses and puts them on.*)

ALAN (*giving her a snapshot*): That's Joan – she's the baby, when that was taken she was only three.

LOTTA: She looks a sweet little thing.

ALAN (*producing another*): That's Eileen, she's at boarding school.

LOTTA (*scrutinising it*): A nice, sensible face. Does she have to wear those glasses?

ALAN: Yes. She had an astigmatism, they're supposed to correct it.

LOTTA: Poor child, let's hope they do.

ALAN (*producing the third*): And this is Ronnie, the eldest. He's quite grown up. He's going to be a chartered accountant.

LOTTA: How tall he is, isn't he?

ALAN: Nearly six foot already. He has a wonderful head for figures.

LOTTA (*turning away, finding the whole situation too much of a strain*): Why didn't you let me know you were coming?

ALAN: I wanted it to be a surprise.

LOTTA (*drily*): You got your wish. It is.

ALAN: A not too unpleasant one, I hope?

LOTTA (*with a sigh*): Oh Alan – why on earth *did* you come?

ALAN: I came – to get you out of this place. I had no

idea you were in it until a friend of Cynthia's sent her a cutting from the *Sunday Clarion*. It was months old of course, but that was the first we knew of it. Cynthia was terribly upset, really she was.

LOTTA: Why?

ALAN: Well, hang it – you are her mother-in-law after all.

LOTTA: We've never set eyes on each other in our lives.

ALAN: That's not her fault.

LOTTA: I didn't say it was. I was merely stating a fact. I only heard from her once and that was seventeen years ago, just after you were married.

ALAN: Well, at any rate we had a long talk over the whole situation.

LOTTA: Situation?

ALAN: Well, you living here, in a charity home. I had no idea, neither of us had, that things had gone so badly wrong with you.

LOTTA: Things haven't gone so badly wrong with me as all that. I'm quite content here. It's a very comfortable house.

ALAN: Why didn't you write to me when – when the break-up happened?

LOTTA: I think I'd mislaid your address.

ALAN: You're being very hard, Mother. I'm trying to do my best. Please help me.

LOTTA: It was kind of you to come, Alan. At least I think it was – I'm not even sure of that.

ALAN: I *am* your son.

LOTTA: Yes, I know. Does that sound as strange to you as it does to me?

ALAN: I'm sorry for having hurt you all those years ago, please believe me.

LOTTA: I believe you, Alan. I'm sorry too. I expect there were faults on both sides, but I think it is a little late now to try to bridge the gulf. I'm a selfish old woman and set in my ways.

ALAN (*producing a letter from his pocket*): Here's a letter from Cynthia. (*He hands it to her.*) She asked me to give it to you.

LOTTA (*taking it*): Thank you. (*She slits it open and reads it in silence.*)

ALAN: She means every word of it.

LOTTA (*finishing the letter and putting it carefully back into its envelope*): It's a very kind letter. I'll write to her to-morrow.

ALAN: Do you agree with what she says?

LOTTA (*looking at him*): Do you?

ALAN: Of course. That's why I'm here.

LOTTA (*rising distractedly and walking about the room*): This is a dreadfully difficult moment, Alan – full of sadness and regret and a sort of hopelessness. I can't find any words to deal with it. I wish you hadn't come – I wish you'd stayed out there in your own life and left me to finish mine here in my own way, in peace and quiet.

ALAN: Living out your last years on public charity.

LOTTA: Does that sound so very humiliating to you?

ALAN (*irritably*): Of course it does. Cynthia was genuinely horrified when she heard it, so was Myrtle.

LOTTA: Myrtle?

ALAN: Cynthia's sister. She's married to one of the most prominent gynaecologists in Toronto.

LOTTA: How convenient.

ALAN (*patiently*): Please try to see my point, Mother.

LOTTA: I see it clearly enough, dear. Cynthia suggests in her letter that I come and live with you both. That would be private charity. Is there so much difference between that and the public sort?

ALAN: Of course there is. You are my mother. There is no question of charity.

LOTTA (*with a slight smile*): You keep on making almost defiant statements. 'I am your son.' 'You are my mother.' Do you really believe that they mean much?

ALAN: I'm doing my best to prove to you that I believe it.

LOTTA (*patting his arm*): Yes – yes – I know you are, and I am being very churlish and disagreeable. But it won't work, my dear, really it won't. You and I may be mother and son in actual fact, but spiritually we're two strangers shouting to each other across a void of thirty-three years. When you were young we managed to draw close to each other every now and then, but not for long, your father saw to that.

ALAN: It wasn't all father's fault.

LOTTA: I never said it was. It was mine too, and also the fault of circumstances. I was away on tour a great deal and beginning to do well in the theatre, your father, on the other hand, wasn't. He was a very jealous man, not only personally jealous but professionally jealous. I don't blame him for taking you from me, knowing his character, it was inevitable. But I couldn't have stopped working then even if I had wished to. If I had we should all three have starved.

ALAN: There's not much point in raking all that up again, is there?

LOTTA: I think it is most important that we should both remember exactly where we stood in a very critical moment of our lives. After the divorce you had to make your choice and you made it. You were certainly old enough to know your own mind. Please don't think that I'm reproaching you, I'm not. I'm merely trying to make you see that certain gestures in life are irrevocable.

ALAN: Do you mean that you won't come, that you won't accept the home that Cynthia and I offer you?

LOTTA (*wearily*): Of course I won't, my dear. It would be insupportable for everyone concerned. You must know that in your heart, you must. One day, if I live long enough and you can afford it, I would like to come to you for a visit and meet Cynthia and — and my grandchildren.

ALAN: Mother – please don't be hasty over this. Think it over carefully before you decide absolutely.

LOTTA: Very well.

ALAN: I shall be here until the end of next week. I have some business to do for my firm.

LOTTA: I don't even know what your firm is.

ALAN: It's called the 'O.T.B.' The Ontario Travel Bureau. It's a steady income, nothing spectacular, but there are chances of advancement – and if I hang on long enough I get a pension when I retire.

LOTTA: Like me.

ALAN: I think I'd better be going now. I've got a taxi outside.

LOTTA: Wouldn't you like to send it away and stay to tea? We're quite a cheerful little group.

ALAN (*embarrassed*): No, really – I'd rather not. (*He hesitates.*) Shall I come and see you again?

LOTTA (*looking at him. Her eyes suddenly filling with tears*): Yes dear, do, please do, just once more.

ALAN (*going to her*): Mother——

LOTTA (*warding him off*): Go now – go at once – there's a dear boy.

347

ALAN: But Mother——

LOTTA: Please do as I ask. It's been rather a shock seeing you again so – so – unexpectedly—— (*She gains control of herself.*) Where can I get in touch with you?

ALAN: I'm at the Cumberland Hotel.

LOTTA: The Cumberland. I'll remember. Good-bye, dear. (*She kisses him, holds him tightly for a moment and then pushes him gently away.*) Go now.

ALAN: Will Wednesday or Thursday be all right?

LOTTA: Wednesday or Thursday will be fine.

ALAN: Let's say Thursday then. If I came about noon I could take you out to lunch.

LOTTA: Yes. That would be lovely. I shall look forward to it.

ALAN: *Au revoir*, then.

LOTTA: *Au revoir.* (*He smiles at her, a little nervously, and goes out. She sinks on to the sofa, buries her face in her hands and bursts into tears.* MAY *comes in from the television room.*)

MAY(*gently*): Don't cry, Lotta—— Please don't cry.

LOTTA (*in a muffled voice*): I'll be all right in a minute.

MAY: Why did he come here?

LOTTA: He brought me a letter from his wife inviting me to go and live with them in Canada. It was quite a kind letter – and very carefully written.

MAY: And you said no?

LOTTA (*sitting up and speaking without emotion*): Yes. I said no.

MAY: I see. (*A slight pause, she puts her hand on* LOTTA's *shoulder.*) Is there anything I can do to help?

LOTTA (*resting her hand for a moment on* MAY's *hand*): Yes, dear May. You might pass me my knitting, it's on the piano.

There is a noise of a motor-bicycle outside.

348

MAY (*going to the piano*): That's Perry. He'll be able to tell us how rehearsals are going for the matinée. (*She brings* LOTTA *her knitting.*)

LOTTA: Thank you. If anyone had told me a year ago that a time would come when I should really enjoy knitting, I should have thought they were mad.

MAY: It's a very pretty colour. What's it going to be?

LOTTA: A bed-jacket. The one I have is Alice blue and too ingénue. It's also falling to pieces.

ALMINA, ESTELLE, MAUDIE *and* BONITA *come in from the solarium.* ALMINA *and* ESTELLE *go to their usual chairs.* MAUDIE *settles herself on the sofa next to* LOTTA.

ALMINA: It's really almost too hot out there. You'd hardly believe it, would you?

CORA *comes out of the television room.*

CORA: That damned machine has started wobbling again. Fortunately it's only a Welsh choir.

ALMINA (*complacently*): Miss Archie will fix it.

PERRY *comes in from the hall.*

PERRY: *Bonjour, Mesdames – comment ça va?*

BONITA: Ever so *trè bien*, thanks.

PERRY *comes over to* MAY *and gives her a small parcel.*

PERRY (*kissing her*): Many happy returns.

MAY (*severely*): Perry. You are breaking the rules again. You know perfectly well that any mention of birthdays is forbidden in this house.

PERRY: It's just a little something to make you smell pretty.

BONITA: Many happy returns, May. Why didn't you tell us——

Everyone murmurs 'Many happy returns' *and* 'Happy birthday'.

MAY: Thank you – thank you all very much. (*She has*

by now undone the parcel and holds up a very small bottle of
'Arpege.') Oh, Perry, you really shouldn't have. I am most
displeased – and very touched. (*She kisses him.*)

PERRY (*pats her hand affectionately and turns to the others*):
Has Topsy Baskerville arrived yet?

BONITA: No. Miss Archie went up this morning. She's
bringing her down on the two-five, so they ought to be
here at any minute.

MAUDIE: Poor old Topsy! I wonder how she feels.

CORA: There's no need to wonder, we all know how
she feels.

BONITA: I was with her at the Hippodrome during the
First War in 1915. She sang 'Oh Mr Kaiser'.

MAUDIE (*laughing*): Yes – I remember that——
    She hums.
    'Oh Mr Kaiser
    Call your legal adviser
    You've bitten off far more than you can chew
    When Mister Tommy Atkins comes a-marching to
        Berlin
    You'll be gibbering like a monkey in the zoo
    (Have a banana!)
    Oh Mr Kaiser
    When you're older and wiser
    You'll learn some things you never learnt at school
    When we've wound up the Watch on your dear old
        Rhine
    You're going to look a Potsdam fool!'

MAY (*leaning over to* CORA, *in a booming whisper*): Who is
this Topsy? I've never heard of her.

CORA: Topsy Baskerville. She was in musical comedy
and revue mostly.

MAY: Poor thing. So exhausting.

PERRY: She's a sweet old girl. You'll love her.

LOTTA: I'm sure we shall, Perry dear. I'm sure we shall. (*She puts down her knitting and gives a wry smile.*) I expect that's exactly what you said a year ago when I arrived.

BONITA: Yes, I expect we did. A whole year ago! It doesn't seem possible, does it?

LOTTA: I was in deep despair, lonely and hopeless and feeling as though I were going to prison, and now, after a year of prison, I feel suddenly free. Isn't that curious? (*She returns to her knitting.*)

MAUDIE *strikes up the song 'Oh Mr Kaiser' as* MISS ARCHIE *comes in from the hall with* TOPSY BASKERVILLE. TOPSY *is a small, frail old lady in her seventies.*

TOPSY (*in a tremulous voice*): My song!

BONITA *runs forward to meet her, everybody is singing 'Oh Mr Kaiser' and*

THE CURTAIN FALLS

SUITE IN THREE KEYS

A SONG AT TWILIGHT
SHADOWS OF THE EVENING
COME INTO THE GARDEN MAUD

A SONG AT TWILIGHT

A COMEDY IN TWO ACTS

CHARACTERS

Hugo Latymer
Hilde, his wife
Carlotta Gray
Felix, a waiter

The time is the Present.

The action of the play passes in a private suite of the Hotel Beau Rivage, Lausanne-Ouchy, Switzerland.

ACT I

The action of the play passes in a private suite in a luxurious hotel in Switzerland.

The scene is the sitting-room. The suite is occupied for two or three months each year by SIR HUGO LATYMER, *an elderly writer of considerable eminence.*

The conventional hotel furnishing has been augmented by some of SIR HUGO'S *personal possessions which include an impressive writing-desk, a special arm-chair by the side of which is a small table. On this are books, bottles of medicine and pills, a small gold clock and a slim vase containing a number of ball-point pens. On the walls hang some of* SIR HUGO'S *favourite Impressionist paintings.*

On stage Left there is a door leading into the bedroom. There are double doors at the back which open onto a small lobby and then the corridor. HILDE'S *room also opens off the lobby.*

HILDE LATYMER *is a faded woman in her early fifties. She has been married to* SIR HUGO *for nearly twenty years and was originally his secretary. Apart from being his official German translator, she is capable, dedicated, and orders his life with considerable efficiency.*

When the curtain rises she is seated at the writing-desk. Standing near her is FELIX, *the floor-waiter. He is a startlingly handsome young man of about twenty-eight and there is already in his manner that subtle blend of obsequiousness, authority and charm which, if he does not allow his good looks to lead him astray, will ultimately carry him to the top of his profession. At the moment he is holding a notebook and listening to* HILDE *with polite attention.*

HILDE: That will be all for the moment Felix. Sir Hugo's guest is due at eight o'clock but it is possible that she might be a little late so I think you should be prepared to serve the dinner at about eight-thirty but not before.

FELIX: A touch of garlic in the salad dressing as usual?

HILDE: Yes. But only the smallest touch. We don't want a repetition of last Friday, do we?

FELIX: Friday night is much to be regretted Milady. But if you will remember I was off duty. Giovanni is a most willing boy but he is not yet accustomed to Sir Hugo's tastes.

HILDE: You will warn him to be more careful next time.

FELIX: Very good Milady. (*He bows and goes out.*)

HILDE (*lifting the telephone. She speaks with a rather heavy German accent*): 'Allo, Mademoiselle. J'ai demandè un prèavis a Londres il y a presq'une demi'heure. Est ce que vous en avez des nouvelles? – Oui – Oui merci j'attendrai. (*She hangs up the receiver and devotes her attention to some letters on the desk. After a moment or two the telephone rings.*) Hallo – is that you Carl? – This is Hilde Latymer speaking. I have been trying to get you all the afternoon. First of all regarding the lecture tour in the States——Yes I know——But Sir Hugo really isn't up to it.——Oh yes, he is much better but the doctor insists that my husband must not undertake anything that is not absolutely necessary. Yes. He will accept the Doctorate at the University and make a speech as arranged, but nothing more than that. After it's over we will either come straight back here or go to Arizona for a rest. ——No I am truly sorry but it can't be helped.

——No, he's resting at the moment otherwise he would speak to you himself. ——Now then, regarding the film proposition for 'The Winding River'. You will have to put in the contract that he has complete veto on the script and the adaptor. Well he certainly won't sign it unless that is confirmed in writing. ——On the contrary I think it matters a great deal. It involves his name and reputation——

At this moment SIR HUGO LATYMER *comes out of the bedroom. He is a distinguished looking elderly man. His figure is slim and erect. Sometimes, when he is in a good mood he looks younger than he actually is by several years. At other times, when upset over some triviality or worried about his health, he becomes suddenly enfeebled and deliberately ancient. This of course is a pose but it works like a charm on doctors and nurses or whoever happens to be looking after him at the moment. It even works on* HILDE *occasionally, notwithstanding the fact that she has had twenty years to grow accustomed to it.*

SIR HUGO *is wearing a dressing-gown, his white hair is slightly tousled and he looks irascible.*

HUGO: What involves my name and reputation?

HILDE (*putting her hand over the telephone*): It's Carl. We're talking about 'The Winding River' contract.

HUGO: Then you are both wasting your time. I have no intention of signing it whatever concessions they make.

HILDE: But Hugo dear you did say that providing they gave you complete veto of script and adaptor that——

HUGO (*snappily*): Well I have changed my mind. I have had no less than three novels and five of my best short stories massacred by the cretinous medium. I

360

refuse to have any more of it.

HILDE (*at telephone*): I can't talk any more at the moment Carl. Ring me in the morning at eleven o'clock. ——Very well ten o'clock but be sure to have it put through to my room. Yes 355. Good-bye. (*She hangs up.*)

HUGO (*sitting in his chair*): Carl's getting out of hand. He needs a serious talking to. All he thinks about is his damned percentage.

HILDE: You can't altogether blame him for that. He *is* your agent.

HUGO: What time is it?

HILDE (*glancing at her watch*): Nearly half past seven. Isn't that clock going?

HUGO: I haven't the faintest idea. It's so exquisitely made that I can't see it without my glasses.

HILDE: You said you were delighted with it when I gave it to you.

HUGO: Well I'm not now.

HILDE: I'm sorry. I'll try and change it.

HUGO: And please don't look martyred. It draws your mouth down at the corners. Like a weary old camel.

HILDE: Thank you.

HUGO: With two unsymmetrical humps.

HILDE: That's a dromedary. Have you had your bath?

HUGO: No I have not had my bath.

HILDE: Well don't you think you should? She's due at eight.

HUGO: If I'm not ready she can wait for me can't she? An extra ten minutes tacked onto all those years can't matter all that much.

The telephone rings.

Damn that bloody instrument! Why can't you have it switched into your room and go and sit by it?

HILDE: You're in a very disagreeable mood.

HUGO: I'm nervous.

HILDE: It's your own fault if you are. You needn't have agreed to see her.

The telephone rings again.

HUGO: For God's sake answer it.

HILDE (*lifting the receiver*): 'Allo 'allo. Oui, a'l'appareil——Mariette c'est vous!——Non je ne suis pas certain, si vous voudrez attendre pour un petit moment je vais voir. (*She puts her hand over the receiver.*) It's Mariette.

HUGO: Curiously enough I gathered that. Why didn't you say I was out?

HILDE: I can still say you're being massaged.

HUGO: You said that last time. She'll think I spend my whole life being massaged. Here——give it to me . . .

HILDE (*into telephone*): Un instant Mariette. (*She brings the telephone over to his chair.*)

HUGO (*his French of course is excellent*): Ma chere Mariette – enfin! Je suis absolument ravi d'entendre ta voix. Comment va tu?——Alas no my dear I cannot possibly. I already have a rendézvous this evening. No, no, not that kind at all. ——No, this is a rendézvous with the past, the very very far distant past. ——No, no nobody you've ever heard of. It was all over and done with before you were born. ——Not another word, I have said far too much as it is. ——Very well, luncheon on Tuesday. (*He raises his eyebrows at* HILDE *who glances quickly at his engagement pad and nods*)——Until Tuesday ——A bientot cherie. (*He hangs up.*)

HILDE *relieves him of the telephone and takes it back to the desk.*

There was no getting out of that. I've put her off three times in the last month. You're looking sour, Hilde. What's the matter now?

HILDE: I think you were indiscreet.

HUGO: Stop nagging at me.

HILDE: It is not nagging to say that I think you are indiscreet.

HUGO (*with almost a conscious smirk*): I have been feeling indiscreet all day.

HILDE: Have you indeed?

HUGO: Yes. And wrapped in an agreeable anticipatory glow until your screeching down the telephone woke me from my nap.

HILDE: Mariette is the most incorrigible gossip. Do you want the whole of Switzerland to know about your private affairs?

HUGO: Switzerland must have a pretty shrewd idea of them by now anyway.

HILDE: I was not speaking financially.

HUGO (*with a complacent smile*): No Hilde, I didn't think you were.

HILDE: Do go and have your bath and dress.

HUGO: I only said I had a rendezvous with the past, which is perfectly true, I have.

HILDE: You made it sound furtive, almost romantic.

HUGO: Perhaps it will be.

HILDE: You would wish it to be romantic?

HUGO: No Hilde, I have long ago given up wishing that anything could be romantic.

HILDE: I find it difficult to believe that you ever did.

HUGO (*irritably*): Ever did what?

HILDE: Sigh for the moon and the stars, open your heart to illusion.

HUGO: I admit that I have always preferred realism to fantasy.

HILDE: Even when you were young and in love – with Carlotta?

HUGO: Even then.

HILDE: I still think all this is a great mistake.

HUGO: Yes I know you do. You've made that abundantly clear during the last three days. You've never been exactly adept at hiding your feelings.

HILDE: On the contrary, Hugo, that is one of the things I do best. Living with you for twenty years has been excellent training.

HUGO: Why are you so frightened of Carlotta?

HILDE (*calmly*): I am not in the least frightened of Carlotta.

HUGO: Oh yes you are. The very idea of her fills your soul with dread. Come on now, admit it.

HILDE: It is time for your blue pill. (*She goes abruptly into the bedroom leaving the door open.*)

HUGO (*enjoying himself*): You'd better take a tranquilliser to calm your desperate fears.

HILDE (*returning with a pill and a glass of water*): Whatever fears I may have about Carlotta are entirely on your account. She is bound to upset you in some way or other. She wouldn't suddenly reappear in your life like this unless she wanted something. Here you are. (*She hands him the pill.*)

HUGO (*taking it*): Perhaps she wants a reunion.

HILDE: Money more likely. She has not been very successful during the last fifteen years.

HUGO: Have you been following her career?

HILDE (*taking the glass*): There hasn't been much career to follow lately. (*She goes off into the bedroom again.*)

HUGO (*complacently*): Poor Carlotta!

HILDE (*returning*): She will upset you. I feel it in my bones. It is like the weather. I can always tell when it is going to rain.

HUGO: That particular form of prescience is rheumatic rather than clairvoyant. In any case it is within the bounds of possibility that I might upset her.

HILDE: She doesn't suffer from your particular form of nervous indigestion.

HUGO: She might be riddled with ulcers for all you know.

HILDE: She didn't sound as if she were on the telephone.

HUGO: Why should she? Gastric ulcers have little or no relation to the vocal chords.

HILDE (*turning away*): I will say no more.

HUGO: Turn round Hilde. I don't like talking to your back. It's such a Teutonic, uncompromising back.

HILDE (*turning*): Is that better?

HUGO: Give me your hand.

HILDE *comes over to him reluctantly. He takes her hand and looks up at her with a quizzical smile. The charm is on.*

HILDE: A lump of sugar for a good little dog?

HUGO (*letting her hand go*): I see you're determined to be tiresome.

HILDE: It's unfair of you to say that. It's you I'm thinking of. You've been so much better lately. Doctor Benoist says your blood pressure is back to normal, you're sleeping well and you haven't had any pains for three weeks. I just don't want you to have a relapse. You know that any sort of excitement is bad for you.

HUGO: Do you seriously believe that seeing Carlotta again will excite me to the extent of sending up my blood pressure?

HILDE: You've been giving every indication of it.

HUGO: Oh Hilde – Hilde. What an egregious ass you are.

HILDE: You have now called me a camel, a dromedary and an ass within the last ten minutes. Your normal dialogue is less zoological. You have worked yourself up into a state about seeing Carlotta again and it's no use pretending you haven't. I know the symptoms. I haven't been with you for twenty years for nothing.

HUGO: Am I so transparent?

HILDE: To me – yes.

HUGO (*petulantly*): It's you who are sending my blood pressure up, not Carlotta . . . Give me a cigarette.

HILDE (*reluctantly handing him a cigarette box*): It will be your seventh today.

HUGO: No it won't, it will be my sixth. I only had one after lunch.

HILDE (*lighting a cigarette for him*): Be careful. That's all I ask of you. Just be careful. She made you unhappy before. I don't want you to give her the chance of making you unhappy again.

HUGO (*patiently*): Now listen to me Hilde. My affair with Carlotta lasted exactly two years, and we parted in a blaze of mutual acrimony. That was many years ago and I haven't clapped eyes on her since except once on the cinema screen when she appeared briefly as a Mother Superior in an excrutiatingly bad film about a nun with a vast bust. Nor have we corresponded. This sudden request on her part to see me again has not unnaturally filled me with curiosity. It is quite possible that your surmise is right and that she wants to borrow money. If that is so I will lend her some for old time's sake. On the other hand she may merely want to see me for sentimental reasons. Time and the difficult years may have mellowed her, or she may even wish to gloat over my age and infirmity.

HILDE (*sharply*): You are *not* infirm.

HUGO: After all you must remember that she was very much in love with me.

HILDE: And you with her?

HUGO: Of course.

HILDE: Was she beautiful?

HUGO: Not in the classical sense. But she was extremely attractive and her vitality was inexhaustible.

HILDE: I suspect that it still is.

HUGO: Even so, the chances of a passionate, physical reunion are remote.

HILDE: So I should hope. The very idea would be ridiculous.

HUGO: Not quite so ridiculous as all that. Anyhow you cannot deny that the possibility crossed your mind.

HILDE (*hotly*): I most certainly do deny it.

HUGO: Isn't that over vehemence a trifle suspect?

HILDE: Suspect! What do you mean?

HUGO: Quite frankly, I suspect you of being jealous.

HILDE (*quietly*): No Hugo I am not jealous. I realised many years ago that I had no right to be jealous.

HUGO: Since when has jealousy been so law-abiding? Is it an emotion that obediently sticks to the rules?

HILDE: I have no wish to argue with you.

HUGO: You are jealous of all my friends, of anyone who is close to me, and you always have been.

HILDE (*with a show of spirit*): You have not so many friends for me to be jealous of.

HUGO: You hate Mariette. You are barely civil to Cedric Marcombe and David when they come here.

HILDE: They are barely civil to me.

HUGO: Cedric Marcombe is a man of brilliant intelligence and exquisite taste. He is also the greatest connoisseur of modern art alive today.

HILDE: And what is David?

HUGO (*defensively*): David is one of the most promising young painters that England has produced in the last twenty years, he also happens to be the son of Lord Tenterden.

HILDE: In that case he should have better manners. And his paintings I do not care for at all. They are ugly and cruel.

HUGO (*viciously*): As a full-blooded German you are scarcely in a position to object to cruelty in art or anything else.

HILDE: It is wrong of you to speak to me like that Hugo, and most unkind. When you are in a better mood you will see that this is so and be sorry. In any case this sort of argument is waste of time and energy. You cannot, after all these long years, seriously imagine that I am jealous of your friends or your heart. If I am jealous at all it is for your well-being. You really must try not to get cross so easily. You know what it does to your acids. Remember what Doctor Benoist said.

HUGO: Now you're talking like a district nurse.

HILDE: No district nurse would have had the endurance to put up with your sudden tempers for as long as I have.

HUGO: Do you wish to leave me? Are you giving me

a month's notice?

HILDE: If I wished to leave you I should have done so long ago. Now it is too late.

HUGO: For God's sake stop looking hurt Hilde. It infuriates me.

HILDE: If you do not wish me to look hurt you should not try so hard to hurt me. I do my best to help you with the business of your life, even to love you as far as you will allow me to. But you make it most difficult for me, sometimes almost too difficult to be borne. (*She turns away.*)

HUGO: Oh Lord! Now I suppose you are going to cry.

HILDE (*turning*): No Hugo. I am not going to cry. That too is waste of time and energy. I am going to put on my hat.

HUGO (*realising that he has gone too far.*) Hilde——

HILDE: If you are determined to receive your long lost love in a dressing-gown with your hair all rumpled, that is entirely your affair.

HUGO: Hilde, I'm sorry. I'm sorry that I upset you.

HILDE: It is nothing new.

HUGO: I am beginning to feel those palpitations again.

HILDE: I am not surprised.

HUGO: I wonder what she looks like? She's been in America most of her life. She'll probably have bright blue hair. Or else she'll be defeated and grey and bedraggled and make me feel old.

HILDE: Do not be foolish. You know perfectly well that you only feel old when you wish to.

HUGO *rises and goes over to the window.*

HUGO: I don't feel now that I can face her alone.

You'd better stay after all.

HILDE: Certainly not. I've already arranged to dine with Liesel at the Grappe d'Or and go to a cinema afterwards.

HUGO: Liesel is a weather-beaten old German lesbian.

HILDE: She is also highly intelligent.

HUGO: Is she in love with you?

HILDE: Not in the least. She lives with a Chinese student who paints butterflies on glass.

HUGO: Whatever for?

HILDE: Actually she's very talented.

HUGO: Put Liesel off – don't go – Stay with me, I need your support.

HILDE: I can't. She's already booked the tickets and reserved a table.

HUGO: Cut the film then and come straight back here after dinner.

HILDE (*firmly*): No Hugo. You've brought this situation on yourself and you will have to deal with it yourself.

HUGO: You have ordered the dinner?

HILDE: Yes. Felix will bring it when you ring.

HUGO: I think I should like a drink, to fortify me.

HILDE: I'll ring for some ice. (*She does so.*) It had better be Vodka. You're having it with the caviar anyhow.

HUGO: I never told you to order caviar.

HILDE: No. It was my own idea. I ordered pink champagne too.

HUGO: Pink champagne! Good God. Why?

HILDE: You're always accusing me of not having a sense of humour. I thought I'd like to prove you wrong.

Hugo: Is the rest of the menu equally plutocratic?

Hilde: No, comparatively simple. Steak Bearnaise, green salad and a chocolate soufflé.

Hugo: I shan't sleep a wink.

Hilde: I shouldn't count too much on that anyhow. The Maalox tablets are in the table drawer if you should need them.

Felix *enters with a bucket of ice.*
Give Sir Hugo a Vodka on the rocks, will you Felix.

Felix: Very good Milady.

Hilde (*at the door*): I won't be more than a few minutes. (*She goes.*)

Hugo (*with charm*): I missed you sadly last evening Felix. Where did you disappear to?

Felix (*mixing the drink*): It was my half-day off sir.

Hugo: Your substitute lacked charm, he also breathed like an old locomotive.

Felix: That was Giovanni Sir. He comes from Calabria.

Hugo: The railway journey must have made a profound impression on him.

Felix: Your Vodka sir. (*He hands it to him.*)

Hugo: Thank you. Did you enjoy your half-day off?

Felix: Oh yes sir. We went to swim in the piscine at Vevey, it is not so crowded as the one here, and then we came back and went to a movie.

Hugo: We?

Felix: My friend and I. He is the assistant bar-man at the Hotel de la Paix. He is a champion swimmer and has won many trophies.

Hugo: You look as though you should be a good swimmer yourself, with those shoulders.

Felix: Not as good as he is, but I myself love to

371

water-ski, it is a great sport.

HUGO: It must be. Water-ski-ing was not invented when I was your age. (*He hears* HILDE *returning.*) Thank you Felix. You will bring the dinner when I ring?

FELIX: Very good sir.

HUGO: It should be in about half an hour's time, depending on when my guest arrives.

FELIX: Bien monsieur. (*He bows and goes.*)

HILDE: Are you feeling more relaxed?

HUGO: More resigned at any rate. That's quite a masculine looking little hat, almost a bowler. Are you wearing it as a subtle gesture to your hostess?

HILDE: You know I dislike that sort of joke Hugo. Liesel has been a good friend of mine for many years. I am very fond of her. The other side of her life is of no interest to me.

HUGO: Give me another cigarette.

HILDE: Certainly not! You've already had too many today.

HUGO: I tell you I'm nervous.

HILDE: Such nonsense. You will probably have a most delightful evening, looking back into the past, remembering little jokes——

HUGO (*interrupting her*): Why have you so suddenly changed your attitude? A short while ago you were moaning and groaning and saying that you didn't want me to see Carlotta again because she would upset me and probably give me a relapse. Now you seem determined to turn the whole occasion into a sort of gruesome 'gala' with your damned caviar and vodka and pink champagne.

HILDE: I've changed my mind. I think she might do you good.

The telephone rings.

HUGO: There now!

HILDE (*answering it*): Oui Gaston. Demandez a Madame de monter toute de suite. (*She hangs up.*)

HUGO: The tiresome woman is early.

HILDE: No. It is you who are late. Go quickly. It would be inelegant to receive an ex-mistress in your dressing-gown, however old she is. I will talk to her until you are ready – go along.

HUGO: Promise me you'll cut the cinema and come straight back here after dinner.

HILDE: That all depends. I'll think about it. Go along – hurry.

HUGO *goes into the bedroom.*

There is a knock at the door. HILDE *goes to open it.*

CARLOTTA GRAY *comes into the room. She is an attractive woman who at first glance would appear to be in her late Forties or early Fifties. She is heavily made up and her hair is expertly tinted. She is wearing expensive costume jewellery, perhaps a little too much of it. Her dinner-dress is simple and well cut and she carries a light coat over her arm.*

HILDE (*holding out her hand*): I am Hilde Latymer. How do you do.

CARLOTTA (*taking it*): Of course. I recognise your voice. You were so kind on the telephone.

HILDE: My husband is dressing, he won't be more than a few minutes. May I take your coat?

CARLOTTA (*handing it to her*): Thank you.

HILDE: Please be so kind as to sit down and take a cigarette if you should care to smoke. They are in that tortoiseshell box.

HILDE *disappears into the bedroom with the coat.*

CARLOTTA *goes to the box, takes a cigarette and lights it, and looks round the room.* HILDE *returns, closing the bedroom door carefully behind her.*

CARLOTTA: What a delightful 'Renoir'! – and a 'Boudin' too! His skies are always so lovely, aren't they?

HILDE: You are interested in painting?

CARLOTTA: Oh yes, immensely interested, but I fear not very knowledgeable.

HILDE: Would you care for a drink?

CARLOTTA: Perhaps not quite yet. I would rather wait a little. How is he, Hugo? (*she corrects herself*) Sir Hugo?

HILDE: He is almost completely well again. He has of course to take care not to overdo things and not to become agitated or unduly excited. He has always been nervously overstrung, as you may probably remember.

CARLOTTA: I don't remember him being overstrung exactly. On the contrary his studied calmness used occasionally to irritate me. It was as though he had made a private vow to remain Captain of his Soul no matter what emotional hurricanes he might encounter. But it was all so long long ago. He has had ample time to change, as indeed we all have.

HILDE (*with a faint smile*): I agree that Hugo has not the sort of temperament to be easily battered by 'emotional hurricanes' as you put it, but that is not quite what I meant.

CARLOTTA: He has certainly had a wonderful career. It wouldn't be surprising if he sometimes found the burden of his eminence a trifle nerve-wracking.

HILDE (*not quite pleased with this either*): Nerve-wracking?

CARLOTTA: The continual demands made upon his

time, the constant strain of having to live up to the self-created image he has implanted in the public mind. How fortunate he is to have you to protect him.

HILDE: He isn't I think, in quite such urgent need of protection as you imagine.

CARLOTTA: You've been married for twenty years haven't you?

HILDE: Yes. He engaged me as his secretary in January 1945 and a few months later we were married.

CARLOTTA (*smiling*): I remember the headlines. It caused quite a sensation.

HILDE (*turning away*): Yes, I know it did. There was much foolishness written in the papers.

CARLOTTA: You are not in the least like I thought you'd be.

HILDE (*politely*): Indeed? – What did you expect?

CARLOTTA: Someone more grim, less vulnerable. A dragon guarding the throne.

HILDE: You put things so picturesquely Miss Gray. Perhaps you should have been a writer yourself.

CARLOTTA: The idea has crossed my mind. Hugo used to accuse me of being garrulous and over-articulate long ago. How does he feel about seeing me again, after so long?

HILDE: I cannot say. He is curious, naturally.

CARLOTTA: And you? What are your reactions to this – this rather peculiar situation?

HILDE: I have no feelings about it one way or the other.

CARLOTTA: I will accept the snub but I am not entirely convinced by it.

HILDE: It was not intended to be a snub. You will please forgive me?

CARLOTTA: There is nothing whatever to forgive. I find it perfectly understandable that you should be suspicious of me. It is the duty of even the kindliest protective dragons to be wary of strangers. It is sad that we did not meet in earlier, different circumstances. We might have been friends.

HILDE (*melting a trifle*): Thank you Miss Gray.

HUGO *comes out of the bedroom. He is wearing an emerald green velvet smoking jacket over dark trousers. He has a cream silk shirt, a black tie and his slippers are monogrammed in gold.*

CARLOTTA *rises and looks at him for a moment. Then she goes to him.*

CARLOTTA: Hugo! What a strange moment this is, isn't it? I had planned so many things to say and now they've gone clean out of my head. Do we embrace?

HUGO (*with a slightly self-conscious smile*) Why not? (*He kisses her formally on both cheeks.*)

CARLOTTA (*drawing away*): How well you look! Slim as ever and so distinguished. White hair definitely becomes you.

HUGO (*with splendid chivalry*): The years seem to have forgotten you Carlotta.

CARLOTTA: Oh no my dear. It isn't that they have forgotten me, it's that I have remembered them and taken the right precautions.

HUGO: You and Hilde have already made friends I see.

CARLOTTA (*glancing swiftly at* HILDE): Yes. As a matter of fact we have.

(*To* HILDE) It's been puzzling me where I could have seen you before but now I remember. There's a photograph of you in Hugo's autobiography. You are leaning against a pillar and shading your eyes with your hand as though you were worried about the weather.

HUGO: The pillar was one of the columns of the Parthenon.

HILDE: The light was very strong.

CARLOTTA: Alas. There is no photograph of me in the book. At least, only a verbal one. (*She looks at* HUGO) The light was a little too strong in that too.

HUGO: Can I offer you a drink?

CARLOTTA: Oh yes – by all means. I should love one.

HILDE (*going to the drink table*): Whisky, Brandy, Gin, Vodka?

CARLOTTA: Vodka please, on the rocks. (*To* HUGO.) I expected you to look much older. But that's beside the point nowadays, isn't it? I mean – people hardly ever look their real age any more. Time is learning to accept a few defeats. It's rather fun frustrating the old monster.

HILDE (*bringing her drink*): Your Vodka Miss Gray.

CARLOTTA: Thank you so much.

HILDE (*to* CARLOTTA): I am afraid I must leave you now. I have a dinner engagement.

CARLOTTA: Oh how disappointing. I had hoped to get to know you better.

HILDE: We shall probably meet again.

CARLOTTA: Of course. We're almost bound to. I have moved into this hotel.

HILDE (*caught unawares*): Oh!

CARLOTTA (*putting out her hand*): Don't be alarmed. I shall only be here for a few days. I am having a series of injections at the Clinique and it's more convenient to be here than in Vevey.

HILDE (*shaking her hand*): Aurevoir then Miss Gray.

CARLOTTA (*smiling*): A bientot Lady Latymer.

HILDE *shoots an equivocal look at* HUGO *and goes*

swiftly out of the room. CARLOTTA *strolls over to the window.*

CARLOTTA: How lovely it is with the lights glittering in the distance. I went over to Evian the other evening on the little steamer and won nearly a thousand francs.

HUGO (*slightly shocked*): Can you afford to play so high?

CARLOTTA: Oh yes, I have a certain amount put by. I also still get alimony from my last husband.

HUGO: Have you had many others?

CARLOTTA: Two before this one. They both died. One in an air crash and the other in the war.

HUGO: Did you love them?

CARLOTTA: Oh yes. I shouldn't have married them if I hadn't.

HUGO: Have you any children?

CARLOTTA: Yes. I had a son by my second husband. He's twenty-four now and very attractive. You'd love him. He's an entomologist.

HUGO: I don't believe I've ever met an entomologist. That's insects, isn't it?

CARLOTTA: Yes. There's a great deal more in insects than meets the eye.

HUGO: I'm sure there is. Personally I've never felt particularly drawn to them.

CARLOTTA: I expect you thought that the bombardier beetle shoots compressed air from its intestines, whereas in actual fact it is highly explosive rocket fuel which it produces in two of its glands.

HUGO: I must admit that has been baffling me for some time.

CARLOTTA: And grasshoppers! You must like grasshoppers!

HUGO: I'm sorry to disappoint you, but I don't.

CARLOTTA: They converse by rubbing their back legs together.

HUGO: I'm beginning to wish we did.

CARLOTTA: Am I to drink alone?

HUGO: Too much alcohol is bad for me.

CARLOTTA: Too much alcohol is bad for everyone. Just pour yourself a teeny weeny one to keep me company.

HUGO: Really, Carlotta, you're too absurd.

CARLOTTA: She's nice, your wife. I like her.

HUGO: I'm so glad.

CARLOTTA: In spite of the fact that she doesn't care for me much. I don't think you quite did her justice in your book. But then, you weren't very nice about anybody in your book, were you?

HUGO: You were under no obligation to read it.

CARLOTTA: There was no warning on the cover. You take a fairly jaundiced view of your fellow creatures, don't you, on the whole?

HUGO: Perhaps. I prefer to see people as they are rather than as more sentimental minds would wish them to be. However, I am a commentator, not a moralist. I state no preferences.

CARLOTTA: Admirable!

HUGO: I would hate you to imagine that I am unaware of the mocking expression in your eye.

CARLOTTA (*with a smile*): Don't worry. I would never suspect you of missing a trick. Except perhaps the most important one of all.

HUGO: And what might that be?

CARLOTTA: The knack of discovering the best in people's characters instead of the worst.

HUGO: Without wishing to undermine your radiant self-confidence I must break it to you that that has been said often before. Usually by ardent lady journalists.

CARLOTTA: One two – One two – and through and through – the vorpal blade went snicker-snack.

HUGO: My dear Carlotta. I had no idea you had such a thorough grounding in the classics. You were virtually illiterate when we first met.

CARLOTTA (*laughing*): It was you who set my stumbling feet upon the path of literature, Hugo. It was you who opened my eyes to many wonders.

HUGO: Don't talk such nonsense.

CARLOTTA: You worked assiduously on my virgin mind. And now I come to think of it you didn't do so badly with my virgin body.

HUGO (*turning away*): Please don't talk like that, Carlotta. I find it distasteful.

CARLOTTA (*gently*): Try not to be so easily cross with me. It's almost too reminiscent. You always told me I was vulgar. According to your lights that is. But your lights are so bright and highly placed that they bring out the bags under my eyes and the guttersnipe in my character. They always did and they always will. There's really nothing I can do about it, except perhaps go away. Would you like me to go away, now, this very minute? I promise I will if you truly want me to. You don't even have to answer. A valedictory little nod will be enough.

HUGO: Of course I don't want you to go away. With all my faults and in spite of my 'jaundiced' view of my fellow creatures, I am seldom discourteous.

CARLOTTA: I would like it to be something warmer than your courtesy that wishes me to stay.

HUGO: I fear I can offer you little more at the moment, Carlotta, except perhaps curiosity, which is even less complimentary. I have reached a stage in life when sudden surprises stimulate me less agreeably than they might have done in my earlier years. I am what is called 'set in my ways' which at my age is not entirely to be wondered at.

CARLOTTA: It implies resignation.

HUGO: Resignation has much to recommend it. Dignity for one thing, a quality, alas, that is fast disappearing from our world.

CARLOTTA: I think I know what you're up to.

HUGO (*still secure on Olympus*): I am open to any suggestions.

CARLOTTA: You are remodelling your public image. The witty, cynical author of so many Best Sellers is making way for the Grand Old Man of Letters.

HUGO: Supposing your surmise to be accurate, do you consider such a transition reprehensible?

CARLOTTA: Of course not, if the process is inevitable and necessary. But aren't you jumping the gun a little?

HUGO (*patiently*): No, Carlotta. I am not jumping the gun, or grasping Time by the forelock, or rushing my fences.

CARLOTTA: You must be prepared for a few clichés if you invite retired actresses to dinner.

HUGO (*ignoring her interruption*): I am merely accepting, without undue dismay, the fact of my own mortality. I am an old man and *I* at least have the sense to realise it.

CARLOTTA: Don't be waspish, my dear. Just as we are getting along so nicely. At least you can congratulate yourself, on having had a fabulously successful career. How wonderful to have been able to entertain and amuse so many millions of people for such a long time. No wonder you got a Knighthood.

HUGO: I'm beginning to suspect that you are here as an enemy. I hoped for a friend.

CARLOTTA: Did you, Hugo? – Did you really?

HUGO: Perhaps I was wrong?

CARLOTTA: No. You were not wrong. I think I am more friend than foe, but I suppose there must still be a little bitterness left. After all we were lovers once, for two whole years actually. Our parting was not very happy, was it?

HUGO: Fairly inevitable at any rate.

CARLOTTA: I really was very much in love with you.

HUGO: And I with you.

CARLOTTA: How convincingly you said that.

HUGO (*turning away irritably*): Oh really, Carlotta! Shall we stop sorting out our dead emotions now? I dislike looking at faded photographs.

CARLOTTA: Why did you write so unkindly about me in your memoirs?

HUGO: Aha! Now I'm beginning to understand.

CARLOTTA (*cheerfully*): Oh no you're not. You're merely jumping to conclusions. That was always one of your most glaring defects.

HUGO: Why can't we concentrate for a moment on some of my glaring assets? It might lighten the atmosphere.

CARLOTTA: We will, when you've answered my question.

HUGO: My autobiography was the assessment of the events and experiences of my life up to the date of writing it. I endeavoured to be as objective and truthful as possible. If in the process I happened to hurt your feelings, I apologise. There was no unkindness intended. I merely wrote what I thought to be true.

CARLOTTA: Your book may have been an assessment of the *outward* experiences of your life, but I cannot feel that you were entirely honest about your inner ones.

HUGO: Why should I be? My inner feelings are my own affair.

CARLOTTA: In that case the book was sailing under false colours.

HUGO (*nastily*): And all this because I described you as a mediocre actress.

CARLOTTA (*laughing*): Did you really say that? I'd forgotten. How catty of you.

HUGO: I've already said I was sorry.

CARLOTTA: No, my dear. You apologised. It isn't quite the same thing.

HUGO (*a little guilty*): I'm sorry then. There – will that do?

CARLOTTA: Yes. That will do for the moment. Are you working on anything now?

HUGO: Yes, a novel. Unfortunately I have been a little ill lately which halted progress for a time, but now I am back again to more or less my normal routine.

CARLOTTA: Your self-discipline was always remarkable.

HUGO: It was less constant when we knew each other. (*He smiles*) There were too many distractions.

CARLOTTA: Did you think I was a mediocre actress then?

HUGO: How could I? I was in love with you.

CARLOTTA: It was later, when you laid aside your rose-coloured glasses, that you saw through me?

HUGO: It isn't exactly that I saw through you. It was

that I realised that, in spite of your vitality and charm and outward 'allure', there was some essential quality missing.

CARLOTTA: You mean you guessed that I would never really become a star?

HUGO: I sensed it rather than guessed it.

CARLOTTA: Anyway your diagnosis was accurate. I never did become a star, a real star, but my career hasn't been altogether a failure, you know. I've played interesting plays and travelled the wide world. My life has fascinated and amused me all along the line. I'm seldom bored and I have few regrets.

HUGO: But the one abiding one is that you would rather have been great than merely competent.

CARLOTTA (serenely): You don't happen to have any parchment lying about, do you?

HUGO: Parchment?

CARLOTTA: Yes. When zoological experts extract the venom from snakes they force them to bite on parchment.

HUGO (with a thin smile): I accept your rebuke.

CARLOTTA: How generous of you.

HUGO: It's curious that you should still be able to arouse hostility in me.

CARLOTTA: Not really. As a matter of fact it was always there, just below the surface.

HUGO: When two young people are passionately in love, a certain amount of bickering is inevitable. It even has charm, up to a point. But when the old indulge in it, it is merely tiresome.

CARLOTTA: Speak for yourself. You are the one who has decided to be old. I haven't yet, maybe I never shall. Some people remain young until they're ninety.

HUGO: You see no point in dignified withdrawal, in

'growing old gracefully'?

CARLOTTA: There is little grace in growing old, Hugo. It's a dreary process that we all have to deal with in our different ways. To outside observers my way may seem stupid and garish and, later on perhaps, even grotesque. But the opinion of outside observers has never troubled me unduly. I am really only accountable to myself. I like slapping on the make-up and having my body massaged and my hair tinted. You've no idea how much I enjoy my long, complicated mornings. I admit I'm liable to cave in a bit by the late afternoon, but a short snooze fixes that and then I have all the fun of getting ready again for the evening.

HUGO: And does the evening really justify so much effort?

CARLOTTA: As a general rule, yes. I have many friends, some of them quite young. They seem to enjoy my company. I like to watch them dancing.

HUGO: I detest the young of today. They are grubby, undisciplined and illmannered. They also make too much noise.

CARLOTTA: Youth always makes too much noise. Many of the ones I know are better informed and more intelligent than we were. Also their world is more shrill than ours was. You really must make allowances.

HUGO: I'm too old to make allowances.

CARLOTTA: Oh Hugo! You're positively stampeding towards the quiet grave, aren't you?

HUGO: Shall we change the subject? Shall we try to discover some general theme on which we can both agree?

CARLOTTA: Your indestructible elegance is flustering me and making me talk too much.

HUGO (*without malice*): You always talked too much, Carlotta.

CARLOTTA: Ah yes. It's a compulsive disease. Useful at dinner parties but fatal in the home.

HUGO: As this is neither, you can afford to relax.

CARLOTTA: There's so much I want to know about you, about what's happened to you during these long years, and here I am talking you into the ground. Will you forgive me?

HUGO: Why is there so much that you want to know about me? Why are you so suddenly curious about what has happened to me during these long years? Some motive must have impelled you to come here, some spark must have been struck. What was it?

CARLOTTA: All in good time.

HUGO: I think you will agree that that is an extremely exasperating reply.

CARLOTTA: Yes it is, isn't it? Again I must ask you to forgive me.

HUGO: If our first evening together after so many years is to be devoted entirely to mutual apologies, it may become tedious.

CARLOTTA: I think I can guarantee that whatever the evening may become it will not be tedious.

HUGO: Do I detect an undercurrent of menace? Is it in your mind to revive our dead and forgotten sex duel?

CARLOTTA: Is that how you remember it? How sad.

HUGO: Carlotta! What is it that you want of me?

CARLOTTA: At the moment, dinner.

HUGO (*with irritation*): Carlotta!

CARLOTTA: I only had a salad for lunch and I'm famished.

HUGO (*resigned*): Very well. Have it your own way.

I am prepared to play any game you wish to play, up to
a point. But do remember, won't you, that I tire easily.
(*He rings the bell.*) The dinner is ordered anyhow. I
even remembered that you liked caviar.

CARLOTTA: That was sweet of you. The first time I
ever tasted it was with you. You took me to Ciro's for
supper after the show.

HUGO: Was I still wooing you then, or had I won?

CARLOTTA: You'd already won, more or less, but I
think the caviar clinched it. I can remember what we
had after the caviar too.

HUGO: What was it?

CARLOTTA: A filet mignon with sauce Bearnaise and a
green salad and the – (*She thinks for a moment*) Then a
chocolate soufflé.

HUGO: Did we by any chance have pink champagne
as well?

CARLOTTA: Yes. I believe we did.

HUGO: You will see in a moment with what nostalgic
charm history can repeat itself.

CARLOTTA: I don't believe you're really old at all.

There is a knock at the door.

HUGO: Avanti.

FELIX *wheels in the dinner table.*

FELIX: Good evening, madame.

CARLOTTA: Good evening.

FELIX (*as he comes in*): The table in the usual place, sir?

HUGO: Yes please, Felix.

FELIX (*seating* CARLOTTA *at the table*): Madame.

CARLOTTA: Thank you.

FELIX *goes to open vodka.*

HUGO: You can leave the Vodka, we will serve
ourselves.

FELIX: Bien Monsieur. (*He gives a quick glance at the table to see that everything is all right, then, with a bow, goes out of the room.*)

CARLOTTA: How handsome he is, isn't he? Greek or Italian?

HUGO (*pouring out Vodka for them both*): Half Italian and half Austrian I believe.

CARLOTTA: He has just a slight look of my first husband, Peter. Poor Peter. His feet trod the world lightly and alas, all too briefly.

HUGO: He was the one who was killed in an aeroplane?

CARLOTTA: Yes. He was studying to be a pilot in San Diego. I was trying out a new play in San Francisco. They had the sense not to tell me until after the matinée.

HUGO (*a little embarrassed by tragedy*): How dreadful for you.

CARLOTTA: Yes. It was my first real sorrow. We'd only been married for eighteen months, too soon for the gold to rub away. Then a little while afterwards I had a miscarriage. That was my second real sorrow. It was quite a year. San Francisco is a divine city and I love it, but I always seem to have bad luck when I play there. In 1957 I lost my last remaining tooth in the Curran Theatre.

HUGO (*with a shudder of distaste*): Carlotta!

CARLOTTA: It was a gallant old stump that held my lower plate together. I remember saying to my understudy one day, 'Sally, when this is out, you're on!' And sure enough, a week later, it was and she was.

HUGO: I don't wish to sound fussy, Carlotta, but I really don't care to discuss false teeth during dinner.

CARLOTTA (*cheerfully*): Why ever not? That's when

they're a force most to be reckoned with.

HUGO: Nevertheless, I should welcome a change of subject.

CARLOTTA: Dear Hugo. I am so sorry. I remember now, you always hated spades being called spades. What shall we talk about? Perhaps you would like some further vignettes from my rather ramshackle career?

HUGO: Provided that they are general rather than clinical.

CARLOTTA: Well let me see now. I married my second husband, Vernon Ritchie, in the Spring of 1936. He was my leading man in a ghastly play about the Deep South which ran for ages.

HUGO (*without much interest*): Was he a good actor?

CARLOTTA: No, terrible. But he made up for his performances on the stage by his performances in – (*she hesitates*) – in the boudoir. I didn't say bed in order to spare your feelings.

HUGO: Thank you. I appreciate your delicacy.

CARLOTTA: He was a sweet man and I was very fond of him. He was the father of my son David and then, soon after Pearl Harbour when the war came to us in America, he joined the navy and was killed in the Pacific in 1944.

HUGO: Was that another 'great sorrow'?

CARLOTTA: No. Just a sadness.

HUGO: What decided you to make your life in America rather than in Europe where you were born?

CARLOTTA: Because I happened to be there I suppose. I went there originally on account of you. It was your play, if you remember, that first deposited me on the Great White Way, where it ran exactly ten days.

HUGO (*loftily*): That was no surprise to me. I never

thought they'd understand it.

CARLOTTA: Do you know, Hugo? I have a terrible feeling that they did.

HUGO: Let me help you to some more caviar.

CARLOTTA: Thank you.

HUGO (*serving her and himself*): And your third husband?

CARLOTTA: Dear old Spike.

HUGO: Dear old what?

CARLOTTA: Spike. Spike Frost. Lots of people are called Spike in America. As I told you he's a movie agent, and a very successful one too. He handles a lot of the big stars.

HUGO: That sounds vaguely pornographic.

CARLOTTA (*delighted*): Hurray! A little joke at last. Almost an off colour little joke too. Things are looking up.

HUGO: And you've never appeared in the London theatre since, since my first play?

CARLOTTA: Oh yes, twice.

HUGO: I don't remember hearing about it.

CARLOTTA: Why should you? As a matter of fact on each occasion you were away, in the Far East I believe, on one of your excavating expeditions.

HUGO: Excavating expeditions?

CARLOTTA: Yes, digging for treasure trove in the trusting minds of the innocent.

HUGO: You have a malicious tongue, Carlotta.

CARLOTTA: Yes. I really should learn to keep it between my false teeth. Let's stop talking about me now. Tell me about Hilde.

HUGO: I really see no reason to discuss Hilde with you.

CARLOTTA: Your loyal reticence does you credit, but it is a little overdone, almost defensive. After all I'm not a newspaper reporter.

HUGO: You might easily be, judging by the tastelessness of some of your questions.

CARLOTTA: It's no use trying to intimidate me, Hugo, because it won't work. If you remember it never did work. You have asked me questions about my husbands and I didn't snap your head off. Why shouldn't I ask you about your wife?

HUGO: The analogy is a trifle strained.

CARLOTTA: I truly want to know, not from idle curiosity, but because I liked her. She has wisdom and repose and her eyes are kind, a little sad perhaps, but kind. I suspect tragedy in her life.

HUGO (*giving in*): There *was* a tragedy in her life. She managed to escape from Nazi Germany in 1940, soon after the 'phoney' war began. She left the love of her life behind, a young poet called Gerhardt Hendl. He died two years later in a concentration camp. Now are you satisfied?

CARLOTTA: Satisfied is not quite the word I would have chosen. But I am pleased that you told me.

FELIX *comes in wheeling a table on which are the covered dishes for the next course.*

FELIX: Am I too early, sir?

HUGO: No, we have finished. You'd better open the wine.

FELIX: Bien monsieur.

CARLOTTA: Champagne! Oh Hugo, I have a feeling that it is going to be pink.

HUGO: It is.

CARLOTTA: How disarming of you to be so sentimental. It must be that evanescent nostalgia. Do you remember the cottage at Taplow and driving down together on summer nights after the Show?

HUGO: Yes. Yes, I remember.

CARLOTTA: And how cross you were that night at the Grafton Galleries, when I appeared in a red sequin frock that Baby Briant had lent me. You said I looked like a Shaftesbury Avenue tart.

HUGO: You did.

FELIX, *having cleared away the first course and opened the bottle of champagne, pours a little into* HUGO'S *glass.* HUGO *sips it and nods his approval.* FELIX *then fills both their glasses and proceeds to serve the filets Mignon, salad, etc.*

CARLOTTA: And the weekend we went to Paris, and I got back to the Theatre on the Monday night exactly seven minutes before curtain time. My understudy was all dressed and ready to go on . . . I often wonder why you didn't write any more plays. Your dialogue was so pointed and witty.

HUGO: You flatter me, Carlotta.

CARLOTTA: I've read everything you've ever written.

HUGO: You flatter me more than ever.

CARLOTTA: I only said that I'd read everything you've ever written. I ventured no opinion, flattering or otherwise.

HUGO: The statement alone is flattering enough.

CARLOTTA: Yes. Yes, I expect it is. I suppose Ciro's isn't there anymore? (*She signs.*) Oh, dear!

HUGO: That was a pensive sigh.

CARLOTTA: I've been in America too long. It's so lovely to see a steak that doesn't look like a bedroom slipper. . . .

FELIX (*having finished serving*): Tout va bien monsieur?

HUGO: Oui, excellent. Merci, Felix.

FELIX: A votre service monsieur. (*He bows and leaves the room.*)

CARLOTTA: He really is most attractive, isn't he? Those glorious shoulders.

HUGO: I've never noticed them.

CARLOTTA: They're probably padded anyhow. Life can be dreadfully treacherous.

HUGO (*he laughs quite genuinely*): You really are extraordinary, Carlotta. You don't look a day over fifty.

CARLOTTA: I should hope not. After three cellular injections and two face-lifts.

HUGO (*pained*): Carlotta!

CARLOTTA: It's wonderful how they do it now. You can hardly see the scars at all.

HUGO: What on earth possessed you to tell me that?

CARLOTTA: Oh dear. Now I've shocked you again.

HUGO: Aesthetically yes, you have.

CARLOTTA: I am sorry. Just as we were making such progress.

HUGO: As the object of such operations is, presumably, to create an illusion, why destroy the illusion by telling everybody about it?

CARLOTTA: Quite right, Hugo. As a matter of fact you could do with a little snip yourself. Just under the chin.

HUGO: I wouldn't dream of it.

CARLOTTA: It would do wonders for your morale.

HUGO: My morale is perfectly satisfactory as it is, thank you.

CARLOTTA (*gaily*): Long may it remain so.

HUGO (*after a slight pause*): Why did you come here,

Carlotta?

CARLOTTA: I told you. I'm having a course of injections at Professor Boromelli's clinique.

HUGO (*frowning*): Professor Boromelli!

CARLOTTA: Yes. Do you know him?

HUGO: I know of him.

CARLOTTA: You look disapproving.

HUGO: His reputation is rather dubious.

CARLOTTA: In what way?

HUGO: The general concensus of opinion is that he's a quack.

CARLOTTA: Quack or no quack he's an old duck.

HUGO: Don't be foolish, Carlotta.

CARLOTTA: There's no need to stamp on my little joke as though it were a cockroach.

HUGO: Well? (*he smiles a faintly strained smile*) I'm still waiting to hear the reason that induced you suddenly to make this, shall we say, rather tardy reappearance in my life? It must be a fairly strong one.

CARLOTTA: Not so very strong really. It's only actually an irrelevant little favour. Irrelevant to you I mean, but important to me.

HUGO: What is it?

CARLOTTA: Prepare yourself for a tiny shock.

HUGO (*with a note of impatience*): I'm quite prepared. Go on.

CARLOTTA: I too have written an autobiography.

HUGO (*raising his eyebrows*): Have you? How interesting.

CARLOTTA: There's a distinct chill in your voice.

HUGO: I'm sorry. I was unaware of it.

CARLOTTA: It is to be published in the Autumn.

HUGO: Congratulations. Who by?

CARLOTTA: Doubleday in New York and Heinemann in London.

HUGO (*concealing surprise*): Excellent.

CARLOTTA (*with a trace of irony*): I am so glad you approve.

HUGO: And have you written it all yourself? Or have you employed what I believe is described as a 'ghost writer'?

CARLOTTA: No, Hugo. I have written every word of it myself.

HUGO: Well done.

CARLOTTA: On an electric typewriter. You really should try one. It's a Godsend.

HUGO: I have no need of it. Hilde does my typing for me.

CARLOTTA: Of course yes – I'd forgotten. Then you can give her one for a birthday present.

HUGO (*after a slight pause*): I suppose you want me to write an introductory preface.

CARLOTTA: No. I've already done that myself.

HUGO (*with a tinge of irritation*): What is it then? What is it that you want of me?

CARLOTTA: Permission to publish your letters.

HUGO (*startled*): Letters! What letters?

CARLOTTA: The letters you wrote to me when we were lovers. I've kept them all.

HUGO: Whatever letters I wrote to you at that time were private. They concerned no one but you and me.

CARLOTTA: I agree. But that was a long time ago. Before we'd either of us become celebrated enough to write our memoirs.

HUGO: I cannot feel that you, Carlotta, have even yet achieved that particular distinction.

CARLOTTA (*unruffled*): Doubleday and Heinemann do.

HUGO: I believe that some years ago Mrs. Patrick Campbell made a similar request to Mr George Bernard Shaw and his reply was, 'Certainly not. I have no intention of playing the horse to your Lady Godiva'.

CARLOTTA: How unkind.

HUGO: It would ill become me to attempt to improve on Mr George Bernard Shaw.

CARLOTTA (*helping herself to some more salad*): You mean you refuse?

HUGO: Certainly. I most emphatically refuse.

CARLOTTA: I thought you would.

HUGO: In that case surely it was waste of time to take the trouble to ask me?

CARLOTTA: I just took a chance. After all, life can be full of surprises sometimes, can't it?

HUGO: If your forthcoming autobiography is to be peppered with that sort of bromide it cannot fail to achieve the best seller list.

CARLOTTA: You can turn nasty quickly, can't you? You were quite cosy and relaxed a moment ago.

HUGO: I am completely horrified by your suggestion. It's in the worst possible taste.

CARLOTTA: Never mind. Let's have some more champagne. (*She takes the bottle out of the bucket and pours herself some. She holds it up to him enquiringly.*)

HUGO: Not for me, thank you.

CARLOTTA: There's quite a lot left.

HUGO: Finish it by all means.

CARLOTTA: Professor Boromelli will be furious.

HUGO: I gather he doesn't insist on any particular regime. What sort of injections does he give you?

CARLOTTA (*enjoying her steak*): Oh it's a formula of his

own. Hormones and things.

HUGO: The same kind of treatment as Niehans?

CARLOTTA: Oh no, quite different. Niehans injects living cells from an unborn ewe, and as long as he doesn't pick a non U Ewe it works like a charm.

HUGO: Have you been to him as well?

CARLOTTA: Oh yes, ages ago. He's an old duck too.

HUGO: You seem to regard Switzerland as a sort of barnyard.

CARLOTTA (*raising her glass to him*): Quack quack!

HUGO (*crossly*): Don't be so childish.

CARLOTTA (*laughing*): You used to enjoy my jokes when you and I were young love and all the world was new.

HUGO: Flippancy in a girl of twenty-one can be quite attractive, in a woman of more mature years it is liable to be embarrassing.

CARLOTTA: Like bad temper in a pompous old gentleman.

FELIX *re-enters, wheeling a table on which is a chocolate soufflé.*

Perfect timing, Felix. I congratulate you.

FELIX: Thank you, madame. (*He deftly removes the empty plates, places them on the movable table, places clean ones before them and proceeds to serve the soufflé.*)

CARLOTTA (*after a longish pause*): The lake's like glass tonight. There'll be a moon presently.

HUGO: How clever of you to know.

CARLOTTA: There was a moon last night. I just put two and two together. (*To* FELIX) Sir Hugo tells me you are half Austrian and half Italian, Felix.

FELIX: That is correct, madame.

CARLOTTA: Which half do you like best?

HUGO: Please, Carlotta——

FELIX: I find the two perfectly satisfactory, madame. (*He smiles.*)

CARLOTTA: I expect both the waltz and the tarantella come quite naturally to you.

HUGO (*testily*): That will be all for the moment, Felix. Please bring the coffee immediately.

FELIX: Subito signore! (*He bows, smiles at* CARLOTTA, *and leaves.*)

HUGO: I hate familiarity with servants.

CARLOTTA: Oh eat up your soufflé for God's sake and stop being so disagreeable.

HUGO (*outraged*): How dare you speak to me like that!

CARLOTTA: Dare? Really Hugo. What have I to fear from you?

HUGO: I consider your rudeness insufferable.

CARLOTTA: And I consider your pomposity insufferable.

HUGO (*icily*): I should like to remind you that you are my guest.

CARLOTTA: Of course I am. Don't be so silly.

HUGO: And as such I have the right to demand from you at least a semblance of good manners.

CARLOTTA: 'Semblance of good manners'! Talk about clichés. That's a clanger if ever I heard one.

HUGO (*quivering with rage*): Once and for all, Carlotta——

CARLOTTA: For heaven's sake calm down. Your wife told me earlier on that it was bad for you to over-excite yourself. You'll have a fit in a minute if you don't stop gibbering.

HUGO (*beside himself, shouting*): I am not gibbering!

There is a silence for a moment. CARLOTTA *continues to eat her soufflé.*

HUGO *rises majestically.*

HUGO (*with superb control*): I think, Carlotta, that as we really haven't very much more to say to each other, it would be considerate of you to leave as soon as you've finished eating. As I told you, I have been rather ill recently and it is my habit to retire early. I also feel that I have reached an age when I no longer have to tolerate being spoken to as you spoke just now.

CARLOTTA: If you are determined to decline so rapidly you'll soon reach an age when nobody will be able to speak to you at all.

HUGO: I am sorry if I appear to be discourteous but after all, it was you who forced us both into this – this rather unprofitable meeting. I have done my best to receive you kindly and make the evening a pleasant one. That I have failed is only too obvious. I am sorry also that I was unable to accede to your request. I am sure, after you have given yourself time to think it over, that you will realise how impertinent it was.

CARLOTTA: Why impertinent?

HUGO: Not having read your book I have naturally no way of judging whether it is good, bad or indifferent. I am perfectly aware, however, that whatever its merits, the inclusion of private letters from a man in my position, would enhance its value considerably. The impertinence I think lies in your assuming for a moment that I should grant you permission to publish them. We met and parted many years ago. Since then we have neither of us communicated with each other. You have pursued your career, I have pursued mine. Mine, if I may say so without undue arrogance, has been eminently successful.

Yours, perhaps less so. Doesn't it strike *you* as impertinent that, after so long a silence, you should suddenly ask me to provide you with my name as a stepping-stone?

CARLOTTA (*looking at him thoughtfully*): Am I to be allowed a cup of coffee before I leave?

HUGO: Of course. He will bring it in a moment.

CARLOTTA: Poor Hugo.

HUGO: I am in no need of your commiseration.

CARLOTTA: Think carefully and you may not be quite so sure.

HUGO: I haven't the faintest idea what you are implying nor, I must frankly admit, am I particularly interested.

CARLOTTA: I am implying that a man who is capable of refusing a request as gracelessly and contemptuously as you have done can be neither happy nor secure.

HUGO: Happy and secure? My dear Carlotta, I salute the facility with which you have picked up the glib, sentimental jargon of American women's magazines.

CARLOTTA: Look out, Hugo. You are riding for a fall. Your high horse may suddenly buck and throw you.

FELIX *enters with the coffee*.

FELIX: Coffee- monsieur?

HUGO: For Madame only. You can put it over here and take away the dinner table.

FELIX: Very good, sir.

CARLOTTA: You are afraid of not sleeping?

HUGO (*coldly*): I never drink coffee in the evening.

CARLOTTA: What about a nice cup of cocoa? Inelegant but soothing.

FELIX: That will be all, monsieur?

HUGO: Yes thank you.

FELIX: Good night sir – Madame.

CARLOTTA: Good night Felix. The dinner was delicious and the service impeccable.

FELIX (*shooting a quizzical glance at* HUGO's *stony face*) Madame is most kind. A votre service Monsieur. (*He bows and wheels the table out of the room.*)

HUGO (*pouring out a cup of coffee*): Do you take sugar?

CARLOTTA: Yes please, a little. How long have I got before the curfew sounds?

HUGO (*ignoring this*): Here's your coffee.

CARLOTTA: The letters really are very good Hugo. It's disappointing that you won't allow me to use them. They *are* love letters of course up to a point and brilliantly written. The more ardent passages are exquisitely phrased although they do give the impression that they were commissioned by your head rather than dictated by your heart.

HUGO: I have no wish to discuss the matter any further.

CARLOTTA: It seems a pity that posterity should be deprived of such an illuminating example of your earlier work.

HUGO: I really am very tired Carlotta. I feel that my age entitles me to ask you to leave me alone now. Perhaps we may meet and talk again within the next few days.

CARLOTTA: My wrap is in your bedroom. Hilde put it there. May I fetch it?

HUGO: By all means.

CARLOTTA *goes into the bedroom.* HUGO *lights a cigarette and then immediately stubs it out again. He is obviously seething with irritation. He opens the table drawer, takes two white tablets out of a bottle and crunches them.*

CARLOTTA *returns*.

CARLOTTA: Good night, Hugo. I am sorry the evening has ended so . . . so uncosily.

HUGO: So am I, Carlotta. So am I.

CARLOTTA (*turning, on her way to the door*): To revert for a moment to the unfortunate subject of the letters. You may have them if you like. They are of no further use to me.

HUGO: That is most generous of you.

CARLOTTA: I'm afraid I can't let you have the others though. That would be betraying a sacred promise.

HUGO: Others? What others?

CARLOTTA: Your letters to Perry.

HUGO (*visibly shaken*): My letters to Perry! What do you mean?

CARLOTTA: Perry Sheldon. I happened to be with him when he died.

HUGO: What do you know about Perry Sheldon?

CARLOTTA: Among other things that he was the only true love of your life. Goodnight, Hugo. Sleep well.

CURTAIN *as* CARLOTTA *turns upstage exiting through the door*.

ACT II

Time: A few minutes later. When the curtain rises HUGO *is
sitting in his arm-chair staring into space. Finally, with
an effort, he rises, goes over to the drink table, and pours
out a glass of brandy. He drinks it in one gulp. He walks
over to the window and back again several times. At last,
having made his decision, he goes to the telephone.*

HUGO (*at the telephone*): 'Allo – Gaston? Je veux
parler avec Madame Gray, Madame Carlotta Gray.
– Oui, elle est arrivée cet apres-midi. – Merci, j'attendrai.
(*He waits.*) Hallo – Carlotta? Yes it's I, Hugo. ——Don't
pretend to be surprised. Quite a lot is the matter and
you know it. ——Will you please come back. I must
talk to you. Please Carlotta. ——No, you know perfectly
well that it can't wait until to-morrow. You've won
your point, for God's sake have the grace not to exult
too much. Please come. ——Yes now – immediately.
Very well. Thank you Carlotta.

*He hangs up the telephone and sits for a moment with his
head buried in his hands. Then he gets up, goes slowly over to
the table, takes a cigarette, lights it and resumes his pacing
of the room. There is little energy in his movements. He is a
worried, unhappy man. Presently there is a perfunctory
knock on the door and* CARLOTTA *comes in. He stops his
pacing and they stand looking at each other in silence for a
moment.*

CARLOTTA (*with the ghost of a smile*): I'm sorry Hugo. That was an unkind trick. But you had it coming to you.

HUGO: I would like, if you don't mind, a little further explanation of what you said when you left me a few minutes ago.

CARLOTTA: Shall we sit down? It looks rather foolish standing here and sizing each other up like a couple of Japanese wrestlers.

HUGO: I have no wrestling match in mind, oriental or otherwise. I have already admitted defeat. (*He motions her to a chair.*)

CARLOTTA (*sitting down*): Oh no you haven't Hugo. Not quite yet. But there's no hurry. Oh by the way, I met that charming Felix in the corridor and ordered another bottle of champagne. I do hope you don't mind. I thought we might need it.

HUGO: I see you have decided to set the mood in a light vein.

CARLOTTA: You are the challenged. You have the choice of weapons. We can send the champagne away again if you like.

There is a knock on the door and FELIX enters carrying a bottle of champagne in a bucket of ice and two glasses.

FELIX: The champagne Monsieur.

HUGO: Thank you Felix. You may put it on the table.

FELIX: Would you wish me to open it?

CARLOTTA: Please do Felix. I am sure that neither Sir Hugo nor I could manage it as efficiently as you.

FELIX: Certainment Madame. (*He proceeds to open the bottle.*)

CARLOTTA: I was right about the moon. Look Hugo.

It's making a path right across the lake. How sad for you Felix to have to rush about serving people in this stuffy hotel when you might be dancing your heart away in one of those little open-air cafes on the shore.

FELIX: There is time for everything Madame.

CARLOTTA: But not for everybody Felix. Not for everybody.

FELIX, *having opened the bottle and filled two glasses, brings one to* CARLOTTA.

FELIX: Madame.

CARLOTTA (*taking it*): Thank you Felix.

FELIX (*taking the other glass to* HUGO): Monsieur.

HUGO: Put it down please. I will drink it later.

FELIX (*obeying*): That will be all Monsieur?

HUGO (*irritably*): Yes yes – that will be all, good night.

FELIX (*to* CARLOTTA): I have put a bottle of Evian in your room Madame as you requested.

CARLOTTA: Thank you Felix, Good night.

FELIX: Good night Madame. (*He bows and goes.*)

CARLOTTA: Well I must say it's pleasant to have *one* request granted, even if it's only a bottle of Evian.

HUGO: I am finding the flippancy of your manner extremely irritating.

CARLOTTA: Now that I come to think of it, you always did. In any case this is not a tragic situation Hugo. All the tragedy was drained out of it when poor Perry died. There's only comedy left now. Rather bitter comedy I admit, but not entirely unenjoyable.

HUGO: You must forgive my lack of humour.

CARLOTTA: You never had much anyhow. Wit, yes, a brilliant talent for the sharp riposte, the swift, malicious phrase. But true humour lies in the capacity to laugh at oneself. That you could never do.

HUGO: I fear it is a little too late for me to change.

CARLOTTA: Ah yes. Much too late. It's all too late now. That's the pity of it. I should have sought you out before. Who knows? I might have been able to do a little good.

HUGO: If you had, would blackmail have so strongly coloured your missionary zeal?

CARLOTTA: Blackmail? Really Hugo! I had no idea you had such a highly developed sense of melodrama.

HUGO: You said you were with Perry Sheldon when he died. Is that true?

CARLOTTA: Yes. (*She takes a sip of champagne.*)

HUGO: And you have in your possession letters written by me to him?

CARLOTTA: Yes. Love letters most of them. They are less meticulously lyrical than the ones you wrote to me, but there is more genuine feeling in them. They were written in your earlier years remember, before your mind had become corrupted by fame and your heart by caution. The last ones were written in the last years of his life. There are three of them. All refusals to help him when he was in desperate straits. They also are fascinating in their way, masterpieces of veiled invective. Pure gold for your future biographer.

HUGO (*controlling a quiver in his voice*): Did you steal these letters?

CARLOTTA: No Hugo. I didn't steal them. He gave them to me three days before he died.

HUGO: What do you propose to do with them?

CARLOTTA: I haven't quite decided yet. I made him a promise.

HUGO: What sort of promise?

CARLOTTA: I promised him that if he gave them to me I would keep them safe until the time came when they could be used to the best advantage.

HUGO: Used? To the best advantage! Used in what way?

CARLOTTA: By a suitable biographer.

HUGO: And are you intending to be that biographer?

CARLOTTA: Oh no. I am not experienced enough. It would require someone more detached and objective than I am to write an accurate and unbiased account of you. My personal feelings would be involved.

HUGO: Your personal feelings would still be involved after more than half a lifetime?

CARLOTTA: Memory is curiously implacable. It can forget joy but it seldom forgets humiliation.

HUGO: Your emotional tenacity is remarkable.

CARLOTTA: There is no longer any emotion in my feelings for you Hugo.

HUGO: Wouldn't you consider revenge an emotion?

CARLOTTA (*with a little laugh*): Revenge! You're jumping to the wrong conclusions again.

HUGO: I wouldn't expect you to admit it.

CARLOTTA: You're wrong. I'd admit it like a shot if it were true, but it isn't. As a matter of fact my motives in all this are altruistic rather than vindictive. Suddenly, in my raddled old age I have seen the light. I find myself obsessed with a desire to right wrongs, to see justice done, to snatch a brand from the burning.

HUGO: I am not impressed.

CARLOTTA: Never mind. The night is young.

HUGO: To revert to the subject of my, as yet unnamed, biographer. Have you found one?

CARLOTTA: Of course.

HUGO (*still with admirable calm*): May I ask his name?

CARLOTTA: Certainly. His name is Justin Chandler. He used to be a professor at Harvard. I met him first when I was playing 'Hedda Gabler' in Boston.

HUGO (*fury breaking through*): I don't give a damn what you were playing in Boston.

CARLOTTA: I know you don't, but it was 'Hedda Gabler'.

HUGO: Am I to believe that this eminent Harvard professor is contemplating writing a biography of me without even asking my permission?

CARLOTTA: He'll probably get round to that later when he has completed his notes. He's been planning it for years. He's always been a fan of yours.

HUGO: Has he indeed.

CARLOTTA: He once wrote a monograph on you for the *Atlantic Monthly*. It was called 'Technique and What Next?' He is a fervent admirer of your literary craftsmanship. He said that your autobiography was the most superlative example of sustained camouflage that he had ever read. He certainly is a smart cookie.

HUGO: My knowledge of American slang is limited.

CARLOTTA: The exact English translation would be clever biscuit.

HUGO: And is it your intention to hand over to this – this 'clever biscuit' private letters of mine which were written to somebody else over thirty years ago?

CARLOTTA: You must realise that they are exceedingly valuable documents. Your fame has made them so. Not only financially valuable, although I have no doubt that they'd fetch quite a fancy price at a public auction, but their importance to anyone who wishes to make an analytical survey of your life and career, is too obvious to be ignored. Owing to your own ceaseless vigilance your 'bubble reputation' must be almost as solid as a football by now. You mustn't be surprised that certain people should wish to kick it about a bit.

HUGO: How much do you want?

CARLOTTA: Don't be *silly* Hugo. Give me a little more champagne. I suggest that you'd better have some too while you're at it. It might help to clear your mind.

HUGO (*taking her glass*): I have no alternative but to follow your lead Carlotta. If your object in all this is to humiliate and embarrass me, you have so clearly succeeded that no further comment is necessary. What is the next move? (*He fills her glass and hands it to her.*)

CARLOTTA: Thank you.

HUGO (*with an effort*): The knowledge that my letters to Perry Sheldon are still in existence has naturally come as a considerable shock to me. It would be foolish to deny it.

CARLOTTA (*sipping her champagne*): Also unconvincing.

HUGO: I presume you have taken the trouble to acquaint yourself with the legal aspects of the situation?

CARLOTTA: The legal aspects of the situation are fairly simple. Any letter from the moment it is posted, automatically becomes the property of the recipient. In this case Perry was the recipient. He made the letters over to me in a written statement which was witnessed by a public notary. They now legally belong to me and I am at liberty to do what I like with them.

HUGO: I fear you have been misinformed. The letters may indeed by your property, but according to law they may not be published without my permission or, when I die, the permission of my estate.

CARLOTTA: I am sure you are right, but so far there

has been no question of them being published. The important fact is that they exist, and for so long as they continue to exist they will remain a potential menace to your carefully sculptured reputation.

HUGO: Where are the letters?

CARLOTTA: I have them with me.

HUGO: You have not yet told me what you propose to do with them.

CARLOTTA: Because I have not yet decided. There is still what you describe as my 'missionary zeal' to be taken into account.

HUGO: I don't know what you are talking about.

CARLOTTA: All in good time Hugo. All in good time.

HUGO (*losing his temper*): This is intolerable!

CARLOTTA: Keep calm.

HUGO: I have been calm long enough. I am sick to death of this interminable witless skirmishing. Come to the point, if there is a point beyond your feline compulsion to torment me and insult me. The implications behind all the high faluting rubbish you have been talking have not been lost on me. The veiled threat is perfectly clear.

CARLOTTA: What veiled threat?

HUGO: The threat to expose to the world the fact that I have had, in the past, homosexual tendencies.

CARLOTTA (*calmly*): Homosexual tendencies in the past! What nonsense! You've been a homosexual all your life, and you know it!

HUGO (*shouting*): That is not true!

CARLOTTA: Don't shout. It's waste of adrenalin. You've no idea what it does to the inside of your stomach when you work yourself into a state like that. If you won't drink champagne for God's sake have a little brandy and pull yourself together. Here – I'll get you some. (*She goes purposefully to the drink table.*)

HUGO (*near hysteria*): I don't care what you do – do you hear me? You can publish whatever letters you like and be damned to you.

CARLOTTA (*handing him a glass of brandy*): Here Hugo. Drink this and stop being hysterical.

HUGO (*knocking the glass out of her hand*): Go away – go away from me – leave me alone! (*He sinks into his chair and puts his hand over his face.*)

CARLOTTA: There. Now look what you've done! Brandy stains all over that nice rug. For shame, Hugo! You're behaving like a petulant little boy at a children's party.

HUGO: Go away and leave me alone.

CARLOTTA: Be careful. I might take you at your word. You know perfectly well that if I went away now and left you alone that you'd be on the telephone within ten minutes imploring me to come back.

HUGO: I am an old man, Carlotta, and, as I already told you, I have recently been ill, very ill. I have neither the strength nor the will to continue this, this embittered conflict that you have forced upon me. I am too tired.

CARLOTTA: If I poured you out another glass of brandy, would you again dash it to the ground or would you drink it calmly and sensibly?

HUGO: I am not supposed to drink brandy. It is bad for my heart.

CARLOTTA (*going to the drink table*): I feel on this particular occasion a little licence might be permitted. (*She pours out another glass of brandy and brings it to him.*) Here, I think that your heart, what there is of it, will survive.

HUGO (*taking it and looking at her*): Why do you hate

411

me so? Is it because you once loved me?

CARLOTTA: You've got it all wrong, Hugo. I don't hate you, and loving you I only dimly remember.

HUGO (*taking a swig of brandy*): You underrate my intelligence.

CARLOTTA: Oh no. I may have overrated your stamina but I would never underrate your intelligence. Your intelligence is of a very high order indeed, up to a certain point. It is what happens over and above that point that arouses my curiosity.

HUGO: I don't know what you're talking about.

CARLOTTA: You flew into a fine theatrical passion just now when I said you had been homosexual all your life. Did you consider that an insult?

HUGO: Wasn't it intended to be?

CARLOTTA: Of course not. We are living in the nineteen-sixties not the eighteen-nineties.

HUGO (*nastily*): This sophisticated tolerance hardly fits in with the sneer in your voice when you accused me of it.

CARLOTTA: You are over sensitive. If there had been a sneer in my voice, which there wasn't, it would not have been a sneer at the fact, but at your lifelong repudiation of it. In any case I did not accuse you of it, for the simple reason that I do not consider it a crime. What I am accusing you of is something far worse than that. Complacent cruelty and moral cowardice.

HUGO: On what evidence?

CARLOTTA: On the evidence of every book you've ever written and the dismal record of your personal relationships.

HUGO: You know nothing of my personal relationships. We are strangers.

CARLOTTA: On the contrary I know a great deal about them. I've been making diligent enquiries for quite a long time. It's been rather fun, piecing together odd bits of information, talking to people you've known here and there in course of your travels. Your name is unfailing as a conversational gambit. Your ivory tower is not nearly so sacrosanct as you imagine it to be. You cannot be half so naive as to imagine that a man of your sustained eminence could ever be entirely immune from the breath of scandal, however gingerly you may have trodden your secret paths.

HUGO: I am not interested in the scruffy surmises of the mediocre.

CARLOTTA: By no means all the people I discussed you with were mediocre, and by no means all the things I heard were surmises.

HUGO: Nor am I interested in your opinion nor anyone else's opinion of my character. What I am interested in is the motive that impelled you to come here.

CARLOTTA: I find it awfully difficult to explain even to myself. I suppose basically that it was irritation more than anything else.

HUGO (*outraged*): Irritation!

CARLOTTA: And don't minimise the force of that apparently trivial little emotion. It can be more powerful than anger and more devasting than hatred. It can wear away rocks and stones and human tissues. It can also play merry hell with the kindliest of dispositions. I am not by nature a vindictive character but you have irritated me for years and I am determined to put an end to it before my whole system is poisoned.

HUGO (*with commendable calm*): It might clarify the

situation for me if I knew why I had irritated you for years.

CARLOTTA: Perhaps because I loved you once, and had such high hopes for you.

HUGO: Poppycock! It was because I left you behind half a lifetime ago and your greedy female vanity has never forgiven me for it.

CARLOTTA: I was right about the brandy. You're becoming belligerent again.

HUGO: It isn't irritation that is poisoning your system but envy.

CARLOTTA (*with a sigh*): Oh dear!

HUGO (*with violence*): Envy and bitterness and regret for a life that you just might have shared if you had been bright enough to prove yourself worthy of it.

CARLOTTA: Calm down Hugo. You'll be off the rails again in a minute.

HUGO: Would you be kind enough to get me a little water, I'm feeling suddenly rather ill. (*He sinks into his chair.*)

CARLOTTA: Get it yourself, you're as strong as an ox.

CARLOTTA *strolls over to the window.* HUGO, *after shooting her a baleful look, staggers up from his chair and pours himself out some water with a shaking hand. He returns to his chair and sits down again.* CARLOTTA *comes back from the window and stands silently looking down at him.*

CARLOTTA: That was rude of me, I apologise. After all you are older than I am.

HUGO (*breathing rather heavily*): You haven't won you know. I don't think you ever will.

CARLOTTA: I'm not even sure I want to. I'm not even sure that there's anything to win.

HUGO (*with decision*): How much do you want for those letters?

CARLOTTA: I really am sorry for you, Hugo.

HUGO: That is entirely irrelevent.

CARLOTTA: It must be truly horrible to have gone through life holding your fellow creatures in such bitter contempt.

HUGO: Your present behaviour is hardly calculated to improve my outlook.

CARLOTTA: Bravo!

HUGO: Please stop prevaricating and name your price.

CARLOTTA: The letters are not for sale.

HUGO: I am beginning to think you must be a little unbalanced.

CARLOTTA: I see your point. That would explain away a lot of things, wouldn't it? Unfortunately, it isn't true.

HUGO: We seem to have reached an impasse.

CARLOTTA: Yes, we do rather, don't we? (*She helps herself to some more champagne.*)

HUGO *opens his mouth to speak, thinks better of it, rises from his chair and walks slowly about the room for a moment or two.* CARLOTTA *sips her champagne and watches him. Her face is quite expressionless.*

HUGO (*meeting her eye*): What did Perry die of?

CARLOTTA: Leukemia. He suffered no pain.

HUGO: Oh. I'm glad.

CARLOTTA: He had had a very bad attack of Hepatitis the year before.

HUGO: Brought on by drink?

CARLOTTA: Yes. Yes I think so. But he didn't drink at all during the last months of his life.

HUGO: How old was he? When he died I mean?

CARLOTTA: Late fifties, early sixties, I'm not quite sure. But he looked much older than that.

HUGO: Yes – yes – I expect he did.

CARLOTTA: He was painfully thin and he had become rather deaf. I bought him a hearing-aid.

HUGO: That was generous of you.

CARLOTTA: It was comparatively inexpensive.

HUGO: When did he die?

CARLOTTA: About two years ago.

HUGO: I see.

CARLOTTA: The only vitality he had left was in his eyes, they still retained a glimmer of hope.

HUGO: How do you expect me to react to all this, Carlotta?

CARLOTTA: Exactly as you are reacting. For the moment you are manufacturing a little retrospective regret. It may even be quite genuine, but it isn't enough and it won't last. One swallow doesn't make a summer. You didn't even know that he had died.

HUGO: How could I have known? Two years ago I was a long way away, in West Africa, as a matter of fact. I returned to Rome in the spring. Somebody told me. We were living in Rome at the time.

CARLOTTA: Yes. It was from Rome that you wrote your last three cruel letters to him.

HUGO (quietly): I want those letters back, Carlotta.

CARLOTTA: Just those three? Or the earlier ones as well?

HUGO: All of them of course. You must see how important this is to me.

CARLOTTA: Certainly I do.

HUGO: Was it true, what you told me a while ago about this ex-Harvard professor wishing to write about me?

CARLOTTA: Justin Chandler. Yes – perfectly true.

HUGO (*with an effort*): I have no alternative but to throw myself on your mercy, Carlotta.

CARLOTTA: No. You haven't really, have you? I thought we should arrive at this point sooner or later.

HUGO (*after a pause*): Well?

CARLOTTA: If you had the choice of having the earlier letters back or the later ones, which would you choose?

HUGO (*a little too quickly*): The earlier ones.

CARLOTTA: Yes. I was afraid you'd say that.

HUGO: You can also, I should imagine, understand my reasons.

CARLOTTA: Yes. I understand your reasons perfectly. You would prefer to be regarded as cynical, mean and unforgiving, rather than as a vulnerable human being capable of tenderness.

HUGO: In these particular circumstances, yes.

CARLOTTA: Why?

HUGO: Your mind appears to be so clogged with outraged sentimentality that you have failed to take into account one important factor in the situation.

CARLOTTA: What is that?

HUGO: According to the law in England. Homosexuality is still a penal offence.

CARLOTTA: In the light of modern psychiatry and in the opinon of all sensible and unprejudiced people that law has become archaic and nonsensical.

HUGO: Nevertheless it exists.

CARLOTTA: It won't exist much longer.

HUGO: Maybe so, but even when the actual law ceases to exist there will still be a stigma attached to 'the love that dare not speak its name' in the minds of

millions of people for generations to come. It takes
more than a few outspoken books and plays and
speeches in Parliament to uproot moral prejudice from
the Anglo-Saxon mind.

CARLOTTA: Do you seriously believe that now, today,
in the middle of the Twentieth century, the sales of
your books would diminish if the reading public
discovered that you were sexually abnormal?

HUGO: My private inclinations are not the concern
of my reading public. I have no urge to martyr my
reputation for the sake of self-indulgent exhibitionism.

CARLOTTA: Even that might be better than vitiating
your considerable talent by dishonesty.

HUGO: Dishonesty? In what way have I been
dishonest?

CARLOTTA: Subtly in all your novels and stories but
quite obviously in your autobiography.

HUGO: I have already explained to you that my
autobiography was an objective survey of the events
and experiences of my life in so far as they affected my
career. It was never intended to be an uninhibited
exposé of my sexual adventures.

CARLOTTA: In that case it would surely have been
wiser not to have introduced the sex element into it at
all. It is a brilliant and entertaining book. Your obser-
vations on life and literature in general and the people
and places you've seen are witty and very often profound.

HUGO (*with irony*): Thank you Carlotta. Thank you
very much.

CARLOTTA: But why the constant implications of
heterosexual ardour? Why those self-conscious, almost
lascivious references to laughing-eyed damsels with

scarlet lips and pointed breasts? And, above all, why that contemptuous betrayal of Perry Sheldon?

HUGO (*with anger*): I forbid you to say any more. There was no betrayal.

CARLOTTA (*relentlessly*): He loved you, looked after you and waited on you hand and foot. For years he travelled the wide world with you. And yet in your book you dismiss him in a few lines as an 'adequate secretary'.

HUGO (*losing his temper again*): My relationship with Perry Sheldon is none of your God damned business.

CARLOTTA: Considering that I have in my possession a bundle of your highly compromising letters to him, that remark was plain silly.

HUGO (*with forced calm*): Once and for all Carlotta will you either sell me or give me those letters?

CARLOTTA: No. Not yet – perhaps never.

HUGO: Are you planning to continue this venomous cat-and-mouse procedure indefinitely?

CARLOTTA: No. Not indefinitely. Just until something happens.

HUGO: What in God's name do you mean by that! What *could* happen?

CARLOTTA: Unconditional surrender.

HUGO: Do you wish me to plead with you? To fall abjectly at your feet and weep for mercy? Would that assuage your insatiable female vanity?

CARLOTTA: No. That would get you nowhere at all.

HUGO: What then? What do you want of me?

CARLOTTA: Oh, I don't know. A moment of truth, perhaps. A sudden dazzling flash of self-revelation. Even an act of contrition.

HUGO (*pouring himself some more brandy*): That, if I may say so, is pretentious twaddle.

CARLOTTA: The time has come for me to roll up some heavier ammunition.

HUGO (*evenly*): By all means. I find that I have got my second wind. Fire away.

CARLOTTA: Has it ever occurred to you that you were indirectly responsible for Perry's death?

HUGO: If I had murdered him with my bare hands it would still have nothing to do with you.

CARLOTTA (*ignoring this*): You discarded him ruthlessly, without a shred of gratitude or compassion. Having corrupted his character, destroyed his ambition and deprived him of hope. You wrote him off like a bad debt.

HUGO: He was a bad debt. He became an alcoholic. And alcoholics bore me.

CARLOTTA: And whose fault was it that he became an alcoholic?

HUGO: His own.

CARLOTTA: Do you really think you can shrug off the responsibility as casually as that?

HUGO: You are implying, I suppose, that my tyranny drove him to it.

CARLOTTA: Not your tyranny. Your indifference.

HUGO: Rubbish. Perry took to the bottle because he liked it and because he was a weak and feckless character.

CARLOTTA: And yet you loved him. You loved him for quite a long while. Your letters prove it.

HUGO: I should have thought that even your cheap magazine mentality would have learnt by now that it is seldom with people's characters that one falls in love.

CARLOTTA: Granted. But when the first blind rapture begins to fade, most people have the instinctive grace to accept the situation without rancour; to make adjustments, to settle for a gentler climate.

HUGO: I seem to hear the sound of violins.

CARLOTTA: If they didn't, very few human relationships based initially on physical attraction would
survive.

HUGO: I must frankly confess, Carlotta, that I am
beginning to find your recurrent lapses into tabloid
philosophy inexpressibly tedious. You spoke just now
rather grandiloquently, I thought, of 'rolling up heavier
ammunition'. Is this it? Am I expected to stagger to
my knees, bloody and defeated, under a hail of simper-
ing platitudes? If, for some reason best known to
yourself, you feel it your bounden duty to chastise me,
to destroy my reputation, to batter me to the dust and
to lay bare the quivering secrets of my evil soul, I have
no means of preventing you. So get on with it. Attack
as much as you like. But for Christ's sake don't bore me.

CARLOTTA: Like Justin Chandler you certainly are
quite a smart cookie.

HUGO: I am also an old cookie and it is long past my
bedtime.

CARLOTTA: Are you throwing me out again?

HUGO: Yes I am. The 'impasse' remains. I have
refused to give you permission to publish my letters to
you in your damned book and you have refused to sell
me or give me my letters to Perry Sheldon. There
doesn't seem to be anything more to discuss.

CARLOTTA: You're bluffing.

HUGO: So are you.

CARLOTTA: I have no need to bluff. I hold the cards.

HUGO: For one thing I don't believe that this Justin
Chandler exists.

CARLOTTA: He exists all right. But even if he didn't,

the letters do.

HUGO: I haven't seen the proof of that.

CARLOTTA: Wait and see.

HUGO: You must forgive me if I seem obtuse, but if you have no intention of selling me the letters or giving them to me, what do you hope to gain and why are you here? Your only explanation so far has been that I have irritated you for years because you once loved me and had such high hopes for me, but you surely cannot expect me to accept that as your basic motive for suddenly intruding on my privacy after so long a lapse of time? There must be something more, something deeper, that impelled you, out of the blue, to launch this gratuitous attack upon my peace of mind. Is it perhaps a long-cherished, stale revenge for some imagined wrong I did you in the past?

CARLOTTA: No. It isn't that. Although the wrong you did me in the past was not imagined.

HUGO: Through your relationship with me, you acquired a leading part which up to then nobody else had offered you, reasonably good press notices and, for the time being at any rate, an assured position in the theatre. You were praised and photographed and paid attention to for the first time in your life and you finally went off to the United States in a blaze of gratifying publicity. You cannot blame me for the fact that from then on you did not quite achieve the dazzling prospects that had been predicted for you.

CARLOTTA (*scrutinising her face in her hand-mirror*): I did well enough. I have no complaints. What I am interested in is what you got out of the deal.

HUGO (*witheringly*): In the first place I didn't regard our affair as a 'deal'.

CARLOTTA: Very well, I'll put it more delicately. Let's say a profitable experiment.

HUGO: In what way profitable?

CARLOTTA: That old bubble reputation again.

HUGO: What are you implying by that?

CARLOTTA: I'm not implying anything. Just re-capitulating a few facts.

HUGO (*with irritation*): Unfortunately, I seem to have no way of stopping you.

CARLOTTA: I was twenty-two and, curiously enough, considering that I had been involved with the theatre since I was fourteen, I was a virgin.

HUGO: Are you now casting me in the role of the vile seducer?

CARLOTTA: Oh, not at all. We were both virgins. That is from the heterosexual point of view. (*She pauses.*)

HUGO: Very well. I've registered that. Go on.

CARLOTTA: I didn't realise it at the time of course. You were my first love. I loved you deeply and passionately. I had your photograph on the table by my bed. I used to kiss it every night before I turned out the light. Sometimes I even went to sleep with it under my pillow.

HUGO: I hope you had the sense to take it out of its frame.

CARLOTTA: We had been together for well over a year before I began to realise my exact status in the cautious pattern of your life.

HUGO (*turning away*): Really, Carlotta, do you consider it entirely relevant to continue this musty, ancient, soul-searching?

CARLOTTA: Yes, I do. I most emphatically do. It was

your dishonesty and lack of moral courage in those far-off days that set you on the wrong road for the rest of your life.

HUGO: It is hardly for you to decide whether the course of my life has been wrong or right.

CARLOTTA: You might have been a great writer instead of merely a successful one, and you might also have been a far happier man.

HUGO: And what bearing has all this on that dreadful wound I inflicted on your feminine vanity in the nineteen-twenties?

CARLOTTA: Because you have consistently, through all your glittering years, behaved with the same callous cruelty to everyone who has been foolish enough to put their trust in your heart.

HUGO (*near violence again*): In what way was I so callous and cruel to you?

CARLOTTA: You used me. You used me and betrayed me as you've always used and betrayed every human being who has ever shown you the slightest sign of true affection.

HUGO: In what way did I use you any more than you used me?

CARLOTTA: You waved me like a flag to prove a fallacy.

HUGO: What fallacy?

CARLOTTA: That you were normal, that your morals were orderly, that you were, in fact, a 'regular guy'.

HUGO: Was that so unpardonable? I was young, ambitious and already almost a public figure. Was it so base of me to try to show to the world that I was capable to playing the game according to the rules?

CARLOTTA: It wasn't your deception of the world

that I found so unpardonable, it was your betrayal of
me, and all the love and respect and admiration I felt
for you. If you had had the courage to trust me, to let
me share your uneasy secret, not in the first year perhaps,
but later on when things were becoming strained and
difficult between us, if then you had told me the truth,
I would very possibly have been your loyal and devoted
friend until this very minute. As it was, you let me
gradually, bit by bit, discover what my instincts had
already half-guessed. You elbowed me out of your life
vulgarly and without grace, Hugo, and I can even now
remember the relief in your voice when you said good-
bye and packed me off to America.

HUGO: I didn't pack you off to America. You went
with an excellent contract; and in a first-class state-
room.

CARLOTTA (*with a sigh*): I see clearly that I am wasting
my time.

HUGO: You most certainly are. And mine. The only
interesting fact that has emerged from your impas-
sioned tirades this evening, is that in spite of a full life,
three husbands and an excessive amount of plastic
surgery, you have managed to keep this ancient wound
so freshly bleeding. You must be suffering from a sort of
emotional haemophilia.

CARLOTTA: I salute you. You're an unregenerate old
bitch!

HILDE *comes quietly into the room. She is still wearing her*
hat. There is something subtly strange in her manner. It is not
that she is actually drunk, but she undoubtedly is what is
described colloquially as a little 'high'. She is, of course, aware
of this and is making a gallant effort to conceal it. She
stands by the door for a moment, conscious of the oppressive

silence. She comes forward.

HILDE (*tentatively*): I do hope I haven't come back at an awkward moment. Were you discussing anything of importance?

HUGO: No. Nothing of the least importance.

CARLOTTA: We were just reminiscing.

HILDE: How nice. It's always fun talking over old times isn't it?

CARLOTTA: Enormous fun. Hugo and I have been in stitches haven't we Hugo?

HUGO: I wish you'd take off that hat Hilde, it makes you look like a cab-driver.

HILDE (*with a little giggle*): Certainly dear. (*She does so.*) I don't really care for it very much myself. (*She goes over to a mirror and adjusts her hair.*)

HUGO: I see that you decided not to go to the cinema after all.

HILDE: Yes. Liesel and I just sat on after dinner, gossiping. (*To* CARLOTTA) You have never met Liesel Kessler?

CARLOTTA: No, I'm afraid I haven't.

HILDE: She is a great friend of mine. Hugo always laughs at her, but she is most intelligent.

CARLOTTA: Why does he always laugh at her?

HILDE (*with another little giggle*): I think because he disapproves of her. Hugo is quite old-fashioned in some ways.

HUGO (*irritably*): Please Hilde.

HILDE: But it doesn't really matter. Actually she disapproves of him too.

CARLOTTA: Sacrilege.

HILDE (*laughing*): Forgive me Hugo but that is very very funny.

HUGO (*looking at her searchingly*): Hilde. What's the matter with you?

HILDE: Nothing. Why do you ask?

HUGO (*sternly*): Have you been drinking?

HILDE: Oh yes. We had a bottle of vin rosé at dinner and two stingers afterwards.

HUGO (*angrily*): Hilde!

CARLOTTA (*sweetly, to* HUGO): You seem to have a positive genius for driving those who love you to the bottle.

HILDE: Oh it wasn't Hugo's fault, not really. I just felt like it.

HUGO: You'd better ring for some black coffee.

HILDE: No thank you Hugo. I do not want any black coffee, it would keep me awake. But now that my wicked secret has been discovered, I think I will take another little drink. (*She smiles conspiritorially at* CARLOTTA.) It is as good to be hung for a sheep as for a lamb.

HUGO (*warningly*): Hilde!

HILDE (*going to the drink table*): I would have liked it to have been a stinger because they are so delicious, but we have no creme de menthe and it is too much trouble to send for any at this time of night, so I will make do with just the brandy alone.

HUGO: I absolutely forbid you to drink any more brandy Hilde. I think you had better go to bed.

HILDE (*pouring some out*): 'Entbehren sollst Du! sollst entbehren! – Das ist der ewige Gesang.' (*She looks at them both blandly.*) Das ist von Goethe. He was a great genius.

CARLOTTA (*amused*): What does it mean?

HILDE: 'Deny yourself! You must deny yourself! –

That is the song that never ends.' (*She takes a swig of brandy and sighs contentedly.*) Ach das ist besser, das ist sehr gut.

HUGO (*frigidly*): You are perfectly aware that I do not like you to speak German in my presence. It is a language that I detest.

HILDE: The language of Goethe is not merely German, it is universal. You must not forget Hugo that my translations of your books have earned you a great deal of money in Germany. It is ungrateful of you to turn up your nose. (*To* CARLOTTA) You have no idea of his popularity in my country Miss Gray. *The Winding River* went into three editions in five months.

HUGO: I cannot feel that the subject of my foreign royalties can be of the smallest interest to Miss Gray.

CARLOTTA (*with deceptive guile*): Wrong again Hugo. Everything you have ever done or written is of absorbing interest to me.

HILDE (*pleased*): Now is not that the most charming thing to say?

HUGO: Miss Gray has said so many charming things this evening that I am quite confused.

HILDE: But why are you so suddenly formal Hugo? You were calling her Carlotta when she first arrived.

CARLOTTA: I hope you will call me Carlotta too.

HILDE: But of course. With the utmost pleasure.

HUGO (*turning away*): Oh my God!

HILDE (*cheerfully oblivious of undertones*): Liesel was so amused when I told her about this strange, unexpected reunion you are having with Carlotta tonight, after so many many years.

HUGO: She must have a very warped sense of humour.

CARLOTTA: What was it about the situation that so amused her?

HILDE (*a little giggly again*): Oh I don't know. I expect I was a little indiscreet. But it was such a long long time ago wasn't it? – I mean it couldn't really matter speaking of it now.

HUGO: You had no right to speak of it at all. How dare you discuss my private affairs with Liesel or anybody else!

CARLOTTA: You mean that you told your friend that Hugo and I had once been lovers?

HILDE: Not in so many words——

CARLOTTA: Was that why she laughed?

HILDE (*a little uneasy*): I don't remember. – We were just talking. She has always been most admiring of Hugo as a writer, although I must admit she doesn't care for him very much as a man. But that is largely his own fault because he has now and then been a little offish with her. We were talking in German naturally and she quoted some lines of Heinrich Heine.

> 'Ich weiss nicht, was soll es bedeuten
> Dass ich so traurig bin;
> Ein Marchen aus alten Zeiten,
> Das kommt mir nicht aus dem Sinn.'

CARLOTTA: Please translate.

HILDE (*with a furtive look at* HUGO): 'I know not why I am so sad; I cannot get out of my head a fairy tale of olden times.' That was when she laughed.

CARLOTTA: I wonder why. (*She glances at* HUGO *and laughs herself.*)

HILDE: You are not angry I hope?

CARLOTTA: Of course I'm not.

HUGO: You may not be. But I am.

HILDE: Please don't be Hugo. You know how bad it is for you. You have been looking angry ever since I came into the room. Is there anything wrong – between you and Carlotta I mean? Has something bad happened?

HUGO: Oh no. It has all been delightful. Carlotta came here this evening either to blackmail me or reform me. I have not yet discovered which.

HILDE (*apprehensive*): Blackmail! What do you mean? I do not understand.

HUGO: She is a very remarkable character, a mixture of adventuress and evangelist. Her strongly developed sense of moral rectitude has impelled her to span the grey wastes of the Atlantic ocean in order to confront me with my past misdemeanours and upbraid me for my lack of conscience. The fact that she has an ex-husband living from whom she extorts a regular income on con dition that she no longer shares his hearth and home, she apparently finds in no way inconsistent with her ethical principles. All of which goes to prove what I have always contended, that the capacity of the female mind for convenient rationalisation is unlimited.

CARLOTTA: And what makes you imagine that the male mind is so vastly superior?

HUGO: I don't imagine it. I know it.

HILDE: I do not understand. I do not understand at all what is happening.

HUGO (*savagely*): If you had spent less time guzzling down stingers with that leather-skinned old Sapphist your perceptions might be clearer.

HILDE (*with spirit*): You will *not* speak of Liesel like that. She is my close friend and I am devoted to her.

HUGO: Then you should have more discrimination.

HILDE: Nor will I permit you to speak to me in that

tone in front of a stranger. It is in very bad taste and makes me ashamed of you.

CARLOTTA (*enjoying herself*): Hurray! A 'sudden flood of mutiny!'

HILDE (*in full spate*): When you are ill and in discomfort, I am willing to endure your rudeness to me, but now you are no longer ill, you are perfectly well and I will stand no more of it. This very evening you accused me of being jealous of your friends and of anyone who is close to you, you even said I was jealous of Carlotta. But the truth of the matter is you have no friends, you have driven them all away with your bitter tongue, and the only one who is close to you in the world is me. And I will say one thing more. I will choose whatever friends I like and I will drink as many stingers as I like and so that there shall be no further misunderstanding between us I am at this moment going to have some more brandy. (*She goes purposefully to the drink table.*)

CARLOTTA: This is certainly not your evening Hugo.

HILDE (*having poured herself some more brandy*): Now then. I should like to know what all this is about, this talk of blackmail. What does it mean? What has been taking place?

CARLOTTA: Shall I explain Hugo, or will you?

HUGO: No explanation is necessary. I do not wish Hilde to be involved in anything we have discussed tonight. It is none of her concern.

CARLOTTA: On the contrary I should say that it concerned her most vitally.

HUGO: In addition to which I do not consider her to be in fit state to do anything but go to bed.

HILDE: What nonsense. My mind is perfectly clear. Perhaps a lot clearer than it usually is. It is only my legs that are a little uncertain, therefore I shall sit down. (*She does so.*)

HUGO: In that case I shall retire to bed myself.

CARLOTTA: And leave me in command of the field? I cannot feel that even for the sake of making a majestic exit you would be as foolish as that.

HILDE (*with quiet determination*): I am waiting.

CARLOTTA: Well Hugo?

HUGO: Carlotta is about to publish a book of her memoirs and she asked my permission to include in it some love letters I wrote to her in the nineteen-twenties. I refused my permission.

HILDE: Why? It seems a most reasonable request. (*To* CARLOTTA) Are they nice letters?

CARLOTTA: Charming. They make up in style for what they lack in passionate intensity.

HUGO (*loudly*): I will explain why if you will stop interrupting and allow me to. May I go on?

HILDE (*taking a sip of brandy*): Yes dear, please do.

HUGO: I have no idea of the quality of Carlotta's book and I certainly wouldn't wish to be associated in any way with the type of sensation-mongering, journalistic claptrap which so often passes for literature in the Brave New World.

HILDE: I see no reason why you should think it would be like that at all.

CARLOTTA: Thank you Hilde. (HILDE *nods and smiles at her.*)

HUGO (*glaring at them both*): A little later it transpired that Carlotta has in her possession some other letters, written by me to someone else. These she threatens to hand over to an ex-Harvard professor called Justin Chandler who is apparently planning to write an analytical survey of my life and works.

HILDE (*taking another sip of brandy*): He'll do it very well. He's a very clever man and a brilliant writer.

HUGO (*thunderstruck*): What do you mean?

HILDE: Exactly what I say.

HUGO: You mean that you know him?

HILDE: Not personally, but we have corresponded quite a lot over the last three years. He wrote a monograph on you for the *Atlantic Monthly*. I didn't show it to you because I thought it might make you cross.

HUGO: Do you mean to say that you have been corresponding with this man about me behind my back, without saying a word about it?

HILDE: There is no need to look so agitated. I have said nothing indiscreet. He asked politely for certain information and I saw no harm in giving it to him.

HUGO (*through clenched teeth*): What sort of information?

HILDE: On dates of publication, lists of the places you have visited on your travels, a few small biographical details. He really is one of your greatest admirers. It should be an excellent book when he gets around to writing it. At the moment he is only assembling material and making notes.

HUGO (*furiously*): How dared you! How dared you! You have no earthly right to give out details of my private life to strangers without consulting me first. You have been guilty of the most shameful disloyalty.

HILDE (*rising*): I have never been guilty of disloyalty to you Hugo. Never in my whole life. And you will please never say such a thing to me again. Nor did I give Mr Chandler any details of your private life and you know that I would never do so in a million years. (*She turns to* CARLOTTA) These other letters Carlotta, are they love letters?

CARLOTTA (*extremely embarrassed*): I think – I think I would rather not say.

HILDE: That means they are. Please tell me. It is important for me to know.

CARLOTTA: Very well. Yes – they are.

HILDE: Who are they written to?

CARLOTTA: I really cannot tell you that.

HILDE: Hugo, will you tell me?

HUGO: There would be nothing to be gained by my telling you. They were written many years ago, long before I married you.

HILDE (*with a sigh*): It is of no consequence. I think I can guess anyhow. But I would have liked you to tell me yourself. As a matter of fact I would have liked you to have told me long ago, it would have shown me that even if you didn't love me, you at least were fond enough of me to trust me.

HUGO (*obviously disturbed*): They were no concern of yours. They belonged to a part of my life that was over and done with.

HILDE (*with a sad little smile*): Over and done with! Oh Hugo! Earlier this evening, you called me a camel, a dromedary and an ass, but I would like to point out to you that all those three animals are more sensible than an ostrich.

HUGO (*only a little bluster left*): And pray what do you mean by that?

HILDE: For twenty years I have looked after your business affairs, dealt with your correspondence, typed your manuscripts and shared, at least, the outward aspects of your life. You cannot seriously imagine that in all that time you have been able to withold many secrets from me. The letters were written to Perry Sheldon weren't they?

HUGO (*after a slight pause*): Yes. Yes they were.

HILDE: I thought so. As a matter of interest I found some of his replies, years ago, when we packed up the house in Chapel Street. They were in one of the pockets of that old crocodile leather briefcase you discarded when I gave you the brown one for your birthday present.

HUGO: Where are they now?

HILDE: In your strong box in the bank. I put them into a sealed envelope and wrote on the outside 'Not to be opened until after my death' I signed it Hugo Latymer. (*To* CARLOTTA) I often have to forge Hugo's signature when writing his letters you know. It really isn't very difficult.

HUGO: Why didn't you tear them up?

HILDE: Because they concerned you intimately. You are a great writer and a famous man, nothing that concerns you should be destroyed.

HUGO: Not even compromising letters that could do infinite damage to my reputation?

HILDE: It is your work that is important, not your reputation.

CARLOTTA: Think how surprising it would be for posterity to discover that you had a heart after all!

HUGO: Be quiet Carlotta.

CARLOTTA: Actually I *have* been quiet for quite a long time.

HILDE (*to* CARLOTTA): And these letters you have from Hugo to Perry, you wish us to buy them from you?

CARLOTTA: No. I have already explained to Hugo that they are not for sale.

HILDE: You intend to give them to Mr Justin Chandler?

CARLOTTA: Possibly. I have not yet decided.

HILDE: As you know Hugo's feelings in the matter Miss Gray, that would be a malicious and unforgiveable thing to do.

CARLOTTA: I notice that you no longer call me Carlotta.

HILDE: I called you Carlotta when I thought we were to be friends. But I cannot possibly be friends with anyone who sets out deliberately to hurt my husband.

CARLOTTA: You are certainly magnanimous.

HILDE: It has nothing to do with magnanimity. It is a statement of fact.

CARLOTTA: I was thinking of Hugo's treatment of you.

HILDE: As you have only seen Hugo and me together this evening for the first time in your life, you cannot know anything about his treatment of me one way or the other.

CARLOTTA: You don't find it humiliating to have been used by him for twenty years not only as un unpaid secretary, manager and housekeeper, but as a social camouflage as well?

HUGO (*violently*): Once and for all Carlotta I forbid you to talk like that.

HILDE: There is no point in losing your temper Hugo. We can neither of us prevent Miss Gray from saying whatever she likes.

CARLOTTA: You admitted just now that he had never said a word to you about Perry Sheldon. Has he ever,

in all your years together, done you the honour of taking
you into his confidence about anything that really
mattered to him? Has he ever once trusted you with the
secrets of his private heart?

HILDE: It was not necessary. I knew them already.

CARLOTTA: That is an evasion and you know it.

HILDE: You are a very forceful woman Miss Gray
and Hugo is a complex and brilliant man, but it is
beginning to dawn on me that I have a great deal more
common-sense than either of you. I think I can understand why you came here to-night although I can only
guess at the bitterness that must have passed between
you. Your visit actually has little or nothing to do with
permission to publish letters or threats or blackmail has
it?

CARLOTTA: No. No it hasn't.

HILDE: Am I right in suspecting that you really came
to resolve a problem of your own ego? To redress a
small wrong that was done to it more than half a lifetime ago?

CARLOTTA: In a way you are right.

HILDE: I thought so.

CARLOTTA: But it is not quite so simple as that, nor
as a matter of fact quite so self-centred. I genuinely
wanted to prove something to him. Something that
with all his brilliance and talent and eminence, he has
never yet taken into account.

HILDE: What is it that he has failed to take into
account?

CARLOTTA: You, being the closest to him should
know better than anybody. He has never taken into
account the value of kindness and the importance of
compassion. He has never had the courage or the

humility to face the fact that it was not whom he loved in his life that really mattered, but his own capacity for loving.

HUGO: Hark the Herald Angels Sing!

HILDE: Stop behaving like that Hugo. You should be ashamed.

HUGO: I see that, in addition to being unpaid secretary, manager and housekeeper, you have now elected to become my dear old Nanny.

CARLOTTA: It is clear that my mission has most dismally failed.

HILDE: It could never have succeeded. You are a sentimentalist. Hugo is not. I too am a sentimentalist but then I happen to be a German and sentimentality is ingrained in the German character.

CARLOTTA: There is a wide gulf between sentiment and sentimentality.

HUGO: Turgid mysticism, Santa Claus, Christmas trees and gas chambers.

HILDE: You see. He is quite incapable of recognising people as individuals. His mind classifies all human beings in groups and races and types. Whenever he is angry with me he punishes me for my country's sins. He is a profound cynic which is one of the reasons he has been proclaimed as the greatest satirical writer of our time.

CARLOTTA: Why does he mean so much to you? Why are you so loyal to him?

HILDE: Because he is all I have. (*Ignoring him.*) You have lived so differently from me, Miss Gray, that I quite see why you must find my attitude difficult to understand. I have only loved one man in my life, one of my own countrymen, who was destroyed by my own

countrymen in 1944. When I came to Hugo as secretary
I was desolate and without hope and when, a little
later, he asked me to marry him, it seemed like a sudden
miracle. Please do not misunderstand me. I was not in
love with him and I knew that he could never be in love
with me. I also knew why and was not deceived as to his
reasons for asking me. I recognised his need for a
'facade' and was quite content to supply it. I thought
that it was a most realistic and sensible arrangement
and, what is more, I think so still. I am not pretending
that our married life has been twenty years of undiluted
happiness. He is frequently sarcastic and disagreeable to
me and I have often been unhappy and lonely. But then,
so has he. The conflict within him between his natural
instincts and the laws of society has been for the most of
his life a perpetual problem that he has to grapple with
alone.

CARLOTTA: Wouldn't it at least have eased the
problem if he had trusted you enough to share it with
you?

HILDE: Possibly. But it would have been out of
character. He has made his career and lived his life in
his own way according to the rules he has laid down for
himself. Now, when the passing years have diminished
the conflict, he is growing to rely on me more and to
need me more, and that, with my sentimental, Teutonic
mentality, is the reward that I have been waiting for.

HUGO (*very gently*): Hilde . . .

HILDE: Don't interrupt for a moment, Hugo, I have
not quite finished. (*She turns back to* CARLOTTA.) To
revert to the Perry Sheldon letters. You must, of course,
dispose of them as you see fit. If Mr Justin Chandler
wishes for them and you wish to give them to him, there

is nothing we can do to prevent you. But I must warn you that, according to law, he will not be allowed to publish them without Hugo's written permission. He may possibly quote them and paraphrase them to a certain extent I believe, but I cannot feel that a really good writer would waste time in referring to them at all. If Perry Sheldon had been in any way significant as a human being; if he had been in any way worthy of attention on his own account, apart from the fact of his early relationship with Hugo, there might be some point in disclosing them. But he wasn't. He was a creature of little merit; foolish, conceited, dishonest and self-indulgent.

CARLOTTA: How do you know?

HILDE: Through Liesel. Curiously enough, we were talking about him this evening. She knew him for years when she was a scriptwriter in Hollywood. She lent him money on several occasions but, as she said, it is no use lending money to the morally defeated. They only spend it on further defeat.

CARLOTTA *gets up thoughtfully, and walks about the room for a moment or two.* HILDE *and* HUGO *watch her in silence. Finally, she comes to a halt, opens her handbag, takes from it a bundle of letters and goes over to* HUGO.

CARLOTTA (*holding them out to him*): Here they are, Hugo. Here are the letters. They can be no practical use to me or to Mr Justin Chandler. They might conceivably, however, be of service to you.

HUGO (*taking them. His face expressionless*): Thank you.

CARLOTTA: I cannot say that I entirely regret this evening. It has been most interesting and almost embarrassingly revealing. If many of the things I have said have hurt you, I'm sorry. (*She gives a slight smile.*) I don't apologise, I'm just sorry. I am also sorry for having kept you up so late.

HUGO: I will see that the permission you asked me for earlier in the evening is delivered to you in the morning. Goodnight, Carlotta.

CARLOTTA (*looking at him, still with a quizzical smile*): Goodnight, Hugo. (*She turns to* HILDE.) Goodnight, Lady Latymer.

HILDE: Goodnight, Carlotta. I will see you out.

CARLOTTA: There is no necessity for that. My room is only just along the corridor.

HILDE: Nevertheless, I should like to.

She takes CARLOTTA *by the arm and they go out.* HUGO *stands looking after them for a moment, then he glances at the bundle of letters in his hand and sits down in his armchair. He puts on his glasses, selects a letter at random from the package and begins to read it. Having read it, he takes another. As he begins to read this second one, he frowns slightly and looks up. It is apparent from his expression that he is deeply moved. He starts to read the letter again and then, with a sigh, covers his eyes with his hand.*

HILDE *comes quietly back into the room. She stands looking at him for a moment and then sits down silently on the edge of the sofa.*

HUGO (*after a long pause*): I heard you come in.

HILDE (*almost in a whisper*): Yes. I thought you did.

HUGO *continues reading the letter as —*

THE CURTAIN SLOWLY FALLS

SHADOWS OF THE EVENING

A PLAY IN TWO SCENES

CHARACTERS

Linda Savignac
Anne Hilgay
George Hilgay
Felix, a waiter

The time is the Present.

The action of the play passes in a private suite in a Hotel in Switzerland.

SCENE I

The scene is the sitting-room of a private suite in a hotel in Lausanne, Switzerland. On the right of the audience there is a door opening into a bedroom. In the centre are double doors leading to a small lobby and thence to the corridor. The furniture is conventional and what one would expect to find in an expensive European hotel. On the left of the audience there are French windows opening onto a balcony which overlooks the lake of Geneva. On the opposite side of the lake the high mountains of France stand against the sky.

The Time is the Present.

When the curtain rises, late afternoon sun is flooding through the open windows. It is a day in early summer.

LINDA SAVIGNAC *is sitting in a sofa playing 'Patience' on a small table in front of her. At her right is a trolley-table upon which is a tea tray.*

LINDA *is a handsome well-dressed woman in her forties. There is a knock on the double doors centre.*

FELIX, *the floor-waiter, enters. He is a very good-looking young Italian.*

FELIX: Madame rang the bell?
LINDA: Yes, Felix. You can take away the tea-table

446

now.

FELIX: Very good, Madame.

LINDA (*as he begins to wheel the table away*): And will you bring some ice in a few minutes?

FELIX: With pleasure, Madame. (*He bows and goes out with the table.*)

> LINDA *goes on with her 'Patience' then, after a moment she rests both her elbows on the table and buries her face in her hands. She stays like this for a little and then glances anxiously at her wrist-watch. She gives a deep sigh and begins listlessly to play again. The telephone on the desk behind her rings. She flings down the pack of cards and goes hurriedly to answer it.*

LINDA (*at telephone*): 'Allo – 'Allo – Oui——Voulez vous demander à Madame de monter toute de suite.

> *She hangs up the telephone and stands quite still for an instant with her eyes closed. Then she nervously takes a cigarette out of a box, lights it, and almost immediately stubs it out in an ashtray. She wanders over to the window, stares at the view briefly and then comes back to where she was. There is a knock on the door.*

LINDA (*in rather a strangled voice*): Come in.

> ANNE HILGAY *enters. She is a tall, distinguished Englishwoman. Her age might be anywhere between forty-five and fifty-five. She is dressed in a travelling suit and a light coat. She advances into the room. She and* LINDA *stand looking at each other unsmilingly for a moment.* ANNE *finally breaks the silence.*

ANNE: How are you, Linda?

LINDA: I'm all right, I think. (*She makes a movement towards her but* ANNE *steps back.* LINDA *halts where she is.*) It was good of you to come – so – so promptly.

ANNE: It was a bit of a scramble getting up from the

447

country and one thing and another, but Gillie organised it all with her usual efficiency. I expect you remember Gillie, she was George's secretary for years.

LINDA: Of course. I remember her quite well.

ANNE (*after a pause*): You don't seem to have changed a bit.

LINDA: Neither do you.

ANNE: These are the sort of things people always say when they meet again after a long time. It's almost exactly seven years, isn't it?

LINDA (*mechanically*): Yes. Seven years.

ANNE: Considering that this isn't a particularly comfortable moment, don't you think we'd better sit down?

LINDA: Of course – forgive me. (*She motions* ANNE *to a chair*.) Would you like a drink?

ANNE (*sitting down*): Not quite yet, thank you.

LINDA (*her voice is strained*): I've ordered the ice – I mean I told him to bring it in a few minutes. I didn't think you'd get here quite so soon.

ANNE: Your chauffeur is an excellent driver and, of course, the new auto-route makes a great difference. In my day we used to have to weave along by the lake. It was kind of you to send the car.

LINDA: It was the least I could do.

ANNE: Yes. In the circumstances I suppose it was.

LINDA (*with an effort*): I apologise for being so hysterical and incoherent on the telephone last night. I was in rather a state.

ANNE: You were certainly incoherent, however I managed to gather that something fairly serious had happened. I presume it concerns George.

LINDA: Yes. Yes it does.

ANNE: Has he had an accident?

LINDA: No, he hasn't had an accident.

FELIX *knocks and enters, carrying a bucket of ice. He takes it over to the drink table.*

FELIX: Madame requires anything else?

LINDA: No thank you, Felix, that will be all for the moment.

FELIX: Very good, Madame. (*He bows and goes out.*)

ANNE (*after a pause*): He hasn't run off with anyone else, has he?

LINDA: No, Anne. He hasn't run off with anyone else, and even if he had, you would hardly be the one I should send for to comfort me. I am not entirely devoid of taste or common sense.

ANNE: It is such a long time since I have seen you that I seem to have forgotten both your assets and your defects.

LINDA: I would be the last to complain of your perfectly natural antagonism towards me, but I think you would be wise to submerge it for the moment.

ANNE: I would prefer to decide that for myself when you have explained to me what has happened.

LINDA: Your manner makes it difficult for me to explain anything at all. You must have realised that it wasn't for my sake that I telephoned you last night and asked you to come here, it was for George's.

ANNE: Why?

LINDA: Because he is going to die.

ANNE (*after a long pause*): How do you know?

LINDA: The doctor told me last night. His name is Pasquier. He is a brilliant man. It was he who gave George the check-up last Spring and advised him to have the operation.

ANNE (*sharply*): Operation! – What operation?

LINDA: Didn't George tell you about it when he was in England last summer?

ANNE: No. He did not.

LINDA: It was apparently quite trivial, a small cyst under his left arm. Pasquier said that it would be a good idea to get rid of it, so George went into the clinique for a couple of days and had it cut out. Nobody seemed to attach much importance to it. We stayed on here for about a week so that it could be dressed, then it healed up and we went to Corsica as we had planned.

ANNE: I remember. He sent me the usual routine postcards.

LINDA (*with an edge in her voice*): Would you rather he hadn't?

ANNE: Mind you own business.

LINDA: If I were you, I wouldn't indulge your personal bitterness now, Anne. There's very little time. You will have to make an effort to forgive me my trespasses, outwardly at least, for his sake. He will need you.

ANNE: How flattering of you to be so sure.

LINDA (*angrily*): Once and for all, will you stop talking like that and even feeling like that. This is a desperate emergency.

ANNE: In the circumstances, isn't it a little arrogant of you to dictate to me how I should speak or feel?

LINDA: No, it is not. In these particular circumstances there is no room for wounded pride or remembered heartbreaks or any other form of self-indulgence. The situation between you and George and me has existed for seven years. I said a moment ago that you would have to make an effort to forgive me my trespasses and

I added 'outwardly at least'. That was the operative phrase. I don't give a damn whether or not you truly forgive me or despise me or hate me or love me. You've made your gesture by coming here when I asked you to. For God's sake carry it through.

ANNE: What did this Doctor Pasquier say exactly?

LINDA: He said that there was no hope whatever. That George will die within nine months, possibly sooner.

ANNE: What is the disease? What is he to die of?

LINDA: It's something called 'Melanoma'. He explained it to me carefully but I'm not very good at medical technicalities. It has something to do with 'secondaries' occurring as a result of the cyst being removed.

ANNE: Is Doctor Pasquier infallible? Has he suggested calling in any other consultant?

LINDA: Several doctors have been consulted. George has been in the clinique for the last three days. They performed a minor exploratory operation. The findings were malignant.

ANNE (looking down): I see.

LINDA: That is what Pasquier came to tell me last night. He was fairly blunt and absolutely definite.

ANNE: Has George any idea of this, any suspicion?

LINDA: No - I don't think so.

ANNE: When is he coming out of the clinique?

LINDA: Tomorrow morning.

ANNE: How is he now? I mean - is he in any way ill?

LINDA: No. He feels perfectly all right. I talked to him on the telephone just before lunch. He had had an anaesthetic yesterday for the exploratory examination, but they gave him a sleeping pill last night and he said he'd slept like a log. I asked him if he wanted me to come and see him this afternoon but he said he'd rather be left alone to relax and get on with his James Bond. He was actually being considerate, I think. He knows hospitals and cliniques give me the horrors. – I'm – I'm – glad he was considerate – it would have been a bit difficult after seeing Pasquier last night. I suppose I should have managed all right but I *am* feeling rather strung up and George is awfully quick at sensing people's vibrations and I – I—— (*She bursts into tears. Fumbling in her bag for her handkerchief.*) I'm sorry. I've been so determined *not* to do this.

> ANNE *lights a cigarette. It is apparent that her hand is trembling slightly.* LINDA *continues to sob convulsively for a moment or two and then, with a determined effort, controls herself. She takes a compact out of her bag and dabs her face with a powder-puff.*

LINDA: It won't occur again, I promise you.

ANNE: I'd like to see Doctor Pasquier.

LINDA: Yes. I think you should. We'll telephone him at his home number, I have it written down. He said he'd be in between seven and eight.

ANNE: What's the time now?

LINDA (*glancing at her watch*): Just six-thirty.

ANNE (*returning to her chair*): It is absolutely certain, isn't it? I mean there isn't any hope of them being wrong?

LINDA: He's a wise man, and sensible. I'm sure he wouldn't have been so – so definite if he weren't quite sure.

ANNE: Does he speak English?

LINDA: Yes, perfectly.

ANNE: Did he give any opinion as to whether George

ought to be told or not?

LINDA: No. We talked about that. He said it was one of the most difficult problems that doctors have to cope with. Sometimes apparently, mortal illness carries with it a sort of compensating illusion, a subconscious refusal to face the fact of dying. He said that in such cases it was unwise and cruel to shatter the illusion. With certain people however, he said that not knowing was worse than knowing. Obviously it all depends on character, on individual temperament.

ANNE: I would be inclined to place George in the latter category.

LINDA: You mean you think he should be told.

ANNE: Yes. I suppose that is what I mean.

LINDA: Would you be prepared to tell him?

ANNE: Is that why you sent for me?

LINDA (*steadily*): No, Anne. That is not why I sent for you. I am perfectly capable of telling him the truth alone if it is necessary. But you surely couldn't expect me to make such a decision without consulting you? You would never have forgiven me if I had.

ANNE: I should have thought that by now my forgiveness was immaterial to you one way or the other.

LINDA: You are quite right, it is. It is also irrelevant. What is relevant is that you are still his wife. I am merely his mistress.

ANNE: If I had agreed to divorce him, years ago, when both you and he wished me to, would you still have sent for me? Would you still have needed my help?

LINDA: If I considered that you still loved him enough to be of use, yes.

ANNE: Whether I love George or not has nothing

whatsoever to do with you, Linda.

LINDA: On the contrary, it has everything to do with me. Your love for him, coupled with mine, is all he has to hang on to. For the next few months, all he has left of his life, he is going to need us both, and he's going to need us both on the best behaviour we are capable of. I am well aware that from the obvious, conventional point of view all the rights are on your side. You are his lawful wife and the mother of his children but if, in this intolerable situation, you attempt to trade on those rights, you will not only be cruel but stupid.

ANNE: And what rights are you intending to trade on?

LINDA: None. Beyond the fact that he is still in love with me and I with him.

ANNE: Are you quite sure that this romantic passion you feel for each other will survive the imminence of death?

LINDA (*steadily*): Yes. I hope it will and I think it will. However if I am proved wrong that will be my problem and I will deal with it as best I can. In the meantime you and I have got to come to some sort of an arrangement. When George is dead, when he is no longer here for either of us, we can indulge in orgies of recrimination if you wish to. You can accuse me of taking your husband away from you and breaking up your happy marriage. I can accuse you of vindictive self-righteousness in refusing to divorce him so that he could marry me. We can go through all the hoops and give vent to all the mutual bitterness that has been fermenting in us for years. But not now. Not yet. For so long as George lives, we are going to establish a truce. We are going to be friends, close, intimate, loving friends. Is that clear?

ANNE: Yes. Quite clear. But out of the question. I have no intention of pretending something that I don't feel for George's sake or anyone else's.

LINDA: I think that that sort of stubbornness indicates weakness rather than strength.

ANNE: It is a matter of supreme indifference to me what you think.

LINDA: It isn't what you or I think that counts. It is what George feels.

ANNE: You said just now that he was still in love with you and you with him. That surely should be enough to comfort him.

LINDA: That was cheap and unworthy of you. You had George's wholehearted love for fifteen years, and even now you still have part of it.

ANNE: I really don't care for this sort of conversation, Linda. It's embarrassing.

LINDA: I don't care for it either, but we've got to come to an understanding. You still love George and you always will, otherwise you wouldn't have come here when I asked you to. I love George and I always will. In a way we're both in the same boat and in a moment as tragic and desolate as this, it would be shameful for either of us to allow our personal animosity to rock it. We have no way of knowing how he is going to react to this situation, but we do know that we are the two people he loves most. Surely you must see that if we can make him realise that we are friends again rather than enemies, it will be a little easier for him to face what he has to face. Please, Anne, give in.

ANNE (*after a long pause*): Very well. I'll give in. There really doesn't seem anything else to do.

LINDA: Is it a deal?

ANNE: Yes. It's a deal. (*She closes her eyes miserably for a moment.*) What do we do – kiss?

LINDA: We may need to later on. At the moment I think a strong drink would be more sensible.

ANNE: I agree.

LINDA: What would you like?

ANNE: Brandy, I think, with a lot of ice.

LINDA: Good idea. I'll have the same. (*She proceeds to pour the drinks.*)

ANNE: I suppose I'm beginning to accept the truth of the matter. I don't think I did quite, at first.

LINDA *brings her her drink.*

ANNE: What do you think they told him – the doctors, I mean?

LINDA (*bringing her own drink and sitting down*): I don't know. I expect they just said that the exploratory examination had been satisfactory.

ANNE: He must suspect something. He has a sharp mind. He isn't the type to accept evasions without question.

LINDA: I suppose it all depends on whether he really wants to know or not. Perhaps his sub-conscious has already started the resistance process.

ANNE: I doubt that. Don't you?

LINDA: Yes – yes I do – but we can't tell for certain, can we?

ANNE: I must talk to that damned doctor.

LINDA (*going to the telephone*): I'll call him now.

ANNE: Shall I go to him or will he come here?

LINDA: Whichever you prefer.

ANNE: I think I'd like to see him alone anyhow.

LINDA: Of course. (*At the telephone.*) Mademoiselle – Voulez vous me donner trente-six – quarante-deux –

vingt-trois. – Merci.

ANNE (*rising and walking about the room*): I suppose he's aware of the situation, between you and George, I mean?

LINDA: Oh yes. We haven't discussed it obviously but——(*into telephone*) 'Allo. Puis je parler avec le docteur si'l vous plait? – Il n'a pas encore rentrer de la clinique?——Oui——Dans une demi-heure? – Quand il arrive voulez vous lui demander à telephoner à Madame Savignac au Beau Rivage?——Oui c'est assez urgent – merci beaucoup. (*She hangs up.*) He'll be back within half-an-hour, I've asked for him to call me here. (*Coming away from the telephone.*) You'd better go to him, I think. My car will take you. It isn't very far.

ANNE (*she takes a cigarette from a box and lights it*): How are we to explain to George about me being here? He'll suspect something's up the moment he sees me.

LINDA: I've thought of that. You stopped off here for a few days on your way to Italy and we ran into each other by chance in the foyer downstairs and had a sort of 'rapprochement'.

ANNE: Why should I stop off here on my way to Italy? If I wanted to go to Italy, which I don't, I should go straight there.

LINDA: You came to see Professor Boromelli.

ANNE: Who on earth is Professor Boromelli?

LINDA: He's the new miracle man here. People come from all over the world to see him. He's a highly controversial figure. Most doctors hate him and say he's a charlatan, but he has had a few spectacular successes with his injections, it's a special formula of his own apparently.

ANNE: What sort of injections?

LINDA: I don't know exactly, hormones or something——(*she tails off*).

ANNE: You mean rejuvenation?

LINDA (*weakly*): Yes – something of the kind.

ANNE: What nonsense. George wouldn't swallow that for an instant. He knows perfectly well that I'd never go in for that sort of thing.

LINDA: You might have been run-down and over-tired and in sudden need of some sort of physical reassurance.

ANNE: No, Linda, it won't do, really it won't. We shall have to think of something else.

LINDA: What? – What do you suggest then?

ANNE: When in doubt, stick to the truth, or as near to the truth as possible.

LINDA: You mean tell him I telephoned you and asked you to come?

ANNE: Why not? You were naturally upset and worried about him, and on a sudden impulse you called me.

LINDA: He'd know I wouldn't do that unless it were something really serious.

ANNE: You can't fool George for long. I'm perfectly prepared to believe that in certain cases Doctor Pasquier's theory about the sub-conscious building a deliberate barricade against the truth is accurate, but George would never be one of those cases. He'll see through any foolish little conspiracy we cook up. You must know this as well as I do.

LINDA: Yes of course I do – but we can't be sure, can we – really sure?

ANNE: Of course we can't, therefore we can make no decisions as to whether we should tell him or not.

He must take the lead. He must dictate how we are to behave.

LINDA: I'm so desperately frightened of taking a wrong step, of making a false move.

ANNE: Well don't be. Keep your mind clear. Be vigilant.

LINDA: After you've seen Pasquier, you'll come straight back, won't you?

ANNE: Yes. I'll come straight back.

LINDA: Would you like to dine up here in the suite or shall we go out somewhere?

ANNE: I don't care one way or the other.

LINDA: I think I would rather go out if you don't mind. I'm feeling rather overstrained and there'll be less likelihood of sudden flurries of tears in a public place. There's a little restaurant perched high up in the vines between here and Vevey. The food's good and there's a lovely view across the lake.

ANNE: All right. We'll go there. (*With a wry smile.*) We can talk over old times.

LINDA (*turning away*): Oh, Anne!

ANNE: Don't worry, I wasn't trying to dig up the hatchet again, I gave you my word that it was buried for the time being. (*She holds out her glass.*) I think I'd like a freshener.

LINDA (*taking it*): A good idea. I think I would too.

ANNE (*lighting a cigarette*): As a matter of fact I meant it quite genuinely.

LINDA (*at the drink table*): Meant what quite genuinely?

ANNE: That we could talk over old times.

LINDA: Oh – Oh I see.

ANNE: The future is miserable, the immediate present appalling, so ghastly in all its implications that we can't go on discussing it indefinitely without undermining our self control. The past will be almost a relief, even the painful parts of it.

LINDA (*handing her her drink*): I find it difficult to imagine anything undermining your self-control.

ANNE: I shouldn't bank on that if I were you.

LINDA: I'm sorry. It was a disagreeable thing to say.

ANNE: There's nothing to be sorry about. I quite see your point.

LINDA: I see that this isn't going to be very easy for either of us.

ANNE: I agree. That is why I proffered that rather withered little olive branch. You could hardly expect it to be in full bloom.

LINDA (*with a slight smile*): I didn't expect it at all. It took me by surprise.

ANNE: I was trying to remember that we were friends once, long ago.

LINDA: Not so very long ago.

ANNE: You made this drink extremely strong.

LINDA: Mine is the same. I thought it might uninhibit us a little.

ANNE: Are you certain that that would be an entirely good idea?

LINDA: It's worth trying. It might at least lighten the atmosphere between us a little. We can't spend the whole evening hating each other at full blast.

ANNE: It might on the other hand work the other way and uninhibit us too much.

LINDA (*holding up her glass*): A risk worth the taking.

ANNE (*perfunctorily raising hers*): Have it your own way.

LINDA: Can you remember the very first time we met?

ANNE: Certainly I can. I pulled you out of the Suez Canal in 1943.

LINDA: You always boasted that you did, but it wasn't really as dramatic as that. The brakes failed and I just slid in, lorry and all. I admit that if you hadn't suddenly appeared with that Major what's-his-name, I might have been sitting there now.

ANNE: His name was Edgar Hethrington.

LINDA: It couldn't have been!

ANNE: I was driving him from Suez to Cairo. It was at Ismailia that you skidded. Actually he was rather nice, in a way.

LINDA: I remember he lent me a pair of slacks because mine were sodden and made roguish jokes while I put them on behind the car.

ANNE: I can also remember the orderly's face when we dropped you off at your base and you were trying to hold the trousers up with one hand and return his salute with the other. (*She laughs.*)

LINDA (*also laughing*): What happened to him – Major Edgar Hethrington?

ANNE: The poor beast got Mumps three days later and everything swelled up – they're liable to, you know, if you get it when you're an adult, and he had to be sent home. It's called Hydrosomething-or-other, I believe.

LINDA (*laughing helplessly*): Cele I think – it can't be phobia because that's mad dogs, so it must be cele.

At this moment GEORGE HILGAY *comes into the room. He is a tall man in the early fifties. He stares at* LINDA *and* ANNE *in astonishment. For a moment they don't see him. When they do, their laughter ceases abruptly.* LINDA *jumps up and goes to him.* ANNE *remains seated.*

GEORGE: Anne! What in the name of God are you

doing here?

ANNE (*rising slowly*): Hello, George.

GEORGE: Is there anything wrong with Brian or Margaret?

ANNE: No. Brian's with Andrew in Scotland and Margaret went off to Spain with the whole Chisholm family. They've rented a house near Malaga for a month. I was left alone at home so I thought I'd take a little jaunt.

GEORGE (*looking swiftly from her to* LINDA): Well I'll be damned!

LINDA: Are you all right?

GEORGE: I couldn't stand that damned clinique for another minute, so I nipped out when nobody was looking, got a taxi and came home. What were you both laughing at?

LINDA: Anne pulling me out of the Suez Canal and Major Hethrington having Mumps.

GEORGE: I don't know what the hell you're talking about.

ANNE: We were reminiscing – war experiences – that's when Linda and I first met, you know, during the war. We were both driving people about Egypt.

GEORGE (*with a puzzled frown*): I see. At least I think I see.

LINDA: Sit down and have a drink. You must be tired.

GEORGE: I'm not particularly tired, but I should certainly like a drink.

The telephone rings. LINDA *shoots* ANNE *an agonised look and goes to it.*

ANNE (*calmly*): If it's for me, say I'm out and will call back later. It's probably Mariette de Castries, I ran into

her in the foyer when I came in. She threatened to
telephone about seven thirty. I'll get George his drink.
(*To* GEORGE.) Whisky or Gin or Vodka?

GEORGE (*still puzzled*): Whisky please, with plain
water.

ANNE (*at drink table*): Ice?

GEORGE: No ice – thank you.

LINDA (*at the telephone*): 'Allo – Oui à l'appareil – Oh
good evening – how nice of you to call – yes indeed, I
did leave a message but it doesn't matter now. – Will
you be at home later in the evening? – Oh I see – Just
one moment while I take down the number——(*she
scribbles on a pad*) Soixante-six – seize – cinquante-trois.
Thank you so much. – Yes – yes I'll call later on or
early in the morning. (*She hangs up.*)

GEORGE: That was a mysterious little conversation.

LINDA: It was poor Mr Brevet at the American
Express. I think I'm driving him mad. I keep on can-
celling air tickets and then wanting them again. (*She
lights a cigarette and sits down on the sofa.*)

GEORGE: Well you've got his number in case you
want to cancel anything else.

LINDA: Have you seen Doctor Pasquier?

GEORGE: Yes.

LINDA: What did he say?

GEORGE (*sipping his drink*): Quite a lot of things.

LINDA (*bravely*): Did they find out what was wrong?

GEORGE: Yes. He was very uncompromising.

ANNE (*after a slight pause*): Don't keep us in suspense,
George. It's rather nerve-wracking.

GEORGE: Linda asked you to come, didn't she?

ANNE (*meeting his eye*): Yes. She telephoned to me.

GEORGE: When?

ANNE: Last night. I caugnt the afternoon plane.

GEORGE (*to* LINDA): That was after you had talked to Pasquier?

LINDA (*biting her lip*): Yes.

GEORGE (*getting up and kissing* ANNE): It was dear of you to come, Anne. I'm very grateful –

He leaves her and goes over to the window, patting LINDA *reassuringly on the shoulder as he passes her. He stands with his back to them both, looking out over the lake. They watch him mutely. After a moment or two he comes back to them. He is smiling, as convincingly as he can.*

GEORGE: What had you decided? – Which of you was going to tell me?

ANNE: We hadn't decided anything. We didn't know. We were waiting for you – to – to show us what to do.

LINDA (*firmly*): What did Pasquier tell you?

GEORGE: Exactly what he told you last night. That I am going to die. Within the next nine months possibly, but probably within the next three. I will not confuse and sadden you with the details, but there will be no pain. He promised me that. He's a kindly man and I believe him.

LINDA: He told you all this just now, this afternoon?

GEORGE: I forced him to, because I had already guessed, before they did the examination, while I was waiting to have the anaesthetic I suddenly knew, with all my nerve centres, with all my instincts. It was a curious sensation, remote, detached and without fear, then. I've had a few bad moments since, but I think I'm all right now.

ANNE: You're absolutely certain that Doctor Pasquier is right, that there is no chance of wrong diag-

464

nosis?

GEORGE: Absolutely certain. Several doctors were involved. Of course Pasquier was extremely reluctant to pronounce my sentence. He was faced, poor man, with the most recurrently difficult problem that a doctor has to face, whether or not to tell the truth when a patient insistently demands it. Nine out of ten people believe sincerely that they wish to know their fate, but it is only the tenth who really means it. I finally managed to convince him that I was genuinely one of those tenth men. When he gave in and told me I was shocked beyond measure, and at the same time infinitely relieved. After he'd gone I had a glass of water and smoked a cigarette and lay there staring at the white ceiling, and thought harder than I've ever thought before. You see, I felt it was essential to arrive at a point of view to offer you, Linda — naturally I didn't know that Anne was going to be here too — and I think I've succeeded, temporarily at least. (*He pauses and walks about the room.*) The point of view I want to give you both is that I consider myself to be fortunate rather than misfortunate. These are not merely brave words to comfort you with, but to comfort myself as well. I have had a reasonably happy life, much happier and more secure than the lives of millions of my fellow creatures. I have done my job to the best of my ability . . . and being a publisher has kept me in touch with all the things I love most. I have been neither a spectacular success nor a dismal failure. I have tried to live my life with passable dignity. I have tried to be kind rather than cruel. I have a few regrets, a few remembered follies but I have no complaints. And now, while I have been told that my life must end specifically in such and such a time, I have also been guaranteed that I shall cease upon the midnight with no pain. What more can I ask than that? Of course, I should have liked a little longer but I have at least been allowed time to rally my forces, and so to hell with it. That's all there is left for me to do.

LINDA (*choked*): I'll be back in a minute, don't be cross with me. (*She goes swiftly into the bedroom.*)

GEORGE: Everything forgiven and forgotten?

ANNE (*wearily*): Forgiven at any rate.

GEORGE: I see so clearly why I married you.

ANNE: Can you see equally clearly why you left me?

GEORGE: Yes – that too. Except that I didn't actually *leave* you. I just happened to fall in love with Linda.

ANNE: It's more or less the same thing, isn't it?

GEORGE: No it isn't, and you know it. We went through it all at the time. You accepted the situation.

ANNE: I hadn't much choice, had I?

GEORGE: You could have divorced me.

ANNE: Never.

GEORGE: Why not? I've often wondered why you were so stubborn.

ANNE: The children for one thing, and my pride too.

GEORGE: Wouldn't your pride have been less humiliated if you'd got rid of me once and for all?

ANNE: I didn't want to get rid of you once and for all.

GEORGE: Oddly enough you won your point.

ANNE: That's good news anyhow, a trifle bleak perhaps, but better than nothing.

GEORGE: We should have had this scene before. After all we've seen each other several times over the last years . . . I've been back and forth between my two loves.

ANNE: That's a nauseating little phrase and you

466

ought to be ashamed of such facile vulgarity.

GEORGE (*raising his glass*): I salute you.

ANNE: Keep your damned salutes to yourself.

GEORGE: This is quite like old times, isn't it?

ANNE (*suddenly heartbroken*): Oh no, it isn't. (*She turns blindly away from him.*)

GEORGE (*gently*): I would like you to know that, in spite of all betrayals, you are still a necessary part of my life.

ANNE: Fine words, but curiously arid. They should have been spoken earlier. Seven years is a long time.

GEORGE: Longer than three months.

ANNE: That was cruel of you. I don't need to be reminded that you have so little time left. I am here to help, and I have no intention of confusing the issues by allowing emotion to override my common sense. I'll leave that to Linda. She's bellowing her heart out in the bedroom at this very moment.

GEORGE: I suppose I should be grateful for such stinging astringency.

ANNE: Certainly you should. It will contract your spiritual tissues and help to keep your mind clear. You have to set your house in order. There's no time to sit up in the attic opening up old trunks and sorting out dusty, nostalgic souvenirs.

GEORGE: Were you still in love with me when I upped and left you?

ANNE: What does it matter if I were or not?

GEORGE: I really should like to know.

ANNE: I see that you insist on the attic and the old trunks and the shabby disintegrated gollywogs.

GEORGE: Please, Anne, stop being so defensively articulate and answer my question.

ANNE: Very well. I'll set your mind at rest. The answer is No. I was not in love with you when you 'upped and left me'. Perhaps I was never in love with you in the way that you mean. But I cared for you deeply. There are so many different degrees of loving. How can one tell? One loves as much as one can. As you know I have never been a particularly passionate woman. I see now, in fact I've realised for a long time, that that was where I failed you. But never believe that my heart was frigid. I gave you all I was capable of giving. When you went away from me I was more unhappy than I have ever been in my life. Naturally, after a while, I got over it to a certain extent, but I missed you sadly, I still do. Perhaps I shall miss you less when you are dead.

GEORGE: Fair's fair. But try not to consign me to the limbo too soon. I know I shan't mind then but I do mind now. It makes me feel lonely.

ANNE: None of that, George, none of that. Like the reeds at Runnymede, I may bend but I will not break. So don't waste your time trying to make me.

GEORGE: Have you loved anyone else – since me?

ANNE: Do you mean, have I been to bed with anyone else?

GEORGE: If you choose to put it that way.

ANNE: Yes. Three times.

GEORGE: With different men, or the same one?

ANNE: Different. Three times in seven years isn't an abnormally high percentage.

GEORGE: Maybe not, but it seems oddly out of character.

ANNE: Yes. I suppose it was. But it was a sort of search really. I was trying to find out something.

GEORGE: What were you trying to find out?

ANNE: Where I had gone wrong. Why it was that I let you down.

GEORGE: You never let me down.

ANNE (*with a faint smile*): Of course I let you down, sexually, I mean.

GEORGE: That simply isn't true. I loved your body for many years.

ANNE: Perhaps. But it didn't love you – enough. That's why I went to bed with the others, to discover where the fault lay, with you or with me. But it didn't work really. I proved nothing. I felt nothing, beyond a momentary fleeting physical excitement. I still missed you, and somehow resented you at the same time. I am sure that any psychiatrist could explain it to me in a minute, but I don't want to know, not any more. It's all too far away and the search is over.

GEORGE: I must come back home again soon. To see the house and the garden. How is it all looking?

ANNE: Flourishing. I've planted a row of Tamarisks along the lower lane. They're doing very well.

GEORGE: How's old Tom?

ANNE: Old Tom's been gathered. Just as well really, he was crippled with arthritis and very feeble. Young Tom has taken over, shining with good will and more idiotic than ever.

GEORGE: When was I last there? – Time goes so quickly.

ANNE (*evenly*): Nearly two years ago. You came for Brian's twenty-first birthday and we had a cocktail party on the lawn. Later we dined on the flagged terrace outside the dining-room window, just us and that awful girl friend of Margaret's.

GEORGE: . . . the one with the lisp?

ANNE: . . . Yes . . . It was a lovely warm evening.

GEORGE (*suddenly sitting down*): Oh Christ! (*He covers his face with his hands.*) Fear is an ignoble enemy. It strikes at you suddenly, unexpectedly. (*He looks up.*) I've always rather despised people who were afraid of the dark. Now I begin to see their point. When I was a little boy I was outstandingly brave. I used to force myself to grope my way about the house in the middle of the night touching familiar things, the round silver tray in the hall where people used to leave their visiting cards, the Chinese lacquer cabinet in the drawing room, the china horse on the mantlepiece in my father's study, I had to climb up onto a leather armchair to reach it. I had to prove to myself that these things were still there, although I couldn't see them. I wasn't commended for my bravery because one night my hand slipped and the china horse fell into the fireplace and broke. I was severely whacked for it the next day. But I had at least proved that I wasn't frightened. Now it's different. There'll be no familiar, friendly objects to touch, no china horses to break.

ANNE: Maybe the eternal darkness will be lighter than you think.

GEORGE: No, Anne. That won't wash, you know it won't, not for me. I know you still believe, up to a point, in the things you were brought up to believe in, but I don't – I can't. I've occasionally paid lip service to religious superstition for the sake of appearances and to spare other people's feelings, but my mind refuses to accept hazy, undefined promises of life after death.

ANNE: There is always a chance that you may be wrong.

GEORGE: Of course there is. But I'm quite content to die believing only in life itself which seems to me to be quite enough to be going on with, and I have no complaints either except an immediate resentment that I am only to be allowed to go on with it for such a little while longer.

ANNE: If that's how you feel, hang on to it. No words can help, from me or anybody else.

GEORGE: On the other hand if, in three months' time, I suddenly find myself in some tinsel heaven or some gaudy hell, I shall come back and haunt you. But don't let go of my hand – don't let go of my hand.

THE LIGHTS FADE

An hour has elapsed since the preceding scene. It is dusk outside
and lights can be seen glimmering across the lake. There is
still a slight glow behind the mountains.
FELIX *comes in with a bottle of champagne in an ice-*
bucket and a tray of glasses. He puts the ice-bucket and
the tray down and proceeds to tidy up the drink table.
After a moment or two LINDA *comes out of the bedroom.*
She is wearing a dinner dress and carrying an evening
coat over her arm and a pair of white gloves. These she
puts on the windowseat. She is in perfect control and her
face is calm.

LINDA: Is it the Lanson, Felix, or the Pol-Roget?

FELIX: The Lanson, Madame. Signor Luigi considered it to be the wise choice because it is a most good
year.

LINDA: Thank you, Felix.

FELIX: If Madame would wish some canapés, I have
them prepared.

LINDA: I'll ring if we need them.

FELIX: Va bene, Signora.

LINDA: Has your friend recovered?

FELIX: Si, Signora. It was only a small concussion.
They made three stitches in his head and sent him away,
but he is most low in spirits because the police have

taken from him his driving licence.

LINDA (*with a smile*): Perhaps that is not entirely a bad idea.

FELIX: But it is not quite just, Madame, because it was not all his fault. The young lady in the Alfa Romeo drove across the red lights.

LINDA: Did she get concussion, too?

FELIX: No, Madame, she was not hurt at all, but she was most deeply angry. It was because of her great rage that they took away his licence. She is a Swiss young lady and he is an Italian, so there was no true justice.

LINDA: True justice is a rare thing. It is foolish to expect it.

FELIX (*sadly*): E vero – La Signora a ragione. You would wish anything more, Madame?

LINDA: No, that will be all for the moment, Felix. Wish your friend well from me.

FELIX: Madame is most kind – a votre service.

FELIX *bows and goes out.* LINDA *looks at herself pensively in the mirror and gives her hair a reassuring pat, then she lights a cigarette.* GEORGE *comes in. He is wearing a dinner jacket and there is a red carnation in his buttonhole. He looks at* LINDA *with an appreciative smile and then goes over and kisses her.*

GEORGE: You look wonderful.

LINDA: Thank you, darling. So do you, red carnation and all.

GEORGE: I always wear a red carnation when I'm going to gamble. I have a feeling that it brings me luck. What time does the boat leave?

LINDA: Nine o'clock. I've ordered the car for a quarter to.

GEORGE: It doesn't take more than three minutes to

473

go from here to the Embacadere.

LINDA: There might be a crowd. I always like to play safe.

GEORGE: Did you ring up and reserve a table?

LINDA: Of course. I also ordered a bottle of champagne. We might just as well go the whole hog. Shall we open it now or wait for Anne? She'll be here in a minute.

GEORGE (*sitting down*): Let's wait a while. There's no hurry.

LINDA: Poor Felix has had a trying day. His great friend, the barman at the Hotel de la Paix, bumped into an Alfa Romeo on his motor-bicycle and had three stitches in his head and his licence taken away.

GEORGE: Italians shouldn't be allowed to ride motor-bicycles.

LINDA: Neither should anyone else.

There is a silence.

Do you think this is really going to work?

GEORGE: We must persevere.

LINDA: I'll do my best. I'm quite determined to. But I can't guarantee how long it will last. I'm glad Anne is here. She'll keep me in order.

GEORGE: We must all keep each other in order.

LINDA: She's stronger than I am.

GEORGE: In some ways perhaps, but in others she is more vulnerable.

LINDA: What makes you say that?

GEORGE: Possibly because I've only just realised it. As a matter of fact, I've been realising quite a number of things during the last twenty-four hours. It's extraordinary how swiftly the mind works when faced with sudden urgency.

LINDA: We're on dangerous ground. It may open at our feet and swallow up our little charade.

GEORGE (*gently*): It's more than a little charade, Linda. Don't underrate it. The only alternative is to knuckle under, to abandon ourselves to wasteful tears and emotional chaos. And even that wouldn't last. Grief is no more durable than happiness. We should merely exhaust ourselves and each other. We can't snivel our way through the next few months just because one of us is going to die. We're all going to die eventually. There's too much spiritual defeat in the world today, too much shrill emphasis on fear. Let's stay away from that particular band-waggon. Let's, in fact, try to behave ourselves.

LINDA: Perhaps we'd better open the champagne after all.

GEORGE (*getting up*): I'll do it.

LINDA: I expect Felix has loosened the wire a bit. He's very efficient.

GEORGE (*taking the bottle out of the bucket*): You're quite right. He has.

LINDA: Shall we be going back to London immediately?

GEORGE: No. We'll have our two weeks in Capri, as planned. I shall have to be back on the second of next month anyhow. There's a general directors' meeting. Also, I shall have to do some settling up. I shall take old Fielding into my confidence. I can trust him not to betray it. I don't want to have to face commiserating looks and tight-lipped sympathy.

LINDA: Will part of the settling up include going back to Anne?

GEORGE: Of course. I want to see Brian and Margaret and look through some old trunks in the attic. (*He laughs.*)

LINDA: Why do you laugh?

GEORGE: It was something Anne said. She has a deep-dyed distrust of ancient souvenirs. (*He opens the champagne bottle with a loud pop.*) There. That sounds all right . . . (*He looks up at her while he is pouring the champagne into two glasses.*) Don't look so stricken. I've been back before. Nothing is changed.

LINDA (*vehemently*): Everything is changed, and you know it.

GEORGE (*handing her a glass of champagne*): Heightened perhaps, but not changed. Here you are.

LINDA (*taking it*): I minded you going back before. I shall mind more than ever now.

GEORGE: Don't fuss, darling. I'm still in love with you.

LINDA (*before she can stop herself*): You still love Anne too?

GEORGE (*fetching his own glass from the table*): I've never pretended that I didn't. Have a swig of champagne.

LINDA (*obediently doing so*): I have a ghastly feeling that I am going to be the weak sister in our gallant little trio, the one who can't reach the top notes.

GEORGE: You are so definitely a contralto that it would be foolish to try.

LINDA: I must say something to you, now, urgently, before Anne comes back. You must bear with me. It will be a little sentimental but I promise not to go too far.

GEORGE: Fire away, fire away. I'm steeling myself.

LINDA: I know we made a pact a little while ago, the three of us, after I'd been crying and making a fool of myself. I know we all agreed that the only sensible way to behave was to go on as though there were no shadows closing in on us. I swear I'll keep my part of the bargain for so long as I am capable of it, but I must tell you now, before the performance really gets under way, that the last seven years have been the happiest of my whole life. Before we met and became lovers, I lived in a vapid, over-social vacuum. I went everywhere and I knew everybody and I never once looked clearly at myself. My marriage was a failure, my child miscarried and my divorce was sordid and humiliating. But the fact of you loving me changed everything. It gave me a new point of view and something to believe in. I want you to know that I shall be grateful to you until the end of my days. This is really a sort of spoken bread-and-butter letter and look – I'm not even crying.

GEORGE: Thank you, my love, thank you indeed. (*He hands her his glass.*) You might pop a lump of ice into my drink. It's getting a bit tepid.

LINDA *takes his glass to the drink table and puts some ice in it.* ANNE *comes in. She is wearing a dinner dress and she, too, has an evening coat over her arm.* GEORGE *rises and takes it from her.*

GEORGE: You haven't forgotten your passport, have you? We have to show it when we land.

ANNE: I have it in my bag.

LINDA: Would you care for a little expensive champagne?

ANNE: Very much indeed.

GEORGE (*bringing* ANNE *her champagne*): How are we for time?

LINDA (*glancing at her watch*): Fine. There's no hurry.

ANNE (*sitting down*): I haven't been inside a casino for years. I'm quite looking forward to it. You'll have to give me some money, George. I hadn't time to get any traveller's cheques.

GEORGE: Are you going to stick to Roulette or have a bash at Chemin-de-fer?

ANNE: Roulette. I can never read the cards at Chemin de-fer. I get too flustered. At any rate, I'm much happier just watching. I wish now I'd brought a more glamorous dress. Next to Linda I look like somebody's governess.

LINDA: I know comparatively few governesses who are dressed by Molyneux.

ANNE: It's about a hundred years old.

GEORGE: We shall be the only ones in the casino who are dressed up to the nines. It isn't a Gala night. We shall stick out like sore thumbs.

ANNE: I've always wondered why sore thumbs are supposed to stick out.

GEORGE: For the matter of that, I see no reason why we should be dressed 'up to the nines' as opposed to the tens or the twenties.

ANNE: I expect there *is* a reason for it somewhere. I'm sure Mr Fowler or Mr Partridge would know.

GEORGE: It's curious that our two leading authorities on English idiom should both sound so ornithological.

LINDA: There's always marmalade, for instance.

ANNE: What on earth to you mean?

LINDA: I was thinking of the origins of words that have become common usage. Marmalade goes straight back to Mary Stuart.

ANNE: How?

LINDA: When she was Queen of France she was ill and took a fancy to orange preserve and everyone said 'Marie est malade!'

ANNE (*vaguely*): How fascinating.

GEORGE: Do you imagine that we shall be able to keep the conversation up to this level for the whole evening?

ANNE: You mustn't be crushing, dear. We're doing our best.

LINDA: We agreed to try to behave as usual.

GEORGE: I know we did, and it was a brave resolution, but like so many brave resolutions it is liable to prove impracticable. Heroic gestures, unless they are immediately carried out in the heat of battle with all flags flying, have a nasty habit of degenerating into anti-climax. We are all three of us far too intelligent not to realise that soon, very soon, the pretence may become more of a strain than reality.

ANNE: The reality has struck at us with dreadful suddenness, George. We have had little time to prepare our defences.

GEORGE: I know, darling, I know. But even so, to attempt to silence the enemy's guns by throwing puff-balls is worse than useless. If we try to maintain an attitude of artificial casualness, the tension will become intolerable. The supply of puff-balls will soon run out and the silences between us will lengthen.

ANNE: What do you suggest? A summit conference on life and death?

GEORGE: Not necessarily, but I am definitely against a policy of evasion.

ANNE: We should be going to Geneva instead of Evian.

GEORGE: What about another nip of champagne, there's a lot left in the bottle.

ANNE (*holding out her glass*): Certainly.

LINDA: I'll do it. (*She fetches the bottle of champagne and refills their glasses.*) Shall I ask Felix to bring another bottle?

ANNE: Oh no, please not. I'm not very good at drinking a lot. It makes me sleepy and dull and sometimes rather disagreeable, and I don't want to be any of those things tonight.

LINDA: Quite right. Tonight's going to be difficult enough anyway. Perhaps it would be wiser to go up to that little restaurant in the mountains, after all. To have decided on Evian and gambling seems to me now to be over-ambitious, running before we can walk. We're sure to meet someone we know and have to smile and make conversation; also we may feel claustrophobic, shut up in a hot casino waiting for the boat to bring us back.

ANNE: A quiet, romantic restaurant in the mountains would be more dangerous still. Beautiful views can be melancholy. Moonlight and stars and infinite distance are all right for young lovers, but for three middle-aged people trying to be brave they might be even more claustrophobic than a crowded casino.

LINDA: All right, Anne – I give in. It was only an idea – like the champagne.

GEORGE: I hate to insert a harsh note into this gallant conversation, but your ghastly politeness to each other is driving me mad.

LINDA: Would you rather we snarled at each other?

GEORGE: It would certainly be more convincing, and more honest.

ANNE: Don't place too much value on honesty. In certain circumstances, it can be a very overrated virtue.

GEORGE: It happens to be one of the things I'm fighting to hang on to, and I certainly can't win if I have to face you both cooing at each other like doves. For

God's sake, let's chuck this bloody performance and get down to brass tacks.

ANNE: What particular brass tacks had you in mind?

GEORGE (*suddenly near breaking point*): I don't know – I don't know – and I'm not even sure that I care. All I do know is that this is wrong, deeply wrong. I can't spend the last two months of my life watching you two acting out a loving affection for each other which you neither of you feel and which, considering the situation between the three of us, you could never possibly feel. I resent being treated like an imbecile and I also resent your treacly compassion. I'm going to die – I'm going to die – and, what is more, I'm going to die alone, because everybody dies alone. This fact is hard enough for me to face without your God-damned loving-kindness and pity and synthetic heroics.

LINDA (*emotionally*): You're not to say such things – it isn't fair. Anne and I agreed to a compromise because we considered that our feelings for you were more important than our feelings for each other. There was nothing heroic about it. We did it for your sake, because we wanted to help.

GEORGE: But it won't work! Can't you see? It could never possibly work. I know you both too well and I also love you both too well. I will not put up with tactful deceptions. The moment for me is too bitter.

ANNE (*calmly*): Why, George. You're positively driving us into each other's arms.

GEORGE: Excellent. A little Lesbian frolic might take the burden of emotionalism off my shoulders.

LINDA (*near tears*): You've certainly gone a long way away from us already.

GEORGE: Of course I have. It's train-fever, I expect.

I'm on my way to the station.

ANNE: If that's not synthetic heroics I should like to know what is.

LINDA: I don't think I can bear any more of this, I really don't.

ANNE: You could always retire to the bedroom again in tears.

LINDA: I know I could, Anne, but however much it may disappoint you, I am not going to.

GEORGE: Things are looking up.

ANNE: What more does your obstinate masculine vanity require, George? What do you really want of us?

GEORGE: Truthfulness, a realistic view. Less tender womanly understanding and more horse sense.

LINDA: Do all men who love women despise them so utterly?

GEORGE: That is a generalisation that I am not prepared to analyse at the moment. I have more important things to think about.

ANNE: Are we going to this damned casino, or aren't we?

GEORGE: Of course we are. What else is there to do?

ANNE: Well, I could go back to England, for one thing. I expect there's a night plane.

GEORGE: Do you want to?

ANNE: In one way, yes. But the decision is up to you. You're the dying Gladiator.

LINDA (*violently*): Anne!

GEORGE: What do you think, Linda? Would you like Anne to go back to England and leave us on our own?

LINDA: This is the first time since we've been together that I have ever known you to be really cruel.

GEORGE: That doesn't exactly answer my question.

ANNE: Your question was contemptible.

GEORGE (*inexorably to* LINDA): Would you like Anne to go back to England, now – tonight?

LINDA (*after a pause*): No. No, I wouldn't. I'd rather she stayed.

ANNE: What on earth made you say that?

LINDA (*meeting her eye*): Because I'm too miserable and exhausted to be able to cope with this situation by myself. Whether you go back to England tonight or not, George and I will *not* be 'on our own'. I don't think we shall ever be on our own again. That's all over. You will be with us if you're here or not. Therefore, you might as well stay. The charade's over and everybody has guessed the word.

GEORGE: You're wrong, Linda, you're wrong. You've neither of you guessed correctly. You think the word is 'Death' but it isn't, it's 'Life'. If only I could make you see this there would be no necessity for any more pretence between us at all. Just now, I deliberately destroyed the pattern of behaviour we had set for ourselves because I suddenly realised how completely false it was, and that it could only lead us further and further away from facing honestly the ultimate truth that we have to face. Not only me and you and Anne, but every living human being on this God-forsaken planet. We are all united in the fear of death, we all share it, because, like eternity, it is beyond the grasp of the human mind. It is the unfathomable, the unimaginable and the unknown. But while death is the ultimate reality, it is also a negative one. Courage and honesty and humour on the other hand are positive because they belong to life and life, up until that last bewildering second, is all we have and all we know. It is also our most important responsibility. The heroic figures of our world were not great because of their strength and nobility, but because they had the imagination to deal with their weaknesses. I happen to believe that fear is the most insidious weakness of all, and if you two, during the next few months can help me to battle with that and conquer it, I shall be grateful to you, literally, to my dying day.

ANNE: How do you suggest that we set about it?

GEORGE: By divorcing your emotions from me as much as possible and being yourselves.

ANNE: An interesting performance. I trust you will be ready to correct us when we say the wrong lines.

GEORGE: Why are you so angry?

ANNE: Because I find the situation infuriating.

GEORGE: No longer heartbreaking?

ANNE: No – no longer heartbreaking at all –
(*her voice quivers, she makes a tremendous effort to control herself, but can't quite manage it. She sinks into an armchair, buries her face in her hands, and bursts into tears.*)

LINDA *and* GEORGE *look at her in silence for a moment. George goes to her.*

GEORGE: Oh, Anne, don't, please don't. Forgive me for being so bloody selfish. I didn't mean to be unkind.

ANNE (*in a muffled voice*): I think I'd like a cigarette.

LINDA: Would you care for a nip of brandy, too? The champagne's all gone.

ANNE: Yes, please. I would.

GEORGE *lights a cigarette and gives it to her.* LINDA *goes to the drink table, pours out some brandy and brings it over.*

GEORGE: It isn't unappreciated, really it isn't. All the effort, I mean.

ANNE *searches in her bag, produces a handkerchief*

484

blows her nose.

ANNE: Good, I'm glad.

GEORGE: Do as you want to do, behave as you want to behave, I didn't mean to preach. (*With an effort at lightness.*) You should never have married a publisher in the first place. You always said I was too in love with words.

ANNE: It wasn't your words that defeated me, it was a sudden feeling of hopelessness. Please don't worry. I'm perfectly all right now. Thank you for the brandy, Linda. This isn't strained politeness, it's wholehearted gratitude. (*She pauses and sips her brandy.*) Are the children to be told?

GEORGE: Not yet I think, a little later on.

ANNE: And when the time comes, will you tell them or shall I?

GEORGE: You. You are closer to them than I am. They will be startled and saddened, but no more than that. I have seen little of them during the last few years.

ANNE: I think you underrate their feeling for you.

GEORGE: Brian will mind more than Margaret, which is curious really. It is usually daughters who are nearest to their fathers, but Margaret has never quite forgiven me for going away. Brian has. This is one of my deeper regrets. I love my son and I shall never see what is to become of him.

ANNE: Don't waste any time on guilt, George, what is done is done. Brian will survive, so will Margaret, so will I. We have all three become used to your absence.

LINDA: I envy you, you are better off than I am.

ANNE: Yes. I suppose I am. I have become accustomed to my own kind of loneliness, yours will be a different kind, but it won't last long.

LINDA (*with an edge in her voice*): Why do you say that?

ANNE: Because your temperament is more resilient than mine and your character more adventurous. It always was. Once your immediate grief is over you will begin to look about you, the world for you is still full of a number of things. You will always ask more of life than I shall. My children will eventually marry, I expect, and leave me alone and, oddly enough, the prospect doesn't depress me unduly. I shall be content to pull up a few weeds in the garden, do the *Times* crossword and look at the sea. You will make more flamboyant demands and reap more dramatic rewards, one method is as valid as the other and there is no blame attached to either. It is merely the fundamental difference in our characters.

LINDA (*with a hint of mockery*): Scarlet women are seldom conceded such patrician tolerance. Your manners are certainly impeccable.

ANNE: What nonsense. You are no scarlet woman, you are merely a compulsive amoureuse. Your heart still yearns for passionate love, mine only longs for peace and quiet.

GEORGE: My God! Moments of truth are clattering around us like hail!

ANNE: Which proves that our summit conference is progressing favourably.

LINDA: Later on, when we are alone, will all these wise words still be available to comfort us? Or shall we have forgotten them and find ourselves back where we started, only a few hours ago, when we first knew, when the nightmare began?

GEORGE: Don't minimise the value of words. They are our only currency, our only means of communication.

LINDA: But we can't talk indefinitely. There will be the moments before sleep and the moments just after waking, when realisation comes and we shall be without hope.

GEORGE: Those moments will have to be faced, along with everything else. We can't expect to escape scot free. But the sharp impact will soon diminish, sooner than you think.

LINDA: I am sorry to be a weak sister again, but I was brought up as a Catholic and I have a sudden craving for more dogmatic, more professional consolation.

GEORGE: You mean that a priest's mumbo-jumbo would soothe you more than my graceless agnosticism?

LINDA: Not the mumbo-jumbo exactly, but the feeling behind it, the age-old wisdom, the reassurance.

GEORGE (*gently*): I wouldn't mock at your faith, my darling, or stand between you and your hopeful prayers, any more than I would query Anne's sturdy Church of England rectitude. There is much age-old wisdom at the base of all religions, but for me never enough. Human beings are intrinsically cruel, it is part of their inheritance, so it is not to be wondered at that the gods they set up to worship should be equally so. Some of the old oriental despots are perhaps a shade less bombastic than our ruthless Christian dictatorship, but they one and all smile benignly on pain and suffering and the blood of human sacrifice. Mother Nature, the Life Force, is just as bad, but at least she doesn't wrap her sadistic inconsistencies in an aura of sanctity.

ANNE: You said this afternoon that you were grateful, that your life had been fortunate. Isn't it an abuse of hospitality to speak so bitterly?

GEORGE: One may be received with the utmost

politeness at Gestapo headquarters, but the politeness fails to deaden the screams of the tortured in the rooms below.

LINDA: Oh George, please don't – please don't. I can't bear it.

GEORGE: You mustn't misunderstand me. I am not denying that life can be a wonderful gift. Nor am I denying that man has achieved miracles of ingenuity, courage and loving kindness. I am only bewailing the fact that these achievements should be so perpetually offset by insensate cruelty, greed, fear and conceit. I am not pretending to be infallible. I do not consider that I have been singled out by some celestial agency to set the world to rights. I am merely a reasonably observant man who is about to die and who refuses to be fobbed off with mysticism and romantic fallacies.

LINDA: You can't be sure. The mysticism may suddenly become clear and the romantic fallacies true.

GEORGE: So might heaven, hell, purgatory, the bogey man, Santa Claus and all the other nursery dreams. I make no claim to omniscience. I only know that I *don't* know and that faced with this insoluble mystery all the priests, philosophers, scientists and witch doctors in the world are as ignorant as I am. I have no time to waste on profitless speculation, less than ever now, and I intend to utilise the days that are left by fortifying my mind against fear. Throughout the course of history, many better men than I have confronted the imminence of death with courage, humour and equanimity and I would prefer to die, if my will is strong enough, as a member of their distinguished company. Nor will I permit myself the scared luxury of last-minute death-bed repentance. I propose to greet oblivion without apology. I wish for no cringing, subservient prayers for the salvation of my immortal soul. My immortal soul, whether it is an intricate combination of nuclei, chromosones and genes, or a spiritual abstraction, will have to take its chance, as my mortal body has had to take its chance for over fifty years. Every schoolboy has to face the last day of the holidays. That is how I feel now. I still have enough time to recapitulate a few past enjoyments, to revisit the cove where we had the picnic, to swim again into the cave where we found the jellyfish, to swing once more in the wooden swing and to build the last sandcastle. I still have time to eat and drink and be reasonably merry, say 'Banco' at the chemin-de-fer table, to turn up a nine and win a few coloured plaques. All I ask of you both is perhaps a little additional strength to tide me over a few inevitable moments of weakness. *From outside, on the lake, three hoots of a siren are heard.* That's the steamer. It always does that ten minutes before leaving to warn latecomers. Come, my dear ones, you have your passports. I have mine. It is still valid for quite a while.

GEORGE *helps* ANNE *on with her coat. They collect their handbags, and the three of them go out as —*

THE CURTAIN FALLS

COME INTO THE GARDEN
MAUD

A LIGHT COMEDY IN
ONE ACT AND TWO SCENES

CHARACTERS

Anna-Mary Conklin
Felix, a waiter
Verner Conklin
Maud Caragnani

The time is the Present.

The action of the play passes in the course of one evening.

The scene is the sitting-room of an expensive suite in a luxurious Hotel in Lausanne, Switzerland.

SCENE I

*The action of the play passes in the sitting-room of a private
suite of a luxurious hotel in Switzerland.*

*On stage left there is a door leading into the bedroom. There
are double doors at the back which open into a small lobby,
from which open other rooms and the corridor.*

*The time is about seven o'clock on an evening in Spring.
The windows opening onto a balcony on stage Right, are
open disclosing a view of the lake of Geneva with the
mountains of France on the opposite shore.*

*When the curtain rises, ANNA-MARY CONKLIN is seated
at the writing-desk. Standing near her is FELIX, a handsome floor waiter. ANNA-MARY CONKLIN is an
exceedingly wealthy American matron in her late forties
or early fifties. At the monent she is wearing an elaborate
blue peignoir, blue ostrich-feather 'mules' and a hair-net
through which can be discerned blue hair tortured in the
grip of a number of metal curlers. Her expression is
disagreeable because she happens to be talking to a member
of the lower classes.*

ANNA-MARY: And another thing young man. When
I ask for a bottle of Evian water bien glac*ée* to be put by
my bed every night, I *mean* a bottle of Evian water bien

494

glacée, and not a bottle of Perrier water which is not glacée at all, and gazouze into the bargain.

FELIX: I am most sorry Madame. It shall not occur again.

ANNA-MARY: And you might also explain to that chambermaid, Caterina or whatever her damn name is, that for my breakfast I take prune juice, not orange juice, toast Melba and not rolls and good American coffee with cream, not that thick black French stuff served with luke-warm milk.

FELIX: Very well Madame.

ANNA-MARY: And you can tell her as well that I don't like being nattered at the first thing in the morning in a language that I can't understand. Neither Mr Conklin nor I speak Italian and the sooner the staff of this hotel realises it, the better it will be for everybody concerned.

FELIX (*blandly*): Va bene Signora.

ANNA-MARY: Are you being impertinent?

FELIX: Oh no Madame. I most humbly beg your pardon. It's just a question of habitude.

ANNA-MARY: It may interest you to know that Mr Conklin and I have stayed in most of the finest hotels in Europe and when we pay the amount we do pay for the best service, we expect to get it.

FELIX: Very good Madame.

ANNA-MARY: That will be all for the moment. You'd better bring some ice later. Mr Conklin takes his Scotch with lots of ice and plain water.

FELIX: Madame.

ANNA-MARY: Is the water here all right?

FELIX (*puzzled*): I fear I do not quite understand Madame.

ANNA-MARY: The drinking water? I mean it isn't just

pumped up out of that lake without being properly filtered?

FELIX: There have been no complaints as far as I know Madame.

ANNA-MARY: All right – You can go now.

FELIX (*bowing*): A votre service Madame. (*He goes.*)

ANNA-MARY (*raising the telephone*): Hallo – Operator – Ici Mrs Conklin – Oui, Mrs Verner Conklin, suite 354. Voulez vous me donner le numero de Andre's, le coiffeur? – No, I don't know the number that's why I'm asking you for it – the place is way up in the town somewhere not far from that big bridge, I was there this afternoon. – All right I'll hold on.

> *There is a pause during whcih she scrutinises her finger nails with an expression of distaste. She continues in her execrable French accent.*

'Allo – Je voudrai parler avec Monsieur Andre lui meme – oui, de la part de Mrs Conklin – pardon – il est parti? Vous parlez anglais? – Oh bon – Well I'd like you to tell Monsieur Andre from me that the girl he gave me this afternoon has absolutely ruined my nails. I asked for Carmine fonc*ee* and what I got is tangerine fonc*ee* and they look terrible. I never noticed until I got out into the daylight. I had to take the stuff all off, and what is more she cut my cuticles, and if there's one thing I can't stand it is to have my cuticles cut, I like them pushed back gently with an orange stick and you can also explain to him that when I say I want a blue rinse I *mean* a blue rinse and not a purple dye. I've been under the shower for forty minutes trying to tone it down and– what – ? Well I can't help who you are, you just give him those messages from Mrs Conklin – Yes Conklin – CONKLIN. Thank you.

She slams down the receiver, rises irritably, takes a cigarette out of a box on the table and lights it. She paces up and down the room for a moment or two and then returns to the telephone, lifts the receiver and jiggles the machine impatiently.

'Allo, 'allo – Operator – Donnez moi – hold on a minute – (*She consults a pad on the desk.*) – Donnez moi vingt trois – trente six – vingt deux – merci.

A moment's pause.

'Allo – 'Allo – Ici Mrs Conklin – Je veux parler avec la comtesse si'il vous plait – Oui – Conklin –

Another pause.

ANNA-MARY: 'Allo – Mariette? – Yes it's me – Anna-Mary! – Why it's just wonderful to hear your voice – I can't believe we're actually here at last, I just keep pinching myself, I tried to call you this morning but your number was busy. First of all I want to thank you for those gorgeous flowers, it was just darling of you to send us such a lovely welcome – my dear they light up the whole room, they literally do – I'm looking at them at this very minute. Oh Verner? – He's all right, he's out playing golf somewhere as usual. Now listen honey about tonight – you know about the etiquette of these sort of things much better than I do – ought I to go outside and *wait* for the Prince or will it be all right to have him sent to the bar where we're having cocktails? – Oh – he likes things to be informal! Well all I can say is thank God for that because I simply wouldn't know how to be anything else – I don't have to curtsy to her too do I, – I do? Whatever for? – I mean she was only a commoner after all before he married her – Oh I see – Very well I'll do what you say, but for heaven's sakes get here early to give me moral support. – You're an angel!——How's dear Henri?——Out playing golf too! – Well I suppose it gives them something to do. Au revoir darling – à ce soir. (*She hangs up the telephone and heaves a sigh.*)

At this moment VERNER CONKLIN *comes into the room. He is a tall, pleasant-looking man in his late fifties. There is little remarkable about him beyond the fact that he has spent the major portion of his life making a great deal of money. He is carrying a bag of golf clubs which he flings down onto the sofa.*

ANNA-MARY (*ominously*): So you're back are you?

VERNER: Yeah sweetheart.

ANNA-MARY: You know Verner, try as I may I just *do not* understand you.

VERNER: What's wrong?

ANNA-MARY: Well to start with it's past six o'clock and we've got to be down in the bar and dressed by eight.

VERNER: What for? You said nobody was coming before eight-thirty.

ANNA-MARY: Did you remember about the cigars?

VERNER: Yes, I remembered about them.

ANNA-MARY: Well thank heaven for small mercies.

VERNER: But the store was shut.

ANNA-MARY (*exasperated*): Verner!

VERNER: Sorry sweetheart.

ANNA-MARY: Why didn't you call in on the way *out* to the golf course?

VERNER: I did. That was when the store was shut.

ANNA-MARY: I only have to ask you to do the smallest thing . . .

VERNER: All the stores shut in this lousy town from twelve until three.

ANNA-MARY: Clare Pethrington told me that the Prince likes a special sort of cigar which can only be got at one particular place here, and I, thinking it would be a nice gesture to have them served to him after dinner, am fool enough to ask you to take care of it for me – and what happens . . .?

VERNER: Nothing happens. He does without 'em.

ANNA-MARY: Now look here Verner . . .

VERNER: There's no sense in working yourself up into a state. I guess the cigars you get in this hotel are liable to be good enough for anybody, and if His Royal Highness doesn't fancy 'em he can smoke his own can't he?

ANNA-MARY (*bitterly*): You wouldn't care if the first dinner party we give in this 'lousy town' as you call it, were a dead failure would you?

VERNER: Calm down sweetheart – it won't be. Our parties ain't ever failures, they cost too damn much.

ANNA-MARY: You know Verner that's one of the *silliest* things I've ever heard you say. The sort of people we're entertaining tonight are interested in other things besides money.

VERNER: Like Hell they are!

ANNA-MARY: I can't think what you came on this trip at all for. You can play golf in Minneapolis.

VERNER: And on a damn sight better course too.

ANNA-MARY: You just about sicken me Verner, you really do. Don't you get any kick at all out of travelling to new places and meeting distinguished people?

VERNER: What's so distinguished about 'em?

ANNA-MARY: Wouldn't you consider a royal Prince distinguished?

VERNER: How do I know? I haven't met him yet.

ANNA-MARY: He just happens to be one of the most fascinating men in Europe, and one of the most sought after.

VERNER: Except in his own country which he got thrown out of.

ANNA-MARY: You make me ashamed saying things like that.

VERNER: Listen sweetheart. How's about you just stopping balling me out and ringing for some ice. I want a drink.

ANNA-MARY: Ring for it yourself.

VERNER (*equably*): Okay – Okay – (*He rings the bell.*)
   At this moment the telephone rings.

ANNA-MARY (*answering it*): Hallo – what——Who? ——She's on her way up?——Thank you. (*She hangs up.*) On my God!

VERNER: What's wrong?

ANNA-MARY: It's Maud – Maud Caragnani – I invited her to come and have a drink, and it went completely out of my head.

VERNER: Well – we'll give her a drink. We can afford it.

ANNA-MARY: Here am I with so much on my mind that I'm going crazy and all you can do is try to be funny.

VERNER: Sorry sweetheart.

ANNA-MARY: And take those dirty old golf-clubs off the couch. This is a private sitting-room, not the hotel lobby.

VERNER: I'll take 'em away when I've had my drink. She's the one we had dinner with that night in Rome isn't she?

ANNA-MARY: She certainly is, in that stuffy little

apartment that smelled of fish. I thought I'd die. No air-conditioning and all those ghastly stairs.

VERNER: I thought it was quite a cute little place, kinda picturesque. I like her too, as a matter of fact she was the only one we met in Rome that I did like.

ANNA-MARY (*with an unpleasant little laugh*): Only because she made a play for you. Why, she practically threw herself at your head, it would have been embarrassing if it hadn't been so funny. I remember catching Lulu Canfield's eye across the table and it was much as we could do not to burst out laughing.

VERNER: Well it made a change anyway. Most of the characters we seem to pick up along the line don't even trouble to speak to me.

ANNA-MARY: You've only got yourself to blame for that Verner. It's just that you happen to be a 'taker' and not a 'giver'. You won't make an *effort* with people. You just sit there looking grouchy and don't say a word.

VERNER: Maybe. But I do say the five most important words of the evening. 'Garçon – bring me the check!'

ANNA-MARY: You know something Verner? It's just that very attitude of mind that makes Europeans despise us Americans. Can't you think of anything but dollars and cents?

VERNER (*mildly*): They're my dollars and cents sweetheart and I've spent the best part of my life pilin' 'em up, and if there didn't happen to be a Hell of a lot of 'em you can bet your sweet ass we shouldn't be sitting here worrying about special cigars for Royal Princes and giving dinner parties to people who despise us.

ANNA-MARY: I wish you wouldn't use vulgar expressions like that.

VERNER: And I'll tell you something else. This dame who's on her way up, the one that handed you and Lulu Canfield such a good laugh by 'throwing herself at my head'. She at least took the trouble to give *us* dinner.

ANNA-MARY: Of course she did. It was a sprat to catch a whale. Even I could see that. She hasn't got a cent to her name. She's one of those social parasites who go about living off rich people.

VERNER: Well at least she can't be lonely, the woods are full of 'em. Anyway if you think so badly of her why the Hell did you ask her round for a drink?

ANNA-MARY: After all she knows everybody, and she goes everywhere. She phoned me this morning and I had to think of something.

VERNER: She happens to be a Princess too, doesn't she? That's always a help.

ANNA-MARY (*loftily*): Only a Sicilian one. Princesses in Sicily are a dime a dozen. (*She glances at herself in the mirror.*) My God – I can't receive her looking like this! I must put something in my hair.

VERNER: Try a crash-helmet sweetheart. You're sure in a fighting mood.

ANNA-MARY *shoots him a withering look and goes hurriedly into the bedroom.*

There is a knock at the door. VERNER *goes to open it.* MAUD CARAGNANI *comes into the room. She is an attractive looking woman of about forty-seven or eight. Her appearance is a trifle 'baroque'. She has style, but it is a style that is entirely her own. She wears no hat and a number of heavy gold braclets. She is English born and bred and has acquired much of the jargon of what is known as 'The International Set'. Beneath this however, she is a woman of considerable intelligence. She greets* VERNER *by taking both his hands in hers.*

MAUD: It's lovely to see you again Verner. I hoped you'd be here but I wasn't sure. Anna-Mary sounded a bit 'affolée' on the telephone this morning. I gather she's giving a dinner party this evening for our portly Prince.

VERNER: Do you know the guy?

MAUD: Oh yes he's a horror. A great one for lavatory jokes and a bit of bottom-pinching on the side. The new wife's quite sweet and lovely to look at, she used to be a model I believe. He insists on everyone bobbing to her and when they do she's liable to giggle. You'll like her.

VERNER: Did Anna-Mary ask you tonight?

MAUD: Yes, a little half-heartedly I thought. (*She laughs.*) Not that I blame her, she's probably got all the 'placements' set. In any case I couldn't possibly have come even if I had wanted to. I'm driving back to Rome.

VERNER: It's the Hell of a long trip. Are you driving yourself?

MAUD: Oh yes. I love driving alone, particularly at night. I shall see the dawn come up over the Simplon Pass and probably get as far as Como for breakfast.

VERNER: What kind of a car?

MAUD: Rather a common little Volkswagon, you know, the type that looks as if it were sticking its tongue out, but it goes like a bird.

VERNER (*admiringly*): You certainly are quite a gal!

At this moment FELIX *comes in with a bucket of ice. He sees* MAUD *and bows.*

FELIX: Buona sera Principesa.

MAUD: Buona sera Felix. Come sta?

FELIX: Molto bene grazie, e lei?

MAUD: Bene come sempre. Partiro stanotte a Roma.

FELIX: Che belleza! Come la invidio.

MAUD: E vero.

FELIX: Buon viaggo Principesa e arrividerci. (*He bows and goes out.*)

VERNER: What was all that about?

MAUD: Nothing much. I just told him I was going back to Rome and he said how he envied me and wished me well. He's a nice boy. We're quite old friends. I knew him first when he was at the Excelsior.

VERNER (*at drink table*): What shall it be? Scotch, Gin, Vodka? Or would you like some champagne?

MAUD: No thanks. Vodka would be lovely, with a little tonic and lots of ice.

While he is mixing the drinks, ANNA-MARY *comes out of the bedroom. She is still in her 'peignoir' but she has wound a blue scarf round her head. She kisses* MAUD *effusively on both cheeks.*

ANNA-MARY: Why Maud – isn't this just *wonderful*? I'd no *idea* you were here. When you phoned this morning I couldn't believe it. I had to pinch myself. My! But you look cute as a June-bug with all those gorgeous bangles. Come and sit down right here and tell me all the gossip. How's dear Lulu?

MAUD (*sitting*): I don't know. I haven't seen her for ages. I've been here for the last two weeks staying with my son and his wife.

ANNA-MARY: Why Maud! You take the breath right out of my body! Nobody ever told me you had a son!

MAUD: It isn't exactly a topic of universal interest.

ANNA-MARY: But how old is he? What does he *do*? Is he handsome? Do you adore him? I've just got to meet him.

MAUD: I don't think he's really your cup of tea. He paints abstract pictures and he's a communist.

ANNA-MARY (*shocked to the marrow*): A communist!

MAUD: I don't mean that he's actually a member of the 'party' but he's terribly red-minded. He's also going through a grubby phase at the moment. They have a ghastly little flat in Pully and a lot of Beatnik cronies. It's all quite fun really.

VERNER (*handing her a Vodka and tonic*): Here's your booze Princess.

MAUD (*taking it*): Thanks Pal.

ANNA-MARY: And you say he's got a wife?

MAUD: Yes, she's small and sharp, like a little needle. She used to be a dancer in the Festival ballet and she's just had a baby. That's why I've been here for so long, it sort of hung back. All those 'Giselles' and 'Swan Lakes' make child-bearing a little complicated.

ANNA-MARY: And she had the baby? (*Offering a cigarette.*)

MAUD: Yes. No, thank you. (*Refuses it.*) Late last night, in the hospital. It's a boy and it weighed exactly what it ought to weigh and was bright red, possibly out of deference to its father's political views. Anyhow I am now a grandmother which is a sobering thought.

ANNA-MARY: No one would believe it. You look sensational!

MAUD (*sipping her drink*): So do you Anna-Mary, so do you. That particular colour is very becoming.

ANNA-MARY: Yes, nice, isn't it.

MAUD: Now I come to think of it you wore blue that night in Rome when you came to dine.

ANNA-MARY: And how is that *divine* little apartment? I was saying to Clare Pethrington at lunch today that it was just *the* most picturesque place I ever saw, wasn't I Verner?

VERNER (*laconically*): Yes sweetheart.

MAUD: Clare hates it. She says there are too many stairs and that it smells of fish. Which is only to be expected really because there happens to be a fishmonger on the ground floor. I keep on burning incense and dabbing the light bulbs with 'Miss Dior' but it doesn't do any good.

ANNE-MARY: You know I'm just heart-broken that you can't come to dinner tonight. It's going to be loads of fun. I've got Mariette and Henri, the Pethringtons of course, Sir Gerard and Lady Nutfield, he was the Governor of somewhere or other and he looks so British you just want to stand up and sing 'God Save the Queen' the moment he comes into the room! Then there are the Carpinchos, they're Brazilian and as cute as they can be, and Bobo Larkin who's promised to play the piano in the bar afterwards providing we keep everybody out, and darling old Irma Bidmeyer who lives in this very hotel and plays Bridge with the Queen of Spain, and, last but not least, Their Royal Highnesses!

MAUD: Not Royal, dear, just Serene.

ANNA-MARY (*visibly shaken*): Maud! Is that really true? Are you positive?

MAUD: Quite. But you needn't worry about it, it doesn't make any difference. So long as everybody calls him 'Sir' and bobs up and down like a cork, he's as happy as a clam.

ANNA-MARY: But I could have *sworn* that Mariette said . . .

MAUD (*laughing*): Mariette's terribly vague about that

sort of thing. She once lost her head at an official reception in Geneva and addressed poor old Prince Paniowtovski as 'Ma'am!' – She wasn't far out at that.

VERNER (*with a guffaw*): You know that's funny! That's very funny!

ANNA-MARY (*ignoring this*): Do you mean I have to *introduce* him as His Serene Highness?

MAUD: You don't have to introduce him at all. You just take people up to him and say: 'Sir – may I present so-and-so'. He may buck a bit at Irma Bidmeyer, he's notoriously anti-Semitic, but you can always mumble.

VERNER: Well – what do you know?

ANNA-MARY (*crossly*): Do be quiet Verner and stop interrupting.

VERNER: Okay sweetheart.

ANNA-MARY: Why don't you make yourself useful for once and go down to the bar and ask if they've got any of those cigars. I want to have a little private visit with Maud.

VERNER: Okay sweetheart.

ANNA-MARY: And for heaven's sakes take those golf clubs with you.

MAUD: Oh don't send him away. I've hardly talked to him at all.

VERNER: Don't worry Princess. I'll just set the table, fix the flowers, give a hundred dollars to each of the waiters and be right back. (*He winks at her, picks up his golf-bags and goes out.*)

ANNA-MARY *sighs heavily.*

ANNA-MARY: Verner really gets on my nerves sometimes.

MAUD (*quizzically*): Yes. I see he does.

ANNA-MARY: He's just plain stubborn. He refuses to be interested in any of the things I'm interested in, he doesn't like any of the people I like.

MAUD: He doesn't seem to mind me.

ANNA-MARY: Only because you lay yourself out to be nice to him.

MAUD: Perhaps that's what he needs.

ANNA-MARY: You were just darling to him that night we dined with you. I remember saying to Lulu afterwards, Maud's just wonderful, she's warm, she's human, and what's more, she's a giver and not a taker.

MAUD: You mustn't overrate me Anna-Mary. I'm a taker all right when I get the chance.

ANNA-MARY: Why Maud Caragnani that's just plain nonsense and you know it! You can't fool me. The one thing I flatter myself I'm never wrong about is people. Why do you suppose it is that you're so popular? That everybody's always running after you and asking you everywhere?

MAUD: It's very sweet of you to say so, but I'm afraid you exaggerate my social graces.

ANNA-MARY: I'm not talking about social graces honey. I'm talking about 'character' and 'heart'! You're just basically 'sympathique' and there's no getting away from it! And above all you go through life *making an effort!* Now Verner just will not make an effort. He just stands around waiting for people to come to him, instead of him going to them. Do you see what I mean?

MAUD: Perfectly. But I find it difficult to believe that he could have made the enormous fortune he has, if he were all that lackadaisical.

ANNA-MARY: Oh he's sharp enough in business, I'll

grant you that, but he just won't open his arms out to *experience*. I mean he deliberately shuts his eyes to the *beauty* of things. You'd never credit it but in the whole five months we've been in Europe this trip, he's only been inside three churches!

MAUD (*laughing*): Perhaps he doesn't like churches.

ANNA-MARY: I managed to drag him into Saint Peter's in Rome and all he did was stomp around humming 'I like New York in June' under his breath. I was mortified.

MAUD: Oh poor Buffalo Bill!

ANNA-MARY: What on *earth* do you mean by that?

MAUD: It's how I see Verner in my mind's eye. A sort of frustrated Buffalo Bill who's had his horse taken away from him.

ANNA-MARY (*snappily*): Verner can't ride horseback.

MAUD: There's still time for him to learn.

ANNA-MARY: He's turned fifty-five. His arteries wouldn't stand it.

MAUD: There are different sorts of horses. Pegasus for instance. He had wings.

ANNA-MARY: You know something Maud? I just haven't the faintest idea what you're talking about?

MAUD: Verner. We're both talking about Verner. But from different points of view.

The telephone rings.

ANNA-MARY, *with an exclamation of irritation, gets up and goes over to it.*

ANNA-MARY (*lifting the receiver*): Hallo . . . Yes, speaking – Bobo! My dear – I never recognised your voice. What! – You can't mean it – you can't be serious! – But when did it happen – I mean you sounded perfectly all right on the phone this morning. – Oh my

God!

There is an anguished pause while she listens.

But Bobo you can't do this to me, at the very last minute. I just can't stand it . . . But if you don't come we shall be thirteen at table – But Bobo honey, I was *counting* on you! I've made all the arrangements about the piano in the bar after dinner and everything.——Well all I can say is that it's just disaster that's all, absolute disaster – Couldn't you just manage to come for dinner? That would be better than nothing – A hundred and two! Are you *sure* it's a hundred and two? – When did you take it? – What——the doctor says you're not to talk any more on the phone – but Bobo – Bobo—— (*She closes her eyes in despair and hangs up the receiver.*) He hung up on me – He just hung up on me! After dealing me the worst blow in my life he has the nerve to hang up on me. – I'll never speak to that God damned little pansy again as long as there's breath left in my body.

MAUD: Be reasonable Anna-Mary. You can't expect the poor beast to come to dinner if he's got a temperature of a hundred and two.

ANNA-MARY: Reasonable! Seven o'clock, thirteen at table, and you ask me to be reasonable!

MAUD: Can you think of anyone else?

ANNA-MARY: Of course I can't. We only got here last night. You'll have to come Maud, you'll just *have* to. It'll make one woman too many but that can't be helped.

MAUD: I really can't possibly. I haven't even got an evening dress with me, and I have to drive to Rome.

ANNA-MARY: Oh Maud, go to Rome later, go to Rome any time but just help me out tonight. You don't have to worry about an evening dress. I can lend you a divine Balenciaga model I've only worn twice. Oh Maud – for heaven's sakes I don't know where I'm at. This is a ghastly situation. I think I'm going crazy.

MAUD: Why don't you call up Mariette? She might have somebody on tap for just this sort of crisis.

ANNA-MARY: You really won't come? I'd bless you until my dying day if only you would.

MAUD (*shaking her head*): It's quite out of the question.

ANNA-MARY: You mean you don't *want* to come.

MAUD: To be perfectly frank I don't. In the first place I haven't spoken to either of the Pethringtons for three years, I can't stand the sight of dear old Irma Bidmeyer and I think the Prince is the most lascivious, vulgar old bore it has ever been my misfortune to meet.

ANNA-MARY (*outraged at such lèse-majesté*): Maud!

MAUD: But leaving all that aside I've promised to pick up my son at the hospital and take him to dine at the Grappe d'Or. They probably won't let him in if he looks anything like he looked earlier in the day, but it's the last chance I shall have of seeing him for a long time. Why don't you call up Mariette as I suggested?

ANNA-MARY (*going to the telephone*): This is ghastly – just ghastly!

MAUD: Don't take it so hard Anna-Mary. I'm quite sure the Prince would waive the most atavistic superstition for the sake of a free meal.

ANNA-MARY: I just don't know how you can sit there Maud and say such terrible things.

MAUD: We just happen to be talking about the same person from different points of view again don't we? Only in this case I happen to know him and you don't.

ANNA-MARY (*at the telephone*): Operator – Operator – Donnez moi . . . (*She glances at the pad again.*) Donnez moi – vingt-trois – trente-six – vingt-deux sil vous plait et aussi vite que possible on account of je suis pressé. (*Balefully to* MAUD.) The next time I see that Bobo Larkin, I'll just make him wish he'd never been born.

MAUD: He's probably wishing that at this very moment if he's got a temperature of a hundred and two.

ANNA-MARY (*at the telephone again*): 'Allo – 'Allo – Ici Mrs Conklin, je veux parler avec la comtesse s'il vous plait – what? – I mean comment? – (*She listens for a moment or two.*) Je ne comprends pas – parlez vous Anglais – (*To* MAUD.) It's a different man from the one I talked to before. I can't understand a word he's saying . . .

MAUD (*rising*): Give it to me. (*She takes the telephone.*) 'Allo – C'est de la part de Madame Conklin, est ce que Madame la comtesse est la?——Oui——Elle est sortie? —— Depuis quand? —— Vous savez ou? —— Oui j'ecoute, un cocktail chez Madame de Vosanges – Oui – vous ne savez pas le numero par hazard——Ah bon, je vais le chercher – Merci beaucoup. (*She hangs up.*) She left ten minutes ago to go to a cocktail party and she's not coming back before dinner.

ANNA-MARY: I think I'm going out of my mind!

MAUD: Somebody called Vosanges. I don't know them, but they're sure to be in the book.

She starts to look in the telephone book when VERNER *comes into the room.*

VERNER: What's cooking?

ANNA-MARY: The most terrible thing's happened.

MAUD (*looking up from the telephone book*): Bobo Larkin's got a temperature of a hundred and two.

VERNER: Well – what do you know? Who the Hell's Bobo Larkin?

ANNA-MARY (*with dreadful patience*): It doesn't matter *who* he is Verner. But what does matter is *where* he is. And *where* he is is in bed with a fever which means that he can't come to dinner, nor can he play the piano in the bar *after* dinner.

VERNER: Poor guy. Probably a virus of some sort.

ANNA-MARY: It can be a virus or Bubonic plague for all I care, but what it means is that we shall be thirteen at table.

VERNER: Well – well – well! Boy, are we in trouble? (*He laughs.*)

ANNA-MARY (*icily*): There's nothing to laugh about Verner. It'll *ruin* the whole evening.

VERNER: Sorry sweetheart. It's just nerves. (*To* MAUD.) What about you Princess? How about you pinch-hitting for this Bozo what's his name?

MAUD: Not even for you Verner. Also I can't play the piano, in the bar or anywhere else. I've found the number Anna-Mary, do you want me to ring it and see if I can get hold of Mariette?

ANNA-MARY: No, it's too late. And anyway I couldn't have her just dragging *anyone* along to meet Royalty. There's only one thing to be done. Verner – You must have your dinner up here.

VERNER: Huh?

MAUD: Won't that seem a little odd?

ANNA-MARY: It can't be helped. We'll pretend you're sick or something.

VERNER: You can say I've got a temperature of a hundred and three!

ANNA-MARY: You *could* be waiting for an important business call from New York.

MAUD: No Anna-Mary. I don't think that would do.

A high fever would be more convincing. You can't fob off a Serene Highness with a mere business call. It would be lèse-Majesté.

VERNER: You could always say I've got a galloping hernia.

ANNA-MARY (*losing her temper*): You think this is very funny don't you? Both you and Maud? Well all I can say is I'm very very sorry I can't share the joke. Mariette's been just wonderful making arrangements for this dinner for me tonight. We've been phoning each other back and forth for weeks. She's the only one who has taken the trouble to plan it all for *my* sake, and if only for *her* sake I'm going to see that it's a success if it's the last thing I do. And I'd like to say one thing more because I just can't keep it in any longer. I'm bitterly disappointed in you Maud and it's no use pretending I'm not. I think it's real mean of you not to stand by me tonight and help me out of this jam. You could perfectly easily come to dinner if you wanted to.

MAUD (*calmly*): Certainly I could but, as I have already explained to you, I don't want to, and, as you may remember, I also explained why.

ANNA-MARY: I can remember that you were insulting about my guests and said the Prince was vulgar, and I just don't happen to think that's a nice way to talk.

VERNER: Listen sweetheart, let's not have a brawl shall we?

ANNA-MARY (*ignoring him, to* MAUD): You've hurt me Maud, more than I can say. You've let me down. And I thought you were a friend.

MAUD (*coldly*): Why?

VERNER: Holy mackerel!

MAUD (*inexorably to* ANNA-MARY): We have met

casually three or four times and you have dined with me once. Is that, according to your curious code of behaviour, sufficient basis for a life-long affection?

ANNA-MARY (*with grandeur*): I do not give my friendship as easily as you seem to think Maud, and when I do it is only to those who are truly sincere and willing to stand by me in time of trouble. After all that is what friendship is for isn't it? It's a question of give and take. However I do not wish to discuss the matter any further. I am sorry that there should have been this little misunderstanding between us, and I can only hope that the next time our paths cross, the clouds will have rolled away and everything will be forgiven and forgotten. If you will excuse me now I must go and dress and do my hair. Verner, you will have your dinner up here, and can ring for the waiter and order it whever you feel like it. And I'd be very glad if you would ring down to the Maitre D and tell him I'll be in the dining-room at eight o'clock to re-arrange the place cards. (*She bows coldly to* MAUD *and goes into the bedroom.*)

MAUD (*after a pause*): Well that's that isn't it?

VERNER: She sure is good and mad.

MAUD: Oh I'm sorry. I'm afraid it's partly my fault. I was rather beastly to her.

VERNER: Forget it. Anna-Mary's tough, she can take it.

MAUD: Yes, I'm sure she can. But I hate being beastly to people. It's only that she made me suddenly angry. I wish I hadn't been.

VERNER: Have another drink.

MAUD: No thank you. I really must go now.

VERNER: Come on, just a small one.

MAUD (*glancing at her watch*): Very well, but make it a

really small one. I must leave at a quarter past.

VERNER (*going to the drink table*): Atta girl!

MAUD (*sitting down*): What an idiotic little drama. (*She sighs.*) Oh dear!

VERNER: Snap out of it Princess. It ain't worth worrying about. Anna-Mary always raises Hell when things don't happen to go just the way she wants.

MAUD: Yes. I expect she does.

VERNER: I don't pay no mind to it any more.

MAUD: Are you disappointed? About being forbidden to go to your own dinner party I mean?

VERNER: It's just about breaking my heart.

MAUD (*with a smile*): Yes. I suspect it is. (*She raises her glass to him.*) Well – Here's to the next time we meet. When all those clouds have rolled away and everything is forgiven and forgotten.

VERNER (*raising his glass*): Here's to the next time we meet anyway, whether everything's been forgiven and forgotten or not.

MAUD: Thank you Verner. I'll remember that.

VERNER: Do you want to know something?

MAUD: Shoot pal.

VERNER: That evening we had with you in Rome was the highspot of our whole trip – for me.

MAUD: Only because I 'laid myself out to be nice to you'. That's what Anna-Mary told me earlier on this evening.

VERNER: Well Momma was dead on the nose for once. You sure did.

MAUD: And it worked apparently.

VERNER: Princess it worked like a charm.

MAUD: Would you mind if I asked you a very personal question, almost an impertinent one as a

516

matter of fact?

VERNER: Go right ahead.

MAUD: You really are a very very rich man aren't you?

VERNER: If that's the question. I guess the answer's yes.

MAUD: It isn't. The question is more complicated than that, and I wouldn't even ask it if I didn't like you enough to be genuinely interested. (*She pauses.*)

VERNER (*sipping his drink and looking at her*): Well?

MAUD: Why, when you can easily afford to do whatever you like, do you allow yourself to be continually bullied into doing what you don't like?

VERNER: That sure is a sixty-four thousand dollar question all right.

MAUD: You must have asked it to yourself occasionally. You're nobody's fool.

VERNER (*looking down*): Maybe I have Princess. Maybe I have.

MAUD: And did you give yourself the sixty-four thousand dollar answer?

VERNER (*looking down*): No Princess. I guess I goofed it.

MAUD: Yes dear Buffalo Bill. I'm sadly afraid you did.

VERNER: Hey! What's this Buffalo Bill bit?

MAUD: Just one of my little personal fantasies. I puzzled Anna-Mary with it a short while ago. I said you needed a horse.

VERNER: A horse! Are you out of your mind? What the Hell should I do with a horse?

MAUD (*laughing*): Jump on its back and gallop away on it. Failing a horse, a Dolphin would be better than nothing. There was a little boy in Greek mythology I believe who had an excellent seat on a Dolphin. It took him skimming along over the blue waves of the Aegean, and he never had to go to any dinner parties or meet any important people and whenever they came to rest on a rock or a little white beach, the Dolphin would dive deep deep down and bring him up a golden fish. It's high time somebody gave you a golden fish Verner. It would mean nothing on the Stock Exchange but it might light up your whole sad world.

VERNER (*astonished*): Well I'll be God damned!

MAUD (*rising purposefully*): I must go now. I promised my son I'd be at the hospital at seven-thirty.

VERNER (*with feeling*): Don't go yet Princess. Please don't go yet.

MAUD: I can't. I really can't. But we'll meet again. (*She unexpectedly kisses him on the cheek.*) Goodbye for the moment dear Buffalo Bill. Don't forget me too soon.

She goes swiftly out of the room as –

THE LIGHTS FADE

SCENE II

Several hours have passed and it is now about eleven o'clock in the evening.

When the lights fade in on the scene, VERNER is stretched out on the sofa reading an Ian Fleming novel. He has taken off his tie and his shirt is open at the neck. On stage Right there is a table with the remains of his dinner on it.

There is a discreet knock on the door.

VERNER: Come in – Entrez.

FELIX *comes in bearing a bottle of Evian water in a large bucket of ice.*

FELIX: I hope I do not intrude Monsieur, but Madame requested a bottle of Evian bien glacée to be put by her bed.

VERNER: Okay. Go right ahead.

FELIX *takes the Evian into the bedroom. After a moment he reappears.*

FELIX: I regret not having taken away the table before Monsieur, but I am single-handed on this floor tonight and there has been much to do.

VERNER: Don't worry, that's all right with me.

FELIX: Monsieur has need of anything?

VERNER (*thoughtfully*): Yeah – it seems that I have. I have need of a golden fish.

FELIX: Pardon Monsieur?

VERNER: Never mind. Skip it. Give me a Bourbon on the rocks.

FELIX: Bien Monsieur. (*He goes to the drink table.*)

VERNER: Princess Caragnani said she knew you before. In Rome wasn't it?

FELIX: Yes sir. I served in the bar at the Excelsior for several months. Only as third barman though. The Princess often was there with friends.

VERNER: She has a lot of friends in Rome hasn't she?

FELIX (*with enthusiasm*): Ah si signore, e una donna molto incantevole, tutto il mondo . . .

VERNER: Hey, none of that, stick to English.

FELIX: I was saying that she is a lady much enchanted and that all the world are most fond of her.

VERNER (*a little wistfully*): Yeah – I'll bet they are.

FELIX (*handing him his drink*): Your drink Monsieur.

VERNER: Thanks – (*He takes it.*) Molto gratzie!

FELIX (*delighted*): Ah Bravo! Il signore cominca imparare l'Italiano! Monsieur is beginning to learn my language.

VERNER: I guess it's never too late to try – to try to learn someone else's language.

FELIX: It is difficult at first, but here in La Suisse there is much opportunity because there are so many languages spoken.

VERNER (*with a little laugh*): You're telling me! Have you got a girl?

FELIX: Oh yes Monsieur.

VERNER: Is she here in Lausanne?

FELIX: No signore. She is in Italy.

VERNER: What's her name?

FELIX: Renata.

VERNER: Are you crazy about her?

FELIX: No signore. But we are most fond. I have taught her to water-ski.

VERNER: Are you going to marry her?

FELIX (*with a slight shrug*): Che sa? One day perhaps, but first I must make the money to afford it.

VERNER: Can you ride horseback?

FELIX (*puzzled*): No signore. But in the village where I was born my Uncle had a mule which I used to ride in the mountains. Era un animale molto cattivo. It was a most angry animal.

VERNER: And a dolphin, did you ever try a dolphin, when you were a kid?

FELIX: I fear I do not understand.

VERNER: You know, a porpoise – a kinda fish—— (*He makes a gesture illustrating a porpoise jumping.*)

FELIX *looks at him in some dismay.*

FELIX: Ah si – un porco marino – un defino! Monsieur makes the little joke?

VERNER: Yeah. I guess you're right. It was only a little joke.

FELIX: Is there anything more that Monsieur requires?

VERNER: Yeah Felix. I'm beginning to think there is. You can take away the table now.

FELIX: Bien Monsieur.

VERNER *takes a roll of bills from his pocket and gives one to* FELIX.

VERNER: Here. Buy a present for Renata.

FELIX (*looking at it*): Monsieur has made a mistake. This is fifty dollars.

VERNER: No Felix. It ain't no mistake. I guess the only thing that Monsieur never makes a mistake about is money. Have yourself a ball. Goodnight Felix.

FELIX (*overwhelmed*): Mille mille grazie Signore – Monsieur is most generous. A domani Signore, a domani.

FELIX *bows and wheels the dinner table from the room.*

VERNER, *left alone, returns to his book, tries to read it for a moment or two and then flings it down. He is about to light a cigarette when the telephone rings. He goes to it.*

VERNER (*at the telephone*): Hallo – Yes, speaking – (*His voice lightens.*) – Oh it's you! Where are you? – Here in the lobby ? – Yeah – come on up – come right on up.

VERNER *replaces the receiver and sits staring at the telephone for a second with a beaming smile. He then jumps to his feet, runs to the mirror, smooths his hair and straightens his tie. Then he hurriedly puts on his shoes and his coat, goes back again to the mirror to reassure himself, gulps down the remainder of his Bourbon and lights, with a slightly trembling hand, the cigarette he was going to light when the telephone rang.*

After a few moments there is a knock at the door. He goes swiftly to open it and MAUD *comes into the room. She stands looking at him for a moment with a slight smile.*

MAUD: Hallo Buffalo Bill. How was your lonely bivouac?

VERNER (*grinning with pleasure*): Hi!

MAUD: I'm sure you say that to every taxi you see.

VERNER: Come right in Princess. Come right on in and put your feet up.

MAUD (*sitting on the sofa*): I think it would be more discreet to leave them down.

VERNER: This is great! Just great! I nearly flipped when I heard your voice on the phone just now. I didn't think I was going to see you again for quite a while.

MAUD: No. Neither did I. It seemed a pity.

VERNER: I'd just been talking about you, only a few minutes ago . . .

MAUD: Talking about me? Who to?

VERNER: Felix, the waiter. He's just crazy about you.

MAUD: Is he indeed?

VERNER: He said that you were a lady much enchanted.

MAUD: Italians have a flair for romantic exaggeration Aren't you going to offer me a drink?

VERNER: You bet. What'll it be?

MAUD: Brandy I think, only very little. I have a long drive ahead of me.

VERNER (*going to the drink table*): You really are going to drive all through the night?

MAUD: Yes. I'm looking forward to it. There's a moon and there's not much snow left on the pass, the road will be fairly clear.

VERNER: Do you want anything with the brandy? – Soda or water or ice?

MAUD: No nothing thanks, just neat.

A slight pause.

Why were you talking about me to Felix?

VERNER: I don't know. You said you'd known him in Rome.

MAUD (*taking the glass he hands her*): I see.

VERNER: And I guess you were on my mind.

MAUD: You were on my mind too. I talked about you to my son at dinner.

VERNER: What did you say?

MAUD: I can't remember. Nothing very much. Just that I like you.

VERNER: And what did *he* say?

MAUD: He asked me how long it was before babies

started to talk. I replied that in some cases it took a life-time. (*She laughs.*)

VERNER: Why are you laughing?

MAUD: It's been quite a funny evening one way and another. He's in a state of blissful euphoria. The fact of becoming a father has completely transformed him. He had his beard shaved off this afternoon and his hair cut. He even put on a coat and tie for dinner. He had a bottle of champagne and he babbled away like a brook.

VERNER: Are you very close, you and your son?

MAUD: Not really. But we seemed to be tonight. I don't much care for his wife and I think he knows it. She's actually not a bad little thing au fond but she's a bit neurotic. I expect having the baby will steady her.

VERNER: What's his name? Your son I mean?

MAUD: Faber. His father's name was Fabrizio and Faber was the nearest I could get to it in English.

VERNER: This Fabrizio – what was he like?

MAUD: Handsome, vain, charming and badly mother-ridden. She was an old devil and hated me like the plague. I rather see her point now. Being a mother-in-law isn't all jam.

VERNER: Were you in love with him?

MAUD: Oh yes. But it didn't last long. We'd only been married for a year when he was killed in a car crash. That was in 1940. I managed to get myself onto a ship going to Lisbon, and from there back to England. Faber was born in Cornwall.

VERNER: Did you ever see any of them again?

MAUD: Oh yes. After the war was over I came back to Italy to live. I made the old girl fork out enough money to pay for Faber's education. In the last years of her life we almost became friends.

VERNER (*after a pause*): Why did you come back to see me tonight?

MAUD: A sudden impulse. I was on my way to Pully to pick up my suitcase from Faber's flat and I was driving along, just out there by the lake and I thought of you sitting up here all by yourself, so I turned the car round and came back. I thought you might be lonely.

VERNER: That was mighty kind of you Princess. (*He looks at her intently.*) I was.

MAUD: Aren't you going to have a drink? To keep me company?

VERNER: Yes, in a minute, after I've asked *you* a sixty-four thousand dollar question.

MAUD: Shoot, Pal.

VERNER: Why did you kiss me like you did when you went away before dinner?

MAUD: Another sudden impulse. I'm a very impulsive character. It's often got me into trouble.

VERNER: And you came back because you thought I might be lonesome?

MAUD: Yes. That was one of the reasons.

VERNER: There were others?

MAUD: Yes.

VERNER: What were they?

MAUD: They're difficult to put into words. You have to be a master psychologist to dissect an emotional impulse successfully. Just as you have to be an expert watchmaker to be able to take a watch to pieces and put it together again. I'm not an expert in either of those fields. I'm afraid of being clumsy and making a botch of it.

VERNER: I don't reckon you could ever be clumsy.

MAUD (*with a slight smile*): Thank you Verner. Let's

hope your reckoning is accurate.

VERNER: You said 'emotional impulse'. Was that right?

MAUD: Yes. Up to a point.

VERNER: Do you class 'pity' as an emotion?

MAUD: Yes. But it was more than pity that made me turn the car round.

VERNER: That's what I was aiming to find out.

MAUD: Well now that you've found out, you can get yourself a drink and let me out of the witness box.

VERNER (*going to the drink table*): Okay Lady. You're the boss.

VERNER *pours some Bourbon into a glass, adds ice to it and comes back to her.*

MAUD: That remark is sadly significant.

VERNER: How come?

MAUD: I've never been to America.

VERNER: It's a great country.

MAUD (*thoughtfully*): I suppose American men must like being bossed by their women, otherwise they wouldn't put up with it.

VERNER (*a little defensive*): You can't judge Americans by the ones you meet in Europe.

MAUD: I've heard that said before. I'm not quite sure that I believe it. After all the English and French and Italians seem to retain their basic characteristics wherever they are. I can't see why it should be only the Americans who are geographically unstable.

VERNER: You know Princess. You sure do say the damndest things.

MAUD (*repentant*): I know I do. That's what I meant just now by being clumsy. Please forgive me.

VERNER: There ain't nothing to forgive.

MAUD: I really came back to be a comfort, not an irritant.

VERNER (*looking at her intently*): The fact that you came back at all is good enough for me.

MAUD (*meeting his eye*): Is it Verner? Is it really?

VERNER: You know damn well it is.

He puts down his drink, takes her drink carefully out of her hand and places it on a table, then he lifts her gently to her feet, puts his arms round her and presses his mouth onto hers.

They stand quite still for a few moments, locked in their embrace, then she draws away.

MAUD: I knew perfectly well that that was going to happen, and yet somehow it was a surprise.

VERNER (*a little huskily*): I guess I knew too. But I wasn't quite sure, and I reckon I was a bit scared.

MAUD: Scared?

VERNER: Scared that you'd give me the brush-off, or laugh at me.

MAUD: Why should I laugh at you?

VERNER: I don't mean that I really thought you would. You're too kind to do that, but – well – I'm not the sort of guy who likes to kid himself.

MAUD (*gently*): No. I don't think you are.

VERNER: I mean I've seen too many fellars of my age suddenly go berserk and get themselves into trouble, bad trouble.

MAUD: Would you describe that kiss you gave me just now, as going berserk?

VERNER (*ruefully*): Now you *are* laughing at me.

MAUD: These fellows of your own age you talk about. How old are they?

VERNER (*grinning*): Old enough to know better.

MAUD: And this trouble their sudden madness gets

them into, this bad trouble – what does it consist of?

VERNER: Oh all kinds of things, making fools of themselves, getting in wrong with everyone, waking up one fine morning and realising that they've been played for a sucker.

MAUD: Do you consider, off hand, that I'm playing you for a sucker?

VERNER (*hurriedly*): No Princess, you know damn well I don't – I didn't mean that at all.

MAUD: How old are you anyhow?

VERNER: Fifty-five, pushing fifty-six.

MAUD: Well I'm forty-four and a grandmother. I'm ashamed of you Buffalo Bill, running around making passes at grandmothers.

VERNER (*worried*): What are we going to do?

MAUD: What are we going to do about what?

VERNER: About this! – About us?

MAUD (*putting her arms round his neck*): We could always go berserk again.

VERNER (*after another long embrace*): You're sensational. D'you know that – You're just sensational.

MAUD: I believe you really mean it.

VERNER: Mean it! I'm crazy about you! (*He moves towards her.*)

MAUD (*backing away*): No really – Verner, dear Verner, this has gone far eough. We're both behaving very foolishly . . .

VERNER: What's so foolish about it?

MAUD: It's my own fault I know. I should never have let it get to this point.

VERNER: Why?

MAUD: Because nothing can come of it, there's no sense in us allowing ourselves to get emotionally

involved with each other. There's too much in the way.
You know that as well as I do.

VERNER: I don't know any such thing. All I know is
I've fallen in love with you, and all I *want* to know is
whether you've fallen in love with me. It's as simple as
that. Once that's clear all the other complications can be
taken care of. Have you? – Or rather could you – do
you think – be in love with me?

MAUD (*looking at him*): Yes Verner. I think I could,
and I think I am. Falling in love sounds so com-
prehensive and all embracing and violent. It's the stuff
of youth really, not of middle-age, and yet – and yet . . .

VERNER (*urgently*): And yet – what?

MAUD (*genuinely moved*): I don't know. I'm feeling
suddenly conscience-stricken.

VERNER: About Anna-Mary?

MAUD: No, not about Anna-Mary. You said yourself
earlier this evening that she was tough and could take it.
You're dead right, she's tough as old boots. If any
woman in the whole world asked for this situation to
happen to her she did. I have no conscience whatsoever
about Anna-Mary, but you – It's you I'm worrying
about.

VERNER: Why?

MAUD: I wouldn't like you to get hurt. As a matter of
fact I'm not any too anxious to get hurt myself.

VERNER: There's no fun in gambling on certainties.

MAUD: What exactly do you want of me? – Have you
thought?

VERNER: No. I haven't had time to think. I only
know I want you.

MAUD: You don't know me really at all. You don't
know any thing about me.

VERNER: So what? Come to that you don't know so much about me.

MAUD: I think I know enough.

VERNER: That goes for me too.

MAUD: It's not quite so simple as that. We've lived in completely separate worlds you and I. The standards and codes of behaviour and moral values on this side of the Atlantic aren't the same as those you've been brought up to believe in. I'm not saying that they're either better or worse, but they are profoundly different.

VERNER: It seems to me that people are much the same all the world over, once you get below the surface.

MAUD: That, darling Buffalo Bill, is a platitude and an inaccurate one at that. People are *not* the same all the world over. When you get below the surface of an American you can still find a quality of innocence. There is no innocence left in Europe.

VERNER: What are you trying to say?

MAUD: I'm trying to warn you really. I could never have lived the sort of life I've lived in your country. It wouldn't have been possible.

VERNER: How do you mean the sort of life you've lived? You're scaring the Hell out of me.

MAUD (*with a slight laugh*): Oh it hasn't been as bad as all that, but I am, I suppose, what the old-fashioned novelists would describe as 'A Woman With a Past'.

VERNER (*drily*): I hate to have to admit it Princess, but we have had just one or two of those in the United States.

MAUD: Oh I know – I know. But it still isn't quite the same thing. (*She pauses.*)

VERNER: Okay – Okay – let's let it go at that.

MAUD: Nor do I wish to give you the impression

that my life has been one long promiscuous orgy.

VERNER: Bully for you Princess.

MAUD (*determined to be honest*): But I have had lovers – here and there along the line.

VERNER: If you'd been in America they'd have been husbands and you could have soaked them for alimony and been a damn sight better off.

MAUD: Oh Verner! You really are very sweet. (*She kisses him.*)

VERNER: C'mon (*Holding her*) what's all this about?

MAUD: I just don't want you to be disillusioned.

VERNER: That'll be the day.

MAUD: I don't want you to wake up one morning like those other fellows, those other romantic innocents, and find that you've been played for a sucker.

VERNER (*shaking her gently*): Once and for all will you lay off that kind of talk!

MAUD: Okay pal. I was only trying to be honest.

VERNER (*letting her go*): And get it into your head that it ain't your past I'm interested in, but your future. And that includes me. Do I make myself clear?

MAUD (*looking down*): Yes Verner. Quite clear.

VERNER: Well – that being settled, where do we go from here?

MAUD (*suddenly laughing*): What about Rome? It's as good a jumping off place as anywhere!

VERNER: Whatever you say Princess.

MAUD: When will you come? – This week? – Next month? – When?

VERNER: This week, next month my foot! I'm coming with you tonight.

MAUD: Verner!

VERNER: In that God-damned Volkswagon.

MAUD: It's very small and your legs are so long. I'm afraid you'll be miserably uncomfortable.

VERNER: The seats slide back don't they?

MAUD: Yes. I'm sure they do——(*She breaks off and looks at him.*) On Verner do you really mean this?

VERNER: You bet I mean it. What time do we start?

MAUD (*suddenly turning away*): I can't let you do this Verner, I really can't. It's – It's too sudden. You must give yourself more time to think . . .

VERNER: Are you chickening out on the deal?

MAUD: No. It isn't that, really it isn't. I'm thinking of you, not of myself. I meant what I said just now. You haven't any idea what I'm really like. All you know for certain is that I married a Sicilian, had a son in Cornwall and a grandson in Lausanne.

VERNER: I know what Felix said.

MAUD (*almost crossly*): Did you consult the nearest floor waiter before you took on Anna-Mary?

VERNER (*drily*): Maybe it would have been better if I had.

MAUD (*bursting out laughing*): Oh darling Buffalo Bill, this is ridiculous, it really is. Everything's got out of hand.

VERNER: Now see here Princess. It was you who went on about the horse and the dolphin and the golden fish. How can I get the golden fish if I'm scared of taking the ride?

MAUD: But you must have loved Anna-Mary once, in the very beginning I mean?

VERNER: I guess I kidded myself that I did, but not for long. She got me on the rebound anyway.

MAUD: The rebound?

VERNER: I was married before, to a girl I was crazy

about. (*He pauses.*) Then, just after Pearl Harbour, when I'd been drafted into the Navy, she got stuck on another guy and went off with him to Mexico. The divorce was fixed up while I was in the Pacific. When I got home to Minneapolis in 1946 my old man died and I took over the business. Anna-Mary was there, waiting to greet the conquering hero, I'd known her since she was a kid.

MAUD: Was she pretty?

VERNER: Yeah. That's just about what she was, pretty. Her mother and my mother had been in school together. Everybody put their shoulders to the wheel, it was a natural. We got married and lived happily ever after for all of seven months. There was a good deal of dough around even in those days. Then she got pregnant and had herself an abortion without telling me. I'd wanted a kid more than anything so it was a kind of disappointment. She pretended at the time that it was a miscarriage, but I found out the truth later.

MAUD: What did she do that for?

VERNER: I don't know. She was scared I guess. Also she didn't want to spoil her figure. She was always mighty concerned about her figure. I reckon Anna-Mary's eaten enough lettuce in her life to keep a million rabbits happy for a hundred years.

MAUD: Oh Verner! What a dismal waste of time.

VERNER: You can say that again.

MAUD: And it never occurred to you to break away?

VERNER: Oh yes. It occurred to me once or twice, but it never seemed worth the trouble. We've led our own lives – Anna-Mary and me. She's had her social junketings and I've had my work, and a couple of little flutters on the side every now and again.

MAUD: Well I'm glad to hear that anyhow.

VERNER: We might have jogged along all right indefinitely if we hadn't started taking these trips to Europe. Europe plays all Hell with women like Anna-Mary, it gives 'em the wrong kind of ambitions.

MAUD: I belong to Europe, Verner. I'm a European from the top of my head to the soles of my feet. That's why I said just now that you ought to give yourself time to think – before you burn your boats.

VERNER: My boats wouldn't burn Honey, they're right down on the waterline anyways. What time do we leave?

MAUD (*glancing at her watch*): It's now twenty to twelve. I've got to pick up my suitcase at Faber's flat.

VERNER: I'll pack a few things and meet you in the lobby downstairs at twelve-thirty. The rest of my stuff can be sent on.

MAUD: You're sure? You're absolutely dead sure?

VERNER: Just as sure as I've ever been of anything in my whole life.

MAUD (*going to him*): Oh Verner!

He takes her in his arms again.

VERNER: As soon as I can get a divorce fixed up, we'll be married and . . .

MAUD (*breaking away*): Oh no – don't say that!

VERNER: How come?

MAUD: I don't want there to be any set plans or arrangements or contracts. . . . This isn't a business deal. Come and live with me and be my love for just so long as it works, for just so long as it makes us both happy.

VERNER: But Honey . . .

MAUD: Please darling Buffalo Bill. We don't want to shackle ourselves with promises before we start. Don't let any sense of moral responsibility rub the gilt off our gingerbread. You do realise don't you what a shindy there's going to be? Anna-Mary will scream blue murder. It will be all over Europe and America that Verner Conklin, the millionaire, has left his wife flat and run off with a dubious Italian Princess who runs a shop in Rome and hasn't a penny to her name.

VERNER: I didn't know you ran a shop?

MAUD: Didn't you? It's quite a success really. We sell curious, rather out of the way things, furniture and what-nots and peculiar jewellery. It's called La Boutique Fantasque. That's one of the reasons I have to be back tomorrow. (*She looks at her watch again.*) I must go darling – I must fly like the wind, if I'm to be back by twelve-thirty. Don't forget your passport. Oh! (*She looks suddenly stricken.*) What about Anna-Mary? What are you going to say to her?

VERNER: Nothing much – Just 'goodnight sweetheart' – It's what I've been saying to her for nineteen years.

MAUD: You're not going to explain? You're not going to tell her anything?

VERNER: What would be the sense of explaining? She'll find out in good time.

MAUD (*conscience stricken again*): Will she mind? – Really mind I mean?

VERNER: You bet your sweet ass she'll mind. She'll be so hopping mad she'll eat up the furniture.

MAUD: Oh Verner!

VERNER: Don't you worry about Anna-Mary. It's about time she had a real problem to yak about. Get going Baby and be back in that little old Volkswagon at twelve-thirty sharp.

MAUD: Okay Pal! – Oh a thousand times Okay!

(*She kisses him and goes swiftly out of the room.*)

VERNER, *left alone, walks up and down the room for a moment or two with a springy step. Then he goes to the mirror and examines his face critically. He slaps his hand sharply under his chin in reproval of extra fleshiness. Then, with a sigh, he goes to the desk and sits down by the telephone.*

VERNER (*lifting the receiver*): Hallo – Operator – Give me the bar please. (*He waits for a moment or two, biting his lip thoughtfully.*) – Hallo – is that the bar? – This is Mr Conklin in 354. – Yeah, I know she's there but I don't want you to disturb her – No, there's no need to say I phoned – Is the party still going on——Uh-uh—— The Prince left over an hour ago?——I see – It's breaking up right now?——Thanks – thanks a lot.

VERNER *hangs up the receiver and sits thinking for a minute. Then he quickly takes off his coat and tie, kicks off his shoes, rumples his hair, takes his book from the table where he left it, and stretches out on the sofa. He cocks his ear and listens for a moment then, apparently hearing footsteps in the corridor, he puts his head back, lets the book fall from his hand, and starts snoring gently.*

ANNA-MARY *comes in. She is resplendent in a gown of sapphire-blue satin. She is also wearing a sapphire necklace, earrings and a thick bracelet to match. She is carrying a handbag and a pair of long white gloves. Her expression is grim. She stops short on seeing* VERNER *asleep, and it becomes grimmer.*

ANNA-MARY (*sharply, stamping her foot*): Verner!

VERNER (*waking elaborately*): Why sweetheart – are you back already?

ANNA-MARY (*disagreeably*): What do you mean already? It's five to twelve.

VERNER (*sitting up*): Well who'd have thought it? – I

guess I must have dropped off.

ANNA-MARY: Dropped off! You were snoring like a bull moose.

VERNER: I must have been on my back then. I always snore when I sleep on my back.

ANNA-MARY (*with sarcasm*): That's very interesting Verner, very interesting indeed. But you'd better go and snore in your own room now, I'm tired.

VERNER: Can I fix you a drink?

ANNA-MARY (*sinking down into a chair*): Yes. A Bourbon on the rocks. (*She kicks off her shoes and wriggles her toes.*) These shoes have been murder all the evening. They get me right across the instep.

VERNER (*at drink table*): How was the party?

ANNA-MARY: I just wouldn't know Verner. I'm so darned mad I can't see straight.

VERNER: What's wrong?

ANNA-MARY: Mariette! That's what's wrong. I'll never speak to her again as long as I live. She's nothing more nor less than a snake-in-the-grass.

VERNER (*handing her her drink*): What did she do!

ANNA-MARY (*taking it*): Do? She just monopolised the Prince all evening long. I put him on my right naturally and her on the other side of him and she never gave me the chance to say two words to him.

VERNER: Who did you have on your other side?

ANNA-MARY: That stuffed shirt Sir Gerard Nutfield. He's got one of those British accents that I just can't stand. He kept asking me where I *came* from. (*She gives him her glass.*) Put some more water in that it's too strong.

VERNER (*taking it to the drink table*): Okay sweetheart.

ANNA-MARY: My you look terrible! With no tie on

and your hair all mussed up.

VERNER: I'll have it set and waved first thing in the morning.

ANNA-MARY: I suppose that was meant to be funny.

VERNER (*chuckling*): Yes Anna-Mary, that was supposed to be funny. But Oh Boy! There's better to come!

ANNA-MARY: Have you been drinking?

VERNER: Yeah. Like a fish. A golden fish.

ANNA-MARY (*coldly*): And what, may I ask, does that mean?

VERNER: It means a Hell of a lot of things. A kid riding on a dolphin for instance.

ANNA-MARY: *What?*

VERNER (*pursuing his dream*): And a flat rock and a little white beach and no tie and my hair mussed up.

ANNA-MARY: You've just gone clean out of your mind.

VERNER (*cheerfully*): Way way out. (*He brings her her glass.*) Drink up your booze Ma'am and enjoy yourself.

ANNA-MARY (*taking it*): How often have I got to tell you that I just can't stand the word 'booze' Verner. It's vulgar and it grates on my nerves. You said it to Maud this evening, and I was mortified.

VERNER: *She* didn't seem to mind. Maybe her nerves ain't as sensitive as yours.

ANNA-MARY: I should think not, considering the sort of life she leads. You should have heard what Clare Pethrington was telling me about her tonight. I just couldn't believe my ears.

VERNER: That's the one with buck teeth that we had lunch with today isn't it?

ANNA-MARY: Verner!

VERNER: She looked as if she could eat an apple

through a tennis racquet.

ANNA-MARY: I'll have you know that Clare Peth-rington is a highly cultured woman. She comes from one of the finest families in England. Her Grandfather was the Earl of Babbercombe and her great Grandfather was a close friend of Queen Victoria's. He used to stay at Balmoral every year, regular as clockwork.

VERNER: Bully for him.

ANNA-MARY: Just because she didn't throw herself at your head and butter you up and make you think how wonderful you were like Maud did, you think it's funny to make snide remarks about her.

VERNER (*with deceptive gentleness*): I wouldn't like to make any snide remarks about any of your friends Anna-Mary, but I would like to say, kind of off the record, that in my opinion this dame we happen to be talking about, is a snooty, loud-mouthed, bad-mannered bitch.

ANNA-MARY: Verner Conklin. I just *don't want* to talk to you any more. And that's the truth. I just don't want to talk to you *any more*! I come back worn out after an exhausting evening and find you lying here drunk. Then you start making silly jokes and saying mean things about people I respect and admire. I'll tell you here and now I've had just about enough of it. You've changed lately Verner and it's no use pretending you haven't, you've changed beyond all recognition.

VERNER: You hit it right on the nose baby. I sure have.

ANNA-MARY: You'd better go to your room, order some black coffee and take an Alka-Seltzer.

VERNER (*gaily*): Did His Serene Highness enjoy his God damned cigars?

ANNA-MARY (*furiously*): Go away Verner. Go away

and leave me alone.

VERNER: Okay – Okay – That's just exactly what I'm going to do. Goodnight sweetheart.

VERNER *picks up his tie and shoes, flings his coat over his arm, looks at her quizzically for a split second, and goes swiftly out of the room.*

ANNA-MARY *sits glaring after him balefully as –*

THE CURTAIN FALLS